MORE POWERFUL THAN DYNAMITE

MORE POWERFUL THAN DYNAMITE

Radicals, Plutocrats, Progressives, and
New York's Year of Anarchy

THAI JONES

WALKER & COMPANY
NEW YORK

Image credits: All images are from the Library of Congress, Prints and Photographs Division, except for: **pp. 3, 29, 133, 300:** Rare Book and Manuscript Library, Columbia University; **pp. 66, 95:** Library of Congress, Historical American Newspapers; **p. 73:** "King's View of New York"; **pp. 88, 127, 136, 302:** Library of Congress, Manuscript Division; **p. 104:** No credit; **p. 319:** New York State Archives; **p. 333:** Courtesy of Robert Plunkett; **p. 334:** Columbia University Archives.

Published by Walker Publishing Company, Inc., New York
A Division of Bloomsbury Publishing

All papers used by Walker & Company are natural, recyclable products made from wood grown in well-managed forests. The manufacturing processes conform to the environmental regulations of the country of origin.

LIBRARY OF CONGRESS CATALOGING-IN-PUBLICATION DATA

Jones, Thai, 1977–
More powerful than dynamite : radicals, plutocrats, progressives, and New York's year of anarchy / Thai Jones.—1st U.S. ed.
p. cm.
Includes bibliographical references and index.
ISBN 978-0-8027-7933-5
1. New York (N.Y.)—History—1898–1951. 2. New York (N.Y.)—Politics and government—1898–1951. 3. Anarchism—New York (State)—New York—History—20th century. 4. Progressivism (United States politics) 5. Labor movement—New York (State)—New York—History—20th century. 6. Plutocracy—New York (State)—New York—History—20th century.
I. Title.
F128.5.J728 2012
974.7'1041—dc23
2011033517

Visit Walker & Company's Web site at www.walkerbooks.com

First U.S. edition 2012

1 3 5 7 9 10 8 6 4 2

Typeset by Westchester Book Group
Printed in the U.S.A. by Quad/Graphics, Fairfield, Pennsylvania

To Jeff and Eleanor,
aka my parents

The history of martyrs is the history of people who expanded to their faith. Indeed, men have shaken destiny because they felt they embodied it. Patriotism, the Cause, Humanity, Perfection, Righteousness, Liberty,—all of them large and windy abstractions to outsiders, are more powerful than dynamite to those who feel them.
       —WALTER LIPPMANN, *DRIFT AND MASTERY* (1914)

CONTENTS

FOREWORD

For me, the anarchists came first. I was surprised to discover that three young radicals had been killed in New York City in 1914 when a bomb they were constructing had prematurely detonated inside their apartment. The accident had come in the midst of a national crisis over unemployment and labor rights; contemporaries believed that the dynamite—if it had served its handlers' intended purpose—would have been used to assassinate John D. Rockefeller.

No one I talked to had ever heard of the incident, which had occurred on Lexington Avenue, in East Harlem. This was not far from where I lived, and so it was easy to go and see the building where the blast had struck. The façade had been rebuilt, but a vicious scar still marked the line of devastation where the bricks had come cascading down, along with glass, pieces of furniture, and bits of flesh. Each day, for decades, hundreds of people had walked past the site. Many must have noticed the evidence of damage, but few—if any—could recall its origins or significance. It had taken less than a century for this history to be lost.

At the time, the Lexington Avenue explosion had been the largest dynamite disaster in the city's history. But others would follow. In 1970, a similar accident cost the lives of three young members of the Weather Underground. Their device had been meant for an officer's dance at Fort Dix, in New Jersey, and when its sudden power tore up from the basement, the force destroyed an entire townhouse on West 11th Street, in Greenwich Village.

Whatever differences of ideology and purpose separated the two sets of would-be bombers, I was struck by the similarities that linked them. Having written about the 1960s generation—my parents' generation—I immediately recognized their kinship with the radicals of a half century earlier. These were demonstrations by the young and desperate against the old and entrenched. They were provocateurs. More than anything else, the extremists in these movements had been brought to the same pitch of anger by social injustice. Whether it was the Vietnam War or the daily horrors of industrial violence, both the anarchists and the Weathermen had been prepared to kill in response. And in these two instances—separated by ninety-two blocks and fifty-six years—it was they who died in the attempt.

Investigating the anarchists' deaths unveiled a broader history that had itself largely been effaced by time. As it happened, they were not the only insurgents in New York in 1914. A new mayor had taken office that year, a reformer determined to implement the latest ideas in government, who had surrounded himself with a coterie of nonconformists and social scientists. In Washington, D.C., a sympathetic leader, Woodrow Wilson, had recently begun his presidency. These were the officials tasked with anarchy's containment: not some corrupt political machine that could resort to violence without a qualm, but progressive administrations constrained by their own ideals of civil liberties and impartial justice.

And then there were the Rockefellers. The patriarch had retired but remained the richest man on earth. His son had quit the family business to focus on works of charity. He dedicated his energies to disbursing the money his father had earned, hopeful, perhaps, that if he could do enough good in spending his inheritance, then Americans might forget the ruthlessness that had acquired it in the first place.

Finally, there was New York City itself. Residents saw ball games and went to the movies, rode the subways and watched planes pass overhead. They were assailed by advertisements, and bustled by skyscrapers without caring to look up. They were jammed in the Times Square crush; they cursed the traffic on Broadway. It was, in fine, a modern city. And yet, that same year, a large proportion of tenement apartments lacked private toilets; hundreds died from typhoid, tuberculosis, and diarrhea. Tens of thousands of children labored in sweatshops and factories instead of attending school.

"We live in a revolutionary period," Walter Lippmann, a young journalist, wrote in 1913, "and nothing is so important as to be aware of it." Despite conflicting outlooks for what the nation should become, every political person understood the intensity of the moment. Drastic transformation would come—it was stirring already. On those New York streets, these three blocs—radicals, plutocrats, and progressives—each struggled to impart their own visions of the future onto society as a whole. The issues being contested—free speech, corporate power, industrial democracy—have remained at the storm center of American politics ever since.

In the opening years of the twentieth century, these partisans tested the possibilities and limits of what it would mean to be a modern citizen. Either violent protest would forcibly create a truly democratic society, or the combined restraints of reform, philanthropy, and scientific expertise would prove to be *more powerful than dynamite*.

—Thai Jones, August 2011

INTRODUCTION

December 31, 1913

The masses approached. Wall Street businessmen, wary from past demonstrations, encased their windows behind heavy timbers to protect against the crush. Civic leaders pleaded for restraint. Police made scores of arrests. But for one night the streets belonged to the mob. December 31, 1913, most agreed, was the "wildest" New Year's Eve the city had seen in more than a decade.

By ten P.M., the city air popped with frost. The downtown canyons glowed from the lantern atop the Singer Tower, down past twenty-seven illuminated stories of the Woolworth Building, to the Edison arc lamps on the avenues. Crowds decanted from the cross streets into Broadway—tenement dwellers and denizens of "East Umpety-Umpth streets," gentlemen wearing spats and slender worsted jackets, women swathed in a "kaleidoscope of colored and tinted gowns and wraps." In dark spots where no light spilled, men in long coats discreetly inquired if passersby needed "a nice watch and chain, cheap." And one cherub—quickly escorted to Bellevue—managed to defy fashion, the cold, and moral decency when he appeared wearing "no raiment between a cigar he was puffing and his shoes."

For abstainers, the Society for the Prevention of Useless Noises had organized an edifying program of choral music and prayer. Their "Safe and Sane" celebration drew thousands to a solemn service where any display of verve was quickly throttled by the police. Officers arrested more than a hundred peddlers of rattles, buzzers, and clappers, and even confiscated confetti and false whiskers. But these raids only inflated prices; horns sold for as much as half a dollar, and enough customers

1

New Year's Eve in a New York café.

violated the blockade on these "instruments of torture" that large portions of the city were debauched by the "blare of raspy throated tin horns, a clattering staccato tumult of wooden rattles, jarring bells," as well as numerous other sounds emitted without any discernable purpose.

An hour before midnight, the theaters released thousands toward the restaurants. Celebrants with foresight had reserved their tables a month in advance; throngs overran Reisenweber's and the Marlborough. The owner of Rector's, on Forty-eighth Street, thought he could have filled all of Madison Square Garden with the customers he was forced to turn away. Patrons at Sans Souci and the Café des Beaux Arts received complimentary souvenirs, direct from France. But the food and favors held no interest, and even the champagne sweated alone, untouched. Hurriedly throwing down their coats, the guests rushed the dance floors to fox-trot and tango. Between numbers, they visited their tables for a sip of brut or a nibble of something, but they did so absentmindedly, and only for tradition's sake. "It was dance-dance-dance, everywhere," a

World reporter wrote. "New York literally abandoned itself to the seductive sway and swing and slide of the new sort of dance." Couples spun in the basement wine vaults of the Astor, and they pirouetted on the rooftop of the Belvedere. They would not be refused, and even the fusty Waldorf begrudgingly cleared a small area for those who absolutely had to waltz.

The toughest reservation in town was the Plaza. Two thousand luminaries filled the grillroom and packed the auxiliary salons and ballrooms, so that extra tables had to be placed in the corridors to accommodate the overflow. But hallway seating was not for the honored guests. Harry S. Black, the Realtor, Mrs. O.H.P. Belmont, a millionaire suffrage advocate, Elbert Gary of U.S. Steel, Stuyvesant Fish, the retired president of the Illinois Central—they supped comfortably in the main dining room. Nearby, at a table almost but not quite so well situated, sat a promising young couple: Mayor-elect John Purroy Mitchel and his wife, Olive.

Wiry and tall, at thirty-four Mitchel already looked like a man of authority. He had sharp, focused features and eyes "alive with the joy of fight." This was his night, and these were his people. All round the room they scrutinized his precise, unaffected manners—a reporter for *Hearst's* magazine thought he carried himself with an "almost patrician

Mayor-elect John Purroy Mitchel.

dignity"—and discussed his apparently limitless prospects. As course followed course, coworkers, elder statesmen, and chums from his Columbia days came to offer advice or congratulations. Among his own sort, Mitchel displayed "an infectious kind of gaiety, and an unusual capacity for friendship." He greeted each well-wisher with the just-right tone, switching naturally from deference to bonhomie. "There was kind of an aspect of a young knight in shining armor about him," a colleague recalled, "here was a man who wanted to run out the crookedness and inefficiency and do something brighter and cleaner than had been done for a long, long time." He was master of himself, master of the room, and he would awake the next morning to become master of the greatest city on earth.

No man, whatever his outward composition, could anticipate the prospect without a tremor. And Mitchel, in fact, awaited it with extreme apprehension. The perfect ease he felt with his peers was mirrored by the pure revulsion he experienced among the masses—the very multitudes who were now reveling on the Fifth Avenue sidewalks—who would imminently become the main of his constituency. With them he felt acute and obvious distress; the tension and toll of contact could knock him low with devastating migraines. Tomorrow he faced inauguration. No vision could be more terrifying—the previous mayor had shaken a thousand hands at his swearing-in. But that was tomorrow. As another acquaintance came to pay respects—or as the Neapolitan singers wandered into the main dining room—Mitchel set aside his shadowed cares. His pearl-and-platinum pocket watch displayed the hour; midnight approached.

ON THE STREETS, celebrations everywhere. Directed by hundreds of policemen, the crowds marched north along one side of the thoroughfares, south down the other. A horn-blowing but genial traffic jam extended, according to the *Sun*, "from Bowling Green up Broadway to Park Row, up Park Row to the Bowery, up the Bowery to Third avenue, up Third avenue to Fourteenth street, and so across Fourteenth street back to Broadway and up that thoroughfare of fun to some place probably near the north pole." Rioting taxicabs and private autos posed an incessant menace. Impromptu parties enlivened the upper levels of the buses as riders traversed the routes back and forth just to view the scenes. Even the unfashionable districts above Central Park South participated. Young couples without the "necessary wherewithal" to afford the exorbitantly priced horns or prix fixe meals promenaded along the boulevards uptown—"125th street, ordinarily a live enough thoroughfare, was in a blaze of glory."

THE NATION'S MOST notorious anarchists were throwing a party in their Harlem brownstone. Notifications had gone out the previous week, inviting friends and comrades to "be among us to kick out the old year and meet the new." By ten P.M., welcoming lights glimmered inside the three-story building at 74 West 119th Street that served Emma Goldman and Alexander Berkman as home, office, and meetinghouse. They had moved there in September and already the location was well-known to the city's radicals—as well as its detectives. But this was the official housewarming celebration. The evening "brought the procession of friends," Goldman recalled, "among them poets, writers, rebels, and Bohemians of various attitude, behaviour, and habit." They climbed the stairs to the main floor and were welcomed into a warm and chaotic sanctum that could easily accommodate a hundred guests. The young people waltzed to the gramophone. German Bundists poured stout brown beer. Italian *sindicalisti* swallowed Chianti. They reminisced; they gossiped. "They argued about philosophy, social theories, art, and sex."

As midnight neared, "everybody danced and grew gay." Typically, the hosts would have been the cheeriest participants. Goldman was known as a "great dancer." Berkman was ever the gallant suitor, typically

Alexander Berkman.

partnering up with one or two young ladies, and sometimes with "scores of other radical women." But not this evening. Suffering through a spiteful separation with a younger man, Goldman felt "lonely and unutterably sad." For Berkman, it had been years since he had surrendered himself to happiness. The arrival of each new year only reminded him of the fourteen that he had lost in prison. One time, in the Western Penitentiary of Pennsylvania, the inmates had stayed up past curfew. They had waited for the sounds from beyond the walls—ship sirens in the Ohio River, church bells, factory whistles—to inform them when midnight had come. The prisoners answered with what they had, and Berkman could hear it still. "Tin cans rattle against iron bars, doors shake in fury, beds and chairs squeak and screech, pans slam on the floor. Unearthly yelling, shouting, and whistling rend the air."

In those years, he had grasped for the mercy of such vivid moments. Now, though he was a free man again, the immediacy of those thrills eluded him. The fanatical revolutionist of his youth had been replaced by this forty-three-year-old gadfly—bald, nearsighted, paunchy. For Berkman, another year meant another year older.

* * *

FROM THE 125TH Street station, it was only two stops on the New York Central Railroad to the village of Tarrytown, forty-five minutes—or "a rubber of whist"—away. A short automobile ride up North Main Street led to arcadian countryside, winding roads, the reservoir, and the well-watched gates of the Rockefeller family estate. Within this private preserve, John D. Rockefeller, Jr.—the thirty-nine-year-old son of the world's richest man—passed the evening with his wife and children.

Their perfect holiday season had begun with stockings before breakfast on Christmas morning, followed by a musicale and gifts beneath the tree. Gathering in the schoolroom of their mansion on West Fifty-fourth Street, they had unwrapped their presents—a new sweater from his wife, for their daughter a bicycle. It was "a noisy, happy time," with paper heaped round them, that lasted until the moment came to assail the turkey. After luncheon, they had crowded the automobile for a ride up to Fort Washington Park, scrambling down around the river just as a light snow began to fall. The next afternoon, the family journeyed to the Tarrytown property for a charmed interlude of "quiet and freedom." They gave concerts for each other on the pipe organ, experimented with the new bike, went ice-skating, and took pony rides. "The children were as happy as their parents," Junior wrote. Everyone was relieved to escape "from the rush and hurry of the city."

Such casual ease was in itself an accomplishment for Junior, who had been drilled in austerity and self-denial. Wealth notwithstanding, the holidays had never brought indulgence. As a child, he once confided a Christmas wish to his mother. "I am so glad my son has told me what he wants," she had then reported to a friend, "so now it can be denied him." As he grew up, the family had kept to little gifts. This year, Senior had sent $1,000; Junior reciprocated with "a dozen white handkerchiefs, a dozen colored handkerchiefs and ten cravats." But when it came to pleasing his mother, the game broke down. "I wanted so much to send you something particularly nice," he apologized, "but have not yet seen just what I thought you would like; so to my chagrin and regret, I am sending you nothing. You know how queer I am about presents."

Junior knew that few would sympathize with the burden of his wealth, but that did not mean it did not weigh upon him. "You can

John D. Rockefeller, Jr., the son of the world's richest man.

never forget that you are a prince, the Son of the King of Kings," his mother had told him once, "you can never do what will dishonor your father or be disloyal to the King." He sometimes felt he was not strong enough to bear the pressure. Shy and directed inward, he had "always had a very poor opinion" of his own abilities. Coming to work for Standard Oil after college, he had felt inferior even to the secretaries. "They can prove to themselves their commercial worth," he explained. "I envy anybody who can do that."

His desperation to show himself worthy led to neurasthenia, breakdowns, and depression. His lone ambition was to earn the name that he had never asked for, to redeem it to a nation that had come to associate "Rockefeller" with the cold villainy of the plutocratic class. To that end, he had quit the business life—retiring from the directorial boards of every company except for one—and dedicated himself to philanthropy. Through gifts and contributions, he was gradually crafting a new family legacy. As he approached middle age, Junior finally felt that he was becoming a substantial man, and no longer merely a man of substance.

A few nagging worries still tugged. There was his mother's illness, which had kept her and Senior in Cleveland for the holidays. Renovations disturbed both his city and country houses. In politics, he had contributed thousands to Mitchel's election fund, only to watch the new administration lure away several of his most valued advisers with the promise of important cabinet positions. And there was a coal miners' strike in southern Colorado, affecting one of the few family concerns in which he was personally involved. Taken together, it was "a busy life" he was leading. But still and all he was confident and secure—at least by his own standards—and capable of heeding the counsel of his minister that "cares should sit lightly upon us at this Christmas season."

By removing himself to the countryside, Junior had also removed another potential irritant. The New Year's Eve celebrations in the city, coursing up and down the avenues near his home, grated on his sensibilities. He had never tasted alcohol, puffed a cigar, or played a hand at cards. It wasn't until his freshman year at Brown University that he had first attended the theater or participated in a dance. The tango continued to be a mystery to him. He found the hotel parties, the mobs in the streets so distasteful that each year he contributed one hundred dollars to the Safe and Sane New Year's Committee, which hoped to "do away with the noisy rowdyism which heretofore has marked New Year's Eve in

striking miners. Ten-foot-high walls of snow flanked the paths that inhabitants had hacked throughout the camp. A large tree had been adorned with Christmas ornaments to give the bleak settlement some approximation of hominess, and supporters had shipped in thousands of baskets, filled with "candies, fruit, and sweets for the children." December 25 had been too cold for a communal celebration, so families had shivered inside their separate tents while a union leader dressed as Santa Claus trudged from door to door, distributing the "goodies."

It was gloomier still in the nearby town of Trinidad, where twelve hundred state militiamen made their barracks. "Lavish" decorations and holiday boxes from home brought scant cheer to men who had just learned of their general's orders to close down all saloons in the area. For employees of the Rockefeller-owned Colorado Fuel & Iron Company, this disappointment had been exacerbated by the news that smoking was now to be forbidden on company property. "If John D. lives much longer," complained an angry employee, "we will start each day with prayers and finish it with a service of song."

For months, these rival encampments had existed in a state of tension, awaiting the catalyst that would instigate unbridled war. The soldiers were supposed to be maintaining peace between the workers and the

In southern Colorado, a months-long conflict between striking miners and the state militia had already resulted in ten deaths.

mine owners, but their officers' loyalty was to the bosses. Ten men had already been killed in the conflict. The jails in Trinidad were crammed with dozens of labor sympathizers, and the strikebreakers—many of whom had not known they were coming to scab—had to be kept under perpetual guard to prevent their escape.

In this gruff and vicious atmosphere, no excuse was needed to go and start a fight. On the morning of December 31—responding to news that the strikers were assembling a cache of weapons—forty soldiers marched from Trinidad to Ludlow. The officers negotiated with union leaders. Behind them, two units of cavalry and several infantry companies stood at the perimeter of the camp, a machine gun trained on the tents. Then the mining families stood by while the troops overturned mattresses and scattered furniture, ransacking their homes for armaments. After an hour's search, which netted fifteen assorted handguns and rifles, the militiamen marched back across the blank tundra, their departure tracked by the eyes of hundreds of resentful strikers.

FROM HARLEM TO Wall Street in New York, Broadway "was a solid lane of noisy, convivial humanity." Midnight approached, anticipated by "a welcoming crowd," a *Tribune* reporter calculated, "whose numbers would baffle an army of census takers." Millions "and then a few" packed the boulevards. At 11:55 P.M., the naval radio towers in Arlington, Virginia, began emitting electric signals—"corrected by stellar observation to the most exact time possible"—over a radius of twenty-five hundred miles. The beats reached ships in the North and South Atlantic; they were heard atop the Eiffel Tower and at the nearly completed Panama Canal. When the last pulse sounded: 1914.

In the streets, the din re-echoed for many minutes past the hour. For participants, wrote a columnist for the *Evening Post*, the experience approached ecstasy:

> The whole city seems half delirious. Five minutes in the crowd and you are half delirious, too—you, a New Yorker, in staid, unfeeling, unemotional old New York—yelling your head off, slapping strangers on the back, talking and shouting at the top of your lungs, laughing endlessly, hysterically.

Gentle applause and tinkling crystal warmed the main dining room at the Plaza Hotel at midnight as the Realtors and railroad executives, the senators' daughters and financiers' widows, toasted success to John Purroy Mitchel and his administration. An hour later, the doors of the Grand Ballroom were thrown open, and a forty-piece string orchestra struck up the night's first two-step. Couples paired around the stone floor—men in white waistcoats and bold-wing collars, women in beaded gowns and chiffon frocks. Taking positions along with the rest, the mayor-elect and his wife clasped each other's hands, locked eyes, and began to move. Mitchel waltzed famously. "He is frankly and openly a devotee of the dance," a reporter wrote. He "can tango *a l'Argentino*, and he is also perfect in the modified one-step and the standardized hesitation, to say nothing of the lame duck, the lively maxixe and the vivacious canter."

Across the city, dancers with far less self-government spun and kept spinning. "Anybody with his ear to the ground," a participant later recalled, "could have heard all over town the sprightly patter and tap of patent leather pumps." Time grew ragged. Lips dried and cracked. Champagne flattened, spilled, and gummed the floors. As the sun rose, rumpled gentlemen and women "whose hair was beginning to sag from the lines of beauty" still lumbered on the mosaic tile in Delmonico's. Across the street, at Sherry's, the rugs were rolled up and tossed aside to make room for the tango. Couples were turkey trotting in the subway stations beneath Times Square.

Dawn approached and the accounting began. "Confetti, broken horns, wrecked rattles, fancy paper caps and other junk lay dismally along" Broadway. An estimated fifty thousand bottles of champagne had been consumed, as well as a "fortune in the more plebeian beer, highballs, and cocktails." Rector's alone had earned ten thousand dollars during the night.

As the sun rose over Brooklyn, the very last stragglers stumbled toward Jack's, the all-night restaurant on Sixth Avenue, to honor one final tradition. Settling in at the oyster counter, they recorded their resolutions for the coming year.

I

We are the workers of the world, but we can't get work.
— FRANK TANNENBAUM

1.

So the New Year Opens in Hope

For twenty-five new years running, John Davison Rockefeller Senior had managed to avoid being in his hometown of Cleveland, and this was why. January 1 was "cold and blustery," with the mercury below freezing, and everyone around him all shivering and snuffles. He himself felt a touch grippey, so he spent the morning by the fire, while outside his private golf course remained exasperatingly unplayed.

Rockefeller had taken up the game around the time of his retirement, more than a decade earlier, and he pursued it with the same focus that had made him such a cunning businessman. He was seventy-four years old, and his stroke was deliberate: "the slowest back-swing I ever saw," a witness said, "it seemed to last for minutes." But more often than otherwise he drove straight, "his clear gray blue eyes" closely following the shot, and he dutifully recorded his penalties, playing each point to its conclusion: "When finally he arrives on the green, he puts the ball painstakingly into the hole if his last stroke covers only two inches."

While playing, he adhered to one rule above the rest: an absolute ban against speaking of business. But it didn't seem to matter. The violation usually occurred "along about the ninth hole." He would be well on in his round, finally relaxing into the game, when out came some proposition—"charitable or financial"—and the day was spoiled. "Neither in the privacy of his home, nor at his table, nor in the aisles of his church, nor on his trips to and from his office, nor during the business hours nor anywhere else, was Rockefeller secure from insistent appeal," a close associate recalled. "He was constantly hunted, stalked and hounded almost like a wild animal." He tried carefully vetting his golfing partners and preferred close friends, but he played daily, requiring a large pool of opponents, and not everyone was discreet.

Though the weather hardly brightened in the week after the new year, Rockefeller just had to play. Doggedly, and despite a "drizzly Winter day," he pedaled over from his mansion toward the first tee. His companions were admitted through the high iron gates of Forest Hill, the family's Ohio property. They drove over his roads, "in and out, through and up and over," among a chorus of songbirds, past pheasants and cottontails, to the golf grounds, where the old man also was just arriving. "On schedule, boys, on schedule!" he called, springing down from his bicycle. "That's the thing!"

But his good humor was ruined, and in the usual way, when one of his playing partners casually asked him to comment on the quality of a certain stock. Rockefeller's spirits wilted, his joy in the game all gone.

The stock, he grudgingly replied, was "as good as eggs."

"Yes," pressed the other man, "but there are good eggs and bad eggs."

John D. Rockefeller, Sr.

"And likewise, my friend," said Rockefeller in a tone that was anything but friendly, "there are good stocks and bad stocks."

WITHIN DAYS, THIS repartee had been published in newspapers from Oregon to North Carolina. JOHN D.'S WIT WELL OILED, exulted the *New York Tribune*. "That mad, mad wag, John D. Rockefeller," marveled Franklin Pierce Adams, had done it again, and this was just his latest oracle to find such wide circulation. Sympathetic reporters waited outside his church on Sundays to record his sunny sentiments about world peace or the weather. His philanthropic gifts—from the one hundred million dollars with which he endowed the Rockefeller Foundation, to the gold coins he bestowed on train porters or the pennies he disbursed to lucky children—always received prominent attention. Readers knew him as a plain country squire, a vestige of a simpler era. They saw photos of him on his bicycle, on the links, pottering in the garden, usually smiling a vaguely senile grin and always wearing some outlandish combination of gaiters, sweaters, and caps. "Mr. Rockefeller is a most kindly, gracious gentleman," the *Fra* magazine enthused, "when he talks to you his countenance beams with animation, friendliness, appreciation, good-cheer." He was harmless and endearing. "Glorious old John D.," concluded William James, the Harvard philosopher, who encountered him at a resort, "a most lovable person."

In his dotage, he had become more popular than he had ever been during his career. And yet just a decade earlier his reputation had stood in ruins, apparently beyond repair. For two years, beginning in 1902, Ida Tarbell's investigative articles in *McClure's* magazine had exposed the lawless schemes by which Standard Oil had trampled its competitors. She had reserved her cruelest testimony for the last two installments of her series, devoted to lengthy character studies of Rockefeller himself. "This money-maniac," she had called him, a disfigured wreck of a man who had squandered his soul, "secretly, patiently eternally plotting how he may add to his wealth."

Rockefeller had been slow to appreciate the damage. He had always kept himself private, rarely appearing in the society pages or attending public events. Once, after a particularly taciturn day of testifying, the *World* had reported, ROCKEFELLER IMITATES A CLAM. This was his way: "Never make friends. Don't join clubs. Avoid knowing people intimately." The *McClure's* articles demanded a rebuttal, a response, but still he kept silent and unapproachable, "the very personification of the Sphinx." City editors sent reporters to see him, not because they thought they could get an interview but "in a sort of hopeless, desperate sense of duty." As Tarbell's stories ran month after month and his son, John Jr., staggered under the attacks and collapsed toward a nervous breakdown, Senior was unmoved. He had the articles read aloud to him, and he chuckled at what he heard. "The world is full of socialists and anarchists," he explained. "Whenever a man succeeds remarkably in any particular line of business, they jump on him and cry him down." His wealth and good fortune had inevitably provoked hard feelings, but he was unapologetic and unconcerned. He would continue to do what was right until he was absolved, and for now he would just "let the world wag."

After the Tarbell stories, two personae vied for dominance: "A Mr. Hyde Rockefeller, who became 'money-mad in his early twenties . . . and the Dr. Jekyll Rockefeller, simple, kindly, courteous, beneficent and broad-minded." He kept to his old ways, as if the opinions of others did not concern him. Sunday church. Morning golf. Holidays with the family, preferably not in Cleveland. But he did make one concession. For the first time in his life, he embraced publicity. He gave interviews to all who asked. If a photographer spied him, he'd pause, pose, smile, and wait till the light was just so. And as he warmed to the press, it warmed to him. "This was the new Rockefeller, the revelation," a journalist wrote. "The man of mystery was talking freely and showing himself utterly unlike the popular perception of him."

By 1914, ten years after the *McClure's* series had ended, most readers assumed that Tarbell had misunderstood—or at least misrepresented—him. The scars were largely effaced. "It is the picture of the diabolical Mr. Rockefeller that has been gradually fading from view," an editor decided, "while that of the simple and human Mr. Rockefeller has been growing clearer and more distinct to the public eye."

In the first days of January, he even went so far as to invite a reporter to join him in a round of golf. They toured his course and, violating all that was hallowed, they discussed serious matters while they played. "We are all socialists in a sense," said Rockefeller. "No man liveth unto himself. The interests of one are the interests of all." Not that he saw a social upheaval on the horizon. "Revolutions come and go," he observed. "This talk of political revolutions has been rampant since I was a boy." At last, the newsman asked what counsel the old squire would offer the coming generation. Rockefeller paused, and when he answered, he spoke slowly and with care: "My advice to the young man at the opening of a new year is to go straight and to do the best you can to make a success for yourself . . . If you make mistakes remember it is human to err, but try again, and try harder. Above all things be honest, honest with yourself and with those with whom you deal."

*   *   *

"SO THE NEW year opens in hope," proclaimed the *Times* on January 1, "with the certainty of good things, good business, and carefree minds." Lately, the nation had been hounded by the baying of critics, the protests of labor radicals, the carping from liberal reformers. Those days, the editors predicted, were over. "We have passed through a phase, uncomfortably prolonged, of resistance to the law. The new phase is that of obedience to law's commands, the hooting down of the agitator."

The ecstatic celebrations with which Americans welcomed 1914 were no reflection on the previous twelve months. "On the contrary," a *Life* editor insisted, 1913 "was easily one of the best old years that we have ever seen, and that is saying a good deal." The newspapers proffered retrospectives, covering entire pages with charts, tables, and coded maps. All in all, the documentation of progress was irrefutable. "Each year contains fewer grafters, fewer trusts, fewer magnates, fewer of everything that is bad," continued *Life*, "and more virtue, more generosity, more amiability, more serums and more of everything that is good."

It had been a remarkable year for harmony. Local fighting had wracked the Balkans for a month or so in the early summer, but no more trouble was expected from the region. The great powers were more congenial than they had been for years. "The war cloud has disappeared from European skies," proclaimed the *Herald*, while the *Times* cheered "the growing rapprochement between Germany, France, and England." In the United States, 1913 saw the fiftieth anniversary of the Battle of Gettysburg, which became a national celebration of unity and reconciliation. Plans were also in place to commemorate one hundred years of amity between English-speaking peoples: A century had passed since the British had burned the White House during the War of 1812. "What 1914 may disclose no man knows," the *Post* acknowledged, but none could deny that "1913 is ending with good hopes of peace."

Fifty-one black Americans were lynched in 1913. "This is the smallest number in any year since these grim records have been kept," announced Booker T. Washington. A mere eighty-eight people were executed legally by the states, with New York leading the way by putting eleven criminals to death. Americans donated $170 million to charity in 1913, and the captains of industry had been particularly generous. John D. Rockefeller was most beneficent of all, distributing $11 million of his private fortune to the commonwealth.

New York's live poultry market showed astounding increase. All the butter packets consumed by metropolitan residents, lined up end to end, would have stretched halfway round the earth. Only 302 people— including 149 children—were killed by automobiles in the streets; 108 others were run down by streetcars, and 132 more perished beneath horse-drawn wagons.* Pauper burials at the potter's field on Hart Island, in Long Island Sound, declined by nearly a thousand to 6,744. Infant mortality dropped substantially, to 102 deaths for every thousand children born—a rate, said the secretary of the Babies' Welfare Association, with which "those engaged in caring for the health of infants had every reason to be gratified."†

The city itself was a statistical wonder. The second-largest metropolis in the world—its population of five and a third million lagging behind only London's seven—it was the fastest-growing, most densely populated place on earth. Its harbor and rail system handled nearly half the national commerce. The municipal budget, around $160 million in 1910, was equivalent to one fourth of all federal expenditures. The city elected twenty-two congressmen to the House of Representatives. The mayor disbursed more than four times as much money as did the governor in Albany; municipal expenses were greater than those of any state in the union and larger than the next fifteen biggest cities combined. Each year, New York's revenues, mostly from property taxes and commercial fees, dwarfed the incomes of such corporations as Standard Oil or the Pennsylvania Railroad.

Municipal government directly controlled the lives of thousands of citizens. The city employed eighty-five thousand public workers, a staff twice as large as the federal bureaucracy in Washington, D.C. Municipal jails held more than five times as many prisoners as filled the federal prison system. The city also kept twelve thousand wards in its almshouses and charity hospitals. Years before New York established its state

---

* The number of annual traffic fatalities has dropped significantly in the past century. Despite having to avoid infinitely more cars, only 269 pedestrians in New York were killed by automobile accidents in 2010. Deaths by horse-drawn wagon have also dropped substantially.

† As of 2009, this infant-mortality rate would have ranked between the nations of Zambia and Mali.

constabulary, the city police force topped ten thousand men, more than could be mustered by any state militia.

Unremitting growth had led to a state of permanent revolution. "New York has had a history," a visiting Londoner wrote in the *Times*, "but it is overlaid and obliterated by the raucous present." The previous generation's marvels—the Tower Building, Everett House, the Fifth Avenue Hotel—had already been demolished and replaced. The Woolworth Building, Grand Central Terminal, and the Williamsburg Bridge were newly completed. Twelve thousand sandhogs blasted and drilled miles of new railroad tunnels through the boroughs and beneath the rivers. Harried residents lived with the frequent echo of dynamite: "One rushes to the window at the first explosion with a mind revolving disaster," the *Times* continued. "There is no disaster of any kind. It is just New York growing; New York tearing down something big to make way for something bigger; New York expressing with all the violence of shattered rock its eternal dissatisfaction with the thing that is, its eternal aspiration toward the new and better."

Broadway and the Woolworth Building.

Such progress in industry and science was to be expected; the United States, after all, was a Christian nation, with the greatest and most vital economy in the world. What made the year especially notable were the advances in politics, a field in which Americans, chagrined by endless revelations of corruption, had long felt inferior to their European contemporaries. The 1912 presidential election had swept the mainstream far to the left; everyone was a Progressive now. Even partisans had difficulty distinguishing Democrat Woodrow Wilson's "New Freedom" platform from Progressive Theodore Roosevelt's promise of a "New Nationalism," while Socialist Eugene V. Debs and Republican William Howard Taft had offered more and less, respectively, of the same. Inaugurated in March, Wilson was following his success with the tariff by directing his energy against the monopolies. Those who had opposed him were acknowledging that he was making headway on the good work of reform, while acolytes credited him with returning "responsible, representative government" to Washington.

These unprecedented gains were fragile, however, and so political contests in 1913 became referenda on reform. Every race—"the election of a university regent in Michigan, or a judge in Illinois, or a mayor in Louisville, or a special election for a congressman in a remote district in Maine"—was scrutinized for larger implications on the national mood, the fate of the Republican Party, the strength of the Socialists. "Politics today," suggested *Current Opinion*, "like modern art, has a distinct 'futurist' quality—one can read into it almost any kind of meaning." With the stakes so dear, New York's mayoral race had taken on national importance, becoming "one of the most heated and enthusiastic ever conducted in the city."

Reformers were preaching uplift at every railroad junction, farming village, and mill town in the country. Chicago, Boston, New Orleans—all were as corrupt as they could be. But New York's fight was different. Its machine was the Machine. "In the American political lexicon," an analyst noted, "Tammany Hall and municipal misgovernment are interchangeable terms." New York's struggle had become synonymous with the whole push toward urban improvement. "If the hold of the strongest and most unscrupulous of municipal machines upon the greatest city in the country can be broken, no lesser task for municipal regeneration is impossible." In short: "If Tammany can be defeated no city need give up hope."

During 1913, the need for reform in New York was imperative. The reigning boss, Charles Murphy—that "terrible ogre of American

The Democratic political machine, known as Tammany Hall, had been a scourge to middle-class reformers for generations.

politics"—wielded more authority than any of his predecessors could have imagined. And worse, he made no secret of it. "A nod from Murphy," it was said, "and kingdoms fall." When the governor he had chosen showed unwonted independence, Murphy had him impeached by his handpicked legislature. For the mayoralty, he nominated another of his creatures, Edward McCall, a candidate with nothing but loyalty to recommend him. "Not since the days of Tweed," claimed the *Outlook*, "has Tammany displayed such confidence in its own power."

In a city of millions, there were scandals for every temperament: outrages ordinary and unique, sentimental and pecuniary. Pickpockets lifted billfolds, aldermen snatched district seats. Builders of railroads and aqueducts filched municipal lands. The Canal Board and Highways Department embezzled civic funds. The Public Service and Interstate Commerce commissions conspired with the industries they had been tasked to scrutinize. Ministers seducing parishioners, doctors' wives murdering their husbands' patients, gun battles on the East Side. Grand juries impaneled, ubiquitous. The state treasurer slit his own throat rather than face investigation. "Graft, graft, graft," declared a witness in a corruption case, "it was a story of graft, graft, graft everywhere."

The Machine had crossed too far into hubris. Most of the press corps, leading civic groups, a united front of Republicans, disaffected Democrats, and Independents all stood together against Murphy's gang. Calling themselves the Fusion Party, they put aside ancient grudges and combined "without regard to party politics."

Then, in mid-July, Fusion announced its nominee and hope vanished. "Of what possible use is it to discuss the candidacy of Mr. John Purroy Mitchel for Mayor of New York?" wondered a *Times* editorial. He was obviously an impressive young man—"Spectacularly, preposterously, young," in fact—but his inexperience made him susceptible to "the adoption of fads and nostrums." He would "embark the municipality upon a sea of Socialist adventure." At Tammany Hall, celebration. Once again, the organization's enemies had blundered; Fusion's nomination, they expected, would "make things easier" for their man, McCall.

Mitchel ignored the lamentations and began preparing a "smashing statement" of purpose. People who doubted him couldn't conceive of the inner force he contained. On a South American vacation he had contracted a fever that left him susceptible to devastating headaches. It was agony when they struck. He never complained, but his friends watched him sit through aldermanic sessions pallid, perspiring, crushing the blood from his strong hands, yet refusing to adjourn the meeting before all business was complete. The same degree of will barricaded his passions behind a temperate exterior. "He wanted to hit the ceiling," recalled Frances Perkins, whose husband had a position in the administration. "He wanted to be dramatic. He wanted to be Irish." He did none of these things. "He is the possessor of an unusually analytical mind," an associate said, "which is always under perfect control."

The strain he felt was tensile and apparent. "When he sits, he sits as if he were just about to spring up," a correspondent wrote in *Everybody's* magazine. "When he walks across a room, he marches. He is nerve. He is wire." Finding release in the strenuous life, he enjoyed vanishing for days at a time on hunting and canoeing expeditions in the Adirondacks. "It's the greatest thing in the world to make a man forget matters that agitate his mind," he told a reporter for the *World*. "Then when the call of the city comes and you get back to New York, with its skyscrapers, its noise and its bustle, you have washed out your brain, so to speak, and

can see things in their right perspective." Mitchel was as aggressive behind the wheel as he was restrained in most of his other pursuits. "He
would drive a car sixty-five miles an hour on a straight stretch of road,"
a friend recalled, and at least once during his mayoralty he was pulled
over for speeding. In the city, dancing allowed for some physical fulfillment. His advocacy of the tango even became the subject of censure
from religious leaders, but he refused to abandon it. "Yes, I dance now
and then," he asserted, "and if some of those who criticize me for doing
so would dance too, their dispositions might be improved."

But no amount of exercise could soothe his ire over Tammany. His
abhorrence for Murphy stemmed from long acquaintance. In fact, everything but John Purroy Mitchel's own determination to avoid it had
steered him toward a Tammany career. His grandfather, John Mitchel,
was a legendary Irish demagogue who wrote revolutionary tracts against
the English in the days of the potato blight. After five years of exile in
Australia, he escaped to New York, where he was hailed and feted at City
Hall. He shook so many burly Gaelic hands during his first week in
America that he had to wear a sling to protect his arm. On the other side
of the family, Henry Purroy, Mitchel's maternal grandfather, had gone
into politics early, exhibiting "a great capacity in 'machine' methods" and
rising to become the chairman of Tammany's General Committee.

With this ancestry, Murphy would have offered him the spoils of the
city, but Mitchel had a "hatred of expediency" and instead forged a career
of opposition. For nearly a decade, he had been lashing out against corruption. As assistant to the Corporation Council, commissioner of accounts,
and then president of the Board of Aldermen, he had conducted inquiries
that resulted in the disgrace of several borough presidents. When a Tammany messenger offered a judgeship if he backed off, his response was to
the point: "Tell Murphy to go to Hell!" Whatever post he occupied, he
was usually the youngest man ever to have done so. By the time of his Fusion nomination, he had become "that new thing in municipal history in
America—a municipal expert." Progressives around the country took notice. Woodrow Wilson watched his success "with growing interest." Even
the *Times*, suspicious of his youth, had to acknowledge that "there is probably no man in an administrative office in this city to-day who knows
more about the detail of municipal government."

Mitchel's candidacy was announced only a few months before the election, and he conducted a "whirlwind" campaign, speeding from borough
to borough in his red automobile, often making several speeches a day.
His opponents attacked him as a stooge to business, a traitor to the party,

a "better-than-thou Democrat." Worried that his orations were beyond the capacity of his audience to understand, he practiced simple words and worked hard to use them. But his topic was straightforward enough. For Mitchel, the main focus, as always, was the Machine. "The issue is Murphy," he told audiences in Washington Heights and the Lower East Side, Chelsea and Flatbush. "We want non-partisan administration in place of petty politics, party spoils and pull. Would Murphy give you that?"

In the early days of the effort he performed dynamically, "with crisp, incisive declarations, emphasized by flashing eyes and telling gestures." But soon he wore down, becoming worrisomely gaunt. By October, his voice was going. He'd grown hoarse, he explained to a crowd, from "telling Mr. Murphy what I think of him." Then his headaches returned and he had to give up speaking altogether. After several days' rest, "evidently suffering from the strain of the campaign," he reentered the fray but had to stand aside while proxies gave his orations. Advisers feared that he presented a distant, somber image. "The electorate chiefly knew him as a man who held and applied convictions as to economy and efficiency," one magazine concluded. "These are not magnetic convictions." A variety of strategies were considered to make him appear more personable. "If possible," advised one of his strategists in a personal memo, "be a 'fan' and *go prominently* to one at least, of the World Series ball games." Another observer reminded the candidate "that he should 'look pleasant' when being *photographed*. Most of his published photos are so stern as to belie his personality and suggest an utter lack of humor."

In the final week before the election, Progressives roused themselves for a last great push. Contributions filled Fusion's accounts. More than a thousand concerned citizens aided the effort, giving nearly $130,000; a large minority of the donors could have been found in the latest edition of *Who's Who in New York*. They were lawyers, bankers, and business executives. The Rockefellers—father and son—gave $3,000.

On Election Day, November 4, additional police officers were stationed at the polling places to prevent fraud. Down on the Lower East Side, Charles Murphy cast his ballot and posed for photos. Mitchel spent the afternoon motoring through Westchester County with his wife and some friends. That night he hosted Arthur Woods, a leader in the local Progressive Party, and a few others for dinner in his home on Riverside Drive; the returns sputtered in through a custom stock ticker. The gathering grew more cheerful as each ward reported. He had won. Tammany was smashed. Half a million celebrants cheered in Times Square; they paraded through Harlem. At ten P.M., the mayor-elect traveled to his

A campaign poster for John Purroy Mitchel.

campaign office in the Fifth Avenue Building, on Madison Square. Hundreds of supporters pressed in on him, grabbing at his clothes, trying to touch his hands. "I have but one ambition," he told the crowd in a rasping whisper, "and that is to make New York City the best governed municipality in America."

When the ballots were tallied, Mitchel had earned the most overwhelming victory since the unification of Greater New York in 1898; he'd won every borough and had a majority of more than 120,000 votes. Second only to Wilson's victory the previous year, this was proof that reform was still rising. From the president he received a telegram reading, I CONGRATULATE YOU WITH ALL MY HEART. The *Morning Olympian*, in Washington State, decreed that "Tammany got a richly deserved licking." The *Grand Rapids Press* celebrated Gotham's liberation as if it was its own. "With this vicious organization kicked out by an overwhelming majority," its editors wrote, "the country's largest city should make a fresh start toward honesty and decency in its civic affairs." Fusion was hailed in Knoxville, Tennessee, and in Cedar Rapids, Iowa. "Mr. Mitchel," punned Montana's *Anaconda Standard*, "seems to be the man who took the many out of Tammany."

* * *

ON THE MORNING of New Year's Day, staggering survivors of the previous night reached out for bromo and bromides, according to the *World*, to "soothe the tired, aching muscles which so gaily tangoed between tables, on slippery floors, in subway stations even, not to mention the humble and unresilient sidewalk." Mitchel had hardly slept—if he'd rested at all—and he had dark circles around his eyes to show for it. Last seen doing the two-step long after midnight in the grand ballroom at the Plaza, he again appeared at 8:52 A.M., when his auto pushed through a small crowd in City Hall Park. Eager, ready, and impeccably dressed, he wore "a black cutaway coat trimmed with braid, dark trousers with a small stripe, and a necktie of mauve, relieved by a pin of pearls." A violet in his buttonhole provided the final touch. Without pausing to banter with the crowd, he escorted Olive into his new office on the northeast corner of the first floor.

Economies began at once. The inauguration ceremony, which began a few minutes after noon, offered a complete break from the traditionally interminable Tammany affair. The outgoing mayor's speech lasted one minute. Mitchel took the oath, his right arm raised high above his head. He looked round the room, crowded with 150 friends and colleagues. Olive and his mother stood in the corner, watching with admiration and concern. Addressing the crowd and the gathered reporters, he began by quieting the expectations that had grown throughout the campaign. "We will develop our program slowly," he said. "I would rather have the government of this city for the next few months inconspicuous than have it heralded from day to day in the papers through promises made as to what will be done."

Then he turned to the commissioners who were to lead the municipal departments. In the past they would have been political functionaries, men whose sole credential was loyalty to the Machine. This was a different group entirely. Mitchel had wanted "persons with special qualifications for the tasks assigned to them." Hundreds had applied for the positions, and sorting them had been a nightmare. "There is nothing in the world worse than trying to select appointees for public office," Mitchel wrote to a former traveling companion. "I would rather go through ten campaigns or a long illness than tackle that job." Still, he

The mayor's first day in office.

had soldiered through, diligently perusing the files, turning away many good choices, selecting only the best. These were the experts he would entrust with the sacred work of reform. For the first time in municipal history, social scientists were going to take their theories into the laboratory of the streets. "Run up and down the names of his heads of department," a reporter wrote with wonder, "and you will scarcely find one which indicates politics, while in case after case the sole suggestion is of special training or highly qualifying expertise."

Standing closest to the mayor was his most talked-about appointee, Katharine Bement Davis, the new commissioner of correction, who had just become the first woman to hold a cabinet post in a city administration. Nearby stood John Adams Kingsbury, a former radical from the Northwest who was the newly named head of the Department of Charities. Arthur Woods, an old friend who as yet had no official appointment, was present, too. To the commissioners, many of whom were already prominent in their fields, Mitchel urged the importance of teamwork, "that each man must not feel that he—or she"—he said, with a laugh and a glance toward Miss Davis—"can regard his—or her—department as apart from the others."

His speech lasted five minutes. Then the reception began. This was the ordeal Mitchel had been dreading. Immemorial custom demanded that he receive his constituents. Thousands had come; they massed in a double line extending through the corridors and out the doors into the park. The first five hundred passed through, shaking His Honor's hand, wishing him well. A headache came on. He paled steadily, and finally could do no more. Two thirds of the visitors were sent away in disappointment and Mitchel retreated to his private office. A half hour later, some Columbia friends found him there still. "As we entered through the door," one recalled, "he was seated before his desk, with his arms resting on the desk and his head buried in his arms. He straightened up as he heard us approach, his face white and drawn." Alone with his peers again, the mayor of New York could finally reveal his thoughts.

"It's been hell," he said.

* * *

FAUGH! STUPIDITY. OFFICIAL WINDJAMMING. Thus thought Alexander Berkman, flipping through the excretions of the plutocratic press in early January. "It is disgusting," he complained, "to witness the brazen hypocrisy" of the newspapers and magazines, and yet compulsively he searched his enemies' propaganda for material to fill his monthly column in *Mother Earth*, the anarchist magazine he edited for Emma Goldman. It was a game he enjoyed—turning their words against them, using the evidence printed daily in the bourgeois journals to show "the utter rottenness of our whole politico-economical life." Some mornings, though, it required "nothing short of heroism" to face the latest batch of lies and half lies. January 1 presented more than the usual measure of irritants. The papers overflowed with the typical buncombe, but in addition the new year had inspired the most miserable sort of dialect pieces and doggerel, Messages of Optimism, paeans to "Progress"—shoddy, threadbare stuff.

The new calendar also brought the inevitable retrospectives and annual reports. Newspaper after newspaper plastered entire pages over with charts, tables, and coded maps. Poultry and dairy records, self-congratulatory discussions of death rates, misleading numbers and pseudo-facts displayed triumphantly as the hard proof of national health and prosperity. Berkman liked to use statistics, too. In the column he was working up for January, he noted that "the United States, according to statistical figures, employs more children in stores, factories, and mines than any other 'civilized' nation." While the press predicted peace, he understood that capitalism and conflict were inseparable. He noted the invention of an improved machine gun that could fire hundreds of rounds a minute. "Think what that means!" he wrote. "A single company of soldiers will, by means of the new Lewis gun, have a destructive power equal to a whole regiment at present. Wonderful human achievement."

The holiday season had been a busy time, though anarchists enjoyed the festivities in their own way. "It is hardly necessary to assure those who attend our affairs," said Berkman, "that they will find there no preachment about peace on earth, good will to all, but, what is more vital in our days, joyous abandon and true comradeship." In October, *Mother Earth*'s annual reunion party had been a "most unique and interesting event . . . so enjoyable was the *camaraderie* that every one stayed until the wee hours of the morning," leaving reluctantly, even then. The Christmas Eve Dance was another tradition. A newspaper reporter had once come to see it for himself. "All the clever girls, all the intellectual girls, all the thoroughly worthy, serious-minded, housewifely girls, sat around the walls most of the evening," he wrote. "All the pretty girls had partners for every dance." Aunts paired with young nieces. Awkward waltzers stomped each other's toes. "In other words . . . the anarchists' Christmas ball was an own twin brother to every other dance that ever was." Except for the hair. No blondes. No "downright, healthy, open-minded, you'd-like-to-play-tennis-with-her" redheads, either. Only brunettes had attended. "Perhaps so much densely, lustrously, trenchantly black hair, and so thickly set," the newsman sneered, "never gathered in a room before."

The city had been especially aggravating in recent months. Since August, the mayoral race had monopolized the headlines. "The political hucksters are tremendously busy these days," Berkman complained. "One gang of grafters supersedes another in an endless round of elections, and no one's the wiser except the politicians." The furious and self-righteous accusations and counterclaims were mere distractions; Fusion and the Machine were equally corrupt. To the workingman, elections were irrelevant. "He may vote blue, white, or red, but however he casts his ballot, he always votes to continue his own slavery."

All this only heightened Berkman's peevishness. He was forty-three years old. Out of prison for nearly a decade, he now found himself trapped in the sedentary life of a publicist and critic. Occasionally he appeared at demonstrations, but his most militant days, he feared, were slipping further into the past. Along with Emma Goldman, he was the face of American anarchism; increasingly, though, his own was becoming the face of a bank teller or a railroad clerk.

He was bald, bespectacled, and short, softening in the middle; he dressed like a dandy, with a particular taste for light-colored suits and panama hats. Ages had passed since he'd last trembled the bourgeois establishment. The only tool that still worked for him was the pen. But even in his columns, his frustrated pessimism revealed itself. Describing movement allies, he used the flattest terms: His friends were all martyrs, comrades, heroes. Only when writing about antagonists did he let fly, creating an elaborate taxonomy of labor fakirs, reformer-mollusks, parasitic speculators, property patriots, hired plug-uglies, pathological degenerates, government squealers, slimy creatures, Judases, Hessians, harpies, troglodytes. Woodrow Wilson was the "Chief of the plutocratic Cossacks." Theodore Roosevelt was "the arch demagogue," the "Tartarin of Oyster Bay," a "Tarasconian Super-Barnum."*

After aiming such vituperation at the capitalist leeches, he did not neglect to chide the anarchists' "step-brothers"—the socialists—as well. Founded at the turn of the century, the Socialist Party of America conceived of itself as the political arm of the labor movement. On many issues the radicals agreed; they were, as Berkman wrote, "friends with somewhat similar aims." Both looked forward to a society where labor was not exchanged for wages, or goods sold for profit, where workers controlled their own lives. But while the anarchists refused to collaborate in any form with the institutions of bourgeois capitalism, the socialists attempted to reform society from the inside by first amassing political power through votes, offices, and the entire panoply of government. For the moment, this strategy was showing progress: The party was at the peak of its power and influence. Eugene V. Debs had polled nearly a million votes in the recent presidential election; it left him a distant fourth overall, but the organization had successfully elected a congressman—Victor Berger, of Milwaukee—as well as scores of mayors and hundreds of minor public officials. But the anarchists believed that to participate in government was to acknowledge its legitimacy. By seeking political offices, the socialists had fatally compromised their revolutionary beliefs. They joined the capitalists in advocating slow reform; reining in the most radical protests, urging the anarchists to "be pa-

---

* The Tartarin of Tarascon—"Traveler, 'Turk,' and Lion-Hunter"—was the title character of an adventure novel popular during the 1880s.

tient, keep quiet." So in all their accomplishments, Berkman saw only defeat. "The present 'victory' will prove the final *debacle* of American Socialism," he wrote in *Mother Earth* at a time when the party was celebrating the latest election result, "if the Socialists at large don't take timely warning against the siren promise of political success at the cost of forswearing their real aims and ideals."

The role of perpetual censor may have inspired his sharpest writing, but it also propelled his most cynical impulses. Comrades saw danger in his "graveyard humor," fearing he might lose the ability to distinguish friends from foes; or, more seriously, that he would fully become the ranting scold he played in his diatribes. Already his most perceptive acquaintances sensed that he was "desperate," unfulfilled, "just full of despair." He skipped from lover to lover and "couldn't be faithful." Anarchism was supposed to be an affirmation, yet increasingly "he really at heart had no faith in himself." It had not always been so; once he had fancied himself a force of pure ego, a true revolutionist.

He had been twenty-one years old in the summer of 1892, handsome, febrile, with lithe muscles and sensual lips. Having immigrated to the

Alexander Berkman in 1892.

United States from despotic Russia four years earlier, he had plunged into the life of his new homeland. Moving in a whirl of passion, his tumescent politics rendered every question crucial, beautiful, simple. He lived in poverty—working as a cigar maker and a shirt packer, sleeping some nights on the steps of City Hall—but it hardly mattered. In the evenings, he joined the radicals at Sach's Café or Mazzini's. These were the most militant activists in New York City, and yet his own commitment far outstripped theirs. He allowed no slippage between ideals and actions. When a sick comrade required treatment, he refused to waste the movement's funds on a cause that was merely sentimental. He had "neither personal interests nor desires above the necessities of the Cause." Moving beyond the world of doubt and regret, he was "revolutionist first, human afterwards."

Yet human, too. He communed with Emma—a year older than he and already gaining notoriety as "An Eloquent Woman"—making love in her apartment for the first time after a particularly inspiring rally. And there had been others: Anna, Masha, Nadya, Kolya. Luba, "with the swelling bosom, the delicate white throat," had let him touch her breasts above, and then beneath, the bedsheets. Flitting about as opportunities demanded, their liberated ménage evolving constantly as friends and lovers passed through, they were inventing a new way to exist, a modern morality. They were enacting in their private lives the future society they hoped to create. Some days brought rapture and others carried pain, but every moment was exquisite.

All this he had voluntarily given up.

With insatiable rage, he followed the events in Homestead, Pennsylvania, where the Carnegie Corporation had locked out the steelworkers in order to destroy the union. The local despot, Henry Clay Frick, hired hundreds of Pinkerton plug-uglies and constructed miles of stockades topped with barbed wire to surround the plant; then he'd shut down the factories and girded for war. Labor offered concessions, but Frick would hear no negotiations. He was Caesar, Baal, personifying the furnace fires of his mills. "No!" wrote Berkman. "There can be no peace with such as Frick," nor with the rest of the bourgeoisie. "Fricks, vampires, all of them . . . they are all one class. All in a cabal against *my* class, the toilers, the producers."

An anarchist lived for the revolution, forging himself into a weapon of defiance, observing society with the patience of a hunter—judging the moment to strike. This was the anarchists' strategy for constructing class consciousness. Propaganda of the word—the work of *Mother Earth* and other radical magazines—educated workers in the theory of revolution. Propaganda of the deed—the assassination of an enemy—displayed those ideas in practice. No one was naïve enough to think that a single action, even the destruction of a tyrant, could instigate an insurrection. But each lone feat served to advance the struggle.

While the socialists amassed votes for their candidates, the anarchists were compiling a tradition of personal sacrifice that would eventually build until it inspired a mass movement of its own. In 1886, a bomb exploded at a labor rally in Chicago's Haymarket Square, killing several policemen. That had been the first step. The next year, when the state avenged itself by executing four well-known anarchists for the crime, that had been another. No uprising had ever arisen spontaneously; the French Revolution, the Paris Commune, each had been precipitated by untold and unremembered deeds. "In the midst of discontent, talk, theoretical discussions, an individual or collective act of revolt supervenes," wrote Peter Kropotkin, a Russian aristocrat who had dedicated his life to the cause. "One such act may, in a few days, make more propaganda than thousands of pamphlets."

The halfway anarchists of the cafés quailed at the thought of propaganda of the deed. "But, the killing of a tyrant," Berkman argued, "is in no way to be considered as the taking of a life." To assassinate such a one as Frick was to attain the highest honor an egoist could demand. The act itself might be "unpleasant," but the test of a true radical was "to sacrifice all merely human feeling at the call of the People's Cause." With his mind fevered with wrathful thoughts, he noticed some fine ladies on horseback. They trotted past him, sharing a joke, their eyes hardly resting on his face. They were mocking him, no doubt, snickering at his ill-tailored clothes, his big lips. "Laugh! Laugh!" he thought. "You despise me. I am of the People, but you belong to the Fricks. Well, it may soon be our turn to laugh." Bound for revenge, he boarded the train for Pennsylvania.

On July 23, around noon, he stopped in a fashionable men's store on Fifth Avenue in Pittsburgh and purchased a lightweight summer suit, almost pure white. Next, he pushed through a few busy blocks to the Chronicle-Telegraph Building, Frick's headquarters during the lockout. Climbing the stone steps to the second floor, Berkman brushed past the porter and crashed through a swinging door to the inner chamber. He saw his enemy seated at a long table studying some documents. Their eyes met. "He understands," thought Berkman, pulling a .38-caliber

Henry Clay Frick.

Hopkins & Allen revolver. Frick moved to flee, but he only had time to turn his head. Berkman fired twice. His first bullet sliced the cords at the back of Frick's skull, grazing the spine. The second cleaved his neck, passing clean through. Frick collapsed to the ground, his head and shoulders beneath the chair on which he'd been sitting. "Dead?" Berkman wondered, when suddenly he was tackled by a second man whom he hadn't noticed. They grappled on the floor. "Help! Murder!" Frick shouted, still alive. Berkman threw off his assailant and triggered again, but the gun misfired. Carpenters and clerks entered the room, pummeling and clawing the assassin; he staggered, carrying them on his back, grabbing Frick, rolling him to the ground. Pulling a dirk from his pocket, he stabbed, convulsively hacking at the screaming man's legs and hips, until at last he was knocked unconscious by a hammer blow from one of the carpenters. Even then the two men remained locked together. Frick was shaking and swashy with blood; red stains covered the carpets and furniture. The new white suit was ruined.

Following a two-hour trial, Berkman was sentenced to twenty-two years in prison. For the *attentat*, the anarchist term for an assassination attempt, he was unrepentant—he regretted only that Frick still lived—but in Allegheny City's Western Penitentiary, depression thorned deep. "At times the realization of my fate is borne in upon me with the violence of a shock and I am engulfed in despair," he wrote. "Existence grows more and more unbearable." Beyond the walls: the Pullman Strike, a nationwide labor battle that paralyzed American railroads for weeks in 1894; Czolgosz's 1901 assassination of President McKinley; Bloody Sunday, in 1905, when the czar's guard massacred peaceful demonstrators in St. Petersburg. Inside his cell, Berkman lost his youth, his physique, his hair. Long months passed when he didn't see a woman at all. Just the sound of a feminine voice could linger in his mind for days. "I long to hear the soft accents," he wrote, "feel the tender touch." After fourteen years, his day of freedom loomed. Overwhelming all other emotions, he felt "the swelling undercurrent of frank and irrepressible sex desire."

In 1906, he returned to New York. "I found the world changed," he wrote, "so changed, in fact, that I am now afraid to cross the street, lest lightning, in the shape of a horseless car, overtake me and strike me down." The one constant he hoped to rediscover was Emma Goldman. But the love affair that had sustained them both during the years of absence barely survived the shock of contact; both expected the feverish child of the other's recollection. Instead, they each confronted a middle-aged adult. She had become world-renowned as a lecturer, not just on anarchism but on literature and drama. Her wider interests antagonized his single-minded devotion to the revolution. Friends and sympathizers offered every consideration, smothered him with generosity and attention.

He resented all these efforts and could hardly stand to be near those who cared for him most. Instead he wandered the city, seeking familiar landmarks. Orchard Street, the primitive ghetto alley where he had attended his first meetings, now "conformed to business respectability." The lecture hall had become a dance studio; the café was a counting house. Most of the old comrades had died or betrayed the faith; the young people didn't measure up. He sensed a "spirit of cold deliberation in the new set" and was estranged by their "tone of disillusioned wisdom." The sum of his bereavement became apparent. "The fervid enthusiasm of the past," he wrote, "the spontaneous comradeship in the common cause, the intoxication of world-liberating zeal—all are gone with the days of my youth."

Despite himself, he could still inspire love and affection, had a magical

Emma Goldman.

effect on children, and could rile a crowd with just an angry gesture and a sharp word. "The red leader," an acquaintance observed of him, "never lost his temper except on the speakers' platform, and there very rarely and only for the purpose of producing a desired effect." Others were less generous: "Phony as a three dollar bill," one rival concluded. Newspaper reporters remarked on his uncanny ability to slip "through the crowd as rapidly as he could" when a situation became truly dangerous. To the mind of a sympathetic friend, Berkman "was of that very rare species of human being, a genuine fanatic."

His beliefs gave him will. He was part of something grand; he was an anarchist.

Of all the many philosophies that emerged from the Enlightenment, anarchism was the purest and most hopeful. Humanity was perfectible. Each could prosper. All were worthy of trust. Self-government was government enough. In a society of equals, there would be no need for any authority other than one's own conscience. The uses of government—

policing, jailing, war making—were all made necessary by the twisted morality of capitalism. After the revolution, when a new generation had been raised without physical want and had absorbed the teaching of anarchist schools, there would be no need for any of it.

THERE WERE ANARCHIST theoreticians who puzzled out the applied details of utopia. But Berkman was not one of them. He left it for others to ponder the intricacies of how—in practice—an egalitarian society would administer justice, coordinate production, and ensure security. Believing that "the principal thing is to get people to rise against the oppressive institutions and that everything else would take care of itself," he had dedicated his energies toward revolution. Destruction would breed construction. "The more radical the treatment," he argued, "the quicker the cure."

Berkman's politics were driven by a need for revenge. His uncle, a Russian radical, had been exiled to Siberia for a decade. The Haymarket martyrs had sacrificed themselves to the spirit of liberty. Frick had been made to suffer for his crimes against the workers. And this determination to retaliate led Berkman from one facet of anarchism to the other—from the humane preachment of human excellence to the violent application of destruction.

"Bombs and anarchists are inseparable in the minds of most of us," a New York journalist wrote. "Mysterious destroyers of life and of property, merciless men who have pledged their lives or their knives or their guns to some nefarious cause or another." For heads of state, anarchy spelled death: In 1881, radicals killed the tsar; in 1894, the president of France; in 1897, the prime minister of Spain; in 1898, the empress of Austria; in 1900, the king of Italy; in 1901, the U.S. president; in 1911, the Russian prime minister; in 1913, the king of Greece. "When compared with the suppression of anarchy, every other question sinks into insignificance," Theodore Roosevelt had warned. "The Anarchist is the enemy of humanity, the enemy of all mankind."

Members of the movement tried continually to separate themselves from this notoriety. It was capitalism itself that was the supreme killer. "Do we build warships for educational purposes?" asked Berkman. "Is the army a Sunday school? . . . Is the gallows the symbol of our brotherhood, the electric chair the proof of our humanitarianism?" The spectacular litany of anarchist attacks was inconsequential compared to the homicides of state and industry. "Our whole social life," he wrote, "is based on murder and mutual slaughter. War, extermination, is its very breath—the war of the classes against the masses, the war of man against man in the perverted struggle for existence." It had taken decades for the radicals to claim a few monarchs and politicians. At any given moment, their enemies could be found to be doing far worse. In spite of such arguments, Berkman and his comrades could never explain away the history they themselves had made.

"Of all paradoxes," Jack London wondered, "is there one that will exceed the paradox of our anarchists—men & women who are so temperamentally opposed to violence that they are moved to deeds of violence in order to bring about, in the way they conceive it, the reign of love and cosmic brotherhood?"

AFTER EIGHT YEARS of freedom, Alexander Berkman had barely managed to accommodate himself to his disappointments. He clung to the potential of his politics; "The times are pregnant with revolutionary thoughts and deeds," he had written recently. But by 1914, his old idealism seemed irretrievable. Caving to fashion, he had adopted an implacable reserve, cultivating a "cool and suave" persona that replaced commitment with distance, zeal with calculation. An interrupted revolutionary, he somehow had to regain what he'd lost. He needed more than a cause to dedicate himself to; the robber system of capitalism provided an endless litany of causes. He required an enemy, a villain who could inspire something other than sarcasm. If he could find another Frick, then he could retrieve some echo of his past. Perhaps he might even recover the sensations of that one afternoon in Pittsburgh, two decades earlier, when he had finally felt like "a *man*, a complete MAN."

Statistical Abstract

T *he Statistical Abstract of the United States for 1914*, compiled by the
Bureau of Foreign and Domestic Commerce and published by the
Government Printing Office, presented a comprehensive accounting of
the nation's productive capabilities. Anything that could be quantified,
inventoried, ranked, or averaged out had a place within the 720 pages of
the report.

Chart Number 16: "Coal." No. 89: "Potato Crop." No. 37: "Foreign-
Born White Paupers Enumerated in Alms-Houses." No. 44: "Religious
Organizations." No. 54: "Marital Condition of Persons 15 Years of Age
and Over."

Chart No. 135, "Summary of Manufactures, By Specified Industry," listed relevant facts concerning the production of Axle Grease,
Buttons, Billiard Tables, Cigar Boxes, Corsets, Crucibles, Grindstones,
Horseshoes, Oakum, Pavers, Peanuts, Shoddy, Whips, Windmills, and
Wall Paper. Chart No. 154, "Population 10 Years of Age and Upward
Engaged in Gainful Occupations," tallied six million farm workers, two
and a half million manufacturers, six hundred thousand coal miners,
three hundred thousand iron and steelworkers, 105,000 bankers, 101,000
bartenders, 98,000 telephone operators, 30,000 newsboys, 25,000 ticket
takers and railroad station agents, 26,000 paper hangers, 21,000 under-
takers, 14,000 bootblacks, 7,000 piano tuners, 5,000 cornshellers, 1,600
lighthouse keepers.

No. 174: "Wireless Telegraph Systems." No. 190: "Traffic on Railroads."
No. 210: "Cattle, Hogs, and Sheep." No. 222: "Panama Canal Excava-
tions." No. 313: "Life Insurance By Fraternal Orders."

An entire chapter belonged to Chart Number 352. Rather than offering a snapshot of a particular commodity, it combined dozens of categories into one agglomerated "Statistical Record of the Progress of the United States." In 1914, the population stood at 98,646,491, of whom more than a million were immigrants who had arrived during the course of the year. The railroads carried more than a billion passengers. The mails delivered 960 million postcards. Wires transmitted ninety million telegraphs. Twenty thousand newspapers published editions. Thirty-two million cotton spindles turned. Two hundred and eighty-six metallurgical furnaces were kept in blast. The government issued forty-two thousand patents. Nineteen million pupils studied in the public schools. Three and a half trillion dollars circulated.

Taken as a whole, these numbers offered objective and undeniable proof of American achievement. Even adverse data—the 18,000 commercial failures that occurred in 1914, the 2,454 fatalities suffered "in and around" coal mines, or the eleven million working days lost to strikes— were merely the inevitable by-products of large-scale enterprise. To anyone who cared to examine them, the figures conveyed the most sensational epic of the age.

But few Americans had patience for the *Statistical Abstract*.

Edward Mott Woolley was typical of the rest in eschewing these "huge volumes" of data. "Ordinarily such books were of no use to me," he wrote, "they lacked altogether the human element which made up most of my work." A magazine writer, Woolley, along with his articles, was everywhere in 1914. He claimed to freelance simultaneously for forty different periodicals, and had ten articles published during the year in *McClure's* magazine alone—a feat of popularity that none of his colleagues could approach.

Of all the magazines in the United States, *McClure's* was most closely associated with the muckraking movement. It was in its pages a decade earlier that Ida Tarbell had pilloried John D. Rockefeller, and Lincoln Steffens had dramatically exposed corrupt urban politics to a scandalized middle-class readership. Like them, Woolley was a skilled reporter who tenaciously pursued his subjects. But he despised the anticapitalist principles of his peers and considered two topics off-limits: "No muckraking or sex stuff," he'd tell any editor who pitched him a sensationalist assignment.

Woolley may not have found the *Statistical Abstract* compelling reading, but he enthusiastically believed in the news value of American industry. He stuffed his notebook with such story ideas as "peanuts, clothespins, buttons, cotton and tin cans." And as dry as the material

Lincoln Steffens.

looked on paper, editors were eager to acquire it. The December 1913 *McClure's* contained Woolley's feature on peanut farming. The next month it was the grocery business. In February, "Buttons: A Romance of American Industry." In March, "Tin Canners: The Story of the Greatest Utility Industry of the Age and the Men Who Built It." Then, beginning in April, the magazine published a seven-part series on executives, including Samuel Insull, the Chicago electricity magnate, and D. W. Griffith, who earned at least $100,000 a year.

Despite his emphasis on industry, Woolley hated to hear the phrase "business stuff" applied to his work. "What I was trying to do went wholly beyond mere business," he wrote. It was nothing less than "the eternal and ubiquitous competition of men for existence and supremacy." Three quarters of a million readers subscribed to *McClure's* or purchased it at newsstands. In each issue they received the same edifying lessons. "There is money sticking out everywhere in this land of ours," Woolley suggested in a story about the grocery business, "but you've got to reach for it quickly or somebody else nabs it." American business—any

Frank Wiegel.

business, no matter how lowly or obscure—offered the chance at success to any individual with the grit to seize it. "Every industry is worth studying, if only to get acquainted with the stayers who have made it," he wrote in an article on button making. "After all, the real inside story of an industry is the story of the men, not the money."

Woolley believed that his own rise from lowly reporter to magazine luminary followed the same trajectory that his subjects had taken. The cold numbers in the *Statistical Abstract* did not convey his story; instead he took the novels of Horatio Alger, Jr., to be his model. Conceding that such works as *Strive and Succeed* or *Andy Grant's Pluck* featured some "crude workmanship," Woolley nevertheless insisted that the tales contained "eternal truths" and "ranked as masterpieces." Even more to the point, Alger's books for boys sold a million copies each year, putting them "easily first among the best-sellers." Every so often, small-town lads, their imaginations agitated by the paperback tales of metropolitan adventure, would run away to New York. The police were used to it. After some bitter lessons, the kids would be put on a train and sent home, chastened and disappointed.

Frank Wiegel had lived in Brooklyn long enough to have abandoned any such naïve ideas. Around eight A.M. on Saturday, January 18, he showed up to work at the Henry Bosch wallpaper company, which had a factory on Thirty-fifth Street, near the East River. At nearly two A.M. on Sunday morning, still at it, he fell asleep at his station; "in some way," speculated the subsequent report, "he knocked against the controlling pedal, and the next thing he knew his hand was caught in the machine." When rescuers finally disentangled him from the apparatus, the index and pinky fingers of his right hand were too badly mangled to be saved. The accident had occurred seventeen hours and fifty-five minutes into an eighteen-hour shift. Frank was fifteen years old.

2.

The Jobless Man and the Manless Job

"I wisht they'd hurry up."
"Look at the cop watchin'."
"Maybe it ain't winter, nuther."
   —THEODORE DREISER, "THE MEN IN THE STORM"

They arrived early at the Municipal Lodging House in January, gathering out front during the afternoon and waiting hours for admittance. By evening they stood ten wide, blotting out the sidewalk, stretching down East Twenty-fifth Street and around the corner to First Avenue. Their hats no longer kept to shape. Fists rooted deep inside coat pockets. On the coldest nights, as many as two thousand men, as well as dozens of women and a few children, queued outside—nearly twice as many as the facility could accommodate. Of all the homeless in New York, these were the neediest cases: They could not afford a dime for a bed at one of Manhattan's hundreds of cheap hotels, they did not possess the pennies it took to sleep in the back room of a saloon. With no friends or relatives to shelter them, they had no choice but the last resort, to ask for the city's charity.

"Ain't they ever goin' to open up?"

Toward the front: smiles and jostling. Fewer jokes further back. There was "no anger, no threatening words," only "sullen endurance." The newspapers called them loafers. College students went slumming to observe them. To sociologists they were "human derelicts and poor stranded flotsam and jetsam." Among the hundreds and hundreds of homeless, perhaps a few deserved these derogations: the rounders, Bowery bums, and "confirmed beggars." Others were broken and without

A crowd of men outside the city's Municipal Lodging House.

hope, the "physically disabled, the mentally deficient, the infirm from age." Many had succumbed to "intoxicating liquors." But most were vigorous "native sons" of New York, "a collection of broad back, red faced, strong armed young men," who had been victimized by a devastating industrial recession. Bakers, barbers, printers, teamsters: Their motive power had built the subways and office towers, unloaded ship cargo onto the piers, operated the machines of production. Chance had not befriended them, and it was their fell misfortune in this grave-cold winter to be "reserve labor out of place and out of season."

At six P.M., the doors opened and the line stuttered forward. There was "push and jam for a minute," but the policemen at the entrance—as well as an attendant with a blackjack—demanded order, and the shoving steadied into a blank progress of "hats and shoulders, a cold, shrunken, disgruntled mass pouring in between bleak walls." Outside, fear increased as the line shortened. At any moment, the gatekeepers would shout, "Beat it!" or "All out!" The door would slam closed, and the unfortunates still on the street would spend the night folded up between the iron armrests of a park bench.

Those who made it inside faced interrogation. "They are told that they must go back to their relatives, or made to feel at once that they can stay but a very short time, or spoken to as if they were not making an effort to get employment." Anyone who possessed twenty-five cents or more was told to leave: The city's largesse was only for the utterly destitute.

Once past the questioners, inmates were taken to the basement and forced to strip and shower. In another room, their pockets were rifled by the orderlies—the unwritten law of the lodging house was "findings is keepings"—and then their clothes were fumigated. Dinner was plain and meager, though a few coins could supplement the fare with a smuggled chop or some eggs.

Not so many years had passed since the city had sheltered its homeless in a boat moored to an East River dock. After that, the derelict were quartered in the city morgue. But those days were gone; the Municipal Lodging House on East Twenty-fifth Street had opened in 1909 at a cost of half a million dollars, and it was "one of the most elaborate of its kind ever erected" with public funds. Containing 750 beds, it was the Department of Charities' most important resource. Visitors on guided tours agreed that it was an "exceptionally fine building," as clean as a hospital. "The food being prepared looked wholesome." The bedsteads were painted white; the sheets, pillowcases, and wool blankets were "freshly creased." It was, a reporter decreed, "paradise for the wanderer." It hadn't taken long, however, for its shortcomings to reveal themselves. In the dormitories there was "rough talk," beatings, bullying, thefts. The bunk beds, rowed from window to wall, were springboards for "tuberculosis, pediculosis, and other communicable diseases." Though the building was just a few years old, it had been constructed without fire escapes.

At five A.M., the boarders were roused up and ushered out to litter the parks and streets. The next evening there would be more of them. The following week more still, too many to ignore. The number of homeless whom the city shelters could not accommodate had grown over the previous three years. In January 1912, the total had been 8,986. In 1913, it was 14,315. For 1914, the figure was predicted to double—to nearly 30,000. Though Mayor Mitchel acknowledged "an unusual condition of general unemployment," which needed to be investigated, quantified, and eased through efficiencies, he saw no cause to entertain "various suggestions of an extreme nature." Childishness, snorted Berkman: The profit system would always demand desperate, available laborers. "Modern civilization spells the paradox: The more you produce, the less you have; the more riches you create, the poorer you are."

* * *

JOHN D. ROCKEFELLER, JR., had been feeling rather homeless himself lately. Workmen had only just vacated his new mansion on Fifty-fourth Street, and though the family had occupied it since September, several rooms remained undecorated. Up north, his lodge on the Tarrytown grounds was undergoing renovations too, and the racket of building emanated from construction sites at the stables and the front gate. Furniture was continually being crated and uncrated, shipped, lost, dropped, chipped, shattered. With all these distractions—the maid had "been rushed from morning till night!"—everyone was exhausted. For a full week after the new year, Junior and his wife, Abby, did not rise for breakfast once. "We slept," he wrote his mother, "as we had not slept for weeks."

But then the vacation was over and they reluctantly returned to Manhattan. The older children—Babbie, John, Laurence, and Nelson—resumed classes and music lessons. Rockefeller went back to his suite of offices on the top floor of the Standard Oil Building at 26 Broadway, where a pile of correspondence awaited his attention.

He had hated working here at first, and had merely come to tolerate it since. For years he had attempted to impersonate a business executive, but the effort had resulted in little more than a succession of nervous collapses. The more he understood the realities of industry, the less capable he was of participating in them. He was an idealist. He was sensitive. Swindled by a stock scam, witnessing his colleagues giving bribes to party bosses at the back door—these experiences led to a crisis of conscience. Even the office furnishings—massive rolltop desks, bare walls, mustard-colored carpets, overstuffed chairs in need of "the attention of an upholsterer"—were abhorrent to his delicate tastes.

After a decade or so, he came to the same conclusion as the muckrakers: Modern corporations were so large that they could not be held to high ethical standards. He sat on the boards of directors for about a dozen companies. Somewhere within these firms, people were offering political kickbacks, manipulating stock, exploiting workers. Whatever misdemeanors they committed, they did so in his name. If there was a scandal, publicity would inevitably focus on the Rockefellers, and it would be the Tarbell series all over again. The thought tormented him. Finally he decided he had "to live with his own conscience," and so, in 1910, at the age of thirty-six, he had announced his retirement from business.

In the four years since, he had continued working in the office, but his focus had shifted to philanthropy and social reform. Serving on a grand jury to investigate the "social evil"—as prostitution was euphemistically called—he had discovered a side of the city never glimpsed during his cloistered Baptist upbringing. At the end of a rigorous inquiry, he presented his findings to the public. There was brief interest, and then nothing. The revelations were sensational, but Tammany, which was complicit in the corruption, had little will to pursue them. Junior did not give up. Realizing a sense of his own mission, he decided to use his family wealth for social causes; the Rockefeller fortune could bridge the gap between "seeing the need for and getting done." He founded the Municipal Research Bureau, which launched studies on prostitution and policing practices. His Bureau of Social Hygiene opened a laboratory to examine the sexual habits of women inmates at the Bedford Hills reformatory.

This was vital labor, and by 1914 Rockefeller was a recognized patron of reform, "a much more important man to the country and to the world," decreed *Current Literature*, "than he ever would have become as a financial magnate." But accolades just masked the fact that the actual work was being done by others, while Junior's time still went to accounting for expenses, signing receipts, and other drudgery. "No one else can do the big things as well as you can," his wife consoled him, "no one has the faith, the courage and the persistent desire that you have." But, she continued, "I have felt with deep regret, that others were doing the inspiring part of your work while you poor dear were looking after the details of the neglected work of some underling." In her opinion, there was no need for her husband "to be quite so modest as he is."

JUNIOR LOOKED TO the letters and memoranda that had crowded on his desk during his absence. It was the usual assortment of looming crises and petty annoyances: Christmas cards, entreaties, expense reports.

Several documents dealt with the incoming administration. Junior admired the new mayor. He had been one of the largest contributors to the campaign and had written a warm letter of congratulations after the victory in November. With the anti-Tammany Fusion candidates elected, he hoped that all the private work he'd done would finally prove useful to the public authorities. "As you know," he wrote Mitchel in December, "the Bureau of Social Hygiene, with which I am connected, has been at work for several years, studying in as thorough and scientific manner as possible the whole question of the social evil . . . It is the desire of the Bureau to render to you any assistance in its power in dealing with this subject."

Before Christmas, he had gone to City Hall to meet with Mitchel, waiting for nearly an hour in an anteroom before being admitted for a few minutes of conversation. This was all that the mayor-elect could spare. He was living a nightmare of importunities and requests: Every-one in New York who had any connection to politics had a friend or rela-tive to recommend for a position. But Rockefeller did not have to discuss appointees, since so many of his own people had already committed to joining the new government. Katharine Bement Davis, manager of his Laboratory of Social Hygiene, was the new commissioner of correction. The director of his Bureau of Municipal Research, Henry Bruère, was now city chamberlain. Raymond B. Fosdick, currently studying law enforce-ment in Europe, was a leading candidate to head the New York Police Department. If anything, Rockefeller worried that too many of his own people would be lured away.

Some on his staff believed that with a Progressive mayor in office, the Rockefeller bureaus had become redundant. A few even suggested that the continued existence of these private organizations would tempt Mitchel to inaction. "They believe," internal memoranda suggested, "that a known large fund in the Bureau's hands will paralyze the initia-tive of the administration." But others—including Junior—thought that since they had already sacrificed Davis and Bruère, their duty now was to support them as fully as possible. A reform regime backed by Rockefeller resources could do unprecedented work for social uplift. "Our effort should be not merely to get an honest and economic administration," Junior's advisers concluded, "but to raise the standard so high as to make the Mitchel Mayoralty a memorable object lesson of Good Government and thereby a substantial asset of the reformer in future Municipal cam-paigns."

Also on his desk was correspondence addressed to stockholders of the Colorado Fuel & Iron Company. This certainly concerned him, since he and his father together owned 40 percent of the shares. In addition, Ju-nior sat on the board; it was the sole directorship he had kept after his retirement from business in 1910. He had decided to stay on because the Colorado mining concern was one of the worst acquisitions the family had ever made. In the decade or so since the Rockefellers got involved, it had never made a profit, or paid a single dividend on its common stock. Junior had remained out of loyalty: He "had to see it through" until it had been put on a sound footing. He eagerly looked forward to the time when Colorado Fuel & Iron would be securely solvent and he could finally relinquish his last ties to the world of business. But that was look-ing like an increasingly distant prospect.

The family's representative on the scene was Lamont Montgomery Bowers, a veteran executive with impressive successes in his past. But

Bowers was a truculent opponent of organized labor, and in September—when miners across the southern Colorado coal fields had gone on strike—he had chosen to take an inflexible line. His was a dominating personality, typical of an earlier generation of business autocrats. Believing that his company treated its employees as generously as could be asked, he was convinced that agitators from the United Mine Workers were fomenting discontent among his uneducated, immigrant workforce. Bowers's "whole attitude was paternalistic in character," Junior recalled. "He had the kindness-of-heart theory, i.e., that he was glad to treat the men well, not that they had any necessary claim to it, but because it was the proper attitude of a Christian gentleman." He hired replacement workers and private detectives and steeled himself for combat. Bowers would stand against the strikers, and from New York Rockefeller would stand by him, even if at times he felt that his older subordinate sometimes treated him like another one of his misguided employees. "You are fighting a good fight," Junior wrote in early December, "which is not only in the interest of your own company but of the . . . business interests of the entire country and of the laboring classes quite as much."

The newspapers were reporting that Mother Jones was back in Trinidad, Colorado, the town nearest to the center of the coalfields struggle. A matronly rabble-rouser, Jones went where the trouble was, traveling from strike to strike, encouraging the workers to rise up against their employers. Bowers had complained to Junior about her back in September, and the governor of Colorado blamed the entire conflict on her "incendiary teachings." This time her visit was brief. Militiamen seized her before she had even stepped off the train, held her for two hours in the local jail, and then deported her to Denver. As the locomotive stirred, she had called out to the miners, promising to return to Colorado "as soon as it becomes a part of the United States."

On the day after Christmas, Rockefeller had sent another letter before leaving for Tarrytown. And there were two new replies waiting for him when he returned to his office. The reports were mixed. "There are several hundred sluggers camped within the strike zone, who have rifles and ammunition in large quantities," Bowers wrote, "we are facing a guerrilla warfare that is likely to continue for months to come." On the business side, however, news was better. "Everything is running along about as usual," the second note said. Men were deserting from the strikers' camps. Nonunion workers were proving satisfactory. The mines were producing as much coal as the market demanded.

With the Colorado matters tended to, there was finally the business of the antiques for his new house on West Fifty-fourth Street. During the previous month, his home had been transformed into a gallery, with dozens of antiques on loan from dealers' collections. Vases and sculptures, beakers and benches—he had arranged and rearranged them. And, unfortunately, he had broken some, too: A teakwood stand had splintered, and a Persian vase had crashed from the mantel in the dining room. Now, after weeks in the presence of these treasures, he was ready to commit to the items that had truly moved him. He struck a bargain, agreeing to pay for the damages in exchange for getting 10 percent off the entire transaction. He commissioned the dealer's secretary to go from room to room, properly bracing and riveting the various stands and cabinets in order to prevent further destruction.

Junior had initially felt a little selfish collecting art objects, worried that he was buying for himself "instead of giving to public need." But over time he had embraced the pleasure that material beauty inspired in him. After all, "he wasn't taking bread from anybody's mouth," and the

Abby Aldrich Rockefeller.

pieces would end up in museums anyway, so surely he was justified in spending some small part of his fortune on things that gave him joy. Wandering the rooms of his new mansion, carefully avoiding any more accidents, he savored the sense of occupying a space that he himself had designed to his own sensibilities. The money to build it may have come from his position in life, but nobody could accuse him of inheriting his taste. It was one of the few things he could truly call his own.

*　*　*

AN INFINITESIMAL MOVEMENT disrupted the predawn stillness. On the roof of the Whitehall Building, 454 feet above Battery Place at Manhattan's southern terminus, the Weather Bureau's thermograph machine took its reading. A trembling brass tube, filled with liquid, jarred a train of levers attached to a pen that bore down lightly, leaving a mark on a slowly rotating drum of graph paper: At seven A.M. on January 12, the temperature was 27 degrees.

Smoke puffed and clotted round the chimneys above a hundred thousand other rooftops. In the barren avenues, the streetlights had just switched off. A suggestion of sunrise showed from the east. Policemen relieved the peg posts, marking the shift change with a single tap of a baton to the sidewalk; in the silence, the thwack of wood on pavement could be heard for blocks. At 7:23 A.M., almanac dawn, the morning gun fired from the military installation on Governor's Island; tugs and schooners in the harbor replied with whistles and jeers of their own. The elevated trains crowded up, rattling windows; subways droned below. From the South Ferry and Bowling Green stations, thousands of men, joined by high-heeled office girls displaying "their cold little legs in cheap bright stockings of imitation silk," rushed toward the office towers. Hundreds made for the Whitehall Building and their desks at the White Star Line, the U.S. Realty and Improving Company, or O'Rourke Engineering.

Above their heads, the Weather Bureau accumulated data. The thermograph's paper drum continued to spin; the line of ink grew jagged and started to descend. Beside it, the anemometer's four gyrating cups creaked and then began to fly. An Arctic gale bore down, a wall of wind amplified and eddying among the tall buildings and narrow streets. The currents "seized old ladies and tangoed with them at crossings." Women near City Hall had their legs knocked from under them; some were carried fifty feet or more until they were dashed into walls and autos. Falling signs and construction debris fractured skulls. A man was blown off an elevated station platform into the tracks; another was chucked into the East River.

A schooner ran aground. Policemen abandoned their fixed posts, fleeing to the safety of the precinct houses. Smoke whipped from the chimneys and vanished in the onrushing currents. At three P.M., with the anemometer spinning nearly out of its socket, the forecaster's register marked the wind's velocity at seventy-four miles an hour.*

By sundown, Battery Park had emptied. Benches in the plazas and promenades sat vacant. "The Bowery was deserted," a reporter for the *Call* described, "and the saloons, restaurants and similar places were filled to capacity with the shivering, emaciated mass of humanity, whose sole thought was to keep out of the cold." Hundreds more went to missions, University Settlement, or the Salvation Army. And in numbers greater than on any other night in its history, they wandered toward the Municipal Lodging House. By eight P.M., the facility's beds were filled. Latecomers received coffee in a tin cup and some hunks of bread. Some were taken to sleep in the city morgue. Others were led to the Charities Department docks, on East Twenty-sixth Street, where three ferry boats were moored. Once aboard they made do "on the benches, in reclining chairs, inside and outside the cabins." They lay close together on the unheated ships, more than a thousand of them, newspapers and overcoats substituting for blankets.

Long after everyone else was settled, John Adams Kingsbury, the newly appointed commissioner of charities, remained active, stalking between the ferries, issuing directives, planning improvements. Until three A.M. he stayed among his charges, and by then he had seen too much to keep still. At thirty-seven years old, he was young even for Mitchel's youthful administration. A leading theorist of philanthropy, he had not yet learned the policy of silence. "I consider that the present provision for this overflow is absolutely inhumane, inadequate, and indecent," he stormed to reporters the next day. "The men are packed like sardines on the floors of the waiting rooms and docks and suffer severely from the cold."

The new administration was stocked with nonconformists, but Kingsbury could be downright unconventional. "He is of medium height," a reporter wrote, "well built, and wears a mustache and short beard, which cannot hide the kindliness of his face." A former socialist, he had spent part of his childhood in an orphanage and took from that experience a

---

* The highest wind velocity recorded in New York City to that point had been eighty miles an hour. At roughly 120 miles an hour, a Weather Bureau anemometer in Galveston, Texas, had blown from its mooring.

John Adams Kingsbury.

deep sympathy for his work. Mitchel had no doubt that he was the "ideal selection" to head the Charities Department. "His good faith," a colleague recalled, "was transparent." If he lacked political experience, he profused good intentions. "Nobody could meet him without realizing he was an idealist, that he was disinterested, that he was an enthusiast in trying to accomplish what he thought to be good things."

It wasn't just the men sleeping in boats that riled Kingsbury. He had occupied his office for less than two weeks and already felt plagued with emergencies. Abuses tainted every division of his department. The Children's Hospital was so polluted that patients arriving with a single illness promptly contracted several others.* Students at the nursing school were dismissed for holding late-night ginger-ale parties. Insubordinate

---

* One infant girl came to have her whooping cough treated and acquired "measles, pneumonia, abscess and possibly erysipelas" as well. A four-year-old boy had been in the wards for more than a year, though his health seemed fine. Doctors diagnosed him with a troubling condition: "no residence, no disease, no friend, no parents."

matrons grumbled at their superiors. The elderly ladies at the Home for the Aged and Infirm had no soft pillows. In the almshouse, inmates complained of fish "served usually in a dried-up condition and without gravy." Embezzlement and peculation—or "honest graft," as the Tammany men said—were as viral as the other ailments. In a single month, ten thousand pounds of bread, three thousand pounds of beef, and one thousand pounds of mutton had to be marked down simply as "not accounted for." In the morgue, keepers sodomized the corpses.

Kingsbury was responsible for the largest social welfare system in the United States. New York City housed and fed one hundred thousand children, which was one third of all the publicly supported minors in the nation. The municipality paid more for its orphans than most states paid for their university systems. During his first days in government, Kingsbury toured all the many institutions of his magistracy. Not content to follow guides on sanitized inspections, he could appear at any odd hour. He wandered "in the dead of night through the hospitals where these poor people lie suffering, frequently on the floors and packed so close as to make it most impossible to step between their prostrate forms." He inspected "the foul smelling wards where little children—sick children—sleep, two in one little crib." He watched "the feeble-minded asleep in beds crowded so close these helpless creatures must crawl over the foot to enter." He tiptoed over the roaches in an asylum on Staten Island. Then, back at home after these Bedlamite visions, he dedicated the remaining "wee small hours" to researching the history of his bureau, tracking the development of the city's welfare facilities, sketching designs to help the helpless creatures for whom he was now responsible.

THE GALE HAD exhausted itself by the morning of January 13, but temperatures were falling toward zero. For the first time in three years, the Great South Bay froze over; ice encased the shore of Long Island from the Rockaways to Shinnecock. Telephone wires grew brittle and snapped. Broken glass crunched on the sidewalks; boarded-up windows became "so common a sight as to escape comment." The Municipal Lodging House was overwhelmed and police considered converting their precinct buildings into temporary shelters. Kingsbury and Mitchel debated a plan to transform Madison Square Garden into a massive dormitory: "The suffering among the poor was the greatest in years and all agencies of relief were taxed to their limit." Six people died as a direct result of the cold; scores more were hospitalized with frostbite. Dozens of fires disturbed the evening as families in unheated tenements burned anything available to generate some warmth. At midnight, temperatures dipped to four below zero, the coldest mark of the century.*

Ten more died the next day. Already undernourished and unhealthy, they no longer possessed the stamina to resist the cold. The city veered toward catastrophe and the Mitchel administration faced its first emergency. Tammany leaders had been able to improvise solutions. When storms came, thousands were crammed into saloons or meeting halls. Unemployment and homelessness were ward problems, resolved through handouts, favors, personal connections—or simply ignored. But the reform government couldn't backslide into these old folkways. Progressive methods were required, and Commissioner Kingsbury had to provide them. He began with the worst abuses. Touring the moored ferries, seeing "the prostrate forms of homeless men strewn over the deck of the boats . . . huddled like hogs on the hard floor, and smelling worse than any hog-pen could," had shocked even his toughened sensibilities. By the night of the fourteenth, he had enclosed an open-air pier and imported hundreds of additional cots. More than that he could not accomplish alone.

On January 16, the mayor attended the theater. Afterward, he was driven to East Twenty-fifth Street, where Kingsbury was waiting to lead him and Katharine Davis, the new commissioner of correction, on a tour of the Municipal Lodging House. For Mitchel, these occasions usually ended with a headache. They passed through all six floors, beginning around midnight, when the dormitories were filled with sleeping men. "Others, awake, sat up and looked hard at the Mayor as he made his way among the long rows of cots. The Mayor smiled at those who spoke to him, but addressed none of them." In a dinner jacket, silk hat, and overcoat, he was profoundly uncomfortable and out of place. Ms. Davis, who had superintended the women at Bedford Hills prison for years, was more at her ease. As the elevator opened at the basement, Kingsbury stepped out first. The others started to follow, when suddenly he turned and rustled them back inside. They had accidentally arrived at the shower room, and it was in use. Luckily, the mayor's—and Ms. Davis's—dignity had been preserved.

Distasteful as it had been—and if not for Kingsbury's sharp reflexes, it could have been much more unfortunate—the experience prompted

---

* The previous time that temperatures had fallen so low had been fifteen years earlier, in 1899.

Mitchel toward intervention. "Times are hard," he proclaimed, "and the city should meet the situation." More soup was to be distributed. A new municipal employment agency would link jobless men with vacant positions. Statistics would be compiled. "Above everything else I believe that it is important that we should not become panicky," he said. "We must be optimistic and go right ahead buying what we need and giving employment so that these conditions will improve as quickly as possible."

UNFORTUNATELY FOR THE administration, goodwill alone could not address these problems. A condition of "industrial leanness" affected the entire country. Everyone remembered the panic of 1893, when prosperity had "collapsed like a house of cards," and the winter of 1908, which had seen "thousands and thousands of people out of employment." It appeared that 1914 would be as hard or worse. Kingsbury's own Association for Improving the Conditions of the Poor, "an old and conservative organization," estimated 325,000 jobless men in New York City alone. Nationwide, the total approached three million; more than one third of all employees were out of work or laboring part-time. Distressing reports arrived from every state:

Kalamazoo, Mich.—A thousand men idle; works closing down.
Pottsville, Pa.—Ten thousand men of the Lehigh Coal and Navigation Co. in the Panther Creek Valley have been laid off.
Washington, D.C.—With the completion of the Panama Canal, about 30,000 workers, a large number of them residents of the continental United States, will be out of employment.
Joplin, Mo.—Two thousand men in the Joplin zinc district are reported out of work.
Schenectady, N.Y.—Three thousand employees of the General Electric company have been laid off till spring.
Pendleton, Ore.—Farmers are furnishing meat for the hundreds out of employment in various small cities near here. Twelve hundred rabbits were contributed in one day.
Los Angeles, Calif.—Mrs. Mary E. Erickson, a widow, out of work and threatened with starvation, threw a brick through a plate glass window so she might be arrested and given food.

But to some, the weather made for a charming diversion. At Pocantico Hills, Junior and his wife had awakened "to find five inches of snow on the ground and every twig of every tree and bush beautifully covered with pure white snow . . . the picture from every window was simply like a fairyland." In New York City, during the most frigid moments of the gale, some wealthy residents had "laughed at the weather and all its works" by strapping into their ice skates and tangoing across the marbled surface of Van Cortlandt Lake in the Bronx. As they danced, others were freezing. Of the dozen or so fatalities that week, one in particular embodied the iniquity of suffering. On January 13, a socialite rode to a Carnegie Hall concert. While she was inside, her chauffeur sat behind the wheel in the open cab of her limousine. Two hours into the performance, a policeman suspected he had fallen asleep and tried to nudge him awake; the chauffeur slumped forward in his seat, dead from exposure.

For revolutionaries, such incidents presented an opportune crisis. Nothing radicalized the working classes like a business panic. "At Rutgers Square, at Tompkins Square Park, in Mulberry Bend, almost anywhere in the tenement districts," recalled a young radical, "a few minutes of speech-making would draw a thousand people together." Pointing out that Congress's new billion-dollar budget had failed to allocate a single penny to "aid the out-of-works," the Socialist Party offered a platform of jobs bureaus and government relief through public projects.

Wealthy residents taking the opportunity to ice tango on the lake at Van Cortlandt Park.

Anarchists scoffed at such reformism, urging direct action. "The problem of unemployment cannot be solved within the capitalist regime," Alexander Berkman noted. "If the unemployed would realize this, they would refuse to starve; they would help themselves to the things they need. But as long as they meekly wait for the governmental miracle, they will be doomed to hunger and misery."

The suffering had forced people to attend to questions that they otherwise might have ignored. For the first time in years, even influential professionals were discussing unemployment, lecturing on the subject, offering advice. When Mayor Mitchel appealed to the public for suggestions, the responses flooded first his office, and then the Department of Charities, so that Kingsbury—who was already holding daily staff meetings on the question—had to request that future letters be forwarded to the commissioner of licenses.

As yet everyone was dictating to the unemployed; no party or group had emerged to speak on their behalf. One potential candidate, the American Federation of Labor, the most powerful association of working people in the country, exhibited scant interest in the task. The organization favored skilled workingmen; it had no place for factory drones, let alone the homeless or jobless. It claimed two million adherents in all regions and industries. But they were sundered into hundreds of competitive subdivisions. In 1913, the A.F. of L. consisted of 110 national and international unions, 22,000 locals, five departments, 42 state branches, 623 city central unions, and 642 local trade and federal labor unions. Organized by trades, the separate units could be insular and competitive. A major industry, such as railroads, could easily be partitioned into a dozen distinct craft associations and brotherhoods, each with its own ambitions and interests. Brakemen, engineers, and conductors thought of themselves as brakemen, engineers, and conductors, not as a unified group of workers with a single set of needs.*

Since the federation was not interested, that left only one group with the potential to transform the disorganized and destitute into a militant

---

* The A.F. of L. annual convention, which had just met in Seattle, had brought together the Alliance of Bill Posters and Billers of America; the International Association of Heat, Frost, Insulators, and Asbestos Workers; the Pocketknife Blade Grinders' and Finishers' National Union; the International Union of Pavers, Rammermen, Flaglayers, Bridge, and Stone Curb Setters; the Travelers' Goods and Leather Novelty Workers' International Union of America; the International Union of the United Brewery, Flour, Cereal and Soft Drink Workers of America; and the International Union of Journeymen Horse-shoers of the United States and Canada.

and coherent force—an organization for which unity was a watchword, that insisted upon local leadership and total inclusiveness. For a decade, the Industrial Workers of the World—or Wobblies—had pushed "straight revolutionary workingclass solidarity."

The Wobblies' membership totaled about 1 percent of the A.F. of L.'s, but they offered "One Big Union" of all the workers, were more welcoming to women and minorities, and had long organized conference committees for the unemployed. While the craft unions focused on workplace issues "pure and simple," the I.W.W. saw these gains as the first step toward industrial democracy. "The final aim . . . is revolution," one leader explained. "But for the present *let's see if we can get a bed to sleep in, water enough to take a bath and decent food to eat.*" This vision transformed the tiny, impoverished, anarchic I.W.W. into a looming menace. Capitalism could survive if the Pocketknife Blade Grinders' and Finishers' National Union won a pay increase, but the fulfillment of the Wobbly dream would mean revolution. "Organized a little we control a little," they liked to say, "organized more we control more; organized as a class we control everything."

The Industrial Workers of the World had been founded in the western timber and mine lands, but most of its victories were urban. It had waged free-speech fights in Denver and San Diego, had organized a triumphant strike versus the textile masters of Lawrence, Massachusetts, and its long battle against the silk lords of Paterson, New Jersey, right across the Hudson River, had just ended. But the Wobblies had not fared well in Gotham itself, and national leaders were grumbling. Big Bill Haywood, the union's most notorious spokesman, was eager for anything that would make "the town rise out of a stupor." And other organizers asked, "Why has not the I.W.W. a stronghold in the greatest industrial center of this country, New York City?"

The metropolis contained several chapters, including Local Number One, but the meeting halls on Grand and West streets were somnolent. "Are they alive?" the leaders wondered. "No—the most of them fell asleep." The problem, reported the official newspaper, *Solidarity*, was solidarity. Meetings were disrupted by discussions "of a purely theoretical nature," and the entire area had become "afflicted with internal discussion." Sections were "worried into a state of inanition" by debates between political actionists and antipolitical actionists, centralizers and decentralizers. Eager recruits who had joined to accomplish "effective, constructive work" discovered an atmosphere of constant "peevish, petulant criticism" and soon dropped out.

Still, many chose to be optimistic. If only you could "fight capitalism as well as you fight one another," a member wrote to his comrades, then the I.W.W. would have already achieved its goals. It was time to "drop all hobbies and get into the harness" for "one big united effort!" A drive to organize restaurant and hotel workers was producing results. And the unemployment situation offered new chances for agitation. "Let us fight against capitalism," wrote a national leader, "as we never fought before; and make the year 1914 glorious in the history of the SOCIAL REVO-LUTION!"

The local ennui had not affected Frank Tannenbaum's faith in the One Big Union. On the contrary, he "took interest in nothing but the I.W.W . . . read nothing but of the I.W.W . . . considered all speech futile which did not ostentatiously expound the unexcelled virtues of the I.W.W." Nineteen years old, he had worked as an omnibus, washing dishes, in a luncheon club in Wall Street until late in 1913, when he—like so many others—had lost his job.* Unable to pay for his room at the Sherman Hotel, in the Bowery, he had taken to sleeping in parks and lodging houses. Increasingly, he found himself in "close contact with the unemployed in New York City." He watched "men pick bread out of garbage barrels and wash it under a street pump so that it might be fit to eat." At night he sat with them, "closely huddled together, with their collars drawn up, their hands in their pockets, and heads tucked in to keep as warm as the conditions permitted." He joined them in their search for a job, standing in line for advertised positions, and never coming close to reaching the window. "Looking for work and not finding it," a former stonemason told a reporter, "is the hardest work I know." These were the same people the papers decried as shiftless loafers, profiting from the city's generosity. "It's a lie," Frank muttered as he read such stories. "A d——d lie."

He had been born in Austrian Galicia in 1894. Ten years later, his family steamed to the United States. Borrowing money from relatives, the Tannenbaums purchased an abandoned farm near the town of Liberty in the southern Catskills. But rural life was "not all honey and flowers, bluebirds and green grass." The apparent freedom of outdoor work tangled with orthodoxy and constraint, "poverty, ignorance, loneliness, and narrowed and blighted lives." Frank felt himself stultifying, and while still a youth he fled the feudal relations of peasant life for greener pastures in the Bronx.

---

* Today, a restaurant "omnibus" would be called a "bus boy."

Frank Tannenbaum.

Tannenbaum had suffocated on the farm, but in the city he remained "restless, dissatisfied." He had come to try and educate himself; his ambition was to earn a high school degree. But conditions did not allow it. He had to find employment to support himself. Working as an elevator operator, he read Plato between ascents and descents. All he knew was that he had to keep learning; he felt "a sort of inarticulate hunger, a longing for books." He took close notes on all he read, and then, at night, he and his friends would walk across the Brooklyn Bridge carrying on passionate arguments about their conclusions. He found his greatest fulfillment in politics. His "best friends and his bitterest enemies" were the comrades in I.W.W.'s Local Number 179. It was "a socializing vortex" of passions and disputes, committee meetings, "picnics, parties, benefits and funerals." When he wasn't down in the hall on West Street, he was uptown with the anarchists at the Ferrer Center, their community school and meetinghouse. He came to know Berkman and Goldman, impressing them with "his wide-awakeness and his unassuming ways," and aided in the chores of publishing *Mother Earth*.

He was quiet and conscientious. Neither he nor anyone else could ever remember him being impolite. With tousled black hair under a floppy woolen cap, a tight smile, and no trace of a beard, there was little to distinguish him from the city's other youths. And his ordinariness was agony. His aspirations mocked him. "What are you doing? What have you done? What are you planning?" These questions he constantly asked himself. Interacting with the elders of his movement, he was self-effacing and deferential, but he persecuted his peers with propaganda. Those who disagreed with him "were stupid, ignorant, useless people." He "scorned the Socialists, the American F. of L.," and "despised their methods."

According to a friend, Frank possessed "three predominant faults, namely 1. a noticeable desire to become popular 2. self conceit 3. too much of the ego." But he didn't see these as flaws: Focus and determination were necessary for success. "Personally ambitious, desirous for place, acknowledgment, and honor," he found, through the I.W.W., "a constant battleground for the attainment, as well as expression, of these ends and motives." He helped to organize restaurant workers, contributed fifty cents to the legal defense fund, and volunteered as secretary for the Industrial Union League. But so far he had done nothing memorable; he had not distinguished himself. In the evenings, he strategized with friends, drafting elaborate plots to further the cause of industrial democracy—and, incidentally, to force the name Frank Tannenbaum into the public mind.

*　*　*

THE NEXT STORM rolled up along the tracks. Following the Atchison, Topeka & Santa Fe lines from New Mexico, it dropped ten inches of snow in St. Louis on the morning of February 13. Three thousand men dug out the Union Station yards, but the switches were frozen and traffic stopped moving east. The weather surged forward, tracing the Pennsylvania Railroad tracks and the New York Central System, through Cincinnati, eight and a half inches; Wilkes-Barre, twelve inches; Scranton, twenty inches. Depending on one's location, it was the worst storm of the year, of the past three, the most snow seen since the "Big White Christmas" of 1912, the biggest in five years, the most destructive since the Great Blizzard of '88.

The first flakes that fell on Grand Central Terminal, in the early evening, were "small and dry and were blown about." At midnight, the storm grew serious. By one A.M., "snow was coming down in blinding swirls." Plows, sand, and channel cars couldn't keep the transportation network running. Streetcars and elevated trains were blocked, autos stalled as "engines tore their hearts out trying to buck their way through drifts, and tires wore to ribbons with mileage that could hardly be measured." Dead machines clogged the streets. In the railroad stations, people escaping the weather mixed with those waiting for friends and relatives to arrive. The Twentieth Century Limited, the Chicago Express, and everything on the Lackawanna lines were hours late. Some companies doubled up their engines, but trapped locomotives blocked tracks throughout Pennsylvania and across the Mohawk Valley. The Erie Railroad was "badly demoralized." The Albany Local was "annulled." Ten inches of loose and powdery "dry sleet" fell in the city, making walking "difficult and treacherous." And then the tempest passed on—along the New York, New Haven, and Hartford tracks—toward Maine.

ON THE MORNING of February 14, during the storm's hardest anger, unemployed men, boys, and one woman, "with collars turned up and hands thrust deep in their pockets as the drifts formed about their feet," queued out front of No. 27 Lafayette Street. Inside, the staff completed its final preparations to convert a giant storeroom into the city's first municipal employment bureau. The mayor was certain that this new institution could lessen the muckery and muddle that lay behind the labor crisis. There were 725 licensed job-placement agencies in the metropolis, but their efforts did not coordinate. Together they had only managed to fill 58.5 percent of all available positions. More than ten thousand jobs remained empty as a result of the scattered system. "The figures show conclusively," Mitchel argued, "the need for a clearing house, so that in some place in the city a man or woman looking for a job can find out whether a job he or she can fill is available anywhere in the city." At eight A.M., the doors opened, and the line of potential workers slogged inside. The examiners took down their pedigrees and the names of their most recent employers. The results revealed a hearty crowd of chauffeurs, clerks, carpenters, and bakers. "There wasn't a single man among them," a reporter thought, "who didn't look as if he had something to offer in return for employment." And, as it happened, New York had suddenly acquired the need for such a crew.

Ten inches of snow lay atop three hundred miles of avenues and boulevards in the greater city. The sanitation department had twenty-three hundred full-time street cleaners, sweepers, and drivers. In a big storm,

SNOWBOUND NEW YORK 2/14/14

February 14, 1914.

that number could be doubled with auxiliary helpers hired through private contractors, but even this force could remove only an inch of snow per day. Barring a thaw, that meant it would take more than a week to clear the streets. In the meantime, the fire hydrants were blocked and streetcar service was in disarray. Extra hands were urgently needed, and the administration knew just where to locate them. On its first day of operation, the municipal employment bureau assigned 570 men to shovel snow, at a salary of thirty-five cents an hour. A temporary solution to the jobs crisis, certainly, but nevertheless the combination of labor and laborers had the aspect of providence.

The slush froze hard. By the afternoon, men were hacking at ice, stretching to lift their loads onto small, high carts and losing half a batch with each shovelful. After two days, with progress finally apparent, another flurry added a new layer of a "fluffy sort" of flake, and everything backed up again. Fifteen inches—three million cubic yards—of snow covered the streets. Twenty thousand men were now at work, and even Mayor Mitchel plied a shovel.

Up in Tarrytown, Rockefeller Senior's golf course lay beneath two feet of snow. He had to keep himself—and a hundred employees—busy by digging out the paths around his house.

After a week, even the city's main thoroughfares remained deranged, the ice skaters had discovered new diversions, and reserves of good humor had emptied. "As a comedy of inefficiency and waste and feebleness, nothing could equal the scenes of overcoming this blockade of New York's streets," griped the *World*. "It is Lilliputians wrestling with a native of Brogdingnag. It is an army of moles working at a mountain."

Thirty-five cents an hour was no fortune, considering the severity of the work. And that old foe, graft, incised deeply into even this meager sum. Each person sent from the employment bureau was directed to a private contractor who took twenty-five cents off the top plus a dime to hire the shovel. After an eight-hour day, and another nickel for the foreman, a man might have a dollar left. But he didn't get a dollar, he got a ticket, which he could use only at a particular saloon. There he was charged 20 percent to cash the thing and was forced to buy a drink. "Well, you are faint, frozen, trembling with weakness and fatigue," a snow digger explained:

You are only human. You may take two drinks, three drinks, four— and your body has paid the toll of toil and you are dazed with bad whiskey that saps what little strength and resolution you have left. The next day, sick, aching, empty, you haven't a penny, you haven't any strength, any heart or any hope—you are only sick, aching and starving; your feet are bruised and wet and cold, your dirty clothes cut and chafe you, the grime and sweat is caked on you—you are a dead man who limps and aches and whimpers!

It only took a few days before protests began to disturb the business of the municipal employment bureau. Sick of shoveling, the men "became obstreperous," and the director called in police reserves to drive them out. Two hundred marched from the exchange to City Hall, denouncing a system that identified a quarter million men out of work, offered a few of them pennies to perform back-destroying labor, and considered the problem solved.

THE LAST OF the snow was gone, washed into the sewers by a blessed rain, when on the morning of February 27 hundreds of delegates crammed City Hall for the first national conference on "The Jobless Man and the Manless Job." Representatives from charity groups in Chicago, Milwaukee, London, and dozens of other municipalities were on hand to share their experiences. John Adams Kingsbury sat on the dais, and Mayor Mitchel offered the opening statements, extolling the success of his new employment office, suggesting mild remedies, cautioning against drastic measures. That evening, the conference held a second session at Cooper Union. The tone became less reserved. There were half a million vagrants and beggars in the United States, a delegate claimed, and each year they caused $25 million in damages to property. "We must do something," cried another. "We cannot let things go on as they have been doing." During the general discussion, an audience member asked William Howard Taft what advice he'd give an able man looking for work; the former president shook his head and replied, "God knows."

Outside the hall, a massing, angry crowd gathered to listen to more constructive suggestions. The principal speaker, a nineteen-year-old boy in a worn-out cap, had a plan. "New York City is full of churches," he explained. "We will march to one of them and go to bed. If they don't like it, they can lock us up and then we can sleep in jail. We will march to the Court Houses and they can lock us up. We must get some food, too. In this city there is plenty of bread and provisions. We have a right to as much as we can eat." And with a thousand men behind him, he led his army of unemployed toward the Old Baptist Tabernacle on Second Avenue. The next morning, New York City would finally read his name, or at least a version of it: "Frank Lenebaum."

The Social Evil

There was a time when Americans had spoken of prostitution as the "Social Evil." Just so, capitalized and with the definite article—the Social Evil—as if all the ills of modern life were reducible to a single Satan. By 1914, such generalities seemed antiquated: Wickedness had specialized. The Social Evil was disaggregated into its constitutive elements: the prostitution evil, the industrial evil, the political evil, the tenement evil, the smoke evil, the divorce evil, the automobile evil, the gang evil, the moving-pictures evil, the cigarette evil, the pushcart evil, the tango evil, "the whiskey evil, the slavery evil, the gambling evil, the living for pleasure evil, and the capital and labor war evil."

Traditionally, curbing vice had been church business. But the calamitous conditions of the cities now sprawled beyond the pulpit's reach. All the best elements rallied, forming a "wave of moral house cleaning," an "organized militia of philanthropy" as various and diversified as sin itself. Chicago, Philadelphia, Minneapolis, Atlanta, Jacksonville, Little Rock: Between 1910 and 1914, each of them sponsored vice investigations of their own. Colorado had a Denver Morals Commission. In Pittsburgh, there was a Moral Efficiency Commission. In Syracuse, the Moral Survey Committee. The trend was ubiquitous. "Everything is being reformed these days," an editor marveled. "Not to reform is out of date."

For someone seeking to "catalogue the eighty-seven or eight thousand and seven societies that have been organized to do New York good," a columnist for the *World* suggested, the place to start was the Charities Directory. The 1896 edition ran to 517 pages; by 1911, the volume was nearly twice as thick, its leaves crowded with handy entries for the New York Cremation Society, the Clean Streets League, the Country Home for Convalescent Babies, the International Pure Milk League, the Society of Sanitary and Moral Prophylaxis, the Committee on the Congestion of Population, the Union of Religious and Humanitarian Societies for Concerted Moral Effort, the Society for the Prevention of Useless Noises.

Whereas previous generations had practiced social reform, the catchword for the twentieth century was "social hygiene." While the former was messy and moralistic, the new discipline was systematized and professional. "Social hygiene is at once more radical and more scientific than the old conception of social reform," Havelock Ellis, one of its leading practitioners, explained. "It attempts not merely a haphazard amelioration of the conditions of life, but a scientific improvement in the quality of life itself."

A geography of uplift overlay the city. Trained agents of sanitary prophylaxis and capable experts in concerted moral effort toiled together within the skyscrapers of the United Charities Building and the Russell Sage Foundation, both on East Twenty-second Street, as well as the

A collage in a contemporary guidebook illustrates the baffling proliferation of charitable institutions.

Hebrew Charities Building around the corner and the Central Civic Hall a few blocks away. The Presbyterian Building on Fifth Avenue housed the Anti-Cigarette League, the Anti-Saloon League, "and half a dozen other anti-leagues" as well. Down in the Village, Theodore Dreiser watched a breadline grow "from a few applicants to many," until it had become "an institution, like a cathedral or a monument." One hundred and nineteen settlement houses operated among the immigrant neighborhoods. Concerned wardens patrolled the corridors of the Home for Friendless Girls, the Home for Intemperate Men, and the Reformatory of Misdemeanants. Young humanitarians led classes at the Institute for Atypical Persons, the School for Stammering, the School to Discipline Wayward Boys, the West Side Day Nursery Industrial School and Kindergarten.

In such a congested field, it was necessary to advertise. Yearly reports and solemn tracts no longer sufficed. "The charity that never is in the newspapers stands a good chance of being forgotten," an executive noted. "A wise board of directors always keeps things on hand to announce in the papers." Full-page proclamations routinely touted organizational accomplishments, while the Association for Improving the Condition of the Poor stumbled on the best gimmick of all: Its list of "New York's 100 Neediest Cases," published around the holidays, brought in thousands of dollars each year.

These business methods sapped philanthropy's credibility as a spiritual, altruistic enterprise. Critics began to discuss the "charities trust," a monopoly of the best-endowed organizations, which—like Standard Oil—would destroy competitors, dictate terms, and wield untrammeled power. An old couplet rose to the lips of more than one disgruntled sufferer:

> *The organized charity, scrimped and iced*
> *In the name of a cautious, statistical Christ.*

The proliferation of unions and associations was baffling. Most contemporaries would have known that the Help-Myself Society promoted temperance, that the Short Ballot Organization favored an easy-to-understand voting system, that the International Sunshine Society offered aid to blind children, and the Simple Spellers advocated typographical reform. But then the various cliques began to blend together. The Union for Practical Progress, the Purity Alliance, the American Vigilance Association: All these did valuable work, no doubt, but of which variety? And what—besides discretion—distinguished the Secret Law and Order League from the Law and Order Union, or the New York Sabbath Committee from the New York Sabbath Alliance? In churches, the pastors were so "distracted" by the various groups jostling for time during Sunday services that they began insisting on "a union of all these societies, which more or less overlap."

The Suppression of Vice was the aim of the Committee for the Suppression of Vice, and it was a laudable aim—in moderation. But others would brook no closure of saloons on Sundays, and any "lot of high toned men" who sought to "make rules and laws for the great masses" would find the German-American Reform Union standing in their way. The Committee of Seventy had to be replaced by the Committee of Fifty, which, proving unwieldy, was pared down to a Committee of Fifteen and then a Committee of Three. Denouncing all these bodies as tools for the four hundred was the Committee of One Hundred, which claimed to speak for the multitudes.

Down that road lay madness, at least in the considered opinion of experts. When a *Times* survey asked leading psychologists, "Is 'Reform' Sensationalism Responsible for the Apparent Increase of Insanity?" the answer was: Yes, oh yes. "There have been Bryanism and free silver, municipal ownership, Socialism, and other insane doctrines," a neurologist complained, "and many persons of weak minds have been so confused by the clashing of opinions that they have become insane."

Before long, many citizens decided: Enough. Too much. Murmured protests against the "pestering and hectoring of the people by flap-mouthed reformers" grew louder and more caustic. "The noble company of the half-baked," complained a *Tribune* editor, "have established themselves as our most active experts on all matters of political and business policy." Walter Lippmann declaimed against "the panacea habit of mind," whereby engineers wanted to reconstruct society, sanitation experts would scour it clean, and lawyers planned to argue it into submission. "No one who undertook to be the Balzac of reform," Lippmann would write, "could afford to miss the way in which the reformer in each profession tends to make his specialty an analogy for the whole of life."

But the social-reform craze had suffered its cruelest setback in the autumn season of 1912, when *The Charity Girl* premiered at the Globe Theatre, on Broadway and Forty-sixth Street. Billed as a "sociological document in musical comedy form," the play opened with a scene in the tenements, peopled with slummers, social reformers, white slavers, and a young girl teetering on the precipice of vice. Over the course of three acts, as many evils as could fit came bustling across the stage while the heroine progressed from the East Side to Fifth Avenue, via an airship and the timely advice of a clairvoyant. Yet despite the antics, as well as vaude-ville and snatches of ragtime, critics feared that *The Charity Girl* was "both too long and too loosely constructed for New York."

The Social Evil had relapsed into Human Comedy, and it was a flop.

3.

A New Gospel

If the ladies will form in line on one side of the room and the gentle-men on the other," the instructor began, "I will explain the rudiments of the steps which make up the new dances."

Fifteen men in tuxedos and fifteen married women ceased chatting and parted to opposite ends of a small ballroom in the Plaza Hotel. It was a Saturday evening, and they—like hundreds of their peers across the city—were here for tango lessons.

The pianist played a few notes, slowly, so that the teacher—a veteran of the Winter Garden and the Folies Marigny—could explain the simplest moves. First came the hesitation. He counted as he demonstrated, "One, one-two-three, one-two!"

"Oh, isn't that pretty?" exclaimed one of the students.

The ladies and their partners pantomimed the steps separately. "Feet together!" he called out. "Ladies forward with the left . . . Balance!" The women were quick learners, the men not so quick. Among the latter, one appeared especially befuddled. After a series of missteps, he finally stopped completely, confessing, "I don't quite get that." The instructor clasped the pupil's hands and practiced with him a dozen times, very slowly, counting aloud: "One, one-two-three, one-two."

When at last all were ready, the piano played "Nights of Gladness," and the couples were permitted to attempt the hesitation together.

"This will be an easy one," the instructor assured his students, as he displayed the next step. Most took to it. The awkward beginner concentrated hardest. Whenever he did something wrong, he would pause, count earnestly and aloud, and repeat the move again and again until he was satisfied.

Then, during the hitch and slide, he stumbled and stopped completely. "I don't quite get that," he said again. Once more the master clasped his hands, danced him round till he had the knack, and returned him to his practice partner.

Afterward, the teacher asked one of the onlookers, "Who is the young man who asks so many questions?"

"Why, don't you know?" came the answer. "That's young Mr. Rockefeller!"

JUNIOR MIGHT NEVER become the most agile dancer, or for that matter the sprightliest wit, the wisest commentator, the most inspiring orator, the best good fellow. In fact, nothing came easily to him. What he lacked in instincts, however, he made back through discipline, pursuing each task with a rapt focus that was utterly unself-conscious. "The annoyances, the obstacles, the embarrassments had to be borne," he believed. Anything that stood in the way of success "became merely details." It was this determination that had steered him to remain on the board of the Colorado Fuel & Iron Company until it turned a profit. It guided his philanthropic work, inured him to the criticism and ridicule of public life. *I don't quite get that*, he'd ask his advisers, attending to their answers until he was confident in his position. And it was effective. Junior made great progress, even at the waltz. "He 'scissors" and 'cortezes' like an adept," the instructor raved at the end of the lessons, "he has every little dip and twist at the tip of his toes—it's a pleasure to watch him spinning about the ballroom, light as thistle-down."

Junior was again immersed in reform work. "The first four days of this week were consumed with all day conferences," he complained to his mother after sitting through meetings for the Rockefeller Foundation and the General Education Board. The new report from the American Vigilance Association, an antiprostitution society, had just arrived. He took this work more seriously than any other; in December he had donated $5,000 to the group, and he personally supervised its team of undercover agents, who infiltrated the city's brothels gathering information on the prevalence of the Social Evil.

The latest revelations were as shocking as ever: New York remained a city of sins. To ensure that the proper officials were made aware of its findings, Junior had the document forwarded, through his Bureau of Social Hygiene, to the mayor and police. Wanting future accounts to be even more persuasive, he asked that the next installment be as far-reaching as possible. "It therefore should cover saloons, with their rear rooms, disorderly cafes and other places where vicious people congregate," he wrote to the investigators. "In view, therefore, of this broader scope of the inquiry, you may think it wise to put another man or two on this month."

Few of Junior's good works meant more—or had caused him more "nervous depression and despondency"—than the Young Men's Bible Class, which he had led, off and on, at the Fifth Avenue Baptist Church for the previous fifteen years. Teaching religion to others had helped him elaborate his own theology of discipline and service. He credited it with guiding his decision to retire from business, and it was his best avenue for interacting with people outside of work and family. But the effort of preparing his speeches had many times threatened to overwhelm him. Three nights a week he would enclose himself inside his study to write out meticulous outlines on index cards. Then, on Sundays, he would pass along his insights. Recently, in a talk on "Fixing Life Standards," he had urged temperance in food, work, exercise, pleasure, and drink. "If a man is unwilling to do small tasks and do them well, he ought not be permitted to do big tasks," Junior had said, "and if he is permitted mistakenly he is most certain to fail."

Under his leadership, the class had grown to hundreds of students. And if some of these merely hoped to benefit from his acquaintance, many had been impressed by the patent sincerity of his lessons. Guest speakers had included Andrew Carnegie, Booker T. Washington, and Mark Twain. He invited the members to his home, gave them individual attention, and sponsored annual banquets. Whatever lengths he went to, however, the press and public were quick with malicious comment. "Every Sunday young Rockefeller explains the Bible to his class," Twain remarked. "The next day the newspapers and the Associated Press distribute his explanations all over the continent and everybody laughs." Condescending headlines—ROCKEFELLER ON LOVE: SAYS MOTHER'S IS NEXT TO GOD'S, or ROCKEFELLER ON RICHES: WEALTH DOES NOT GIVE HAPPINESS, SAYS BIBLE CLASS LEADER—were bad enough, but the implication that his religion was little more than hypocrisy was far worse. "With his hereditary grip on the nation's pocketbook," one newspaper complained, "his talks on spiritual matters are a tax on piety." Junior bravely kept at it, in spite of the humiliation. And by 1914 this determination had finally earned him some respect. "You have borne all the criticism and ridicule that is necessary," his wife reassured him, "to let the world see that you are sincere."

On Sunday, March 1, as yet another incapacitating blizzard reached the city, Junior prepared to lead a Bible class at the Calvary Baptist Church on Fifty-seventh Street, a couple blocks from his home. His father, who had recently come east, motored down from Tarrytown, a drive that took an hour and a half in the rising storm. In their reserved pew, at the center of the second row, the two Rockefellers sat together—Senior in a fur coat and "a pair of old fashioned 'galoshes'"—while several nearby benches remained deserted. Few others had been willing to brave the weather to hear the sermon.

In the late afternoon, as Junior was conducting his class, the Calvary caretaker placed a frantic call to the Forty-seventh Street precinct house: He had heard that the Industrial Workers of the World were coming, and the church needed protection. A guard of reserves hurried over. As congregants arrived for the evening lecture, they passed through a barrier of police guarding the Gothic portico. At the end of the night, as Junior stepped down into the snowy streets, the officers were still there, stomping and shuffling to keep warm after a tedious watch. All across Manhattan that night, policemen promenaded outside of frightened churches. The I.W.W. was on the march, and no one knew where the menace would appear.

BY EIGHT P.M., in fact, they had arrived at Washington Square: a straggling column of nearly a hundred unemployed men with Frank Tannenbaum in the vanguard. "Plodding through the thick slush in downtown streets, with sharp sleet cutting into their faces," the troupe passed beneath the marble arch and paraded up Fifth Avenue. A few blocks north, at Eleventh Street, there appeared the Tiffany windows of the old First Presbyterian Church, "shining through the snowflakes" like welcoming beacons of relief. The minister was preaching "Redemption" to a sparse audience. The main doors crashed wide and in stepped Tannenbaum. Footsteps ringing on the stone floor, the intruders tracked dirty snow down the aisle. They sidled noisily into the front pews, gaping and leering at the gasping congregants, many of whom "were highly excited and apparently half inclined to flee in terror from the horde of ragged and wild-eyed invaders."

The reverend had stood dumbfounded as they had entered. It was the Industrial Workers of the World—and they had chosen his church. "There can be no question of our sympathy toward you on such a night as this," he stuttered, at last, "and no question but that we will give you whatever aid you need."

"I'd like to say a few words," said Tannenbaum, rising from his seat.

"You may, if you say nothing to create disorder in this sacred place."

"Well," he said, "we're cold and we're hungry and we're going to sleep in here where it's warm."

"I am sorry that I cannot invite you to do that."

Then members of the mob leapt up and began to yell.

"You'll have to club us out!"

"We're going to camp right here!"

"Yes, don't worry. We'll take all the responsibility off of your hands."

Fearing a riot, the pastor beckoned Tannenbaum up to the pulpit and offered twenty-five dollars for the men to pay for food and shelter, if they'd only agree to leave quietly. Frank took the money and marched his triumphant mob back through the aisles. As they went, their roar of satisfaction "shook the rafters of the vestry." But in the lobby the sight of a file of policemen quieted them down. The cops had been called during the confrontation. They had their nightsticks drawn; all they needed was an excuse. The unemployed crept past the menacing cordon, just a little chastened.

Out in the "miserable, windy night," they feasted in a Bowery restaurant and then tucked themselves into beds at a nearby hotel. The money was spent down to the last dime.

THIS WAS THE third straight night that Tannenbaum had trespassed against a city church. By the next morning, March 2, the clergy had split in its reactions. Most were outraged. For years they had complained of the drop in churchgoing, but the I.W.W. solution was not to their taste. Several ministers responded to the threat by canceling their evening services, preferring no prayer at all to the possibility of an appearance by the unemployed. A few offered their support, embracing the challenge of caring for the needy in a desperate season. In that morning's *World*, the pastor of St. Mark's-in-the-Bouwerie had even invited the homeless to shelter in his chapel. Tannenbaum decided to accept his offer.

That evening he led more than a hundred followers out of Rutgers Square, one of the few slashes of open space amid the crush of East Side tenements, which served as a meeting place for radical gatherings.* As they passed others along the way, the men called out, "Come on with us

* Rutgers Square is now Straus Square.

and get free food and lodging," so that their ranks had more than doubled by the time the parish doors opened for them at St. Mark's. Churchwomen beckoned them in from the darkness to a large, brightly lit chamber set up with two long tables loaded with coffeepots and piles of bean sandwiches. The men thronged inside, removing their hats, joshing each other. "The great fireplace was piled with burning logs," a reporter wrote, "and for a moment this aimless crowd seemed at peace with all the world."

Frank devoured a sandwich and waited for the others to finish eating before he rose to speak. "We want work, but we will not work for 50 cents or $1 a day. We want $3 a day for an eight-hour day, and any man who works more than eight hours scabs it on us," he said. "They tell us to go to the Municipal Lodging House, but I tell you that it is not fit for a dog to sleep in. Let Kingsbury sleep there. We are going to establish a boycott on the Municipal Lodging House so that no man out of work will go there."

All the time he was talking, more men were arriving; by eleven P.M., the newcomers had filled a second room. Men snored in their chairs by the fireplace. Others stretched out along the floors. All was quiet as the reverend made his final inspection of the night. In the morning there

The Bowery breadline.

was coffee and eggs, and the men scattered in search of work, leaving a few volunteers to tidy up and shovel snow.

Frank woke with the others, and then headed to 214 West Street, the Wobbly headquarters on the waterfront, to read about himself in the papers. Photo insets showed his wavy curls and round cheeks. The newsmen who had once ignored him were now insatiable for answers. "Who is this young Tannenbaum?" they asked. "Where did he come from? Who are his parents, what his boyhood environment? Is he normal or abnormal mentally and physically? What started him on the program begun a few nights ago when he and his 'army of the unemployed' began to raid churches?" Was he "a fanatic or an extremely able propagandist of some special order," was he even a leader at all, or "a convenient catspaw for the invisible leadership which is the inspiring and directing force of the I.W.W. activities"? Reporters competed now to pen vivid portrayals of him. "His black hair blown half across his face, his jaw set and his eyes agleam with determination . . ." one passage began. He was often misquoted, maligned, and misrepresented, but his name was in the headlines every morning. And no one misspelled it anymore. "Now, what is the program, the idea, the definite plan proposed by this smooth faced, slender stripling?" asked the *Sun*. "Why, merely to take possession of New York—that is all."

Each night he told his men: *We are not slaves. We are not accepting charity. What we're getting—they owe it to us.* Not once—despite what the newspapers said—not once had he raised his voice in anger, preached anarchy, or incited violence. Newspapers called them a "ragged regiment," a "mob." Well, they might be a little rough, but he had never felt love the way he did when they were all camping out together at night. Watching them eat a hot meal served on clean dishes in a warm room—it was the most religious thing he'd ever seen. The city knew him now as the "Boy I.W.W. leader," and Frank was happier with that job than with anything else he could think of. He wouldn't give it up for anything— not even for a place in President Wilson's cabinet.

* * *

IT WAS SNOWING that week in Washington, D.C., as well, but inside the Willard Hotel on F Street, it smelled like spring. The foyer was bedecked with flowers: pink azaleas, Richmond roses in crystal vases, tulips and hyacinths in gold baskets. Woodrow Wilson's cabinet members planted themselves amidst this garden in anticipation of their leader's arrival. Around eight P.M., the White House motorcade appeared and the president hurried his two daughters through the weather into the comfort of the parlor. It was March 7, the one-year anniversary of the administration's first cabinet meeting, and everyone felt like celebrating. After collegial greetings, the guests passed into the dining room for supper. "There was no set program," reported the *Washington Post*, "spontaneity being the keynote of the evening." The courses progressed, accompanied by enthusiastic toasts and a serenade by the Marine Band. All in all, it was "as informal as an occasion may be at which the President of the United States is a guest."

For the previous several days, newspapers had been offering end-of-year retrospectives on the administration's progress. Congress had continued in session for eleven of the twelve months of its tenure, and the record of legislative accomplishments was unimpeachable. "It has been a year of incessant activity and of substantial achievement," the *New York Tribune* exulted. "Mr. Wilson has already written his name high on the list of the Presidents who have done things." He had shown himself to be an able executive, a dynamic speaker. "He has always appealed to the 'intellectuals,'" conceded editors at the *Outlook*. "He now appeals to very practical persons and to the man-in-the-street."

If these glowing assessments, along with "an elaborate menu with the usual liquid accompaniments," heightened the conviviality at the Willard Hotel, the president also shouldered some private cares. His wife, Ellen, had felt her health decline alarmingly since the start of the year; having already endured a succession of illnesses, she remained bedridden and in pain after slipping on the polished White House floor a few days earlier. Also, though no announcement had yet been made public, Wilson had just learned that his youngest—and favorite—daughter had broken with a longtime fiancé and was now engaged to marry his own secretary of the treasury, a man more than twice her age.*

And then there was foreign affairs, where a looming crisis threatened to subvert all the administration's domestic gains. In February 1913, weeks before Wilson had even taken office, a Mexican general, assisted by agents of the U.S. embassy, had assassinated the progressive president of that country and then claimed the office for himself. American entrepreneurs welcomed the change; the new leader was the sort of man they

---

* William Gibbs McAdoo, the secretary of the treasury, was a former police commissioner of New York City.

enjoyed doing business with. He had no notion of redistributing land to the peons or of nationalizing the oil reserves. Most of the world's nations had immediately recognized the fledgling government, but Wilson demurred, refusing to partner with the blood-soaked regime. Political turmoil descended into civil war as various insurgent groups took up arms against the illegitimate government in Mexico City. Investors panicked. War correspondents wired back tales of atrocity and outrage.

The president faced a diplomatic quandary. He could relent—as American business interests were howling for him to do—and belatedly acknowledge the ruling clique, or he could throw his support to the rebels, a disparate array of revolutionaries and banditos. Neither side lived up to his high moral standards for governance. It was more or less impossible to differentiate between them. "This unspeakable conflict is not a political quarrel, but a mere fight for power and plunder," a reporter wrote. "It is Jesse James against Tammany."

Unwilling to adopt either faction as an ally, Wilson chose to remain aloof and hope the situation would resolve itself. Thus began a period of "watchful waiting," which lasted throughout 1913 and into the new year. During this time, he had demanded the strictest neutrality, refusing to sell arms to either side and standing firm against ever-more-strident demands for action. When it came to foreign affairs, he was determined to be more than just a director of policy; he would be the self-appointed conscience-in-chief for the nation. But his rectitude did not impress the Mexican combatants, and procrastination was not a program. The president's cool detachment looked like indecisiveness. Friends began to murmur. Opponents sensed weakness and moved to exploit it. Critical committee reports and resolutions appeared daily in Congress. "We have been informed by the President of the United States that the policy of 'watchful waiting' would bring peace results in Mexico," a Republican senator had complained a few days earlier. Instead, Wilson's inaction had "resulted in a 'deadly drifting,' if not in merely wishing."

Finally, in early February, the president relaxed his position by lifting the arms embargo and allowing American firms to supply weapons to the Mexican rebels. If he had hoped this would bring a quick termination to the conflict, that wish was soon dashed. The insurgents had indulged in a spree of atrocities of their own, further eroding their standing as a potential ally in the cause of democratic progress. As March began, only one alternative remained. The United States could cease acting through untrustworthy proxies and involve itself directly. Publicly, Wilson still refused to consider any move toward invasion. At a White House press conference he reminded those "clamoring for armed intervention" to recall the sacrifice involved, urging them "to reflect what such action would mean to brothers, sons, and sweethearts." But a subtle change had shifted in his stance. No longer did he dismiss outright the calls for action. The situation may not have warranted such a move just yet, but if the provocations continued the time might come to adopt "a drastic course."

* * *

IN NEW YORK CITY, the longed-for thaw came on March 3, and—finally—the grimy ice began to yield before ten thousand shovels. Pedestrians stayed to the middle of streets to avoid the deadly icicles that "dropped tinkling to the sidewalks." High-piled snow wagons creaked through the avenues, swerving between trolleys that were running again after days of inactivity. No one talked anymore about a coal shortage, or of milk and egg famines. The heaps of week-old trash began to smell. Stockbrokers, typists, and clerks resumed their commutes.

In the late afternoon, runoff from the remaining piles of gray slush coursed in dark streams through Rutgers Square. Scores of men hid from the wind in doorways; others drifted toward the plaza. By 6:30 P.M., when Tannenbaum paced decisively through the ranks, hundreds were waiting, drawn by the news of his successes. They cheered and gathered in close as he leapt onto the granite rim of the fountain to announce that he had arranged food and shelter for the night. Clambering down again, he shoved his charges into a column two abreast, snarling, "Get in line and be decent," as they left the square and headed west on Canal Street.

Lower Manhattan, hectic with the evening rush, paused to stare at the parade. Thousands of office workers watched it pass; traffic locked up as it went by. "There was a prophetic, peculiarly, significant aspect in the entire affair," an observer thought, "that caused many ordinarily indifferent to the pleadings of the poor to turn and watch the little procession until it faded away in the distance." In the ranks some began to sing "Hallelujah, I'm a Bum," till Frank told them to pipe down. And then they marched in silence toward the Bowery Mission, where more than a hundred men queued on a breadline.

"Is this the I.W.W.?" shouted someone from the sidewalk as they drew close.

"Yep," came the response. "Come on along, we're going to church."

"Jump in, boys!" another marcher shouted. "Get in the real breadline and see what's comin' t'you." Dozens of new recruits rushed to join the parade, leaving only a few grumblers behind to beg a handout.

Turning downtown again and now numbering more than two hundred, they arrived at the parish house of St. Paul's Protestant Episcopal Chapel, at Broadway and Vesey Street, where women church workers passed around pots of coffee as well as platters of bananas and cornedbeef sandwiches. "We are entitled to champagne, roast turkey and a shower bath," Frank said this time.

Every one of us should have a room with a couch and all the comforts of home. Rockefeller and a lot of other people would break the law in a minute if they had to sleep on the floor. We are going to break the law and go to jail if necessary to get what we are entitled to. We are the workers of the world, but we can't get work. I suppose I'll be arrested before this is over. I expect to be, but I'd sooner spend my time in jail, where at least it's warm and where there'll be something to eat, than be put out in the cold without shelter or food or work.

The lights were put out at ten P.M., and the halls quieted down. Across the street, a dozen police officers hid in the shadows, away from sight. Plainclothesmen had been with the men right along—in the crowds at Rutgers Square, on the march to St. Paul's—and their vigil continued still; the ranking officer, hoping for a chance to act, planned to wait throughout the night, "in case he might be needed."

VACATIONING IN THE Adirondacks, Mayor Mitchel was snowbound by the blizzard. His staff could not reach him by telephone; downed wires left him stranded and helpless to intervene in the growing crisis. Without him, the Tannenbaum problem was getting beyond control. Four nights. Four churches. Clergymen panicked. Editorial writers apoplectic. While the mayor went ice-skating on Lake Placid, the unemployed had established "a condition of terror and brigandage" in his streets, and gangs of professional agitators were "terrorizing public assemblies from the Battery to Harlem."

In the mayor's absence, Commissioner Kingsbury had served as the administration's voice on unemployment. And an overflowing font he had been, issuing contradictory statements, flashing from project to project, accomplishing naught. Labor conditions were "abnormal," he confessed, but did not require converting the armories into shelters or opening the churches. "Such action," he believed, "would only bring

Mayor Mitchel in the Adirondacks.

more unemployed to this city and further complicate the situation." Only so much assistance could be offered; too much would foster indigence. "Relief, like cocaine, relieves pain," he said, "but it creates an appetite." The Municipal Lodging House had already received twice as many applicants as in any previous year of its existence. He had expanded the facility, and even if it still didn't have enough beds, it offered every man a meal and "a more comfortable place to sleep than he can find in the basement of any church."

These were temporary measures. Lasting solutions would have to wait until the administration had a comprehensive, scientific understanding of "why some individuals become homeless drifters instead of capable workers"—and that would take at least two weeks. For fourteen straight nights, Kingsbury directed research experiments on the residents at the Municipal Lodging House. On March 2, at the very moment when Tannenbaum was leading his aching cold men into the cozy warmth of St. Mark's chapel, the initial 143 subjects were being selected from the city shelter's inmates. Thirty specialists—ten physicians, ten sociologists, ten psychologists—as well as a regiment of stenographers awaited in telephone-booth-sized consultation rooms. The human subjects were asked probing questions: Did you desert your wife? Have you ever been convicted of a crime? They were measured and prodded by the physicians, and required to recite the days of the week forward and backward. "When the work is finished," Kingsbury promised, "we expect to know the who, the what, and the why of the unemployed problem. Then we will know just how the situation sums and we will know how to go about the work of devising remedies.*

But Kingsbury's ideas were just exasperating now, his ruminations about as welcome as the incendiary speeches of the anarchists. His experiment had a touch of absurdity to it; not even the most committed social scientists really believed that a few questions to a random group of subjects could elicit any fruitful results. The editors of the *New York Herald* were just as sick of "sociological investigators" as they were of "professional agitators." Radical critics joined in, too. "The great man in the City Hall investigates, investigates," sneered the socialist *Call*. "Mayor Mitchel and Kingsbury are largely responsible for present conditions." Big Bill Haywood, the leading national spokesman for the Industrial Workers of the World, stormed to reporters via telephone: "But they are in exactly the same boat with ex-president Taft. He said 'God knows' when asked what ought to be done to remedy conditions. These officials have made no provisions."

It was not until March 4 that Mitchel's overnight train finally sighed into Grand Central Terminal. In public he downplayed the Tannenbaum issue. "I don't think that there is any situation," he reassured reporters. "As a movement, I think it is played out. If it isn't, we'll deal with it, but there is no situation with a capital 'S,' as far as I can see." In

---

* This absurd "experiment" is characteristic of the Mitchel administration's efforts at social science. Combining minuscule research samples, compromised and biased observations, and outrageously broad goals, its uselessness as a practical solution to the structural problems of unemployment is apparent. Just as an example, the men were supposed to be chosen at random but were in fact "typical" cases handpicked by charity experts. The Binet tests, involving reciting the days of the week, could supposedly measure mental acuity. Here is a newspaper's description: "The Binet tests used consisted of noting how rapidly or slowly the mind of the examined man worked. The doctors knew just how long it should take a person of a certain age to answer certain questions, to do simple problems requiring thought, or to run through certain formulae, such as the days of the week, the months of the year, forward and backward."

private, though, he conceded that action was necessary. Hauling his police commissioner, Douglas McKay, down to City Hall, he insisted on a firmer stance. Afterward, the chastened commissioner told reporters, "I will not stand for any high-handed measures by the I.W.W., or any other organization. As soon as they commit any act demanding police action I will be in a position to use the police."

FRANK SET DOWN the morning newspapers on March 5, feeling like the hunt's prey. They were after him now. The editorials bawled for blood, for his arrest, for the police to come and club him down. All week, he had felt those batons hovering. The cops had always been there, waiting, infiltrating, hoping to provoke some trouble that could justify his arrest. Of course, he had given them no excuse. It was against no law to point out the hypocrisy of church and government. Still, the master class would get him. He had always known how his protests would end. In the afternoon he met with Haywood, who couldn't participate himself but who urged Frank to "keep up the damned agitation." And that's what he intended to do—but as he walked once again through the mired streets toward Rutgers Square, it was with the intuition of looming disaster.

The largest gathering yet awaited him. A thousand men, maybe more, applauded his approach, cheering again as he climbed the fountain. Interspersed amongst them, though, was also a large detail of police: detectives whose faces had grown as familiar as his friends', plainclothesmen who stood out from the gray crowd, as well as blue-uniformed regulars who had never been more apparent. "I'm sorry for you fellows," he called to them. "You are only slaves like ourselves." But he knew it was vain to try and reconcile them; the grim cops stood unmoved, waiting.

Tannenbaum climbed down and ordered his men into ranks. He led them along Canal Street past the Bowery, walking quickly. He made no announcements about where they were going, and appeared to be deciding as he went. He turned north onto West Broadway; his followers stretched out over three blocks behind. The police detectives were right beside him, ready to react to whatever he did. He could just give it over for the night and try again some other time. But no, it was better to play it out, as Haywood had said, to "keep up the damned agitation."

Halfway up the block, on the left, Frank's eyes lighted on a church. Drawing level with the stone stairs, he turned without warning and ran up toward the doors. Two plainclothesmen had been marching with him pace by pace, twitchy and sharp for any movement he might make. When he reached the entrance and turned to face his men, the detectives were right behind. His parade had stopped, and the stragglers were still catching up, massing around the foot of the steps. The detectives urged him on, and Frank entered the dimly lit nave of St. Alphonsus' Catholic Church. The policemen followed. The door closed behind them.

Inside, statues of the saints loomed by the doors. It was too dark to see more than a few paces ahead. Frank walked down the center aisle, startling some kneeling worshipers. He didn't have any clear plan. He was just reacting now; the police were in control of the situation. It was the detectives who went and found the priest—the authorities arranged everything.

"Father," said the detective sergeant, "this is Frank Tannenbaum. He wants to speak to you."

"All right, just one moment," said Frank, asserting some free will. "My name is Tannenbaum, and I've led my army here to make one request of you. We want to sleep in the church tonight. Can we do it?"

"No, you cannot."

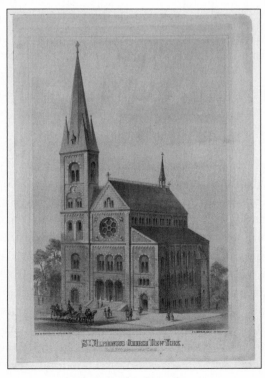

St. Alphonsus' Catholic Church.

"But we're starving. We've come here to spend the night."

"No, you haven't."

"Do you call this living up to the teachings of Jesus Christ?"

"I don't intend to argue with you on ecclesiastical matters," snapped the priest. "You've got to get out."

"Well, will you give us money to buy food?"

"No."

"Will you give us work?"

"No."

Frank offered his hand. "All right, no hard feelings," he said. "We'll go away." The priest refused to shake, and Tannenbaum walked a few steps, before turning to say again, "All right, no hard feelings, now, remember."

They went back into the main hall of the church, which was now crowded with the unemployed. More protesters were filing in. The policemen by the door let them in gladly—once inside, however, no one was permitted to leave. Frank offered to lead the men back to the street, but the detectives told him to stay put. They were being sealed up, trapped. The intruders and the assistant priests were hollering at each other. The men still outside were shouting. Bells tolled on approaching police wagons. The photographers' flashbulbs were firing off like ammunition. It was all so ugly and ridiculous that Frank had to laugh. "This is fine," he said to himself with a wan smile. "This is the best meeting I've had yet." A detective who had disappeared now slipped back inside through the guarded entrance. It was almost a relief when he shouted out, "Frank Tannenbaum! Step forward! You are under arrest for unlawful entry, by order of the commissioner."

"All right," Frank said, and submitted to being led out through the doors into the riotous street. Traffic was blocked. Scores of police officers cordoned off the steps, or filtered through the crowds that had spilled from the nearby tenements to watch. He heard them shouting at him—or for him, he couldn't tell which—as he descended to the street. The detectives lifted him into the green patrol wagon that was backed up to the foot of the stairs, and for a moment he was alone. Then the next prisoners got shoved in with him, and then still more. When the benches were filled, and men were crouching on the floors, the van jolted forward, picking its way through the jammed avenue. At the station house on MacDougal Street, his name was entered in the blotter. For a couple hours they left him waiting in the holding cell while the others were booked, and finally the detectives escorted him uptown to be arraigned.

It was after eleven P.M., when Frank, pale and trembling from exhaustion, was led into a courtroom for the first time in his life. He fidgeted anxiously at the stand, wiping an old kerchief across his face, unconsciously fussing with his wavy hair. Around him, obscure officials spoke in murmurs. "Is that the judge?" he asked the detective, pointing to the court clerk. Then, when the doors opened and the actual magistrate ascended the bench, he was unmistakable—massive and remote, beefy jowls overspreading the high collar of his black robe. He read the charge: inciting to riot, a felony that carried a maximum penalty of five years' imprisonment.

"Do I have to plead now?" asked Frank. The judge was explaining his options, but he couldn't follow. Panic rising. He couldn't answer any of the questions; he didn't know what to do. It was a relief to hear that the proceeding was rescheduled for the following afternoon, but when the bail was announced—$5,000—the sum hit Frank like a hurled weight, and he staggered and gasped. He looked around for friends. But he was alone. The officers led him out from the courtroom to his cell and locked him away for a sleepless night.

IT WAS A late evening—and a long one—for Police Commissioner McKay as well. That morning, he had issued general orders to his men to keep tabs on Tannenbaum. Then he had spent all day detailing his resources for a comprehensive response. Every conceivable precaution was taken. After dark, he lingered at headquarters, waiting by the telephone. Finally, the call. It was Detective Sergeant Gegan. *Tannenbaum was at St. Alphonsus' on West Broadway.* McKay ordered out the reserves, every precinct— Greenwich Street, Elizabeth Street, Mulberry Street, MacDougal Street, Charles Street, Mercer Street, Beach Street—all of them. And then he jogged to his official car and sped to the scene. By the time he arrived, more than seventy-five officers were in action, and the patrol wagons were already being loaded.

One hundred and ninety men and one woman had been arrested, the largest roundup in the city's history. McKay was in amongst it the entire night: From the church he toured the precinct houses, and then made the late-night trip to the Yorkville court, in midtown, to watch Tannenbaum's arraignment. It was exhilarating to see his plan coming to a satisfying end. McKay wanted these troublemakers locked away. "Absolutely nothing but a felony goes," he told a subordinate, "charge every one of them with a felony. We have plenty of room." Reporters crowded round him, asking when he had started plotting his coup, whether the mayor had ordered him to act. McKay jokingly denied any premeditation. It wasn't like that at all, he replied, eyes twinkling: "I just happened to be in the neighborhood."

* * *

ALEXANDER BERKMAN WAS in no mood for anniversaries. And such is life, he marked them everywhere. The March issue of *Mother Earth* celebrated the eighth year since the journal's beginning. It was eight years, also, since Johann Most, a onetime mentor in anarchism, had died. And Berkman did not need the *Revolutionary Almanac* to recall that this was the month that had seen the opening salvos of the Revolution of 1848 in Prussia, or the founding of the Paris Commune a generation later. To spiritually linger in the past was an unpardonable weakness. One should draw lessons from history but live in the present: He despised colleagues who prated forever about their former deeds. But as the commemorations came he could not help recalling the passion of his former self. It was his today, his unbearable today, that made his yesterdays of such concern. If only Berkman could find meaningful work to do—new deeds, new triumphs—then he could release himself at last from this nightmare weight of past generations.

Such despair as he felt was inexcusable. Mere human sentiment was unworthy of the real revolutionist. Detachment in all things was paramount, but he could never quite manage it himself. Not when it came to women. And not when the cause was at stake. Detachment in most things. He was two men. An anarchist philosopher who overflowed with affection for the world, and an anarchist propagandist whose sworn duty it was to inspire rage and goad others to violence. "The propagandist," he wrote, "must, in a considerable degree, be a fanatic and even hate where the human in him yearns to love. This is perhaps the severest struggle in the inner life of such a one, and his deepest tragedy."

He had such a desperate need for a worthy crusade—one that could justify his self-imposed misery—that he almost tried to wish it into existence. "In the whole history of this country," he wrote in the latest *Mother Earth*, "there has never perhaps been witnessed a popular movement of deeper meaning and more far-reaching potential effect than the raiding of churches by the unemployed of New York." The out-of-work army had shown the highest qualities of anarchism. It was spontaneous, nonviolent, dignified, and viciously subtle in its revelations of hypocrisy. A few ragged men at a handful of churches had exposed the reformers and reverends, the socialists and police, for what they truly were. And most of all, it perhaps signaled the beginning of the mass movement he so longed for. "The roots of this crusade go deeper," Berkman wrote, hopefully. "It challenges the justice of the established; it denies the right to starve; it attacks the supremacy of the law; it strikes at the very foundation of THINGS AS THEY ARE."

The aftermath of Tannenbaum's arrest, in contrast, was almost too sordid and predictable. The capitalist press, of course, was all relief and approbation. "Stern and repressive measures," cheered the *Herald*, "yesterday broke the backbone of the mob of church raiders who had been led through the city for nearly a week by Frank Tannenbaum." The Socialist newspapers sniveled in their obnoxious way, offering nothing but condescension and hostility to the prisoners. Thus encouraged, the police forbade all further open-air meetings, arresting more speakers in Rutgers Square on the night following the mass arrests. The only one to behave like a man through it all was young Tannenbaum, who refused his friends' offer to pay his fine, preferring to remain in jail with the rest instead of taking freedom for himself alone.

The city's newspapers reveled in Tannenbaum's arrest.

The remainder of the story was just as foreseeable to Berkman, who had witnessed this all unfold before. The claim by officials to have received scrawled death threats, followed by the suspicious discovery of hidden dynamite. The ludicrous spectacle of police incompetence, the stupor of the courts. Revelations of brutality and barbarous conditions— "scenes that would shock the moral sensibilities of man"—inside the city prisons. The betrayal and cowardice of supposed allies in struggle.

No matter. Tannenbaum had revealed a weakness to exploit. And Berkman took it upon himself to do so. He organized a rally at Union Square to show that the spirit of revolution in New York could not be tamped out by a few arrests. On Saturday, March 21, when he arrived, thousands had already gathered. Emma Goldman, back in the city after one of her frequent lecture tours, was first to speak.

"Your toil made the wealth of the nation," she began. "It belongs to you." The audience crowded in around her, blocking the northern reaches of the plaza. A bright thin sun did little to warm the freezing air. It was the first day of spring. "The rich are keeping it from you. The officials do nothing to help you." The thin trees of the park stood lonely amidst the remaining hummocks of snow. It was twenty-five years now since Berkman had first looked out from this vantage. He had spent chilled nights with no other place to shelter. He had fled from charging phalanxes of police. He had paraded here in triumph with his fellow workers. "March down to the mayor. March down to the police. March down to the other city officials." He had heard Emma make this speech a hundred times. "March upon Fifth Avenue and take that which belongs to you!"

With that, he began to gather the crowds into a loose mass. When they were organized, he strode to the very front. With a pretty young girl on either arm, he led the column up Broadway. He had no permit to parade, but the few detectives assigned to watch the rally followed passively, unable to stop him. Some of the protesters walked in the streets, others claimed the sidewalks, jostling the afternoon shopping crowds in the Ladies' Mile. Discordant shouting. Snatches of song. At Thirtieth Street, they fell still and silent as a man unfurled a black silk banner. Red letters spelled out one word: DEMOLIZIONE. The column closed in, linking arms. Then, in a shrill, high key, a lone woman began to sing "The Marseillaise." After a few notes, other female voices joined, and then the men began. In a moment, the revolutionary anthem was on every lip, echoing in half a dozen languages. The sun vanished ominously behind a wall of clouds. And the parade was moving again.

Anarchists on the march.

Fifth Avenue—"Millionaire Avenue"—and here came Berkman with his army. The Waldorf-Astoria, the Metropolitan Club, St. Patrick's Cathedral, Henry Clay Frick's nearly completed mansion: At each landmark, the demonstrators jeered, chanting, "Down with the parasites! Down with the parasites!" Anarchists took command of every major intersection, halting trolleys, blocking traffic. One rioter, a young woman, rapped on automobile windows, forced open the doors, and spat at the passengers. It was a rout. A revolution. There were no uniformed police on hand at all, just the few detectives, who found themselves helpless to intercede. "Berkman and his followers," a reporter wrote, "were laws unto themselves."

When the parade finally ended with a celebratory dinner at the Franciso Ferrer Center on 107th Street, Berkman felt once more the young man's thrill in combat, "the spirit of revolt that has fired the hearts of the downtrodden in every popular uprising." He judged the city's mood and believed he had thousands with him. From his enemies, he saw only cowardice and panic. "What! The starvelings to be permitted to parade their naked misery, to threaten the moneychangers in their very temple?" he pantomimed disdainfully. "The black flag of hunger and destruction to wave so menacingly in the wealthiest and most exclusive section of the metropolis, the fearful cry of Revolution to thunder before the very doors of the mighty! That is too much!"

JUST ONCE, John Purroy Mitchel wished the citizenry might remain sensible instead of indulging in hysteria at the slightest indication of unrest. But so far during his short time in office, his constituents had shown no inclination to do so. The mayor had been motoring uptown on Fifth Avenue at the time of the anarchist "revolution." He had seen a clump of people on the march, and the sight had been so innocuous that he had driven on without giving it the slightest attention. When newsmen interrogated him outside of his office, he treated the affair as a joke.

"Some of the speakers urged that they should call on you here at the City Hall and demand their share of the world's riches," a reporter asked. "What would you do in a case like that?"

"I would suggest that instead of calling they file their application for the riches."

"I suppose you know that Emma Goldman denounced you in true anarchistic style at the meeting."

"That is habitual and chronic," said Mitchel, "and she would denounce anybody who happened to be in office."

But many of his supporters took the threat more seriously. "It will not be easy for the police to explain their toleration of the disorderly demonstration," complained the *World*. "The procession was worse than disorderly. It was lawless." Once again, just as with the church invasions, he was being pressed to respond with drastic measures. "This is an attack—an attack on the social system," declared the *Times*. "Its aim is nothing less than revolution." The detectives on the scene could not restrain their frustration. "It is evident that the men downtown do not recognize the seriousness of this movement," said Detective Gegan, who had arrested Tannenbaum. "We who follow them from day to day see that they are gaining strength, and unless they are checked serious consequences may result." Panicky rumors were abroad. The word that anarchists had occupied Fifth Avenue had been wired to ships at sea, and some papers were reporting that Mitchel had called on the National Guard to restore order. Finally, the mayor snapped at all the hectoring. "That is all damned nonsense," he said. "The more attention there is paid to such insane stories the more the agitators are helped."

Nonetheless, certain interests had to be placated. On the Monday after the Fifth Avenue debacle, Mitchel again met with Commissioner McKay.

And again they emerged from their conference with strong statements. Alexander Berkman and Emma Goldman were well-known to them; the citizenry could rest easy, knowing that all prominent anarchists in the city were under constant surveillance. "They may have their public meetings," the mayor decreed, "and their speeches may have the widest latitude, but any general disorder or disturbance of the peace will not be permitted."

* * *

ON THE MORNING of March 24, guards scraped open the iron gate of cell number 813 of the Tombs prison, and Frank Tannenbaum was marched to a lavatory, where he freshened up for trial. Around ten A.M., when the heavy wooden doors of the General Sessions Court opened for him, the benches had already filled. There weren't as many friends as he had hoped for, but he showed nothing but composure, nodding to the few comrades he did recognize and taking his seat at the bench.

The attorneys spent hours wrangling over prospective jurors, most of whom freely admitted their biases against him. But they hardly needed to say so. Their smug, well-fed appearances told the same, as did their occupations: real estate, architecture, management, foreman, speculator. These men were not of his class. They would not sympathize with what he had done. He had never wanted to submit to this trial, but his friends had insisted he go through with it and he had finally agreed. Not that he had hope of an acquittal; maybe the publicity would make good propaganda.

On the afternoon of the first day, and all through the second, the state presented its case. The police detectives perjured themselves shamelessly, claiming Frank had entered St. Alphonsus' Church despite their protests, when in fact they had invited him inside—and that he had refused to leave, when, to the contrary, they had barred his exit. The prosecutor called his men "a mob," and the judge overruled his attorney's objections. The defense called as witnesses the newspaper reporters and photographers who had witnessed the arrests. All of them corroborated his story. The unemployed were not violent, no property had been damaged, the police had manufactured the entire episode. By the time the jurors withdrew on the evening of the trial's third day, the truth of the case had been so clearly established that his friends assured him justice would prevail.

Forty-five minutes later, the twelve representatives of bourgeois order returned to pronounce their verdict: guilty, of course. The judge lectured him about American democracy and gaveled him the maximum sentence, a year in the workhouse on Blackwell's Island.

Frank Tannenbaum smiled.

"I would like to make a statement, I think," he said.

"You are," said the judge, "at liberty to make any statement you desire."

Frank told about the men he had met in the Tombs, and how they were as decent as any magistrate or district attorney. He described the rapture he had felt watching his hungry men eat, and how if that feeling wasn't religion, then nothing was. He insisted that he had been polite from first to last. He recalled the first time he had gone into a courtroom and hadn't been able to tell a clerk from a judge, and how now—after nearly a month's experience with the legal system—he knew all he needed to know: that the working class could expect no mercy from the law. When the first man had been convicted in the first court, he said, justice had flown out the window and never returned.

"I suppose," said Frank Tannenbaum, "that the press tomorrow will say I wanted to make myself out a hero or a martyr. I don't know who it was who said, some well-known preacher, that society would forgive a man for murder, theft, rape, or almost any crime, except that of preaching a new gospel. That is my crime."

II

Life in a democracy, where there is progress, where new things are being established, is more or less of a battle and in a battle almost anything is likely to happen.
— MAYOR JOHN PURROY MITCHEL

The Possibility of a Revolution

In the mornings, Mabel Dodge woke amid the mussed white linens of her gray Parisian canopy bed, surrounded by embroidered Chinese shawls and draped silks from Biarritz. Every wall and surface of her boudoir was bleached, snowy, silver, or the color of cream. Rebelling against the grime outside, she could never seem to get enough white into her apartment. The coffee appeared, and she was reaching for the telephone even before she drained the cup, making plans, calling for the automobile, inviting everyone everywhere.

She had lived at 23 Fifth Avenue for little more than a year, and already she knew the most interesting artists and writers. After dismissing her second husband, she had helped to publicize the Armory Show, contributed essays to *Art and Decoration*, and introduced American readers to the poetry of her dear friend Gertrude Stein. "I kept meeting more and more people," she wrote, "because in the first place I wanted to know everybody, and in the second place everybody wanted to know me." Wealthy and independent, she dressed in billowy Grecian robes that were utterly unstylish and yet perfectly becoming. Men, especially, attended to her. Young or middle-aged, married or bachelor, her presence brought out the best and worst in them all. "Their passions become exacerbated," said Max Eastman, editor of the *Masses*, a radical magazine of arts and politics. "They have quarrels, difficulties, entanglements, abrupt and violent detachments. And they like it—they come back for more."

Insurrections were everywhere, in painting and poetry, in perceptions and relationships—somehow they each formed part of the same struggle—and she and her comrades in Greenwich Village were waging

Mabel Dodge.

them all at once, together. "The world could not understand us—not our innermost selves," Dodge recalled. "We could be superior and laugh at the world together in an ecstasy of companionship." The ferment and excitement was leading to an entirely new order of their own creation. To Gertrude Stein, she wrote, "I am following any events which seem to bear on the possibility of a Revolution."

This city of dreams had its landmarks, too. Café Boulevard, on the Lower East Side, had been the site of innumerable raucous parties and late-night celebrations until its closure in January 1914. At Polly's restaurant on MacDougal Street, near Washington Square, the cook delighted his customers by referring to them as "bourgeois pigs"; upstairs, the Liberal Club hosted debates and lectures and was particularly popular among writers for the *Masses* magazine.

For anarchists, however, city life revolved around the Francisco Ferrer Center. Located in a three-story brownstone on East 107th Street, the institution combined "class-room, committee-room, check-room, lecture-hall and library, all in one." The basement held a lunchroom and kitchen. The main floor auditorium featured speeches and lessons nearly every day of the year, and was usually "packed to the doors." Clarence Darrow, Lincoln Steffens, Elizabeth Gurley Flynn all spoke there; Berkman and Goldman were frequent guests and Man Ray occasionally attended the art classes upstairs. On the walls hung portraits of Charles Darwin, William Morris, Leo Tolstoy, and Walt Whitman. Near the lectern, a giant bronze sculpture represented "A Proletariat." But pride of place went to a full-length painting of Francisco Ferrer, an anarchist and educator who had been executed by the government of Spain in 1909.

The center fostered adult education at night, but during the daytime it was home to the Modern School, an educational experiment that drew observers from around the world. A dozen or so children from the neighborhood attended classes conducted in a thoroughly anarchist style. Students arrived when they pleased and studied whatever interested them: writing, singing, piano, drawing, carpentry. Instead of imposing discipline, the instructors used only "patient reasoning" to curb disruptive behavior; at the end of the day the pupils often refused to leave. Field trips to the park or the city's museums formed a central part of the curriculum. And no outings were so highly anticipated as the frequent visits to the nearby offices of *Mother Earth*. "We were sure to get a warm booming welcome from Alexander Berkman," one of the students recalled. "He always had time for a bit of boisterous fun. He was very proud of his physical prowess and loved to indulge in all kinds of contests with the younger men. Often we found ourselves caught up and tossed about in those impromptu acrobatics and we loved it. Then Emma would come out and somehow it grew colder. She never said anything, but we knew that she did not care for children and we soon went away."

Mabel Dodge had scant interest in children, and she considered the Ferrer Center a hub "of social disaffection"—a little too coarse for her and her friends. The mixture of poverty and naïveté did not live up to the standards of Bohemia. Of her acquaintances, few were as dismissive of the anarchists as the devilish Walter Lippmann, a twenty-four-year-old Harvard graduate who carried himself, she wrote, "as one who expects to be president in about 3 yrs from now." He was pudgy, awkward, and contemptuous of everything. Having studied under William James and Lincoln Steffens—as well as serving as aide to the socialist mayor of Schenectady, New York—Lippmann still found himself dissatisfied with the confused philosophy of his elders. To sort the contradictions of modern society required a clarity of mind that no public figure possessed. And so he did it himself. Lippmann set about obliterating all prudishness and romanticism from his thought, leaving only "the cleanest strokes of an edged intellect." His initial book, *A Preface to Politics*, published the previous year, had brought praise—and anxious attention—from his elders. His goal for it had been modest enough: to fundamentally discredit the life's work of the entire previous generation of social theorists.

To accomplish this, he applied the ideas of Sigmund Freud to the study of American conditions. Reformers such as Steffens, or the Reverend Charles Parkhurst, who had founded the Society for the Prevention of Crime, had believed that sin resulted from a logical equation. Poverty, squalid surroundings, and immoral teachings led to vice; by eliminating these factors, a harmonious civilization was attainable. Lippmann revealed this to be a delusion. Once subconscious urges were considered, the notion of rationalizing behavior became indefensible. For proof, one only had to look at New York City. "Men who in their youth took part in 'crusades' against the Tenderloin," he wrote, referring to the section of midtown Manhattan, roughly from Twenty-third to Forty-second streets, that was home to the city's most notorious brothels and cabarets, "now admit in a crestfallen way that they succeeded merely in sprinkling the Tenderloin throughout the city." For Steffens, exposure to these new ideas was a jolting revelation. "I remember thinking how absurd had been my muckraker's descriptions of bad men and good men," he later recalled, "and the assumption that showing people facts and conditions would persuade them to alter them or their own conduct."

Most conversations with Lippmann ended that way—with the interlocutor feeling browbeaten and depressed—but Mabel Dodge still savored their frequent lunches together at the Holland House. He made fun of her intellectual clutter. "Your categories aren't any good," he'd tell her. "They remind me of a Fourth Avenue antique shop." In him she saw "a fine poise, a cool understanding," with "all the high humor in the world shining in his intelligent eyes." But unlike most of his acquaintances, she could prod at his self-importance and laugh when he said things like: "Human nature is a rather shocking affair if you come to it with ordinary romantic optimism."

Inspired by Lippmann and others, Dodge began devoting herself to political pursuits. John Reed, her lover for a time, had convinced her to volunteer with the striking silk workers in Paterson. She had attended each day of Frank Tannenbaum's trial, and spoke publicly in his defense. "I think that the unemployed are justified in doing anything to call public attention to their condition," she told a reporter for the *World*.

Walter Lippmann.

"Anything that doesn't injure people . . . Of course, I don't believe in dynamite and that kind of thing."

Nevertheless, she had still been terribly nervous the first time she visited the brownstone shared by Emma Goldman and Alexander Berkman on 119th Street. Nothing was more precious to her than human life, and the anarchists, she knew, agitated for violence. Not only did they discuss it, they had even committed it themselves. While she and her downtown circle dithered over abstractions, these people had been doing things. "They were the kind that *counted*," she felt. "Their judgment was somehow true. One did not want their scorn." As she climbed the stone steps to their door, thinking about the detectives who were probably watching from the shadows, Dodge was most concerned about making a good impression.

Once inside, "the warm, jolly atmosphere" of the dining room quickly alleviated her anxieties. A vast supper overspread the table, and Emma Goldman bustled about, foisting hunks of beefsteak and fried potatoes on her guests. "She didn't look wild or frightening," thought Dodge, relieved. "She looked to me, from the very first, rather like a severe but warm-hearted school teacher." Berkman made a different impression. Friends assured her that he was harmless, but somehow she never saw it herself. He was heavy jawed, "bald in front, with veiled eyes and thick lips." There was a menace in him that she found repellant.

Since men were always hanging round her anyway, Dodge took to inviting them to her apartment, making sure to mismatch them just so, in order to ensure exciting discussions. She would slouch in her armchair, suggesting lines of conversation, and the guests would pursue these discussions, hoping to impress her. "Poor and rich, labor skates, scabs, strikers and unemployed, painters, musicians, reporters, editors, swells"—all were welcome to participate in her evenings. "It was," declared Steffens, "the only successful salon I have ever known."

At the end of March, excitement surged around a debate between Big Bill Haywood and the anarchists. He would explain the philosophy of the Industrial Workers of the World, while Goldman and Berkman would counter by justifying their own ideologies. But it did not go well. The speakers groped about, Haywood mumbled confusedly, and Goldman fell back on her persona as schoolteacher. Berkman sulked. Lippmann asked questions that no one could answer. Everyone was uncomfortable in the white-on-white rooms, and the audience soon lost interest. At last, a spectator called out from the back of the chamber, "They talk like goddam bourgeois!"

The disappointment added to the reserve Dodge still sensed from the radicals: "I felt they had Plans. I knew they had. I knew they continually plotted and planned and discussed times and places." Berkman was always intimating about "the day when blood would flow in the streets of New York." He seemed to think that this moment would be a "blissful and perfect consummation, to be lived for, to be worked for, and sacrificed for." He would die to bring it sooner. "There was blood in the air that year—there truly was," she recalled. "One was constantly reminded of it."

Lippmann was slipping away from an activist persona in order to adopt the guise of a full-time commentator. The journalist's knack of condemning everything came intuitively to him, and he had already espoused firm prejudices against just about all the factions vying seriously to affect the American scene.

Rockefeller and the plutocrats, he believed, were largely to blame for the ferocity that wracked the labor movement. "As rulers of American industry," Lippmann had declared after the 1910 bombing of Harrison Gray Otis's virulently antiunion *Los Angeles Times*, "Otis and his kind have exhibited the same sort of incompetence as the rulers of Russia." As for President Wilson, those who decried him as a socialist—or worse—had little understanding of his true beliefs. "Wilson doesn't really fight the oppressions of property," Lippmann noted. "He fights the evil done by large property-holders to small ones." The anarchists, on the other hand, were too undisciplined to accomplish much; in Lippman's mind, they were "wild in their dreams and unimportant in their deeds." As far as he was concerned, all the anarchists' bluster, and even their occasional forays into violence, amounted to a case of overcompensation. "It is the weak unions, the unorganized and shifting workers," he wrote, "who talk sabotage and flare up into a hundred little popgun rebellions. Guerrilla warfare is the only tactic open to weakness."

But Lippmann was not opposed to plans as such. Though reviewers were still grappling with the arguments of his previous book, he had already moved on. Freudianism, socialism, syndicalism—these ideas were all passé. There could be no solution to societal questions until all parties were ready to consider the situation rationally. "You cannot plan a civilization on a heated powder mine," he argued. "You cannot rearrange industrial processes, lay out cities, solve the problems of food and work, devise uses for leisure, breed finer strains of men, on a battlefield."

His new project was to be a manifesto called *Drift and Mastery*. In it he planned, at last, to explain without prejudice or sentimentality the entire complex of problems that comprised modern life. It would offer the prescription for a future founded on a humane science that was self-aware and not self-deceiving. "This is what mastery means," he revealed, "the substitution of conscious intention for unconscious striving." But Mabel Dodge defined his undertaking differently. Writing of Lippmann to Gertrude Stein, she explained, "His second book is called 'Drift & Mastery' & is about everything & everyone contrasted with himself! The world he represents as Drift, himself as Mastery."

THOUGH THEY KEPT trying, Dodge and Berkman just could not communicate. When she purchased a copy of his *Prison Memoirs* and asked him for a signed dedication, he wrote:

TO MABEL DODGE, FOR A DEEPER SOCIAL CONSCIOUSNESS AND A MORE PERFECT CRYSTALLIZATION OF A DEFINITE GOAL TO

MAKE THE WORLD A BETTER PLACE TO LIVE IN FOR MEN AND
WOMEN.

Which was nice enough. But, as with everything about him, it irked
her. In particular, there was something in the word *crystallization* that
she objected to. "I cannot imagine myself ever crystallizing into an anarchist," she responded, brutally. "Any crystallization seems to me only an
opportunity for further disintegration . . . no sooner has an idea become
crystallized into an institution, a habit, or even a *party*, than it is ready
for some spiritual dynamiting." The same rules applied to affairs of the
heart. "I do not believe or disbelieve in marriage," she continued, "but I
do believe in love, which may exist either within the institution or outside of it, provided it is free."

Stung and a bit confused, Berkman was all contrition. "Words indeed
are poverty-stricken things," he wrote. "I despair of clarifying myself to
you on paper." Instead, he suggested they might communicate through
"presence" and "personal contact." But his attempts in the flesh were
even worse. Soon after their exchange of letters, Dodge and Berkman
found themselves alone with each other in a taxi. She had written insou-
ciantly about free, unfettered love, but during the ride she was appalled
to realized he was flirting. Then he leaned over to assay a kiss, and when
she saw "his eyes half closed, his red mouth expressing nothing but an
impersonal hunger" as it lunged for her lips, she was filled with fear and
indignation. She recoiled, aghast. In the panic of the moment, she blurted
out the most conventional phrase imaginable: "I am not that kind of a
girl."

Later, she tried to analyze this reaction. It wasn't just that he was a
would-be murderer, or that he was so much older, and so unstylish, or
his ludicrous accent. It was the disrespect implied by his assault. Despite
all her experiments with independence, Dodge still felt the burden of being an unprotected woman. No one realized how brave she was to do the
things she did. And she could not tell them, since then they would have
understood how scared she was in the first place. "I did not want them to
know that *ever*," she decided. "They had to be content with my mystery."

4.

"Three Cheers for the Cops!"

At one thirty in the afternoon on the fourth of April, crowds enjoying the Saturday half-holiday in Union Square were startled at a sudden incursion by a massive contingent of police. Four hundred officers hurriedly deployed, asserting control over the area. Some patrolled the outer boundaries. Others swept up and down along the pathways of the park, warning idlers to "move on." Fifty uniformed men filed into hiding within a pavilion at the north end of the plaza; scores more concealed themselves inside a construction shed, and another hundred or so plainclothesmen mingled among the spectators.

Commissioner McKay arrived in his green automobile and established a command post on Seventeenth Street, between Broadway and Fourth Avenue. During the previous two weeks he had endured ceaseless criticism for having failed to prevent the anarchists' last parade through the wealthiest neighborhood in Manhattan. This morning, he had received word that they were planning to repeat the performance, and he was absolutely determined to forestall them. To do so, he called on all the department's resources. Besides the men on the scene, he had two hundred more officers dispersed among the basements of every fashionable club and hotel from the Ladies' Mile to Harlem. One thousand more reserves stood ready in the precincts to act as reinforcements. A general order issued to all these forces that morning was terse and direct: "Break 'em up!"

There were two rallies planned for the afternoon. The Central Federated Union, a conglomeration of A.F. of L. locals, had received official approval from the city to hold their meeting. The anarchists, as usual, had not deigned to beg for "the kind permission of the master class and its armed hirelings." Berkman suspected that the police were intentionally pitting the groups against each other, using the moderate trade unionists to discredit the radical unemployed. Newspapers, he knew, would gleefully exaggerate any conflict between rival labor factions. So he had two choices. He could march and face accusations of fomenting dissension within the working class, or he could postpone his parade.

It was after two P.M., and no one outside Berkman's inner circle yet knew what he had decided. Six or seven thousand demonstrators were milling around at the northern edge of Union Square, where the trade-union meeting was just being called to order. Spectators hovered on the periphery or watched from windows, hoping to see some excitement. Three motion-picture cameras swept the scene. McKay and his inspectors surveyed the crowd, while reporters and photographers scrambled to cover any potential outbreak. Lincoln Steffens stood on tiptoe trying to get an adequate view. Everyone kept sharp for the anarchists.

And then with shout and shove, they were there. The group surged forward in a tight, organized mass, "seeming to spring from the ground," wrote a reporter, "so rapid was their approach." The militants pushed through the crowd, distributing propaganda as they forced a path toward the speaker's platform. The mob tightened in, cheering crazily. At the front, Berkman scaled a stacked tower of lumber that served as an improvised stage. As the highest spot in the area, the platform also happened to be the police operations center, so as he turned to address the demonstrators he was just a few feet from McKay and his inspectors. Everyone craned closer to hear.

He started with his usual imprecations against labor fakirs and the "capitalist class." Then came the substance of his address. "We will postpone our meeting," he said, "because we want the people of New York and of the country to see our solidarity with labor, whether organized or unorganized." As Berkman clambered down to the sidewalk, the police inspectors momentarily relaxed.

At the very moment their attention lapsed, they lost control of the situation. A different group of radicals—either unaware that their rally had been put off, or unwilling to abide by the decision—chose this instant to raise signs reading HUNGER, UNEMPLOYED UNION LOCAL NO. 1, and TANNENBAUM MUST BE FREED. Seeing the placards, policemen at the boundaries of the demonstration thought a parade was forming and recalled their orders to "Break 'em up." Forming wedges, they sliced into the throng. Commanders signaled frantically, but whether to stop the assault or urge it on, it was impossible to know. "The crowd jeered and yelled and the banners continued to wave for a moment or two," a reporter wrote. "Then the flags were jerked from the hands of the color bearers, and a minute later those color bearers . . . were on their way to the East Twenty-second Street Police Station."

Riotous demonstrators trailed the officers and their prisoners to the upper edge of the park, shouting threats and turning back only when a line of mounted policemen cantered over to block their path. Facing south, the leaders improvised a new plan. "Come on, men," shouted an unemployed anarchist named Joe O'Carroll, "We'll march to Rutgers Square." With him in the lead was Becky Edelsohn, "a comely young woman" of "electric vitality" in her mid-twenties, who was a former lover of Berkman's and was becoming a leading campaigner for militancy. During the previous parade up Fifth Avenue, she had been the one who shocked even some of her own cohort by prying open the door to a limousine to spit at the faces of the women inside.

Arm in arm they showed the way, and within a minute, hundreds had fallen into line behind them. The column soon stretched the entire length of the park. Demonstrators shouted "Kill the capitalists!" and "Revenge Tannenbaum!" Detectives scurried to head off the leaders, while the mounted patrol trotted menacingly on the parade's flank and the hidden officers streamed out from their concealed positions. For a few moments, the two sides marked each other. Then, at Fourteenth Street, the detectives ordered the protesters to disband. The crowd responded with taunts and hisses. And, at last, detectives Gegan and Gildea—the officers who had been pining for this moment since early March—ordered the attack.

The horsemen formed a column, drew their batons, and spurred directly toward the middle of the parade. "Invective and imprecations hurled at the policemen changed to yells of alarm and terror" as the surging cavalry struck the mass of demonstrators. Protesters fled, if they could, or were ridden down. Horses wheeled and charged, wheeled and charged, knocking dozens to the sidewalks, raising a clamor that could be heard for blocks around. At the front of the march, plainclothesmen and uniformed policemen pushed their way toward the heart of the mob. "The officers fought coldly, contemptuously, systematically, shoulder to shoulder and elbow to elbow," a reporter wrote. "The I.W.W. and anarchists battled wildly and lost all judgment in a furious rage." Each side unleashed its resentment and hatred on the other. "The yells of defiance, the curses, the screams of pain from men and women, the clacking

Mounted officers disperse the anarchists.

of galloping horses, the curt orders from police commanders made a chorus which overwhelmed the ordinary song of the streets."

In the first moments of fighting, detectives had grabbed O'Carroll and dragged him, struggling, from the melee. His friends chased behind, cuffing and shouting at the arresting officers, pulling their hair in a wild attempt to pry him free. The panicked and outnumbered cops lashed out indiscriminately, beating the thin, sickly O'Carroll on the head until a deep gash opened across his scalp and blood was pouring over his face and soaking his clothes. Becky threw her body over his, shielding him as best she could from the policemen's blows and shouting desperately, "Save Joe from the oppressors of the poor!"

Hearing her calls for help, an unemployed radical named Arthur Caron moved to intervene. Within seconds, he too was on the ground, being struck again and again with blackjacks and fists on his head and legs. "For Christ's sake," he pleaded, "stop hitting me." They grabbed him up, manhandled him toward a patrol wagon, and threw him into the hold. O'Carroll was already in the back, two officers rode up in the cab, and several plainclothesmen stood out on the running board. The door slammed shut as the vehicle coughed into motion. A cop hissed at Caron, "You bastard, we've got you now," and punched him in the face. He tried to get up, blood racing from his nose. "You bastard, lie still!" they yelled, as they all beat him on the back of his skull. O'Carroll staggered over and cradled Caron's wounded head. "Poor boy!" he muttered in shock. "Jesus! You're getting it awful."

At the East Twenty-second Street station, the two crushed protesters were dragged from the wagon and shoved down onto opposite ends of a long bench. Before they could be booked, the detectives made them wash the blood off their faces, necks, and hands to make them presentable to the magistrate. Then they had to think of what charges they would file against their prisoners.

"That's O'Carroll," one of them said. "We'll charge him with striking an officer and resisting arrest."

"What'll we charge that big bastard with?" asked another, gesturing to Caron.

"Charge the fuck with trying to take him away from the police and yelling, 'Kill the bastards!'"

"NO SCENE IN New York for years has approached the violence of the outbreak in Union Square yesterday," proclaimed the next morning's *Sun*. There had been eight arrests and dozens of injuries. For more than a week, newspaper editors had been calling for stern measures against protest demonstrations, and for now the press seemed satisfied with the result. "The police," a *Times* reporter wrote, "led by a detachment of mounted men, wielded their clubs right and left, and left many aching heads in their wake." The *World* expressed similar contentment at seeing "a couple of hundred vile-tongued I.W.W.'s . . . routed by unmerciful clubbing." After the battle, Commissioner McKay surveyed the scene of his masterstroke with complacency. "Though what did happen was bad enough," he told reporters, "anything might have happened, and we were prepared for it." Surely, no one would now accuse him of overindulging these anarchists.

* * *

THE TONE OF the telegram from Washington hinted at what was to come:

COMMITTEE ON MINES AND MINING DESIRES YOUR TESTIMONY ON COLORADO STRIKE WILL YOU APPEAR IN WASHINGTON WITH BOOKS PAPERS AND LETTERS WITHOUT FORMAL SERVICE AND WHEN ANSWER.

This seemed brusque even for a cable message, but John D. Rockefeller, Jr., refused to be baited. YOUR COURTEOUS TELEGRAM OF MARCH 31ST I FIND UPON MY RETURN TO THE OFFICE THIS MORNING, he replied. IF IT SUITS YOUR CONVENIENCE I WILL BE GLAD TO APPEAR BEFORE YOUR COMMITTEE ON MONDAY MORNING, APRIL 6TH, AT ANY TIME AFTER NINE O'CLOCK.

He was not sure why the investigators wanted to see him in particular. After all, he was merely one of several directors who sat on a board of one of many companies involved in a nearly statewide coal-mining strike. There must have been dozens of business leaders with more knowledge of the situation. Though it was true that he exchanged weekly—and at times daily—correspondence with his executives at the Colorado Fuel & Iron Company, he himself had not even visited the state in a decade. "What possible value any knowledge which I may be able to impart may be to this inquiry, I do not know," he wrote to his father. "However, since the invitation has been extended, I felt it wise to accept it without hesitation."

The five congressmen on the subcommittee had just returned from Denver themselves. During their three-week visit to Colorado, they had conducted hearings throughout the troubled districts, interviewing company bosses and union leaders as well as dozens of individual miners and other locals. Through these meetings they had uncovered a "system of feudalism" reinforced through violence, corruption, and coercion. The state militia was controlled by the mine operators, while the strikers in their tent encampments were armed and organized as well. Every hand gripped a shotgun or rifle, and twenty-two people had by now been killed.

The committee members had found no blameless parties, but they had been particularly irritated by the stubbornness of the corporate executives—men like L. M. Bowers, the Rockefeller-appointed chief at Colorado Fuel & Iron. He had reiterated for them his belief that the company treated its workers as well as they had any right to expect. "The word 'satisfaction,'" he wrote to Junior, "could have been put over the entrance to every one of our mines." If it wasn't for the interference of agitators, the miners would be calm as cattle. The only thing worse than a union organizer, in his mind, was the "goody, goody, milk and water" brand of reformer. "It will be a happy day for the business man," Bowers had written in 1912, "when a lot of these social fanatics are placed in lunatic asylums, and the muckrakers, labor agitators and the grafters are put in jail."

The congressmen saw that this intransigence was hindering any chance of industrial peace in Colorado. "Society in general cannot tolerate such conduct on either side," they decreed. "The statement that a man or company of men who put their money in a business have a right to operate it as they see fit, without regard to the public interest, belongs to days long since passed away."

Thus the antagonism that Junior had detected in the telegram, and which manifested itself as soon as he arrived in the Washington, D.C., hearing room, was not entirely unexpected. Still, he indicated no apprehensiveness as he settled in at the witness table with his lawyer and a sheath of documents. At ten A.M., on April 6, the chairman—Martin D. Foster, a Democrat from Illinois—initiated the proceedings.

THE CHAIRMAN. You may give your name and residence to the stenographer, Mr. Rockefeller.

MR. ROCKEFELLER. John D. Rockefeller, Jr., 10 West Fifty-fourth Street, New York.

And that was just about the last collegial exchange of the day.

From then on, Junior was peppered with hostile questions, mockery, and hectoring. The congressmen repeatedly interrupted and challenged him on every last little detail of fact. He had wondered what he—who'd had so little direct contact with the strike situation—could add to the investigation. Now it was clear that the interrogators had no interest in his expertise; they intended to showcase his ignorance.

THE CHAIRMAN. You know when the strike started, do you?

MR. ROCKEFELLER. I could refer to the exact date in this correspondence. It was in September or October, some place along there: but the date I would not have retained.

MR. BYRNES. We can all tell you it was the 23d of September.

MR. ROCKEFELLER. Well, you see, you have been there.

THE CHAIRMAN. Do you realize that since last September this strike has been reported in the press throughout the country, that the governor of Colorado has called out the militia to police the disturbed district, and that the conditions prevailing in that district were shocking, according to such reports, and that the House of Representatives deemed it a duty to undertake this investigation?

MR. ROCKEFELLER. I have been fully aware of all those facts.

THE CHAIRMAN. And yet you, personally, nor the board of directors, have not looked into the matter?

MR. ROCKEFELLER. I can not say as to whether the board of directors has—

THE CHAIRMAN (*interposing*). Whether conditions were correct as reported in the press?

MR. ROCKEFELLER. I can not say as to whether the board of directors have looked into the matter or not, their meetings being held in the West.

THE CHAIRMAN. What action has been taken personally to find out about the trouble in Colorado?

MR. ROCKEFELLER. This correspondence will give the whole thing.

THE CHAIRMAN. Personally, what have you done, outside of this, as a director?

MR. ROCKEFELLER. I have done nothing outside of this; that is the way in which we conduct the business . . .

THE CHAIRMAN. You do not consider yourself a "dummy" director in the Colorado Fuel & Iron Co.?

MR. ROCKEFELLER. I do not.

This was how all the family's operations worked, as Rockefeller patiently explained. Trusted operatives handled daily affairs, with only minimal interference from 26 Broadway. Senior had run Standard Oil that way, and it was hard to cavil with its effectiveness. New York received intelligence from the local proxy—in this case, L. M. Bowers. If he reported that the miners were treated leniently, and had been bullied and preyed upon by alien agitators into striking—that, as one of his associates had claimed, "the strike of our coal miners was literally forced upon them against their wishes by people from the outside"—then that information was considered reliable.

THE CHAIRMAN. What, in your judgment, should be the relation between employee and employer?

MR. ROCKEFELLER. That is a pretty big and broad question, is it not?

THE CHAIRMAN. . . . Yes; I am getting your opinion, because you have had a good deal to do with the civic uplift of the country, and you ought to have a good idea and an intelligent opinion of those matters. I think it would be valuable to have it in the record.

MR. ROCKEFELLER. If you can make the question at all concrete, I should be glad to try to answer it.

THE CHAIRMAN. You know there has been growing in the country a belief that there does not exist between employers and employees the relation that there should be between the two. What do you say as to that?

MR. ROCKEFELLER. I believe that the employer and the employee are fellow men, and I see no reason why they should not each treat other as a fellow man. You are asking a broad question, and I am giving a pretty broad basic reply. It is difficult to get closer to the subject.

THE CHAIRMAN. That leads me to ask this question: As a director of the Colorado Iron & Fuel Co., and representing a large interest in that company, have you personally taken the trouble to know any of those miners or to look into their conditions there, their manner of living, and all that?

MR. ROCKEFELLER. Oh, when I was investigating vice in New York I never talked with a single prostitute. That is not the way I have been trained to investigate. I could not talk with 10,000 miners.

THE CHAIRMAN. No; you could not.

For hours he parried these attacks with a civility that soon attracted the sympathy of the reporters who witnessed his performance. "Never ruffled," they wrote, "polite and thoroughly suave," he was "at ease throughout." Few public men had so much experience in facing derision. Junior's position as his father's son had meant he'd been perpetually underestimated his entire adult life. This session ranked as a minor irritation compared to some of the barbs he'd already endured. He did not stammer. He did not dodge or sidestep. Instead, he waited to make his own case against organized labor. And, finally, he did.

THE CHAIRMAN. But the killing of these people, the shooting of children, and all that that has been going on there for months has not been of enough importance to you for you to communicate with the other directors, and see if something might not be done to end that sort of thing?

MR. ROCKEFELLER. We believe that the issue is not a local one in Colorado; it is a national issue, whether workers shall be allowed to work under such conditions as they may choose. And as part owners of the property, our interest in the laboring men in this country is so immense, so deep, so profound that we stand ready to lose every cent we put in that company rather than see the men we have employed thrown out of work and have imposed upon them conditions which are not of their seeking and which neither they nor we can see are in our interest.

THE CHAIRMAN. And you are willing to go on and let these killings take place—men losing their lives on either side, the expenditure of large sums of money, and all this disturbance of labor—rather than to go out there and see if you might do something to settle those conditions?

MR. ROCKEFELLER. There is just one thing, Mr. Chairman, so far as I understand it, which can be done, as things are at present, to settle this strike, and that is to unionize the camps; and our interest in labor is so profound and we believe so sincerely that that interest demands that the camps shall be open camps, that we expect to stand by the officers at any cost. It is not an accident that this is our position.

THE CHAIRMAN. And you will do that if it costs all your property and kills all your employees?

MR. ROCKEFELLER. It is a great principle.

THE CHAIRMAN. And you would do that rather than recognize the right of men to collective bargaining? Is that what I understand?

MR. ROCKEFELLER. No, sir. Rather than allow outside people to come in and interfere with employees who are thoroughly satisfied with their labor conditions—it was upon a similar principle that the War of the Revolution was carried on. It is a great national issue of the most vital kind.

The hearing was adjourned at 2:25 P.M. If Junior was concerned about his performance, he was reassured the next morning by the newspaper headlines. For the first time in his life, the press treated his words seriously, taking note—with a certain surprise—of his gravity and poise. And then the congratulations began to arrive. "Nothing I have read or heard in recent years," wrote Charles M. Schwab, "so fully and clearly and logically expresses the views that I hold with reference to a situation of this kind, as the testimony you have given." J. P. Morgan, Jr., sent a letter saying, "It was exceedingly amusing to see the common-sense business point of view as opposed to the political and excited sociological point of view which all members of Congress appear to occupy."

The most welcome notes came from his parents in Tarrytown. "It was a bugle note that was struck for principle yesterday before our country," wrote his mother. His father bragged to a friend, "He expressed the views which I entertain, and which have been drilled into him from his earliest childhood." To show his gratification, Senior presented his son with a generous gift: ten thousand shares of Colorado Fuel & Iron

Company stock. "Nothing could give me greater satisfaction," Junior replied to his mother, "than to feel that you and Father are satisfied with my effort of yesterday."

But in fact his conscience was disturbed. One exchange, in particular, had touched on his most delicate feelings.

> THE CHAIRMAN. Do you think that a director like you are of a company such as the Colorado Fuel & Iron Co. should take the responsibility for the conduct of the company?
>
> MR. ROCKEFELLER. Mr. Chairman, in these days, where interests are so diversified and numerous, of course, it would be impossible for any man to be personally responsible for all of the management of the various concerns in which he might be a larger or smaller stockholder . . . I do not know of any other way in which a company can be run except by putting the responsibility upon the officers, and then holding them to it, and seeing that they perform in a proper way the tasks imposed upon them.

Junior was profoundly aware that modern industrial organization was incompatible with individual responsibility. This was the very realization that had prompted him to retire from business four years earlier. Colorado Fuel & Iron was the one directorship he had retained, and he had done so only out of a feeling of duty to his father. Now he was in the exact predicament he had hoped to avoid, publicly vouching for the choices of others—men he trusted, but whose actions he could not control.

The congressmen had nudged him toward uncertainty. Perhaps he had delegated too much responsibility. From L. M. Bowers he had received a vehement, almost feverish, letter of congratulations. It worried him. Hearing that Bowers happened to be visiting his home in upstate New York, Junior sent him an urgent cable: THINK IT IMPORTANT TO SEE YOU BEFORE YOU GO WEST. If they could meet personally, maybe he could convince his subordinate to offer some concessions, or at least assure himself that the man was still qualified to lead.

But the telegram arrived too late. Bowers had already entrained for Colorado.

*   *   *

THE POLICEMEN'S TESTIMONY was disjointed and contradictory. Their assailants came from uptown; no, from the downtown side; they had yelled "Kill the Cops!" and some other such unlikely things, and had initiated all the fighting. The presiding magistrate shook his head throughout, with a baleful smile.

And then Arthur Caron took the stand: his eye swollen shut, his face checkered with bruises. "The next thing I knew I got a blow over the back of the head with a blackjack," he said. "I tried to straighten my hat, which was knocked off, and I received a blow over the wrist. A blow was struck into my kidneys at the same moment. I dropped to the sidewalk, but I tried to get up, and then I was shoved into an automobile. Policeman Dawson jumped on the running board and hit me twice in the face, while somebody else hit me on the back." After he had finished, the magistrate acquitted Caron of all charges, and urged his defense attorney to launch an investigation of the police department. "The condition of these prisoners," the judge admonished the officers, "is enough to make us feel ashamed."

On April 8, when Arthur Caron walked out of the courtroom at 300 Mulberry Street, his derby was battered through in three places. But he was a free man.

COMMISSIONER MCKAY HAD helplessly watched the burnish fade from his coup. The same public that had chided him for inaction now complained of his exuberance. The *Tribune* demanded an official inquiry into the violence at Union Square. "Disapproval of the methods and purposes of the Industrial Workers of the World," wrote an editor at *Outlook*, "so far from affording an excuse for brutal police conduct, should make the police authorities the more scrupulous in seeing that the rights of such people are maintained." The *Times* alone continued to support the commissioner and his men. "It is nonsense to say that the police made too free use of their heavy clubs," the paper insisted. After all, "none of the malcontents was disabled."

Mitchel had spent the weekend in Atlantic City, but he sent an emissary to witness the trial where Caron was vindicated, lending "weight to rumors that I.W.W. sympathizers had gained the Mayor's attention." On his return he attempted to restore composure to the metropolis, claiming for the second time in a month that there was "no such thing as an 'I.W.W. situation'" and reiterating his commitment to principled government. "I want the police to take all necessary steps to prevent breaches of the peace and law," he said. "On the other hand . . . there must be no unnecessary clubbing."

These speeches were eagerly accepted as a sign of coming peace. But it was Mitchel's second act that really indicated his attitude. He fired the police commissioner.

The mayor had always intended to replace McKay, who was hired by the preceding administration and had never matched the profile of a Mitchel appointee. He made no claims to social-scientific expertise, had not published any studies, nor conducted sensational experiments. If he had shown a knack for leadership, perhaps he could have remained longer, but the only flair he had revealed was for mismanagement. On April 1, he received a letter from the mayor that acknowledged his "efficient and faithful" service—and that also accepted his resignation. The debate over his replacement, which had begun even before Mitchel's Fusion government had taken office, now intensified into a public canvass of suitable candidates for what was widely considered to be "the hardest job in the entire city government."

Some of the most prominent administrators in the nation saw their names mentioned in connection to the post. G.W. Goethals, engineer of the Panama Canal, William J. Flynn, head of the U.S. Secret Service, and General Leonard Wood, the U.S. Army Chief of Staff, were all courted in turn. And each eagerly declined to serve. "The surest way to be out of a job within a year," people said, "was to become Police Commissioner of New York." Fifteen men had already come and gone in the sixteen years since the position was created—"Commissioner had succeeded Commissioner at the same reckless pace"—and if not all had been downright crooked, neither had they especially distinguished themselves. "Few have had time to learn more than routine," an editor wrote, and "none has stayed long enough to impress upon the department a continuous and consistent policy." Of all the men to lead the police force, only one had not been ruined by it—Theodore Roosevelt—and he had served from 1895 to 1897, before the consolidation of the five boroughs into Greater New York.

Ask most New Yorkers to define *police*, and the response, according to the *Outlook*, would go like this:

police (*noun*) — a blackhander to whom the use of bombs is forbidden, but otherwise fully authorized by the state. (*v. t*) — to beat, club, shoot, bulldoze, threaten, or graft. (F. < L. *politia*, state; < Gr. *politeia*, city.)

Of the city's many failures of governance, none had caused more chagrin than its "corrupt and disorganized Police Department." The cops were considered to be "the dirtiest, crookedest, ugliest lot . . . outside of Turkey or Japan." Outrages from the force had been so common during the previous twenty years that by the 1910s they elicited little more than a shrug. "Once more New York City has set the Nation by nose and ears with a scandal of police corruption," sighed a longtime critic of the department, with absolutely no surprise.

In a typical year, New Yorkers committed six times as many murders as the residents of London, and could almost match the combined homicide totals for all of England and Wales. Prisoners waited months to be tried, and conviction rates were appallingly low. The civil service procedure was faulty, and politicians played favorites anyhow; promotion was haphazard and often found the wrong man. No one thought to maintain adequate files; "our criminal statistics are so crude and incomplete," complained the Bureau of Social Hygiene, "that deductions are difficult to make and when made are little better than rough estimates." Every sort of depravity was sanctioned by grafting cops, and "collusion between exploiters of vice and officials in the Police Department" was common knowledge.

Every decade or so an investigation would reveal the dirty details of these operations—the Lexow Committee in 1894 and 1895, the Mazet Committee in 1899—but they had no discernible effect. The public had more or less given up on reform; it would have been satisfied if law-enforcement officers would just conduct their crooked business out of sight. Lincoln Steffens described New York–style Good Government as "clean streets, and well lighted; an orderly police department, with well-ordered blackmail and corruption (of which people don't hear), and general comfort and cleanliness." But even that was too much to ask.

There were irregular, spectacular occasions of depravity, and these could still raise a newspaper reader's eyebrows. But far more detrimental to morale and efficiency was the quotidian influence of habit, suspicion, silence, and self-interest that was universally known as the System. "The police 'system' in New York, as the man-on-the-street understands it," explained a muckraking reporter, "consists of a cohesive group of men who sell the privilege of breaking the laws, surrounded by a larger group which, while honest, is stultified by the tainted spirit of the powerful and corrupt few." Take care to sustain the System, and it would take care of you. Every few years a commissioner might pass through with some improvements in mind, but the policemen knew enough not to worry. The reformer would be gone and the System would remain.

"I believe it is essential that the police commissioner should have a long term of office," a progressive activist had told a conference in 1913. "Today he is a bird of passage. And usually he flies so fast that the men on the force have hardly time to determine his species. The policy of the force, when a new commissioner is given them, is to try to size him up—what kind of man he is—and then to humor him as the occasion calls for." The speaker's name was Arthur Woods, and on April 8, the same morning that the I.W.W. agitators were being acquitted in the Magistrate's Court, Mayor Mitchel swore him in as the tenth police commissioner in the history of Greater New York.

Waving off his chauffeured car, Woods walked up from City Hall to police headquarters at 240 Centre Street, arriving a few minutes before noon. As cameramen snapped photos for the next day's papers, he chatted with the outgoing chief. Best wishes were exchanged; the "room filled rapidly and every one was as happy as if the occasion were a picnic." At precisely twelve o'clock, Woods sat at his desk for the first time and signed general order No. 15, finalizing his "assumption of the government and control of the Police Department" and placing its nearly

Arthur Woods.

eleven thousand men under his authority. "Is there anything I can do for you?" McKay asked, preparing to leave.

"I wish you'd pray for me," Woods replied.

"I HAVE DONE a good many things," Arthur Woods once said of himself. "I have been a newspaper man, and I have been a schoolmaster, and I have been a business man. It is pretty hard to generalize from all those three."

He was the great-grandson of the founder of Andover Theological Seminary, the grandson of a president of Bowdoin College; his father had earned a fortune in textiles. After graduating Harvard in 1892, he spent a year at the University of Berlin, and then returned to teach English literature at Groton, where Franklin Delano Roosevelt numbered among his students. When the classroom became too confining, he contemplated a missionary's life in the Philippines but instead asked his friend Jacob Riis for a position on the *Evening Sun*. As a police reporter, he covered grafting officials, the Black Hand, pickpockets, and safe breakers—taking lessons from the Other Half that he could never have acquired as a prep-school don.

Eager to apply this experience to a useful cause, he agitated for municipal reform. In 1907, the city created a new position for him—the Fourth Deputy Police Commissionership, with jurisdiction over the Detective Bureau—so that it could benefit from his expertise. He accepted, deferring the appointment to steam to England at his own expense to study the methods of Scotland Yard. For two years he pushed innovations, reorganizing the undercover branch and introducing the use of police dogs. But when the commissioner he served under was replaced by a Tammany functionary, he returned to private life. In 1913, the potential of a Fusion victory brought him back to politics. Becoming a top strategist for Mitchel's campaign, he served for a few months as the mayor's official secretary. When everyone else turned down the thankless position of police commissioner, Arthur Woods jumped at the job that nobody wanted.

He was forty-four years old in 1914, tall, with graying hair and strong features that were just starting to sag. To one reporter he seemed "a keen, dark, alert, well-groomed gentleman—very much the gentleman." Photos made him look severe, but acquaintances described his "crust of levity" and a "light and airy way of talking." He lived at the Harvard Club in midtown with other wealthy bachelors, and his peers judged him an awfully good fellow. "Just as he was in school, so he is to-day," a member said. "Whenever a man's in trouble and needs a confidant, he goes instinctively to Woods." Since his college days, he had been "engrossed," even "obsessed" with theories for "municipal progress and social betterment." Having mastered the literature of reform, he understood the connections between crime and housing conditions, employment opportunities, or social neglect. "Arthur Woods had ideas of his own," Edward Mott Woolley would write in a profile for *McClure's*. "The traditional scheme of a police department is to delve out crime and abet the punishment. Commissioner Woods saw an additional function in the department: the prevention of crime through the removal of the impulse of people to commit it. He believes that crime is due largely to environment."

"There has never been a Police Commissioner quite like him," gushed a reporter for the *Times*. "He may not succeed in carrying out his ideas, but he can never be charged with a lack of them, or an unwillingness to fight for them." In Arthur Woods, New Yorkers believed they had

SIZING HIM UP.

Commentators wondered if the new commissioner could make any headway against the "System."

found the leader to transform their police department into an efficient, twentieth-century force. "Few men," proclaimed *Outlook*, "have come to municipal office more fitly trained for its duties than he."

On the evening of his first day in command, Woods ate dinner with Chief Inspector Max Schmittberger, the highest-ranking uniformed officer on the force. Afterward, taking a police automobile, they toured several uptown station houses. At each precinct he made "quick upstairs, downstairs, into-the-cellar explorations," examining cells and blotters, explaining to the anxious men on duty that he was "just getting acquainted."

Down on East Fourth Street, meanwhile, five hundred angry, excited radicals—as well as an undetermined number of plainclothes police—were crammed into the Manhattan Lyceum to discuss the next phase of the anarchists' campaign against the city. O'Carroll and Caron sat onstage, where their wounds could be most effectively displayed. Becky Edelsohn spoke first, arguing that it was the newspaper editors and the Rockefellers who were the real inciters to riot. "It is difficult for me to speak in moderation of these cowardly police," she went on, "who for a few measly dollars . . . beat and almost kill the working classes." Berkman, who had disappeared just at the moment when the previous Saturday's violence was commencing, spoke with even more fury. "If I had seen the brutality of the police," he sputtered, "if I had seen it with my own eyes right on the very spot, and if I had had a revolver, I would have used it." Rage sent his rhetoric right over the threshold of decency. His bloodcurdling climax was all but unprintable. The morning papers transcribed it as "To ____ with all the ____ ____ ____!"

Berkman ended with a promise to return to Union Square on Saturday, April 11, for a "monster mass meeting" to assert the right of free speech. "I believe in resistance!" he shouted. "I claim the right to preach riot if I want to!" And in three days' time, he intended to see if anyone—including the new police commissioner—would attempt to stop him.

ARTHUR WOODS KNEW the potential gravity of Berkman's threat as well as any officer in the department; he was familiar with the anarchist's methods and considered him an "auld acquaintance." The two had first confronted one another six years earlier, in 1908, during a similarly miserable winter when mass joblessness had again posed a desperate crisis.

In late March of that year, thousands of unemployed protesters had crammed into Union Square for a socialist rally. Within minutes, the police had arrived to break up the demonstration. Inevitably, resistance led to clubbing and scuffles. At the height of the violence, Woods, in his role as fourth deputy commissioner, had arrived with a detachment of reinforcements. With his help, the officers cleared the square and the danger appeared to have subsided. Only a few reporters and some stragglers remained. A contingent of twenty cops lined up. Their work done, they formed ranks prior to being dismissed.

As the men stood in two smart rows, a young immigrant dashed at the formation from the rear. Pausing a few steps away, he fumbled with a parcel and raised it chest-high. "There was a splutter of sparks," a witness said, "and then an explosion like the report of a 6-inch gun." Through the smoke, the unharmed officers sought their assailant. They found him, a Russian-born anarchist, wounded on the pavement. His hand had vanished and half of his body was in tatters. The bomb—a brass bed knob crammed with broken nails, nitroglycerin, and gunpowder—had detonated a moment early.

"A second Haymarket horror was averted yesterday by the narrowest of margins," the *Tribune* reported the next morning. Woods took charge of the investigation; his detectives sped through the city after leads. One of his first measures was to arrest Alexander Berkman, who had

An anarchist bomb in Union Square.

had no connection with the riot and who was released with a warning from the magistrate.

But if Woods's first instinct was punitive, on reflection he had come to a different understanding of what had occurred at Union Square in 1908. The police, he realized, had initiated the violence by storming a peaceful rally. At one point, a protester had demanded that Inspector Schmittberger respect his right to free speech. The veteran officer had motioned icily with his baton and said, "The club is mightier than the Constitution." The quotation had become a rallying cry for the radical opposition, and the whole affair had turned into a political embarrassment.

Six years later, as he took up the commissionership himself, Woods recalled the lessons he had learned. Although certain newspapers were calling once again for repressive measures, he had the confidence to follow his own experience. On his second day as commissioner he addressed the upcoming demonstration, meeting with Lincoln Steffens to discuss a possible truce and making reassuring statements to the newspapers. "The fact that a man talks on the subject he is interested in, and even uses profane language in punctuating his remarks, is not a breach of the peace," said Woods. "The speakers will be allowed to do their oratorical best if they do not violate the law. I do not expect any trouble."

Rather than sending hundreds of menacing police, he assigned just a few officers to the square. McKay had exhorted the troops to "Break 'em up!" Woods instructed his men to adopt a radically different approach. "It was pointed out that the crowd would undoubtedly be most provocative," Woods later recalled of the briefing he gave to his men,

> that many in it would try to make themselves martyrs and desired nothing more ardently than to have the police assault them; that they would tempt the police to take what would seem to be the initiative. It was explained to the police that their great effort should be to prevent trouble. If trouble should arise they were to suppress it, and to use whatever force might be necessary for suppression. But their aim was to be to prevent it from arising . . . Beyond this, however, they were charged with the duty of radiating good nature, of trying to maintain an atmosphere of quiet and calm. For a smile is just as infectious as a sneer.

Most of the city expected bloodshed at Union Square. The agitators were hinting at more trouble. "What are we going to do Saturday, huh? You wait and see." The Socialist *Call* warned its readers to stay away. Big

Bill Haywood refused to attend. A rumor circulated that the anarchists had recruited gunmen from around the nation to retaliate if and when the police made their assault. Anticipating a spectacular battle, the *World* assigned a special correspondent to the scene—John Reed.

By two P.M. on April 11, thousands had already gathered. They arrived in separate groups, organized and ardent. The unemployed marched in from one direction. Anarchists appeared as a separate unit. Men wore hatbands that said BREAD OR REVOLUTION. Speakers attracted attention in all parts of the square. "The whole place was murmuring and boiling with low-voiced propaganda," Reed reported. "Free speech was beginning." "Little east side radicals, quacks, social service workers and even politicians were the centre of eager little tight-packed groups, arguing and preaching . . . One saw Lincoln Steffens plunging through the mob . . . shoals of strange radical women in the Greenwich Village uniform, and others in civilian clothes. All the intellectuals were there. Then there were hundreds of Socialists, although their official daily paper had warned them to ignore the meeting. And many I.W.W.'s who had also been told to hold aloof."

Just a few score uniformed officers spectated from the sidelines, stirring only to prevent marchers from parading out of the square. Berkman spoke and no one moved to silence him. Leonard Abbott, a founder of the Ferrer Center, proclaimed that "the whacks of the police clubs that fell upon the head of Arthur Caron a week ago have already been

I.W.W. meeting in Union Square.

Alexander Berkman in Union Square, April 11, 1914.

heard around the world." Still, the cops kept their distance. It gradually became clear that new guidelines were in effect. "These people have faith in Mayor Mitchel, and faith in the new Police Commissioner," Abbott confessed, "and it seems to have been justified . . . You can fairly feel the ugliness of the crowd's mood seeping out of it."

Woods, who had been receiving regular updates from Schmittberger, arrived just as the demonstration was breaking up. Even he was surprised at the results of his own orders. "The change of method was almost unbelievably successful," he realized. "There was no disorder." Emboldened, he mingled with the protesters. "I was not recognized," he recalled. "I went up toward the crowd of one or two hundred people, perhaps, and their orator got up on the billboards, and as I went up he called out, 'Well, boys, the cops certainly have made good today. Three cheers for the cops!'"

* * *

"WITH SUCH A man as police commissioner," said a relieved John Purroy Mitchel, "I'll have no police problem. I can just stick him up in headquarters and forget him." One less cause for nerves, however, still left far too many worries and did little to ease his overall anxiety. The imperturbable "young knight in shining armor" who had taken office four months earlier had grown pale and thin; the black hair around his ears was turning gray.

Mitchel's workdays usually began at breakfast, with one or more cabinet heads joining him in the wainscoted dining room of his apartment in the Peter Stuyvesant, an elegant building on Riverside Drive at Ninety-eighth Street. The upper-story windows looked high over the gray waters of the Hudson to the trees and cliffs on the far shore, offering a brief promise of serenity. But then the telephone would ring and city business pressed again. Downstairs, he and his subordinate would climb into the open tonneau of his automobile—the chauffeur draping a fur robe over their legs to protect against the cold—and they would accelerate out onto the drive. Often they would stop by some other commissioner's apartment and pick him up, too, before speeding downtown to City Hall. By the time the mayor arrived at his office, he had already done an hour's worth of work. And many nights he wouldn't leave again until nine or ten in the evening. "Mayor Mitchel's friends," a concerned *Sun* reported in May, "say he is burdening himself with the pressure of work such as few men stand for more than a limited period."

Mayor Mitchel en route to City Hall.

Mitchel, who prized efficiency first and last, felt himself everywhere thwarted. He employed two full-time secretaries—one for official business, another for the private obligations engendered by his position—and they each placed about a hundred telephone calls a day. Still, nothing got done. Or it was done, and then undone, and had to be done over. Newspapers magnified any misstep into a ruinous lapse, and saw disaster in every portent. If there happened to be a real problem—as, for instance, with the unemployed—it was inevitably exacerbated by the press. It felt as if his five and a third million constituents had nothing to do but lodge bitter complaints, request impossible favors, waste his days with eccentric schemes. He received between two hundred and three hundred letters a day, asking for matrimonial advice, offering headache remedies, challenging him to a tango competition. "Quite a lot of time of this office," he complained to an interviewer, "is taken up by matters that never ought to come before the Mayor at all." Unable to mask the frustration he experienced around constituents, he became increasingly impatient, "and not seldom too curt," with citizens who behaved "captious and unreasonable."

Doctors had promised that his migraines would gradually diminish, but thanks to the stress of his responsibilities the attacks were in fact occurring with greater frequency and severity. His bodyguard would find him in his office, prone on the couch, head in hands, in "bending pain." On the worst days, he would vanish into a secret hideaway in the Municipal Building to recover alone. In March, a headache forced him to retire from a meeting of the Board of Estimates. When newspapers published exaggerated articles about his "collapse," the mayor warned reporters: "If you are going to write such stories, you will have to do it about twice a month."

There were an estimated two hundred thousand "mental incompetents" in the country, and a disproportionate number of them, it seemed to Mitchel, must have been resident in the five boroughs. The city had an inexhaustible stock of neurasthenics, dipsomaniacs, hypochondriacs, and plain old "bugs"; "There are thousands of people who write threatening letters," Mitchel testified. "The Mayor is always receiving threatening letters." Of course, the majority were harmless, and there was really no way to protect against the rest, anyway. But he couldn't completely ignore them. His predecessor, William Gaynor, had been shot in the throat by a deranged assassin; the wound had festered for years before killing him. With a growing sense of his own vulnerability, Mayor

Mitchel took to carrying a revolver in a shoulder holster whenever he ventured out on public business.

IT WAS ABOUT ONE P.M. on April 17 when Arthur Woods appeared in the mayor's office. While they prepared to leave for lunch, he described the scene of a lodging house fire he had just toured. Together with Frank Polk, the corporation counsel, and George Mullan, Mitchel's former law partner, they left the building, descending the marble steps onto City Hall Plaza. The afternoon was cloudy but warm, and the old elm trees were just showing yellow buds. Office workers on their midday break jammed the square. A group of socialist orators gathered, as always, around the plinth of the Benjamin Franklin statue. As the officials walked south toward Park Row, many in the crowd paused to get a close look at their mayor.

A police department automobile was idling at the curb. Mitchel clambered first into the narrow rear seat, followed by Polk and then Mullan. The chauffeur reached across to cover them with the fur robe. Woods, who was to ride up front, ventured round to the street side, carefully avoiding the nearby trolley tracks. A shabbily dressed old man approached, threading through the traffic. Woods stepped onto the running board and was about to climb inside. The old man had reached a distance of about five feet. He raised an arm, revealing a snub-nosed revolver. Woods, two jumps away, was already in motion when the first round fired. There was no second shot. Woods, an expert in jujitsu, grabbed the attacker by the shoulder, tackled him to the ground, and pinned his arms.

In the car, Mitchel thought for a confused moment that he had heard a muffler explosion. But then he felt the burning in his ear. To his right, the corporation counsel coughed blood and teeth. The mayor was unscathed except for some scorches from the gunpowder. Gathering himself, he drew his blue-gray revolver, enraged, eager to retaliate. He made a survey of the crowd, looking for assailants, hoping to trigger off some revenge. But Woods and the chauffeur had disarmed the shooter. They had him on his feet and were leading him away. Thousands of civilians were mobbing the car. Police whistles blared from every corner, and Polk was gagging with pain. Mitchel, still brandishing his gun, supported the wounded man back inside City Hall. Even then, in the throes of excitement, he was already experiencing relief. For months he had anticipated this moment; the burden of dread had grown excruciating. Finally, instantaneously, it had been removed, and he could proceed with the work he had to do.

The assassin fired from about five feet away.

Only a few hours later, the mayor faced an audience of hundreds at a Press Club dinner. "Calm, smiling, cool," he displayed "a jaw of steel," wrote a witness, and was "totally unlike a man who had escaped a funeral." He rose to speak, and the thankful crowd offered a five-minute ovation before he could say a word. "The experience of this afternoon is, of course, one to impress itself on any man's mind," he began. "I had been almost expecting some such thing, not because I had any reason to expect it, not because there is any reason why such a thing should happen in a civilized community ordered by laws, as is ours, but because I know that life in a democracy, where there is progress, where new things are being established, is more or less of a battle and in a battle almost anything is likely to happen."

It was midnight when the mayor eventually got home to Riverside Drive. By 8:30 A.M. the next day, he was already dressed and breakfasted. Riding the elevator down to his waiting auto, Mitchel arranged himself to confront the business of a new morning.

Chief-Inspector Judas

On May 3, 1903, he parades through a perpetual ovation. Stock-ticker tape slips in helixes through the skies from Bowling Green to Trinity Church, and confetti cloaks his uniform. The jammed spectators at Houston Street refuse to let him pass until he tips his cap three times to them. Every block reserves its loudest huzzah for his approach. From both sides of the boulevard, they surge against the police line, stamping and calling out, "Max!" "Schmitzy!"

Eyes front, Inspector Max Schmittberger nudges his horse from Fortieth Street onto Fifth Avenue. After twenty-nine years of service, he is still the "Police Samson," a "big, burly six-footer." In the late-afternoon light, the brass buttons and gold oak leaves on his coat no longer shimmer as they had at midday, but his gloves and cap remain pure white. A fine hussar's mustache overtops his small, tight-lipped mouth. He wears the Prussian Order of the Black Eagle and has invoked the diktats of Field Marshal von Moltke to many a subordinate. Even on station duty he demands a crisp salute. The handiest horseman in the department, he is its truest sharpshooter and "an artist" with a baton. "He is not only the equal of any man on the force," a former chief declared, "but I cannot think of any one who is his equal."

The reviewing stand is in Madison Square, near the foot of the new Flatiron Building. The police commissioner and mayor are in the first row on the flag-strewn platform. Distinguished guests are massed twenty deep, and the colorful din belittles all that has preceded it. Schmittberger draws even with the dignitaries. For nearly a decade, these men and their predecessors have humiliated and ostracized him. They have "cuffed and cursed" him, accused and slandered him with "nasty and

INSP. MAX SCHMITTBERGER

Max Schmittberger.

vindictive" attacks. Until this year—his year of redemption—they have
forbidden him even from marching in the annual policemen's parade.

He turns his blue-gray eyes on them. He salutes. And then, eyes
front.

*   *   *

SUCH CURSES HAD covered him in the previous decade, such obloquy
and derogation. The newspapers called him "liar" and "grafter." Church-
men took him for a "thief and a crook." An "everlasting disgrace," said
the district attorney. Socialists jeered him as an anarchist, and anarchists warned he was a "marked man." His fellow policemen—the honest and dishonest alike—loathed him, one and all. He was "Judas," a
squealer who had "split on his pals," and many officers refused to serve
under him. He should be in Sing Sing, not in uniform, ran the everlasting outcry. "Schmittberger will never do police work of any kind

again." "Schmittberger will get a hard drubbing." "Schmittberger has got to go!"

A DECADE EARLIER, in 1894, he had been a recently promoted captain with a record "unmarred by a single complaint." He was a shrewd and patient investigator, a fearsome pugilist, and a modest subordinate who had personally accounted for nearly a thousand convictions and had arrested more murderers than any other man in uniform. And, like every other officer of his rank on the force, he was corrupt, in a good-natured sort of way. He would collect payoffs for his superiors and rake off his due portion. He was selective about the brothels and illegal saloons he busted up: Proprietors who were paid up with the police tended to stay in business longer than those who fell behind. It wasn't corruption so much as it was tradition. These were established practices, and Schmittberger was a firm believer in upholding them.

Sometimes the private business of the System would escape the shadows into the public eye, and then the reformers would be involving themselves. Every ten years or so, some impaneled bluebloods came around scratching for trouble. In 1894 it was the Lexow Committee, state investigators hoping to irritate the city bosses. It looked, at first, to be the usual nothing: a circus for the papers, a political career for a prosecutor, some catharsis for the Society for the Prevention of Crime. But witnesses sometimes say funny things—like, in this case, about handing a $500 bribe to a captain named Schmittberger. Subpoenas ensued. Still, even this was no source of worry; the captain was known as a dependable fellow with a small mouth, the taciturn type.

Nevertheless, every seat was occupied in room 1 of the Tweed Courthouse on the morning of December 21, 1894. A long delay heightened anticipation, and a "loud buzzing" greeted Schmittberger's entrance. He wore civilian clothes and had "dark rings about his eyes, which told of sleeplessness and mental suffering."

Q: You are a police captain of this city?
A: Yes, sir.
Q: In command of what precinct at the present time?
A: The Nineteenth.
Q: Now, captain, you are called here as a witness on behalf of the
    State of New York to testify in relation to matters in the police

department of this city . . . you appreciate the obligations which rest upon you, do you?

A: Yes, sir.

Q: You know that the oath administered to you is binding absolutely upon your conscience?

A: Yes, sir.

Q: To tell the truth, the whole truth and nothing but the truth?

A: I have come here to tell the truth wholly and truly, without any promise of any kind.

No more buzzing. "Half a dozen police captains who were in the room opened their eyes wide, and bent forward to hear what was coming next."

And then Schmittberger talked. He tallied the bribes he had taken, the payoffs and political contributions he had disbursed. He explained how patrolmen purchased their appointments and then paid again to be promoted. He sketched the system of coercion and collusion, from chief to roundsman, that was ruining discipline in the department. And he revealed the crowning exposure of all: that protection for any "vice and crime" in the city could be purchased at an established price. When he had told enough to fill seventy pages of testimony, he descended from the stand, a "broken man."

At every place where New Yorkers gathered to talk, they spoke that night of Schmittberger, "in all the hotel corridors, the social clubs, the political organizations, the theatres, the fine cafés in the fashionable streets and avenues and the rumshops and 'dives' of the East and West side." The lone exception was 300 Mulberry Street—police headquarters— which wreathed itself in silence.

* * *

HE "WAS A villain in two ways, in two worlds," wrote Lincoln Steffens, his friend and adviser. "The good were against him for his grafting, the underworld for squealing." Schmittberger remained with the department, as an outcast. He was stripped of his posting in the glamorous, roaring Tenderloin and sent to the wasteland of the Bronx, where "the chief business of the police is said to be watching for stray goats." Languishing in Goatville, he waited for the officers he had exposed to get their transfers to Sing Sing. But no indictments appeared. The worst of the thieves retired on comfortable pensions. All the rest retained their

rank and standing, determined to see him break. His "years of purgatory" had begun.

AT THE DINNER table, in his apartment on East Sixty-first Street, his
eight children sat in silence. They nudged one another, passing the question along to the oldest son. "I say, Pop," he blurted out at last, "is it
true this stuff they are saying? It's all lies, ain't it!"

He would redeem himself through labor. He followed cases overnight,
two nights in a row, stealing home after sunrise to burgle a few hours of
sleep. Newspapermen found him composing reports simultaneously on
seven different typewriters. He was a good cop, and these were not so
plentiful. Antivice forces could not afford to waste an honest police captain
who was estranged from the System and desperate for forgiveness. They
pardoned his faults and convinced themselves of his repentance. Theodore
Roosevelt, in his years with the police, used Schmittberger as a "broom"
to sweep out whatever districts his constituency happened to find most
appalling. The Reverend Charles Parkhurst, whose Society for the Prevention of Crime had urged on the Lexow investigations in the first place,
met with him almost daily to discuss the condition of his conscience. But
the reformers never lasted longer than one election. The Tammany men
always returned, and then Schmittberger's torments would begin again.

Early in 1903, Schmittberger took the exam to qualify as an inspector,
scoring higher than any other captain in the rolls. His opponents rallied
their last reserves to slander him. But his repentance and redemption had
won the "support of the best people in the country." Roosevelt, now president of the United States, wrote him a letter of endorsement and shook
his hand in public during a visit to New York. With no other recourse,
the police commissioner regretfully granted him an inspectorship.

The triumphal procession in May 1903 was his reward. When the
multitudes cheered his apotheosis, they also celebrated the charity of
their own forgiveness. Their clemency had lifted him up again to the
position he had forfeited. They had redeemed him, themselves, their
city. Applause from the Battery to Madison Square, huzzahs from here
to heaven: It could never be too much.

IN 1909, WHEN he alone remained from the scandalous nineties, he was
promoted to chief inspector, the city's highest-ranking uniformed officer.

"I think I can safely say that it has been a long, hard fight, honorably and honestly won," he said. "Victory has come to me because I have 'made good.'"

After nearly a decade as chief inspector, Schmittberger caught cold while watching a Liberty Loan parade. When he died a week later, the flags at every precinct in New York marked mourning for the "Grand Old Man" of the police department. Thousands followed his casket to St. Patrick's. Mayor Mitchel and Commissioner Woods marched in the procession. As did Frank, his trusted mount. After Schmittberger's death, reporters found in his apartment half a dozen rooms crowded with commendations and trophies, ornaments from foreign governments, his Slocum Medal, notes of thanks from the neighborhoods he had patrolled. And, on his bookshelves, intermixed with the rest, the five black volumes of testimony from the Lexow Committee hearings.

5.

Somebody Blundered

Aﬅer the magistrate had disclosed his sentence, Frank Tannenbaum, the dangerous I.W.W. agitator, returned to his cell in the Tombs Prison to settle some outstanding business. He asked a comrade to please return a library book he had borrowed. And he scrawled a quick note to his mother and father.

Dear Folks,

I have just been committed to serve 1 year in jail. Don't worry. My friends will take care of me. I will not be able to write to you, only once in a few months. But when I come out I will spend some time at home. With regards to all at home.

I remain your loving son,
F. Tannenbaum

That done, he was ready for transportation.

Guards bused him from the jail to an East River dock and led him down the gangplank to a Department of Correction ferry. From there it was just a short steam upriver to Blackwell's Island, where he marched in a column across the yard toward the administrative building. In the photographic room, he was ordered to undress and was slammed down into a chair. A keeper slapped an iron hood over his head, barking, "Stretch your arms!" "Put out your foot!" while posing him in various positions. Then he was issued prison stripes, coarse undergarments, and a filthy blanket before being led to a shadowy three-foot-by-seven-foot cell, possessing neither toilets nor windows.

Until then, none of Tannenbaum's experiences had affected his inner man. Through it all, he had remained "aggressive, defiant, uncompromising." In the Tombs, he had enjoyed amiable relations with the guards, and even the wrathful magistrate had treated him with a certain respect. Now—hooded, prodded, and penned on the island—he finally felt the burden of circumstances. "I had ceased to be a human and had become a number," he recalled. "For at least the next few hours I was the most humble, obedient, I might almost say the most broken-spirited person imaginable."

Blackwell's Island did that to people. A narrow two-mile-long shard of earth between Manhattan and Queens, it was blessed with refreshing breezes, as well as lawns and gardens that made it "one of nature's beauty spots." Reformers spoke of turning the whole area into a park, and Jacob Riis prophesied that someday it would be "the most marvelous public playground in the world." In the meantime, the city had found a different use for it. Since the early decades of the nineteenth century, the island had served as a quarantine for New York's sinners and sufferers. Charity and smallpox hospitals, asylums, orphanages, prisons, and almshouses interposed themselves among the fields and forests.

Prisoners returning from work on Blackwell's Island.

From the water, these solemn structures made a "fine show," and the penitentiary in particular had "the pathetic beauty . . . of an 18th century print." But any grandeur vanished on acquaintance. Within the picturesque walls, inmates discovered "conditions in daily operation quite at variance with the dictates of humanity and the ordinary laws of health." In the 1880s, Nellie Bly had spent ten days in the madhouse on assignment for the *World*. Riis had devoted a chapter of *How the Other Half Lives* to "The Wrecks and the Waste" of the charity wards. Through these revelations, the island had acquired indelible connotations of brutality and squalor. It was a way station toward purgatory. "When they move out of the Fourth Ward they will move into Bellevue Hospital," went a typical jeremiad, "when they move out of the Bellevue Hospital they will move to Blackwell's Island; when they move from Blackwell's Island they will move to the Potter's Field; when they move from the Potter's Field they will move into the darkness beyond the grave!" By the twentieth century, the name was so blemished that the newly constructed Blackwell's Island Bridge was quickly renamed the Queensboro, and an effort was gaining impetus to rechristen the island itself.*

A few days before Tannenbaum's arrival, Commissioner of Correction Katharine Davis had presented Mayor Mitchel a report on the penitentiary, revealing a facility dysfunctional in every facet. The cornerstone had been laid in 1828, and the buildings had long since become obsolete. With an intended capacity of eleven hundred inmates, the actual population averaged around eighteen hundred. Cells were "wet, slimy, dark, foul smelling, and unfit for pigs to wallow in." Hardly large enough for a single person, overcrowding meant that more than half of these chambers held two occupants. Treatment of the prisoners was "vile and inhuman." On the whole, Davis concluded, the facility "belonged to an era of general political unenlightenment that was long out of date." In her opinion, the entire edifice should be abandoned as soon as possible, and emergency renovations totaling $32,000 had to be pursued immediately.

Prisoners' sentences ranged from one to twelve months, meaning thousands of inmates cycled through the penitentiary each year. Though new people arrived daily, outside contact was strictly curtailed: Convicts were allowed one visitor each month, and there were harsh limitations on correspondence. Pencils and newspapers, toothpaste and soap, were contraband; it was against regulations to hang a photograph on the walls.

---

* A successful movement: Blackwell's Island was renamed Welfare Island in 1921; since 1973, it has been known as Roosevelt Island.

And it wasn't even necessary to commit a violation to receive discipline. "If a keeper doesn't like your face, he punishes you by standing you against the wall, depriving you of food, or shuts you up in the cooler."

Despite all this, Tannenbaum's initial discouragement did not last long. Discovering a camaraderie among his fellows, he soon returned to the accustomed role of instigator. "No matter how many rules you make in jail," he soon learned, "the men will find a way to break them." Before his first day had ended, he himself had transgressed every one. Stolen newspapers were passed around until they fell to pieces. Underground networks smuggled letters in and out. Within a few hours of his arrival, Tannenbaum had already received several illicit notes through these secret means. "My dear Frank," a note from Alexander Berkman began,

Need I waste words to assure you of my deepest sympathy? You have acted like a *Man*, and that is the very highest I could say—as a man and true revolutionist. Never mind the barking of the curs—it is their insignificance + cowardice.

I am proud of you. For I am sick of the crawling and kowtowing—before the court—by those who are so loud when it is safe to be. The time has come when we need, most urgently, men—men who will measure up to the need of the hour and stand up as men at the critical moment.

When you get a chance, let us know how you are getting along + how you are treated. You have friends who will remain true to you + who will not stand for any abuse of you by the authorities . . .

Fraternally,
Alex Berkman

Frank had arrived on the island with a reputation as a troublemaker, and it did not take long for him to confirm it in the minds of his keepers. Every time the guards passed his cell, they discovered him reading an illicit newspaper. Finding the prison library needlessly inefficient—inmates had no choice in what books they were issued, and were often presented with volumes they couldn't read—he volunteered to reorganize the meager assortment. "Any time, Tannenbaum," snapped Warden Hayes in response, "that we want your help to run this institution, we will call for it." Soon, however, he was amassing a private collection of his own.

The way the newspapers had portrayed him, as "only an ignorant boy," had renewed his commitment to educating himself. "I determined," he recalled, "no one ever again could call me ignorant of the education of books, no matter what the cost." He had left his supporters a list; the first consignment of materials contained dense tomes on economic and political theory, including several works by Peter Kropotkin, the Russian anarchist. Tannenbaum would spend his time in prison studying the theories of revolution that he had already attempted to put into practice on the streets.

At the same time, his correspondents kept him informed about their progress. "We held a fine meeting at Franklin Square today," a friend wrote. "At Rutgers Square meetings are being carried on regularly." After the riot in Union Square, he read that "Gegan and Gildea as usual were on the job. The police bore down and beat up the crowd and arrested O'Carroll . . . and Caron and several others." In this way, he also was able to follow the continued violence in the coal regions of Colorado. And he learned of growing tensions between the United States and Mexico. As Tannenbaum's days passed, however, more and more of his correspondents began excitedly to discuss the next big local event, "a giant protest meeting to be held at Carnegie Hall on April 19."

*   *   *

NEW YORKERS WERE by now accustomed to wake each morning and find another headline describing the latest provocations by the Industrial Workers of the World: I.W.W. DEFIES POLICE, I.W.W. FREE SPEECH TO BE INVESTIGATED, I.W.W. SLURS MAYOR: CALLS HIM "BELL HOP." Considering that the local chapters had been nearly defunct at the start of the year, this could have been seen as a triumph of propaganda. "For two months and over the I.W.W. has kept itself on the front page of the metropolitan dailies, and that surely is going some," a comrade boasted in a letter to Tannenbaum. "Now, of course, if it were Carnegie's Peace Society or Rockefeller's Educational Board, that would be different. Their every meeting, their every proceeding, would be reported if so desired. But the I.W.W., never!"

The publicity had done little, however, to clarify the actual goals or doctrines of the Industrial Workers of the World. Politicians and newspapers were content to affix the I.W.W. label to the unemployed, the anarchists, or any of the city's other radical leagues and councils. The Wobblies were "credited with the doings of everybody, no matter whom, so long as the doings take on the appearance of the I.W.W. in the editor's mind," Tannenbaum's correspondent wrote, and if trends continued, "the Republicans and the Progressives will yet get to be classed with the I.W.W.s." It was infuriating to the socialists and trade unionists whose actions were continually attributed to their rivals. And to those who feared that agitators posed a real threat, the willful misidentification seemed to verge on recklessness. "It will be very much to the advantage of the conservative people of this town to learn more than they have yet taken the trouble to learn" about the I.W.W., a *Times* columnist urged. "It is always to the advantage of a person who is attacked to know why he is attacked, who is attacking him, and where he may expect the next blow. And this is an attack—an attack on the social system. Its aim is nothing less than revolution."

But it was the radicals themselves who finally took steps to rectify these misperceptions. "We wanted to present our aims to the public dramatically," an organizer recalled. Assuming "that everybody really wanted to hear the truth about labor," activists began to promote an educational evening at Carnegie Hall. Unlike the street demonstrations, where multiple speakers competed in issuing contradictory statements, this occasion would offer a single coherent message. There would be no sensationalism or controversy. The biggest difference of all: There would be no scare headlines the next day.

Handbills and posters advertised the topics to be discussed: "The outrages at Union Square . . . The outrages at Trinidad, Colorado . . . the severe sentence inflicted upon Tannenbaum." To afford the theater, and to raise money toward paying Frank's $500 fine, the organizers had to charge admission. For a quarter, spectators could pack into the gallery; a dollar afforded a box seat. Promoters canvassed Manhattan, selling tickets to chorus girls on Broadway and to officials at City Hall. When Lincoln Steffens suggested peddling some on Wall Street, one of the volunteers borrowed a presentable coat from Mabel Dodge and managed to sell several seats to the J.P. Morgan Company.

By 8:15 P.M. on the evening of April 19, Carnegie Hall had begun to fill with a curious assortment of people. "Although the crowd was small," a witness observed, "it amply made up for that deficiency in enthusiasm and variety." Actresses in cerise evening cloaks milled about the lobby while laborers looked starchy in new-bought suits. Steffens and Mrs. O.H.P. Belmont, a noted suffrage advocate, attended, as did "practically everybody in I.W.W. and anarchistic circles." About one third of the audience was in stylish evening dress, and if some of these had a serious curiosity, most had come on a lark, "obviously hopeful that something would happen, something lively but not too strenuous." Police Commissioner Woods, who had reserved a prime, first-tier box, casually appraised the scene, laughing when a pretty usher put some radical literature in his hand. Chief Inspector Schmittberger commanded a detail of nearly a hundred men, but the directive to "keep peace with a smile" remained in place, and the police were in gentle temper. Not that they had neglected their preparations; reserves stood ready at the Forty-seventh Street precinct, and "the block would have swarmed with them at the blowing of a whistle."

Fashionable couples were still filtering in from dinner when Max Eastman, editor of the *Masses*, called the meeting to order. The stage was crowded with martyrs of the movement, including Joe O'Carroll, Arthur Caron, and Becky Edelsohn. To accurately convey the feeling of an authentic I.W.W. meeting, the program began by putting two resolutions to the vote. The first concerned the injustice of Frank Tannenbaum's sentence, and it was ratified easily. Only two nays were heard, and both came from occupants of the J.P. Morgan box. The second resolution, opposing the looming war with Mexico, sparked pandemonium. "In a few minutes the hall was in an uproar, men shaking their fists and shouting that there should or should not be war, according to their ideas." The carefully scripted pageant edged toward disarray, but it was not yet lost. Big Bill Haywood was the next speaker, and the audience quieted while he shambled toward the rostrum.

No one else was so identified with the I.W.W. in the public mind. Haywood, a journalist for *Metropolitan* magazine had written, was the "prophet of Industrial Unionism, leader of all poor devils." A youth spent in the hard-rock mines of Idaho had left him with one eye, "the physical strength of an ox," and a "face like a scarred mountain." Now forty-five years old, he still affected a black Stetson and cowboy twang, but he had forsworn his old .38 Colt. If the Big Bill legend persisted, the man himself had mellowed. "Haywood is long on talk, but short on work," sneered the bulletin of the Western Federation of Miners, a union that had expelled him. The *Sun* was even less sympathetic. "When bullets are flying in Colorado, Big Bill is in New York," an editor wrote. "When heads are being broken in Union Square he is detained elsewhere; when anybody starts a fight Big Bill is recorded among the absent." In labor circles, it was murmured that Haywood had gone soft through spending too much time around the bourgeoisie. The "two-gun man from the West" now kept an apartment down on West Fifteenth Street

Big Bill Haywood, the face of the I.W.W.

and was a fixture at Mabel Dodge's evenings. He preferred discussing poetry to politics, and could sometimes be found sitting on the benches in Washington Square, scribbling out verses of his own.

At the moment, a lecture on the future of proletarian painting or a rumination about the poetry of work would have entirely satisfied the organizers who had staked so much on the Carnegie Hall meeting being successful. Anything would do, so long as it helped to ease the "undercurrent of feeling" in the theater that had manifested itself as soon as the discussion turned to Mexico, and which now "threatened to break out at any time." But Haywood chose this opportunity to flash some of his old belligerence. He decided to talk about Mexico.

"Sherman said, 'War was Hell,'" he bellowed. "Well, then, let the bankers go to war, and let the interest-takers and the dividend-takers go to war with them. If only those parasites were out of the country it would be a pretty decent place to live in." The laboring classes would never support President Wilson's imperialism, he continued. "The mine workers of this country will simply fold their arms, and when they fold their arms there will be no war." Three sentences into his speech, everyone was shouting. From the galleries came cries of encouragement. Derision raged from the boxes. "You may say that this action of the mine workers is traitorous to the country," he shouted back, "but I tell you it is better to be a traitor to a country than to be a traitor to your class."

When he lumbered away from the podium, any potential for reconciliation that evening had disappeared. The next morning, New Yorkers would wake to the usual array of panicky headlines: IGNORE CALL TO WAR SAYS BILL HAYWOOD, STRIKE THREAT IF WAR IS DECLARED, HAYWOOD OPENLY STIRS SEDITION.

THE ATTORNEY GENERAL in Washington, D.C., proposed filing an indictment against Big Bill, newspapers demanded reprisals, and even labor leaders rushed to distinguish their positions from his. But Commissioner Woods calmly refused to overreact. He had heard every word spoken at Carnegie Hall, and as far as he was concerned nothing had crossed the boundary separating free speech from sedition.

Meeting in Mayor Mitchel's office on April 22, Woods had other matters to discuss. Commissioner Polk was healing well after surgery to mend the wounds he had received in the murder attempt. At first it had been supposed that the gunman from the previous week had been a radical assassin, with Alexander Berkman and his cadre the most likely source. "The Anarchists have no particular feeling against Mayor Mitchel, and do not consider they have any feud with him," Berkman had insisted. "Anarchists do not resort to assassination for fun, and the only time when it might occur would be when an individual Anarchist in a time of great political or revolutionary excitement might select a much-hated man for a mark." Although this may not have been wholly reassuring to authorities, a short interrogation of the shooter satisfied them that he was no radical, but rather an unstable former city employee with a grudge. Currently, he was under the supervision of alienists in the Tombs, and a transfer to the Matteawan State Hospital for the Criminally Insane was imminent. Mitchel asked Woods to examine any more messages that arrived from "nuts," and also suggested "a plan for looking up the writers of threatening letters and committing them to Bellevue."

Among other immediate topics, Woods and Mitchel had to consider the local impact of a looming war with Mexico. After more than a year of idleness—Woodrow Wilson called it "watchful waiting," while his opponents preferred to think of it as "deadly drifting"—military intervention was now at hand. Finally convinced that action had become a moral necessity, the president had deployed the North Atlantic fleet to blockade the Gulf Coast city of Veracruz. He would deploy force of arms not for conquest or profit but out of compassion. The specific incitement—a minor diplomatic transgression, for which the Mexican government had speedily apologized—hardly mattered now that he was bent on war. The important thing was the greater message his new decisiveness would impart. "I hold this to be a wonderful opportunity," Wilson explained, "to prove to the world that the United States of America is not only human but humane; that we are actuated by no other motives than the betterment of the conditions of our unfortunate neighbor, and by the sincere desire to advance the cause of human liberty."

If fighting began, repercussions in the city would go far beyond Haywood's speech. And indeed while the two officials spoke, the first dispatches started to arrive from Veracruz: FIRING COMMENCED AT DAYBREAK. SHIPS NOW SHELLING SOUTHERN PART OF CITY. The long standoff between Mexican leaders and the U.S. government had finally erupted in gunfire. Personally, Mitchel thought the affair had been bungled. Woodrow Wilson had dithered for months instead of taking action. The mayor would have opted for a direct declaration of war weeks earlier. But now that troops were committed, he wired Washington immediately, promising the president that "the people of the City of New York are with him and behind him in this crisis." Locally, it would mean political posturing—Tammany Hall had just announced it would be raising a regiment of its own—antiwar protests, angry tempers, and patriotic outbursts. Recruitment centers would be jammed; the Brooklyn Naval Yard would have to expand operations.

While they talked, the officials heard some sudden commotion coming from outside the building. Commissioner Woods rushed out to City Hall plaza, where he found a mob of a thousand people roiling round the statue of Benjamin Franklin. They circled the area, pressing in almost to the pedestal, where some unseen instigator plied his trade. Calling the reserves from the Oak Street precinct, Woods forced his way through to the front of the crowd. And there he found Becky Edelsohn antagonizing the throng of hecklers.

At that moment he joined a widening circle of city residents suddenly concerned about her activities. "It is little more than a month since the newspapers began printing the sayings and exploits of one Becky Edelsohn," the *Tribune* announced. "Besides being an agitator, who and what is this person who, bursting out of obscurity, has caused more editorial comment for and against than any woman since Emma Goldman? . . . What has this young girl endured to make her ready to outface street rowdies, to criticise the government and laugh in the face of recognized authority?"

Becky was young and shocking. "She was a tremendously fiery person," a friend recalled, "always two steps ahead of Berkman or Goldman." Her good looks and bright red stockings made a striking impression. "She was five feet four inches tall," a comrade recalled, "moderately plump, with black hair; she was very pretty—beautiful I should say." But most people remembered her for her fearless self-possession. "Becky's eyes," a reporter wrote, "were built to flash, not to weep." In court, she once leveled her hardest stare on a judge who tried to silence her. A member of the audience caught the look. "I knew she was not one of the inarticulate mass," he later wrote, "but a girl with power."

Born in Ukrainian Odessa on Christmas Day 1892, she had come to the United States with her family two years later, and had battled with parents, teachers, and everyone else who claimed authority ever since. She spent a year in high school and tried to train as a nurse, but in each instance had found the discipline unbearable. An elder brother introduced her to politics, and she soon became one of the many strays gathered up in Emma Goldman's extended family of anarchists. She left her family to live with the radicals at the age of thirteen, and a year or two later, in 1906, she had her first chance to display her antiauthoritarian inclinations. When cops raided a protest meeting, the *Tribune* recounted, she "was roughly handled and put under arrest, because she failed to leave the hall as quickly as ordered." Though she was still "a little girl with short skirts," she was accused of assaulting a policeman. The magistrate took one look at the 250-pound arresting officer and dismissed the charges.

She was fifteen when Alexander Berkman, then in his late thirties, was released from prison. Becky comforted him through his first years back in the world, and before long they had become lovers. This was the first of a series of relationships. Becky's sexuality exerted a fascination on outsiders, who let their lascivious imaginings cloud their appreciation for her leadership abilities. A clandestine informant who infiltrated the radicals' circle sniped to handlers that Edelsohn had a "reputation among the anarchists of being able to be 'intimate' with more men in a day than any woman." She underwent an abortion in 1911, and though this would not have been a scandal in the circles she frequented, her general behavior had led to some disquiet; "her lack of responsibility and perseverance in her personal life," Emma Goldman would later write, "had for years been a source of irritation to me."

Now, at the Franklin statue, she was doing her utmost to irritate the hostile crowd.

"It's all a frame-up by the capitalists," she was yelling, "so that good workingmen's blood will be spilled to protect the investments in Mexico of Hearst, Rockefeller, and the Guggenheims."

"Ah," people were laughing, "cut that out, kiddo."

"Show your American citizenship papers," someone called. "And if you haven't got 'em, then shut up."

"How many of you would fight for the flag?" she asked.

Every hand shot into the air.

"A flag isn't anything to fight for!" she cried out. "The American flag isn't fit to defend!" No one was laughing anymore. Clerks and office boys shouted her down. "Hooray for Wilson!" they called. "Hooray for the flag! Down with the greasers and the I.W.W.!"

"Lynch her!"

"Kill the reds!"

Rotten fruit started flying round her head. "War is hell," she yelled, "but when you attack a poor little woman like me it is worse than hell!" The mob pressed forward until it had her pinned against the railing at the base of the statue. And at that moment—"just in time" to save her "from rough treatment"—the Oak Street reserves appeared. "The police formed a flying wedge" and pushed up to the center of the ruckus, "shoving the crowd back, using their sticks now and then as persuaders."

Officers lined up in front of Becky and some other speakers, cordoning them off from the hostile throng. The captain urged the radicals to make their escape, but, led by Becky, they refused to desist. They would test the police department's commitment to free speech in the most dramatic way possible. For the next hour, the speakers railed against the war while the police held off the crowd. Finally, the spectators had had their fill: "Lashed to fury by the tongue of Reba Edelsohn," they attempted one last sortie, charging the cordon, squirming between the uniformed officers. No longer able to protect either the speakers or his own men, the captain ordered the anarchists' arrest. Most submitted meekly, but when a six-foot-tall patrolman tried detaining Becky, she struggled so ferociously that a paddy wagon had to be called in to transport her to the precinct.

A COUPLE OF weeks earlier, police had trampled and clubbed dissenters into the hospitals. Now officers were risking their own safety to assure that all points of view were heard on the city's streets. "In New York," Arthur Woods would later tell an investigating committee, "we not merely permit free speech and free assemblage and picketing, but we protect it." In less than two weeks as commissioner, he had already done much to prove the truth of this statement. He was establishing a novel set of protocols; no longer would the policeman be the instinctive enemy of the protester. Demonstrations would be condoned as long as they did not incite listeners to immediate acts of violence or seriously impede traffic. "If we don't have unrest," Woods had come to believe, "if we don't agitate for better things, if there is not a wholesome discontent, we shall not make progress."

These broad-minded policies had won over some of New York's most skeptical observers. "Commissioner Woods has nerve," judged Lincoln Steffens, who had been a leading critic of the police department for the previous twenty years. The veteran journalist had been especially impressed by the triumph at Union Square. "There was no show of force at all, and no abridgment of free speech," he wrote. "It was an experiment in liberty, and liberty worked." Walter Lippmann was so enthusiastic about Woods's success that he quickly redrafted the opening paragraph of *Drift and Mastery*, his work in progress. "In the early months of 1914," he wrote, "widespread unemployment gave the anarchists in New York City an unusual opportunity for agitation." Newspapers and government officers had succumbed to hysteria and violence, but then there was an about-face: "The city administration, acting through a new police commissioner," ordered an end to repression. "This had a most disconcerting effect on the anarchists. They were suddenly stripped of all the dramatic effect that belongs to a clash with the police . . . their intellectual situation was as uncomfortable as one of those bad dreams in which you find yourself half-clothed in a public place."

Woods himself did as much as anyone to promote his own ideas. A onetime newspaperman, he wrote punchy and dramatic essays about his experiences with the police. Lecturing to society audiences, he portrayed himself as a cosmopolite of crime, cracking wise with seamy characters that his audience would have crossed the street to avoid. He titillated listeners with tales of Lefty Louis, Hunchy Williams, and other criminals of his acquaintance, then left them sobbing over the sacrifices and simple wisdom of his patrolmen. Over and over again he spoke of the Union Square demonstration and described how his men had protected antiwar speakers, including Becky Edelsohn, from angry mobs in Lower Manhattan. These parables of toleration soon earned him a reputation as one of the nation's leading advocates of civil liberties.

In all his speeches, however, he never mentioned another aspect of his practice, the tactics he referred to—when he mentioned them at all—as "graveyard work." This was no oversight. Arthur Woods believed in clandestine policing with the same conviction he showed for free speech. To him they were two sides of the same strategy. But he had learned through harsh experience that secret practices were best kept private.

IT WAS IN 1900 that the police department had first felt its lack of an effective plainclothes branch. That year, Italian anarchists living in Greenwich Village and New Jersey sent an assassin back to the home country to murder King Umberto I. Learning of the attack, a shocked New York police chief at first denied that the plot could have originated in his jurisdiction. "He had heard nothing of a local group of Anarchists for the past two years," it was reported. "If such a group did exist he would have known about it." Once he accepted the fact, however, a second truth became apparent: He was helpless to investigate. In the entire force, there were only a few Italian-speaking detectives. One of them, Giuseppe Petrosino, a brilliant young sergeant who had immigrated from Campania twenty-five years earlier, was immediately assigned to the case.

The city had changed, but the police had not. Officers patrolling the old beats found transformation at every storefront and corner. Kleindeutschland teemed with Russians; Italians pressed the Chinese in Mott Street. "Within a few minutes' walk is the Hebrew colony of the great East Side. Within half a mile is the German colony to the northwest, while to the west are the colonies of Assyrians, Egyptians, and Arabians." Eighty-five percent of all residents were either foreign-born or the children of immigrants. "The Irish patrolman," commented a reporter for *McClure's*, "watched curiously over this half million of queer, jabbering foreigners like a child regarding a strange bug."

More than a million and a half Italians would process through Ellis Island during the next ten years, nearly a third of them settling in Manhattan and Brooklyn. "Generally speaking, they are gentle drudges—honest, faithful, and inoffensive," *Munsey's* magazine assured its readers. "As to their alleged proneness to crimes of violence, there has been much exaggeration." Compared to the Irish, for instance, they were less

Lieutenant Giuseppe Petrosino.

disposed to pauperism, drunkenness, or suicide. "In 1904, only one in every twenty-eight thousand Italians in New York was sent to Black-well's Island," reporters noted, and most of these had been charged merely with disorderly conduct.

If crime existed in the Italian colonies of Mulberry Bend, Williams-burg, and Eastern Harlem, that hardly separated these areas from other densely packed and impoverished districts in the city. But the Italians soon found themselves encumbered with an extraordinary reputation for delinquency. Every trespass in their neighborhoods was attributed to the actions of a mysterious criminal syndicate—the Black Hand. Po-lice officials and newspaper reporters stoked fears over what they dubbed "perhaps the most secret and terrible organization in the world," and endowed the situation with the appearance of a crisis. "The city is con-fronted with an Italian problem with which at the present time it seems unable to cope," the *Tribune* had complained in 1904. Those same detec-tives who had been helpless in the anarchist investigation found them-selves confounded by the rash of bombings, kidnappings, and blackmail that constituted the Black Hand crime wave. With community leaders calling for protection, and newspapers filled with chilling stories, the police commissioner announced the creation of an Italian squad solely dedicated to infiltrating the mafia. Petrosino took command; under him was every detective in the force who could speak the language. There were nine of them.

For secrecy, Petrosino and his men avoided headquarters, at first operating out of his two-room apartment. But there were so few of them working the same streets day after day that secrecy was impossible. "Every New York detective is more truly a public character than the Mayor is," a reporter observed. The elected leader of the city "could walk a thousand miles up and down his five boroughs without being recognized by more than a handful of citizens . . . But let a 'plainclothes man' sally forth, and patrolmen will nod to him, streetcar conductors will ask no fare, hallboys will pick him out, janitors will make a sign, bootblacks will look eagerly about for his quarry, politicians will wink patronizingly, barbers will stop in the midst of a shampoo." When new criminals arrived, old hands taught them straightaway to recognize all the undercover operatives on the force, and Petrosino himself "was probably the most widely known Italian in New York."

With no hope, then, of operating in secret, they resorted to publicity and "brass band" methods, developing a large network of contacts and sources, working with leaders in the Italian colonies to bolster community resistance against criminals. Over time, Petrosino concluded that secret policing, even done effectively, would never solve the ills that had befallen Little Italy. He coordinated neighborhood vigilance committees and urged settled immigrants to shepherd new arrivals through the process of assimilation. "There is only one thing that can bring about the end of the Black Hand," Petrosino explained to a reporter from the *Times*, "and that is enlightenment."

Lacking this more general approach, the secret branch made hundreds of minor arrests but did little to address the root causes of crime. Most of the time, the suspects they did manage to detain were released by the magistrates. With no reason to believe that the police could protect them, witnesses were hard to come by in Black Hand prosecutions. After two years, the squad could claim few successes. "The number of crimes attributed to the Black Hand society . . . has grown," the *Tribune* reported. "In the more serious cases, such as murders and fires, there have been no convictions." The initial enthusiasm for the unit dissipated;

its members were ridiculed by the rest of the Detective Bureau. By 1906, only "a dejected pretense of an Italian squad was in existence."

But that year a new police commissioner arrived. Theodore Bingham was an ex-army engineer with a wooden leg and a determination "to put the town under martial law." Enemies denounced him as "autocratic and severe," while even his friends conceded that "there is a decisive and a soldierly directness about Gen. Bingham which has often been mistaken for abruptness or brusqueness." An amateur genealogist, he boasted of ancestors who had come from England in the seventeenth century to help settle the village of Norwich, Connecticut. He had little affection for anyone whose forebears had arrived much later than that—which included nearly every immigrant in his constituency. "Predatory criminals of all nations" had infiltrated the city, he wrote, "the Armenian Hunchakist, the Neapolitan Camorra, the Sicilian Mafia, the Chinese Tongs . . . the scum of the earth." His aversion to Hebrews would make him a loathed figure in the Jewish community, but this was as nothing compared to the revulsion he felt for "the Italian malefactor," who Bingham asserted was "by far the greater menace to law and order."

Having alienated 90 percent of the electorate, Bingham proceeded to lose the sympathy of subordinates by incessantly harping on the deficiencies of his department. "I have done all in my power with the force at my command," he complained, demanding funds for more than a thousand new recruits. In a memorandum to the mayor, he proposed dissolving the existing detective branch and starting over with a new secret service modeled on the Italian Carabinieri, the Sûreté of Paris, or England's Special Branch. "The crowning absurdity of the entire tragic situation in New York lies in the circumstance that the Police Department is without a secret service," he insisted in a notorious article in the *North American Review*. "In the one city in the world where the police problem is complicated by an admixture of the criminals of all races, the Department is deprived of an indispensable arm of the service."

Annoyed by the commissioner's griping, the Tammany mayor at the time ignored all of his pleas except for the least expensive one. Bingham was granted the right to assign a new assistant to his staff. In June 1907, he created the position of Fourth Deputy Commissioner and chose Arthur Woods to fill it. Not just another underling, Woods took charge of the Detective Bureau. To him would fall the day-to-day responsibility of implementing Bingham's vision of an American secret service.

Lieutenant Petrosino also hoped to contribute to the new commissioner's efforts. He presented Bingham with a far-ranging report, offering his multifaceted plan to curb the lawlessness of the Italian colonies. While it did include repressive measures, such as mandating deportation for anyone convicted of a crime, many of his suggestions were broadly ameliorative: educating the Italian community about the American legal system, reducing population density in the tenements, and controlling the sale of explosives. "It's our own stupid laws," Petrosino believed, "that have allowed them to organize."

But Bingham had no interest in anything for the Italian colonies but secret policing, or, as he described it, "rigorous punitive supervision." Petrosino's advice was brushed aside; he was ordered to focus on clandestine work alone. Moved to a larger—though still inadequate—office on Elm Street, he was granted more resources: Every Italian-speaking patrolman in all five boroughs was reassigned to his supervision, until the branch contained about eighty men. Knowing that the unit could never expand enough to keep pace with the increasing rates of crime, he nevertheless had no choice but to grind on. "Petrosino and his men have been worked beyond their endurance," a *Times* reporter wrote. "Some of them sleep on the tables in the dingy little room which is their headquarters. Petrosino himself has seen little of his home and family for six months." Still, results from the added labor remained elusive.

Bingham found yet another justification for why the city needed a real undercover force in 1908, with the botched attempt of a Russian anarchist to assassinate a phalanx of policemen in Union Square. "Americans have never been brought to consider anarchism seriously," the commissioner grumbled. "There is always the possibility of some crack-brained fanatic being influenced by the anarchist . . . to a desperate deed." He estimated that at least a thousand radicals currently resided in the city, and to counter their plans he again demanded $100,000 and the creation of a secret service on the French or Italian model. Critics pointed out that despite their renowned clandestine organizations, these nations had been subject to a litany of assassinations during the previous decades. "Secret police have not stopped 'Anarchist' outrages in the Continent," noted David Graham Phillips, a famed muckraker. "Why should they here?" But Bingham was unmovable in his determination to infiltrate the city's "gangs of Italian criminals and their anarchist accomplices."

Another year of frustrating Tammany obstructions would pass before he finally got the chance to put his theories to a street test. Then, in February 1909, a *Times* article conveyed the startling news that "police commissioner Bingham has a secret service of his own at last." The mood was jubilant at headquarters. "I have money and plenty of it," the commissioner crowed, "and it didn't come from the city." Coy about specifics, he let it be known that he had obtained most of the financing from bankers and merchants in the Italian community, people who had been subjected to blackmail and other Black Hand predations and believed plainclothes police were the solution. But not all the money had come from Little Italy; there was a mystery benefactor, "said to be the head of one of the great industries of this country, whose great wealth has made him the target for all sorts of letters." Most assumed this meant John D. Rockefeller.

The money went to hire a score of special officers, including men who had once served in the Italian Carabinieri and who would now act as a paid private investigative force under the supervision of the police department, answerable only to Petrosino and the commissioners. Hoping to deport anyone from New York who had a criminal record in Italy, Woods traveled to Washington, D.C., to seek President Roosevelt's assistance in negotiating a repatriations treaty with the Italian government. As for Petrosino, nobody had seen him. Pressed on the lieutenant's whereabouts, Bingham coyly replied, "Why, he may be on the ocean, bound for Europe, for all I know." As it turned out, he was. And the commissioner's slip was an unpardonable indiscretion. Petrosino had traveled to Sicily to gather the criminal files needed to begin deportation proceedings. Word of his arrival spread. Only two weeks after Bingham announced the creation of his new secret service, Petrosino was shot dead, with four bullets in his back, on the streets of Palermo.

The experiment of using privately financed special agents faltered after Petrosino's death. Sensing another setback, Arthur Woods wrote an article in *McClure's* to argue Bingham's position that America was vulnerable to the plots of criminals and anarchists. "Here the police are local," Woods noted. "We have no national police force." The absence of a federal investigative bureau put more emphasis on the city's efforts. All resources should be in play. If the Italian squad had failed, he believed, it was only because it had not been ambitious enough. Regular detectives could never succeed on their own, but "if they could be supplemented by a dozen or twenty men," Woods argued, "working always under cover, never appearing in court or at headquarters, there would be fewer mysterious stories in the newspapers, and the jails would be more full of swarthy, low-browed convicts."

But neither Bingham nor Woods would be in office long enough to implement these plans. Fittingly, it was their commitment to surveillance that resulted in their downfall.

For the previous fifty years or so, every person arrested in New York had been photographed, and their portrait added to the Rogues' Gallery at police headquarters. Over time, the collection had expanded to encompass more than thirteen thousand images. It had grown so unwieldy that suspects often had to be released because investigators could not sort through the mess and locate the proper picture that would have incriminated them. Arthur Woods's first assignment as deputy commissioner had been to reorganize the entire system.

Among the thousands of other photographs, there appeared the face of George Duffy, a milkman from Brooklyn, who two years earlier had been seized as "a suspicious person," held overnight, and then released without charges. It had been a simple case of wrongful detainment, but because he was in the Rogues' Gallery, police detectives now recognized him on sight, and his life became a nightmare of constant harassment and arrests. Duffy's father complained to New York State Supreme Court justice William Gaynor, an inveterate critic of policemen, who agitated to have the picture removed from the collection at headquarters. When Bingham refused, the judge penned a public letter censuring the police commissioner. "He is possessed of the most dangerous and destructive delusion that officials can entertain in a free government," the note concluded, "namely, that he is under no legal restraint whatever, but may do as he wills, instead of only what the law permits."

Rather than admit their mistake, Bingham and Woods attempted to convince the public that Duffy was, in fact, what they said he was: a criminal whose picture belonged in the gallery. While reporters interviewed his parents, employers, and even former teachers—all of whom confirmed the milkman's good character—the police attempted to link him to prostitution and fraud, slandering him as a "degenerate." The cover-up drifted over toward intimidation; Gaynor, and Bingham's other critics, believed that they were being followed by detectives.

The commissioner had made too many enemies to survive the Duffy Boy scandal. On July 1, 1909, Bingham was dismissed. His replacement dismantled the secret service squad two weeks later, and the men of the Italian branch were put back on common patrol duty. Judge Gaynor used the popularity he had accrued as Duffy's defender to mount a successful campaign for the mayoralty. For Arthur Woods, who resigned in solidarity with his chief, the warning was clear. Secret policing had to be conducted discreetly. He would write no more articles praising the idea of clandestine surveillance. Henceforth the graveyard work would be conducted out of sight, where it belonged.

* * *

JOHN D. ROCKEFELLER, JR., glanced up from his four-by-six-inch note card and scanned the audience in the Pocantico Hills Lyceum, just down the road from his estate. The small stone building served the village as library, theater, and dance hall. On Sunday evening, April 19, the folding chairs were arranged in neat rows and the Lyceum had been transformed into a church. Junior was presenting the vespers talk on the subject of "workaday religion." Amongst the gathering, he recognized Abby and the children, neighbors, employees: friendly, familiar faces all.

"Workaday religion," he continued, "is not primarily to die by but to live by. It is not primarily for old age but for youth." He looked back at his notes.

Workaday Religion
1. *its uses*
    a. not primarily to die by but to live by.
    b. "   "   for old age " for youth.
2. *everyone needs it*
    A Christian but not doing anything about it.
3. *they need it now*
    What if all Pocantico had this religion.

After propounding these ideas, he offered a sort of test his listeners could use to tell whether they possessed the faith that he had been talking about. There was a passage in the Book of Matthew describing Judgment Day, when the Lord would divide the charitable from the selfish and reveal that every compassionate act on earth had been a mercy to God. This was the origin of the Golden Rule, the foundation of his beliefs. "Verily I say unto you," quoted Junior at the conclusion of his speech, "In as much as ye have done it unto one of the least of these my brethren, you have done it unto me."

The next morning—Monday, April 20—was cold and blustery in the Colorado coalfields. Linens twisted and wracked on the clotheslines of the Ludlow encampment, the temporary headquarters for the United Mine Workers in its campaign against Colorado Fuel & Iron. Not far from the border with New Mexico, and fifteen miles from the militia barracks in Trinidad, Ludlow itself was little more than a railroad depot

flanked by a huddle of houses. The strikers' tents, imported from a previous labor conflict in West Virginia, were laid out in not-quite-military
precision across a flat patch of prairie.

More than a thousand people had lived there since the previous September. Fitted out with wooden walls, plank floors, and coal stoves,
the bivouacs were grim, if scarcely less comfortable than the company-
owned shacks the workers had been forced to leave when the lockout
had commenced. After eight months of blizzards and rainstorms, the
canvas had grayed and worn out; but the inhabitants had managed to
add some personal effects, a few sticks of furniture, silverware and china,
some photographs. Frequent gunfire had inspired many families to for-
tify; some had dug pits under the floorboards, and beneath one structure
there was a large bunker meant to serve as a maternity ward for the pregnant women of the settlement.

Those precautions now seemed excessive. The violence that had marked
the earliest phases of the conflict had dissipated; months of nearly constant warfare had been replaced by a lull. No one had been killed on either
side for more than a month. "On the whole, the strike, we believe, is
wearing itself out," an optimistic L. M. Bowers had written to Junior on
April 18, "though we are likely to be assaulted here and there by gangs of
the vicious element that are always hanging around the coal-mining
camps."

Most of the militiamen had withdrawn, leaving only two companies
to protect replacement workers and patrol the mine operators' property.
Though their numbers had been reduced, the troops who remained were
among the most belligerent. Their ranks included former mine guards,
soldiers of fortune, ex-convicts, and deserters from the regular army. These
men, whom Bowers especially praised, made no pretense of impartiality.
Other units had mingled freely with the people of Ludlow, but these
combatants were on the side of the operators; they unequivocally viewed
the miners as "the enemy."

Early on April 20, a detachment of soldiers visited Ludlow on the
pretext of asking about a man whose wife believed he was being held
against his will in the camp. The union leader informed them that the
woman's husband had left the previous day, but the soldiers refused to
accept his answer. Using this excuse as a way to aggravate tensions, the
troopers gave an ultimatum: Produce the missing person by noon, or
submit to a search of the settlement. The militia then returned to their
headquarters and geared up for combat, marshaling forces and positioning

a machine gun—which, like the miners' tents, had also been imported from a previous strike—on a high spot of ground commanding the level plain where the tents stood.

Sensing an attack, the residents of Ludlow hustled their families into the nearby hills. "The prairie was covered with human beings running in all directions like ants," one of the miners' wives recalled. "We all ran as we were, some with babies on their backs, in whatever clothes we were wearing." The union men snatched up hidden rifles and flung themselves into defensive trenches outside the camp. The two sides began shooting at just about the same moment. Refugees were still in flight when the first bullets fired; those who had not been quick enough to flee pried open their floorboards and scrambled into the pits beneath the tents.

Gunfire continued for several hours, with casualties on both sides. By the early afternoon, though, militia reinforcements had arrived, bringing with them an automobile fitted out with a second machine gun and seven thousand rounds of ammunition. "Go in and clean out the colony," their commander told them, "drive everyone out and burn the colony." When these soldiers attacked, the defense cracked; "both machine guns," wrote John Reed, "pounded stab-stab-stab full on the tents." Inside, the bullets shattered mirrors and splintered furniture. By sunset resistance had been subdued, and the soldiers roamed unhindered, ransacking the settlement. The "men had passed out of their officer's control," investigators would later conclude, "had ceased to be an army, and had become a mob." They looted "whatever appealed to their fancy of the moment . . . clothes, bedding, articles of jewelry, bicycles, tools and utensils," and then began to systematically burn the tents, dousing the canvas with oil before tossing on the matches.

Most of the remaining families were soon smoked out: Unearthly, screaming figures appeared suddenly from their subterranean pits and ran from the scene, refusing any offer of assistance by the soldiers. But the women and children who had chosen to conceal themselves in the maternity bunker decided to stay, even after the tent above them began to crunch with flames. They coughed in the smoke, and their prayers came shorter as the fire drew out the oxygen from their hiding place; the floorboards above them were too hot to touch.

At dawn the next day, soldiers were still passing torches round the camp, firing the rest of the tents, so that, barring a few camp stoves and iron bedsteads, nothing of Ludlow would be left standing. The sun was

Ruins of the Ludlow Colony.

well up before anyone discovered the charred bodies of two women and eleven children who had been suffocated in the pit.

L. M. BOWERS WIRED his summary of the battle to Junior while the smoke still hung over the burnt tents. Describing AN UNPROVOKED AT-TACK UPON SMALL FORCE OF MILITIA YESTERDAY BY 200 STRIKERS, he suggested that the Rockefellers tell the news to some FRIENDLY PAPERS, in order to begin influencing the press coverage. But this time it was Bowers's telegram that arrived too late. NEW YORK PAPERS HAVE PUB-LISHED FULL DETAILS, a distressed Junior snapped back. TO-DAY'S NEWS IS APPEARING ON TICKER. WE PROFOUNDLY REGRET THIS FURTHER OUTBREAK OF LAWLESSNESS WITH ACCOMPANYING LOSS OF LIFE.

Having tried desperately to secure his personal integrity from the discord inherent in economic practices, Junior now faced his worst fears. He would be faulted for what had just occurred. The Rockefeller name would again be condemned to vicious hatred. Hoping somehow to prevent this, he grasped at any chance to clear himself of blame. Per-haps the recent battle had not directly involved the Colorado Fuel & Iron Company; there were other operators in the region, after all. On April 23, he demanded a clarification on this point from Bowers:

HAVE ANY OF THE DISTURBANCES REPORTED IN YOUR TELE-GRAM OF YESTERDAY OR THOSE REPORTED IN TO-DAY'S PAPERS

OCCURRED IN CONNECTION WITH MINES OWNED BY OR WITH FORMER OR PRESENT EMPLOYEES OF THE FUEL COMPANY? PLEASE ANSWER.

His subordinate's response evaded the question, asserting that NONE OF THE THREE MINE TOPS DESTROYED OWNED BY ANYONE CONNECTED WITH THIS COMPANY NOW OR FORMERLY. But Junior had not asked about "mine tops." What he needed to know was whether the women and children in the pit had been his responsibility. He immediately wired another cable:

REFERRING TO MY EARLIER TELEGRAM, WERE ANY OF THE PEOPLE KILLED OR INJURED OR ANY OF THOSE TAKING PART IN THE DISTURBANCES OF THE LAST TWO OR THREE DAYS PRESENT OR FORMER EMPLOYEES OF THE FUEL COMPANY? PLEASE WIRE FULL REPORTS DAILY.

Bowers's reply—NONE OF OUR EMPLOYEES INJURED NOR PROPERTY DESTROYED YET—was either willfully or wistfully inaccurate. Concerned by Rockefeller's preoccupation with the victims, Bowers tried to recall his attention to workaday matters. MUCH LESS DISTURBANCE TO-DAY THAN WAS ANTICIPATED, he wrote on April 24. TRAIN WITH SOLDIERS ON WAY TO STRIKE DISTRICT IS CAUSING ANXIETY. FEARING DYNAMITING OR OTHER MISCHIEF.

Meanwhile, the censure had already begun. In *Mother Earth*, Alexander Berkman called for vengeance: "What are the American workingmen going to do? Are they going to palaver, petition and resolutionize? Or will they show that they still have a little manhood in them, that they will defend themselves and their organizations against murder and destruction? This is no time for theorizing, for fine-spun argument and phrases. With machine guns trained upon the strikers, the best answer is—*dynamite*."

And Berkman, for once, was not the only recriminatory voice. Even the *Times* conceded the enormity of what had occurred in the coalfields. "Somebody blundered," wrote the stunned and anxious editors after catching the first horrific rumors of the bloodletting. "Worse than the order that sent the Light Brigade into the jaws of death, worse in its effect than the Black Hole of Calcutta, was the order that trained the machine guns of the State Militia of Colorado upon the strikers' camp of Ludlow, burned its tents, and suffocated to death the scores of women and children who had taken refuge in the rifle-pits and trenches."

Labor radicals, who had for years preached the righteousness of violence against capital, would now see their doctrines justified. Each street-corner agitator who had ever denounced the Rockefellers as murderers would believe that judgment confirmed. Before Ludlow, revolutionists had occasionally attacked with bomb and flame and pistol. And now the government had responded in kind. After "a sovereign State employs such horrible means," the editors asked, "what may not be expected from the anarchy that ensues?"

III

This is no time for theorizing, for fine-spun argument and phrases. With machine guns trained upon the strikers, the best answer is—dynamite.

—ALEXANDER BERKMAN

The Lid

The illuminated sign for Rector's cabaret rose seventy feet above the entrance on Broadway at Forty-eighth Street. At night, keen crowds pressed against the doors: "They jammed, fought, and tore to get inside." Those with reservations squeezed past the crush into the lobby. Coats and hats were tossed away; eager feet flew forward, through the French doors, into the main dining room—and chaos. "Bedlam was nothing. This was a twin Bedlam." People who had worked for decades in the city's kitchens had never seen anything like the 1914 class of patron: "Nobody went into Rector's to dine," the owner recalled. "All they wanted to do was dance." To placate them, four bands played in relay, beginning with afternoon *thés dansants* and carrying on almost till dawn. "The diners would drop their knives and napkins the minute the orchestra broke loose, and stampede for the dancing area." Chefs abandoned the stoves; waiters paired up with coatroom girls. Guests swirled together until "the couples were jammed back to back, elbow to elbow, and cheek to neck."

Boasting "the finest ball-room in America," Rector's was more infamous than Jack's, the scene of many a scandal, and more profitable than Delmonico's. *The Girl from Rector's*, a 1909 sex farce, had been so outrageous that it took three rewrites before it could be performed in Boston. And a 1913 Ziegfeld hit had only added allure with its prophecy that

> *A lot of men would pony up a lot of alimony*
> *If a table at Rector's could talk.*

Sarah Bernhardt and Enrico Caruso were favored guests, but anyone was welcome who could spend $7.50—the equivalent of a tenement family's weekly rent—on a quart of Pol Roget 1900. It was the premier restaurant in the Tenderloin, "the spot where Broadway and Fifth Avenue met."

On April 21, advertisements in all the major newspapers touted the evening's entertainment, which included a "Spectacular Sword Dance" and "many other superb attractions." Cocktails and tango kept the patrons enthralled until the last ones staggered through the doors to find a taxi at 3:30 in the morning. Outside, an undercover policeman noted the exact moment—which was two and a half hours after the legally mandated closing time for cabarets in New York City.

EVERYONE KNEW THAT restaurants brazenly flouted the curfew law. "Poor Old Father Nick is supposed to stop eating, dancing and drinking at 1 A.M.," a columnist for the *World* observed, and yet "more people are to be found after that hour in restaurants . . . that are legally closed than in the streets, which are legally open." But it was equally notorious that the statute, as it stood, was in need of reform. One in the morning was just too early, especially in the theater district. If a show ran late, audience members were left with scant time for supper. "A man gets into a restaurant after midnight and must get out by 1 o'clock," a cabaret owner complained. "What chance has he to masticate his food?"

The previous mayor had been in his sixties, and in poor health, and such arguments had failed to engender his sympathy. He had put "the lid" on tight, ordering police to drag patrons from their tables, if necessary, so that the last guest would be in a taxi home by the stroke of one. But Mitchel was only thirty-four, and an eminent practitioner of the tango to boot, and he was convinced that his predecessor's "stringent measures" had gone too far. "I don't believe in taking any diner by the shoulder and shoving him into the street," he explained. "It is one extreme to put people out of restaurants at 1 A.M. It is another extreme to let the restaurants run wild." Understanding that "all rules must be enforced with common sense," his administration hoped to chart a middle course.

Back in January, Mitchel had assigned Arthur Woods the task of finding a satisfactory solution. Woods had then spent weeks consulting with department commissioners, the district attorney, magistrates and aldermen, temperance advocates and cabaret owners. In March he presented his conclusion: that the curfew for cabarets should be extended by one hour, to two A.M., "for the purpose of giving plenty of time for persons after the theatre to get a comfortable supper without being hurried."

An array of clamoring citizens, with various complaints, hurried to voice their opposition to the plan. "This proposed extension is not for good morals," a leader of the Church Temperance Society remonstrated, "not for good order and the quiet of the city, but in the interests of undesirable things and undesirable persons." The waiters union testified that shifts already stretched sixteen or seventeen hours, and later closing times would only mean longer and more inhumane workdays. Proprietors of Bowery dives complained that the mayor was unjustly favoring the wealthy entrepreneurs of Broadway. "There are hundreds of strangers who come to this city who can't afford to pay $3 for a meal," an East Sider argued, "and if only the big restaurants are allowed to keep open, it isn't fair. I'd call it class legislation."

Cabaret owners kept quiet while the opposition railed, confident their interests would be protected in the end. The clientele they served made their status sacrosanct. For years they had enjoyed special privileges—violating the liquor laws, affronting public decency—and hardly any action had been taken against them. While high society blithely gambled thousands of dollars in their private back rooms, police had busied themselves elsewhere, "raiding corner saloons and arresting sailors for shaking dice for five-cent beers." As the restaurateurs expected, the administration spent two weeks listening to all objections, and then proceeded to ignore them, officially confirming the two A.M. extension. "The vote showed that the hotel and restaurant men got nearly everything that they asked for," the *Times* concluded. "The objections of church representatives, reformers, and temperance workers did not figure in any compromise."

The government then began vetting applicants for the extended licenses. Each prospective restaurant would be "investigated in two separate ways," Arthur Woods explained, "one by the Inspector in command of the district and the other by the Special Squad under the command of the First Deputy Commissioner." Beginning in early April, the detectives began their clandestine visits.

At 10:30 P.M. on April 7, an investigator entered the Marlborough-Blenheim, on Thirty-sixth Street. "The patrons . . . appear to be respectable people," he observed. "There were no unaccompanied women present and no drunkenness or disorder." That same week, an inspector visited the Kaiserhof, a German restaurant on Thirty-ninth Street. "The place is well managed," he observed. "The food is good and prices reasonable." He was especially impressed by the "very good string orchestra."

Most restaurants fell short of these standards. At Café Regent, the entertainment was not in good taste. "A female with transparent drapings and her hair down her back performed a dance that consisted mostly of kicking," an inspector complained. "Another female sang a tiresome ballad." In Bustanoby's, the patrons consisted of "a respectable class, mingled with showgirls and prostitutes." At the Princess, on Twenty-ninth Street, an agent griped that one of the coat-check girls "flirts with patrons."

But the worst evaluations went to eateries that catered to working people. Schulz Café, on Fiftieth Street, was "frequented by many women of questionable character." The Circle Hotel was dismissed as "a typical corner saloon." At the Whip, a rathskeller in Brooklyn, the inspectors observed that "the patronage is not high-class." Six sailors and two soldiers were present, and though "all were well behaved," he nevertheless urged denial of a permit.

Then, one night in early April, the official made his quiet entrance into Rector's. It was a relief to be back amongst "wealthy and respectable people," even if they were enjoying themselves a little freely. "While no persons were present who could properly be said to be drunk, there were a number that were mellow and happy," he observed. While he watched, one young couple almost fell down the stairs. The entertainment was "high class vaudeville." Dancing was close but not particularly indecent. "The food and drink is of the best and the prices while moderately high are not prohibitive." On the whole, the investigator concluded, "This is a desirable and high class place."

Rector's was granted its extended license, and policemen were detailed to ensure it honored its commitment to close at 2:00 A.M. Officers waited outside to record the minute when the final patrons departed: 5:00 A.M., 5:15 A.M., 3:30 A.M., 2:45 A.M., 2:25 A.M. Again and again, Rector's was among the last cabarets to close. In September, despite "friendly admonishings and warnings," it defied the curfew on eighteen out of thirty nights. "Some of the other restaurants have violated their agreement in this respect but none so bad as Rector's," a detective reported. "It is the most flagrant violator of the two o'clock stipulation." Chief Inspector Max Schmittberger recommended to Arthur Woods that the restaurant's extension "BE REVOKED, for the reason that said provision has been persistently violated."

But even the most senior policeman in the city could not prevail against the tango gang. Rather than closing down, Rector's expanded. On September 28, nearly a thousand celebrities and socialites attended the grand opening of the restaurant's new colossal "Ballroom de Luxe." The walls were decorated in gaudy pink and gold; distinguished and eminent guests waltzed beneath "a maze of colored lights," while bartenders distributed slingers and manhattans.

It was six in the morning when the last patron left.

6.

Free Silence

Spring had not arrived with the equinox, and April was proving to be "a dreary period of chill rains and raw winds." A brilliant Easter, a few teases of sunshine: These did little against the run of pinched and pallid days. Weeks passed without a hint of change, particularly in those districts where no greenery survived to mark the rhythms of nature. "New York's landscape is red," observed a tenant on Thirty-fourth Street, "brick red or brownstone red . . . Manhattan spring is red." A month of this had sapped the city's patience. "When after a long and bitter winter," an editor at the *World* complained, "the calendar promises grateful relief, and the elements deliberately proceed to falsify the season's prospects, a harassed people have a moral right to rebel."

When renewal began to appear, it came gradually and in private moments: "with a bit of slanting sunlight," the *Evening Post* suggested, or "the glimpse of some flower on a windy street-corner." Warmth interspersed among chill days as "little by little, the sun was getting the better of his enemies." The starlings were singing again near Riverside Drive. On Broadway, "fur coats alternated with gray flannel suits," and winter hats gave way to derbies. The tune of hand organs brought dancing children to the East Side streets. "It was that time of the year when all the world belongs to poets," Upton Sinclair had written in one of his early novels. "There are two weeks, the ones that usher in the May, that bear the prize of all the year for glory."

The hazel was thriving at the uptown end of Central Park, near 110th Street, where Sinclair and his second wife had recently taken an apartment at the extortionate rate of ten dollars a week. Eight years had passed since the publication of *The Jungle*, and the dividends from that success were gone. His writings had brought stingier advances—and critical praise, too, had diminished. A review of his latest novel in *McClure's* had ended by reflecting: "You may search your soul for a tenable reason why Mr. Sinclair thrust this impossible brew upon the public."

He was thirty-five years old, bookish and slight, with "large, earnest eyes" and an "almost girlish face." Rarely wasting a thought on his unkempt hair or clothes, he was modest in manner, "by instinct shy." He had no fondness for "the turmoil of the crowd," and yet he always ended up at the center of controversy. He possessed an empathy and anger that overruled his reticence, compelling him out into the forum whenever injustice appeared. "I clench my hands," he wrote, "and bite my lips together and turn on the fierce and haughty and powerful men with a yell of rage."

His zealous interventions were a constant exasperation for his allies. To Walter Lippmann, who had known him since their days in the Intercollegiate Socialist Society, these passionate furies had become

Upton Sinclair.

embarrassing. "Mr. Upton Sinclair's intentions are so good," the cynical, aloof Lippmann had written, "his earnestness so grim, and his self-analysis so humorless" that he "is forever the dupe of his own sincerity." Victor Berger, the Socialist congressman from Wisconsin, was even less charitable. "Sinclair is simply an ass," he confided to reporters. "He is not recognized by any Socialists that I know of as their representative." The writer's antics were a godsend to reporters, who made him "the butt of countless jokes and the target of much ridicule." Everything he did, they turned against him; "the fact that Upton is for it makes one loathe it," sneered a columnist for the *Chicago Tribune*. Nor had he helped his own good name with a quest for perfect health that had embraced prolonged fasting, frequent sanitarium stays, and a brief experiment with the "monkey and squirrel diet."

In April 1914, Sinclair celebrated the one-year anniversary of his second marriage, to Mary Craig Kimbrough—or Craig—an aspiring writer who came from an aristocratic Mississippi family. They had met during one of his sanitarium stays, and she had already spent much of their married life restraining her husband's crusades. Then, on April 27, he attended a meeting of socialists at Carnegie Hall, where Laura Cannon—wife of the president of the Western Federation of Miners—told the story of the Ludlow Massacre. Sinclair had been following the events in Colorado, but he had not yet heard the pathos of the details. Along with three thousand other members in the audience, he jeered and hissed at every mention of "Rockefeller."

Sinclair's novels featured figurative characters, each representing broad social categories. Workers were innocent and often heroic, bosses were cynical or brutal; whatever their personal qualities, individuals stood for large ideas. He thought of John D. Junior, in his office above Broadway, blithely condemning hundreds of families to starvation and death. He recalled that the man professed himself a Christian, and even led a Bible class to teach morality to others. Here was a character worth confronting. Picturing this parasite, this hypocrite, Sinclair had the nearly uncontrollable desire "to wait for Mr. Rockefeller at the entrance of his office and publicly horsewhip him."

Back home in the apartment, at 50 110th Street, near Madison Avenue, Sinclair declared that that night's supper would be his last: Henceforth, he would fast in solidarity with the strikers. Pacing and ranting, he flatly refused to come to bed. His wife tried to calm his excitement, but he was already planning his next outrages. Visions formed in his imagination: a picket line in front of the Standard Oil Building, grave and picturesque protesters mourning the deaths in Colorado. Junior would become a pariah, abandoned by friends, unwelcome in society. "Now, we don't need to kill Rockefeller," he decided, "no, not even if the worst thing his worst enemy might think of him should be true. Giving him the 'social chill' will count more than death would."

"They will surely arrest you," Craig observed.

"Of course they will; and that is what is needed."

She reminded him of the state of their bank account: There were no funds left to pay the fines. "Someone will put up the money," he reassured her. Finally, she offered a compromise. Rather than picketing, they should go together and pay a visit to Rockefeller in person. If he refused to see them privately, then they could demonstrate in public. Grudgingly agreeing, Sinclair finally permitted himself some sleep.

The next morning, husband and wife appeared at the entrance to 26 Broadway, the "severe but imposing" fifteen-story skyscraper that was "known in every part of this broad world as the headquarters of the Standard Oil." Inside, they handed the secretary a note, informing Mr. Rockefeller that Upton Sinclair had arrived to see him. The secretary vanished briefly and returned, asking them to come back in an hour for a reply. They did, only to be told there would be no meeting. Sinclair presented a second note, prepared in advance. "Do not turn us away," it read, "but let us tell you what we know. You will find us quiet and courteous people. We ask nothing but a friendly talk with you."

The clerk returned again, with Junior's final word: "no answer."

The next morning, April 29, Sinclair returned to the Standard Oil Building. He and the four women who had agreed to join him as mourners wrapped black crepe bands around their right arms. Then they linked hands and began solemnly to pace the thirty feet of sidewalk that stretched before the entrance to 26 Broadway. A small crowd gathered to watch. After about five minutes, a clutch of patrolmen came over to suggest they take their little walk somewhere else. They refused. A police officer grabbed Sinclair by the arm and began shoving him forward.

"Please behave like a gentleman," Sinclair hissed in his ear. "I have no idea but to go with you."

At the precinct house, he told the desk sergeant the story of the Ludlow Massacre, then he repeated the narrative again to the magistrate who arraigned him on charges of disturbing the peace. Having been ordered to return to court the next day for sentencing, Sinclair hurried back to Broadway, where he found his wife in command of a new group of mourners. All afternoon, the protest continued to grow. Alexander

In a light suit, with a black mourning band on his arm, Upton Sinclair paraded solemnly in front of the Standard Oil Building on Lower Broadway.

Berkman, who had been leading his own rally with Becky Edelsohn near City Hall, came to take his turn among the pickets. Volunteers kept arriving, and confidence was high. That day, Sinclair somehow found funds to rent an office in a nearby building. He had telephones delivered, and was about to order stationery when he realized the movement needed a name. "We had to fight it out for free speech," said Leonard Abbott, a leading anarchist from the Ferrer Center. "Now we will fight it out for free silence." The letterhead would read, FREE SILENCE LEAGUE.

AS PROTEST PLANS coalesced in New York City, the slaughter climaxed in the coalfields. In the week following the assault on Ludlow, avenging miners had counterattacked, and dozens more combatants and innocents had been killed. With the state militia on the defensive, L. M. Bowers and Junior now demanded that Woodrow Wilson send federal troops to protect their property in the mines. Hesitant to let Colorado Fuel & Iron executives employ U.S. soldiers for their own ends, the president had tried to compromise. If Rockefeller would submit to arbitration, or otherwise demonstrate his goodwill in settling the strike, he offered, then Washington would consider sending military assistance.

To conduct negotiations, Wilson dispatched Representative Martin Foster, the leader of the committee that had called Rockefeller to testify earlier in the month. For three hours on April 27 the two sides discussed possibilities, but the bloodshed had done nothing to alter Junior's position. He still refused to budge on the only substantive issue—the miners' right to unionize—and the congressman departed in frustration. "The attitude of the Rockefellers," he told reporters afterward, "was little short of defiance, not only of the Government, but of civilization itself." In the end, Wilson conceded to Rockefeller's demands anyway. He had no choice. Violence had spread more than 150 miles north, nearly reaching Denver, and civil unrest was tending toward civil war. On April 30, both sides watched with relief as U.S. troops detrained at Trinidad, fifteen miles south of the ruined Ludlow tent colony. Miners and militiamen alike turned over their firearms to the federals. The truce did nothing, however, to end the strike—nor did it placate the Rockefellers' critics.

IT WAS SOPPY and bleak in New York on Thursday, April 30, a day of chastisement for the Rockefellers. Upton Sinclair left his apartment before nine A.M. and traveled to court for his sentencing. Having eaten only an orange and some ice cream since Monday night, he was "working under high nervous tension." In front of the magistrate downtown, he rambled and protested so much that the court had to forbid him from launching into any further orations.

"I had a moral purpose when I went to 26 Broadway," explained Sinclair. "I wanted to bring home to Mr. Rockefeller the feeling that he is responsible for the murders in Colorado."

"You are making a speech," chided the judge.

"This is a serious crisis of my life. I am facing a physical breakdown."

He so disrupted things that the proceeding, which usually took a few minutes, lasted nearly two hours. For disorderly conduct he was given the choice between paying a three-dollar fine or spending three nights in a cell. Not believing they would dare send him there, he chose prison.

"I say to you that I will go to jail," raved the defendant, "and lie there till I am carried out dead, if need be!"

"All right," replied the exasperated judge, "if you like." And, before

he quite realized what was happening, Upton Sinclair was being escorted across the Bridge of Sighs, the notorious passageway leading from
the courthouse to the Tombs.

With Sinclair incarcerated, the leadership of the protests fell to Leonard Abbott, who served as a link between moderates and anarchists. He
spent Thursday morning in the newly acquired office, a converted bed-
room up four flights of shaky stairs. His assistants—the students of the
Modern School at the Ferrer Center—scampered around performing
chores. On the wall, a warning had been posted:

IF YOU WANT TO BRAWL OR FIGHT, GO TO COLORADO, BUT
DON'T HURT OUR MOVEMENT BY TRYING IT HERE. WE WANT
ONLY MEN WHO WILL PLEDGE THEMSELVES TO SPEAK TO NO
ONE AND GO QUIETLY WITH THE POLICE IF ARRESTED.

He told newspapermen that their readers would be amazed if they
could hear the names of the prominent citizens who had telephoned
during the day to offer donations and support to the Free Silence
League. The effort to "send the social chill" to Rockefeller Junior appeared to have the backing of everyone of importance in New York.
Even the police department had agreed to give the radicals at least its
tacit support. Abbott had spent part of the morning at headquarters talking to Commissioner Woods, who had authorized him to publicize the
government's position: "The city administration considers this a period
of intense public feeling, due to the killing of men, women, and children
in Colorado. It is the intention of the administration in this crisis to permit the fullest possible play of public emotion through free speech, free
assemblage, and free passage through the streets of all persons not engaging in organized parades."

"So long as we only wear crepe on our arms and do not display banners," Abbott elaborated, "we may walk up and down in front of 26
Broadway as long as we want to."

Around midday, however, a group of protesters that refused to bind
themselves by rules of any kind were beginning their own demonstration. At noon, the anarchists harangued a sodden, angry crowd at their
usual setting, the statue of Benjamin Franklin near City Hall. Berkman
and Becky ceded the rostrum to Marie Ganz—an East Side anarchist
whom the press had dubbed "Sweet Marie"—who stood on a ledge inciting the audience.

"I haven't come here to talk about the flag or Mexico," she began.

CROWD BEFORE ROCKEFELLER OFFICE

Crowds swarmed the front of the Standard Oil Building each day.

"I'm going to lead a delegation against John D. Rockefeller, Jr. I want you to come along and wipe him off the face of the earth. I want you to show him that he's got to take action in the Colorado strike . . . Follow me!" With a shout, she leapt down to the sidewalk, and, with Berkman and Becky at the lead, began to march down Park Row toward Broadway. Hundreds of rain-soaked demonstrators fell in behind them; scores more joined as they proceeded. With a thousand followers, the anarchists dashed down to Standard Oil headquarters, where the silent mourners were still pacing the sidewalk.

As the police rushed toward Berkman, Ganz slipped through the line of pickets and darted into the building. With a cursed threat, she ordered the elevator operator to take her to the top floor. Bursting in on the startled employees at the innermost sanctum of the corporation, she demanded to see John D. Rockefeller, Jr. He wasn't in, a nervous secretary stuttered. "Tell Rockefeller," screamed Sweet Marie, within the echoing walls of the office, "that I come on behalf of the working people, and that if he doesn't stop the murders in Colorado . . . I'll shoot him down like a dog." And before anyone thought to stop her, she turned and fled back into the elevator.

Down on the street, Berkman and Becky had found a raised platform,

"Sweet Marie" Ganz.

and they were hollering protests at a throng of angry clerks and messenger boys. Shards of wood, paper bags, and sand flew at their heads as the police struggled to hold off the mob. Becky, who had just been released from jail for her disorderly conduct arrest from the previous week, was firing up the audience in her indomitable manner. "A crowd of two thousand gathered, jeering and yelling at her," a reporter wrote. "Twice the crowd surged forward and swept her and her friends off their perch, but they fought their way back, their voices breaking shrilly through the roar." Finally, using a cordon of officers as a barrier, the anarchists were able to escape down into the Bowling Green subway station.

That evening, reporters visited Upton Sinclair in prison. He paced his small cell on the lowest, most fetid tier of the institution. Finally, he rested on the edge of the narrow cot. "I guess I can sit down," he said, uncertainly. "The keeper assures me this cell is sterilized." He had once spent a night in a Delaware workhouse, jailed for playing tennis on a Sunday, but the rancid and filthy Tombs presented a different degree of penance. The keepers had been by with supper, a bowl of stew with some potatoes and bread. "I took one look at it," Sinclair told the newsmen. "It didn't interest me."

He had been too listless to write much that day, scratching out only two lines of a poem. He languidly watched a slant of sunlight falling across the floor and pulled his overcoat around his thin shoulders. Outside, the rainy morning had cleared into a fine, temperate evening. "Do you know that you have the queerest feeling when you're locked up?" he said, at last. "Gee! But it's awful." Only when his visitors described the riotous antics of Berkman and the anarchists did he recover some of his lost energy. "Oh, dear me," he exclaimed, "these fools! They kill the whole business." As the reporters started filing out, Sinclair roused himself for one more blast. "I hope you will give this message to John D. Rockefeller, Jr.," he called after them. "Tell him I hope he enjoys his meals enough for both of us while I am languishing in jail."

Night was falling in midtown when the ruckus out on Fifty-fourth Street brought Abby Rockefeller, Junior's wife, to her window. The chauffeurs at the University Club, across the way, were being more than usually boisterous. She peered out onto the sidewalk in front of her mansion and saw a group of men marching back and forth before her door. Black crepe ribbons circled their arms, and they wore pins on their lapels that read THOU SHALT NOT KILL. The mourners had come uptown. Reaching for the telephone, she called Arthur Woods and asked that he send over some protection for her and the children.

When the police hurried over from the Sixty-seventh Street station, they found half a dozen or so I.W.W. men pacing, silent and grim, while onlookers jeered and women taunted them from passing automobiles. Arthur Caron tramped in the lead, his face jaundiced and swollen from the beating he had received at Union Square three weeks earlier.

"What do you want in this neighborhood?" the detective asked him. "Move along."

"I'm here to walk up and down," Caron replied, without breaking his pace. "And I won't move on at all." More police arrived, until the cops outnumbered the protesters. With the orders from headquarters urging restraint, there was nothing they could do. And so Thursday, April 30, ended with Arthur Caron pursuing his lonely demonstration, east and west along the row, scrutinized by the butlers and servants in the mansions.

"JOHN D. ROCKEFELLER, JR., had yesterday the busiest day he has experienced since the outbreak of the Colorado strike," declared the *Tribune* the following morning. "He left a trail of riots, threats and arrests wherever he went." The next day, which was the first of May—the international workers' holiday—saw even greater demonstrations: protesters in the public squares, pickets at 26 Broadway, mourners on Fifty-fourth Street, disruptors in Calvary Church, where Junior sometimes led his Bible class. Diffuse anger from months of agitations now converged on one man. Banners in the labor parades accused him of being a "multi-murderer." Berkman decried him as a coward with a "guilty conscience." From the West, the president of the United Mine Workers observed that more Americans had been killed in Colorado than in Mexico. "As to John D. Rockefeller, Jr.," he continued, "his life, in spite of his riches, is empty."

Attacks from professed enemies he could withstand, but condemnation was spreading far beyond the usual coterie of radicals. Acquaintances and colleagues spoke out against him. Mayor Mitchel's administration, which he had done so much to encourage, now acquiesced to his tormenters. Pastors in Manhattan took "Rockefeller's War" as their text; in Brooklyn, a minister "denounced the outrages against the miners." Newspapers reveled in his mounting unpopularity. "The suspicion is beginning to grow very strongly," an editor at the *Herald* surmised, "that the leaders of the strikers rely on the name of Mr. Rockefeller to win their struggle for them."

Throughout the week, demonstrators haunted his home and office. They terrorized his secretary, his pastor, and even his wife. But none, so far, had seen Junior himself. His movements, and the condition of his nerves, became the subject of widely divergent speculation. Sinclair had heard rumors that Rockefeller was sneaking in and out of 26 Broadway through a back door. The family claimed he was bedridden with bronchitis. Certain sources insisted that the "social chill" had not affected him; according to others, he was "seriously troubled by the agitation at his office and elsewhere by sympathizers with the Colorado strikers."

In fact, anxious and wounded, Junior had avoided the office all week. On May 1, around noon, he was spotted arriving at Tarrytown, where he spoke briefly with his father, and then retired to his quarters. The next morning, his wife and children joined him behind the walls of the Pocantico Hills estate. Detectives from the William J. Burns agency had been hired to provide extra security; they patrolled the family's miles of private roads and guarded the gates, accosting anyone who approached. Senior continued playing his habitual round of golf each day, but now he was accompanied at all times by two bodyguards, who "followed him around the course and kept a sharp outlook for strangers."

Junior found himself housebound and helpless, reduced to scanning the newspapers each morning for signs of approval—and finding little of it. "He has been much affected by the things said and printed concerning him," his secretary admitted. Junior himself confessed that "the last two weeks have been trying ones, for no man likes to be blamed and criticized, when he feels that such public censure is unfair and unmerited." He was mortified to think that anger toward him was inadvertently affecting others. "I profoundly regret to bring so much notoriety and discomfort to the Class and the Church," he wrote to officials at Calvary Baptist, "and hope that this period of public hysteria may soon subside." To intimate advisers he admitted the strain he was under. "Those who are closest to us," he wrote to his pastor, "realize how trying the present situation is, for they know its injustice."

Junior's detractors did not understand the conflict he was suffering. In public, for the sake of Colorado Fuel & Iron, he had to maintain a unified front with his subordinates. He could not be seen harboring critics of the company, and therefore he had rebuffed not just Upton Sinclair but official union delegates, congressmen, the secretary of labor, and the president of the United States. His press statements reiterated the testimony he had given to Congress. It was the same official position that had been passed down from management: The company treated its workers generously, most employees had no interest in joining the union, labor agitators were responsible for most of the violence. But Bowers, who had always patronized him, had been lying to him as well, and Junior was catching on.

Privately, Rockefeller attempted to ameliorate the situation in the coalfields. The telegram he had sent to Bowers before the massacre ordering him back to New York had arrived too late. Then, in the immediate aftermath of the assault on Ludlow, he had probed suspiciously at Bowers's crafty omissions concerning the battle. Now, with hatred pouring in on him, Junior kept seeking for a moral policy. He wanted to accept the government's offer to arbitrate the strike. Bowers refused. When Rockefeller broached the idea of sending "disinterested men" to serve as mediators, Bowers replied that "such a scheme would be most unwise." Distraught by what he was reading of the violence, Junior's thoughts turned to the sufferers. IF IT IS TRUE AS REPORTED IN THE PAPERS THAT ANY OF OUR EMPLOYEES HAVE BEEN INJURED IN THE RECENT DISTURBANCES, he cabled to Colorado, I TRUST THAT YOU HAVE ALREADY TAKEN STEPS TO PROVIDE FULLY FOR THEM AND THEIR FAMILIES. This last telegram was simply ignored.

Bowers had one care: to defeat the strikers. The struggle, for him, had grown beyond an industrial dispute. He believed himself to be the leader of the "conservative, level-headed, patriotic business men of the country" in their crusade against "labor union agitators" and "the political muckraking rabble." Each gesture toward mediation, every suggestion that reforms were necessary—even an offer to reimburse the victims—was an admission of error that would harm the company's efforts to vanquish the union. Once the miners had surrendered, then and only then would it be appropriate to assess managerial practices. Until that time, unwavering support was necessary.

Junior might have acted on his growing doubts. He could have admitted his mistakes, confessed to having been misled, and set about redressing the wrongs that had been committed in his name. But he did not. Betraying his own better judgment, he relapsed into nervous tension and wiled away his days petulantly griping about the treatment he was receiving in the press. "To describe this condition as 'Rockefeller's war,'" he complained, "as has been done by certain of the sensational newspapers and speakers, is infamous."

In order to painstakingly—obsessively—follow the coverage, he had all the New York dailies forwarded to his sickbed in Tarrytown. Grateful for compliments, he wrote one editor to thank him for his paper's "fair and broad-minded" reporting. He congratulated Adolph Ochs, publisher of the *Times*, for an editorial on labor unions. But he was just as quick to protest against any perceived offense. When the *World* published a few critical pieces, he was particularly upset. "I tried to get you on the telephone today but was informed that you were away," Junior wrote Ralph Pulitzer, the publisher, who was an old friend.

I simply wanted to inquire whether the editorials regarding the Colorado situation which appeared in the WORLD of this morning, and one or two previous editorials of a somewhat similar tenor, represent your views and were published with your approval. In view of the pleasant relationship which has existed between us I can only assume that these editorials have been written without reference to you and have escaped your notice, for I cannot believe that . . . you could have authorized the editorial of this morning.

Pulitzer's response could not have been what Junior had expected:

I have always felt it my duty to accept responsibility for what appears on the editorial page of "The World". In view of the pleasant relationship which you mention, I will depart from this principle to the extent of saying that had I written or edited the editorials to which you refer, I would have qualified one statement of principle and would have modified certain expressions which might have been construed to contain personal animus, but with these amendments the editorials would have expressed my own views regarding the Colorado situation.

When he was done examining the newspapers, Junior found comfort in the correspondence arriving daily from friends and strangers across the country. "I wish to tell you how deeply . . . I sympathize with you in your present position—Be patient," wrote Andrew Carnegie. A note from Oswald Garrison Villard, publisher of the *Evening Post*, began, "I hope you will let me say how genuinely I have sympathized with you in the annoyances of these past weeks, and that I admire the dignity and self-restraint with which you have borne yourself." And then there were the letters from supporters he had never met. Most began by apologizing for the intrusion, and many came around to ask for a job. Junior read each one, marking his favorite passages in pencil:

I feel that every man in the Country should write you a short note, congratulating you on the stand you are taking in relation to the strike in Colorado.

Don't be distressed by those crazy anarchists, etc., who threaten you. Right is right, and will conquer in the end.

What this country needs is a few more Americans like yourself + no more "Americans" of the Sinclair, Edelsohn + Ganz type.

Ahead of all this trouble is the issue of God vs. Anti-God . . .

I am prepared to assert that all the labor unions in the United States, including the I.W.W., with the exception of the railroad orders, are controlled by the Order of Jesuits . . .

* * *

Times Square was lonely and forsaken at 7:45 in the morning on May 3, when Arthur Caron met the six anarchists who were to join him for a day's excursion. The empty theaters and cabarets were shuttered and dark. At the newsstands, the headlines had to do with Colorado and Mexico, or the previous day's suffrage parades. Stepping down into the station, the little group rode the Broadway subway to its northern terminus in the Bronx. From there, a fifteen-cent trolley fare carried them past the hamlets and farmsteads of Westchester County. At eleven A.M., they disembarked in Tarrytown.

It was Sunday morning, and the sidewalks were packed with families on their way to church. The party asked passersby for directions to the Rockefeller estate, and curious stares followed them as they went. A few blocks took them from the village center onto a quiet country road. The rural setting, and the sunshine, put the leader in a jovial mood; Caron

The great iron gate to Pocantico Hills.

kept up a steady patter of encouragement as they made the two-mile walk. Then the great iron gate to Pocantico Hills emerged into view. The anarchists fell quiet, their eyes following the walls that disappeared from sight in both directions. The estate was enormous, far more imposing than they had imagined.

Patrolling automobiles noticed the approaching group before it had reached the gates. Workmen scrambled to lock and chain the entrance. Guards hustled over. They scowled through the iron bars, while others crouched, heavily armed, behind nearby hedges. Junior's children were called in from their play; pausing for a moment to stare at the protesters, their anxious nurses shooed them on. The radicals did not say a word. In the drive, they paused to tie black crepe to their arms—one woman affixed a card to her hat that read I PROTEST AGAINST THE MURDERS IN COLORADO—and then they started marching with the same "slow, steady tramp" that had resounded across the city.

"We came up here to-day to worry Rockefeller and we have him worried," Caron told the newspapermen who had come along. "It is a peaceful demonstration, but we intend to keep it up every day. Tomorrow we will have double the number, and we will follow Rockefeller wherever he goes. We have him thinking." For two hours, they continued their mourners' march, and then they trudged back into town for an ice cream soda before beginning the long trip home.

The next day, every gate at Pocantico Hills was locked and guarded, and Rockefeller Senior, was laying plans to construct a new main entrance to the estate: It would be "one of the most pretentious in the country," and utterly unassailable to invaders. Armed men tailed the children in their play. Detectives and workmen patrolled the perimeter, but no I.W.W. assault materialized. Instead, Caron had gone to 26 Broadway to take his turn among the mourners, explaining that he had postponed his next visit to Tarrytown until he could raise a larger corps of volunteers.

Released from the Tombs and eating again, Upton Sinclair was crafting plans of his own. He sent telegrams to leading socialists across the nation, suggesting they add their protests to the New York agitations. THERE ARE BRANCH OFFICES OF STANDARD OIL IN EVERY TOWN, he cabled to party officials in all the major cities. CANNOT YOU OR THE NATIONAL EXECUTIVE COMMITTEE RECOMMEND THAT MOURNING PICKETS APPEAR BEFORE THESE OFFICES? CANNOT ALL SOCIALIST LOCALS PUT CREPE BEFORE THEIR DOORS? The answer came back: No. "The Socialists here are decidedly tired of this cheap clap-trap of Sinclair's," a party secretary informed reporters. "They know it is the quiet work of organizing that counts and never this self-advertising noise. Sinclair's noise is his own personally organized affair, and we have nothing to do with it."

Without national support, the ardor drained from the movement. When it rained, the makeshift office became a jumble of drying lines crowded with musty, sagging garments. Hostile passersby shoved mourners to the ground. Businesses complained that the protests were hurting commerce. The granite silence from 26 Broadway persisted, and Junior kept out of sight. "You may judge that it was rather a dull day," a reporter joked midweek, "the loquacious-lipped and prolific-penned Upton Sinclair didn't issue a single voluminous statement, and the fair but fiery Marie Ganz didn't make a solitary murder-threat." Derision poured in from everywhere. "Why should the authorities of New York interest themselves in trying to prevent Upton Sinclair from his 'silence' strike against young Mr. Rockefeller?" asked the *Seattle Post-Intelligencer*. "The more silence there is around Mr. Sinclair's neighborhood the larger the relief to the rest of the country."

After a few more days of this, Sinclair decided he was "through with the Free Silence mourning." It had been intemperate, perhaps rash, to think he could be of service here in New York. He could do more good in Colorado. On Saturday, May 9, he boarded a train for Denver at Pennsylvania Station, leaving his wife and the others to carry on—or not—as they so pleased.

On Sunday, Leonard Abbott disbanded the organization. "The reason there is no more need for the Free Silence League," one leader explained to the public, "is that the Anti-militarist League, headed by Alexander Berkman, and the I.W.W. forces, headed by Arthur Caron, have taken hold so successfully that we may as well drop out." But Craig disclosed the true motivation to her friends. She feared the movement was plunging toward bloodshed; not a day passed without at least one visitor appearing at her apartment door, asking her to "give them some job of violence to do."

The Rockefellers had decided to abstain from Sunday services for a second week in a row, but the pews at Calvary Baptist Church, on West Fifty-seventh Street, were crowded on May 10 with a congregation boasting "the wealthiest and most influential people in the city." Conspicuous among them were detectives Gildea and Gegan and a squad of plainclothesmen. As the final notes of the organist's prelude faded off, the pastor stood at the lectern to announce the text of his sermon: "Samson, the Man of Sunlight, the Man of Tact." But before he could continue, a middle-aged gentleman in a white suit bounded from his seat and hurried toward the altar. "I am here to speak the truth," he called out. And then a gang of ushers grabbed him by the arms and began hustling him up the aisle toward the exit. Slipping their grasp, he clung to the back of a pew. They pried at his fingers as he thrashed and kicked. Parishioners shrieked. "I want you to let me speak," he cried, "so that I can tell you about one member of your congregation who is guilty of the murder of women and children in Colorado." They pulled him loose, and he stumbled to the floor. As he struggled, his scattered followers rose to their feet and shouted—"Let him speak!" "Shame!"—while the rest of the audience cheered the ushers with cries of "Put him out!"

On the street outside, the disruptor's white suit was torn by police as he and ten supporters were manhandled into waiting vans. At the Forty-seventh Street station house, he identified himself as Bouck White, a Harvard graduate, author, and founder of the Church of the Social Revolution in Greenwich Village. It was as a fellow man of God that he had risen to challenge the pastor at Calvary Baptist. As a socialist and Christian, he had hoped to redeem the wealthy congregation with a message of poverty and brotherhood. Hundreds of fervent acolytes gathered in the courtroom for his arraignment. When the magistrate released him, pending trial, they threw their hats in the air and hoisted him on their shoulders, rapturous with joy.

For White, the foray into the temple had been a holy mission. "The real God of the Bible," he explained, "is on the side of the workers and the poor, against the privileged class at the top." But for most observers, his antics indicated yet another escalation in a months-long series of radical outrages. Allusions to the Haymarket Riot and the Paris Commune began appearing frequently in the press. "Have we not had almost enough of the I.W.W. agitation in this peace loving city of New York?" asked the editors at the *Sun*. "Is it not time that means were found of stopping malignant provocation to riot?" The *Herald* offered simple remedies—"A quick application of nightsticks, a proper use of the patrol wagon"—and posed a provocative question: "*Is Mr. Mitchel a Mayor or a mouse?*"

Arthur Woods had theorized that promoting civil liberties would prevent eruptions of violence: agitators would exhaust themselves with words, instead of pursuing more inflammatory tactics. After a triumphant beginning, this doctrine now appeared more tenuous with every protest action. The invasion of Calvary Church discredited any standing it retained, and Mitchel moved to distance himself from his commissioner.

"Mr. Woods's ideas on the subject of free speech are known to be extremely liberal," a reporter explained, "considerably more so than those of the Mayor, who believes that 'incitement to crime is not free speech.'" For Mitchel, the time for social experimentation was done. "You cannot handle with kid gloves" an occurrence like the attack on Calvary Church, he declared. Radical provocations henceforth would be met with "vigorous methods." The noonday meetings at the Franklin statue, which had instigated such nuisances over the previous weeks, were banned. Mourning marchers on West Fifty-fourth Street were detained. Marie Ganz was arrested and given sixty days in the Queens County Jail; it took a magistrate only twenty minutes to sentence Bouck White to six months on Blackwell's Island.

The severity of these measures was partly due to the imminent arrival of the president of the United States. Just a few days after presiding over his daughter's marriage to the secretary of the treasury, Woodrow Wilson was coming to the city for a memorial service honoring the casualties of the Veracruz invasion. The attention of the entire country would be fixed on the ceremony. For the Mitchel administration, it was a chance to demonstrate the capacities of honest and efficient government. The agitators hoped it would be the perfect occasion to foist their grievances on a national audience. To prevent this, Woods and Schmittberger made elaborate plans for security. By the morning of May 11, the city's worst troublemakers had been locked away, and New York was as secure as the police department could make it.

THE GATE TO Pier A, in Battery Park, scraped open at nine A.M., and a squad of marines placed the first coffin onto an artillery wagon and draped it with a flag. Spectators clutched their hats to their chests. Warships in the upper bay stood silent; skiffs and tugs in the rivers refrained from the usual bawling and whistles. Sixteen more caskets followed, and when they had assembled, the parade commenced. Mounted policemen led the way, followed by the honored dead and then Wilson, somber and introspective, in an open carriage. Thousands upon thousands of onlookers filled the Broadway sidewalks "from curb to building line." Up above, they thronged in the windows and crowded the rooftops. Police in dress uniform were stationed every twenty feet. At the Standard Oil Building, the officers lined up shoulder to shoulder. Security agents had observed the demonstrations out front of 26 Broadway for days, and as the president's carriage approached, "there was a visible increase in the vigilance of his guards in that troubled zone." Then it was behind them, and there had been no incident.

Business was suspended at the cotton and produce trading floors, the curb market, and the New York Stock Exchange. At the Equitable Building, construction workers paused in their riveting; high up on the steel frame, they gripped the bare girders with one hand and doffed their caps with the other. No one had known beforehand whether or not the crowd would cheer. The answer was now apparent. "The roll of muffled drums," a reporter wrote, "the soft tread of feet, the gentle tap-tap of the horses' hoofs, and the rumbling of wheels were the only sounds." The bell at Trinity Church tolled as the procession neared Wall Street, then St. Paul's joined in. But the spectators maintained their quiet witness.

Mayor Mitchel, in top hat and formal attire, was waiting on the steps to City Hall as the horses appeared in the plaza. Hundreds of school-children offered a hymn of mourning. The mayor approached a podium, and the singing stopped. "The people of New York pay their solemn re-spect to these honored dead," he began. "These men gave their lives not to war, but to the extension of peace. Our mission in Mexico is not to engage in conquest, but to help restore to a neighboring republic the tranquility and order which are the basis of civilization." When he had finished, Mitchel advanced with long strides forward into the quiet square and set a wreath of orchids on the coffin of a nineteen-year-old seaman from Manhattan.

The choirs took up a new song as the mayor clambered into the president's carriage. Seated there, he appeared even younger than usual. The military spectacle had him fired with a craving for action and sacri-fice, and his excitement made it difficult to maintain the proper dignity. In contrast, Wilson—wearing a pince-nez, and with wispy gray hair protruding beneath his hat—had a haggard look. "The President was silent and very grave," a reporter observed. "His square jaw was set . . . and his eyes were misty." He had toiled through months of personal anguish before ordering the marine expedition to Veracruz, and now he faced the awful results of that decision. With thoughts of death upon him, he congratulated the mayor on his fortunate escape from assassina-tion. Then he relapsed into somber introspection. The leaders of the two largest governments in the United States rode up Centre Street to-gether, past the Tombs, without a word.

The invasion of Veracruz had not lived up to the president's hopes. Never imagining that the Mexican garrison would resist American

The president and mayor shared an open carriage during the procession.

incursion, he had expected his troops to be greeted as liberators and friends. Instead, it had taken three days before the city was pacified, hundreds of civilians had been killed, and Wilson was being cursed as an aggressor throughout most of Latin America. The statue of George Washington in Mexico City had been pulled from its pedestal and dragged through the streets. Stunned by the response, the administration retreated from any plans involving further, prolonged occupation.

The greatest shock for Wilson had come at the news of the American casualties. Back in March, he had worried over the impact of combat on the sweethearts and relatives of the stricken boys; now he had to confront the reality of his fears. "The thought haunts me," he confided to the White House physician, "that it was I who ordered those young men to their deaths." Determined to take responsibility for what had occurred, the president had called a press conference to personally announce the results of the fighting. "I remember how preternaturally pale, almost parchment, Mr. Wilson looked when he stood up there and answered the questions of the newspaper men," a witness recalled. "The death of American sailors and marines owing to an order of his seemed to affect him like an ailment. He was positively shaken."

As the president's meditation continued, the carriage turned right onto Canal Street, the main thoroughfare through the Lower East Side.

The security detail scanned the crowds with special vigilance. Because of the recent protests in New York, Wilson's advisers had pleaded with him to avoid the parade. But he had seen it as his duty and insisted on participating. Now the procession was entering the tenement districts, which harbored so many "avowed enemies of government." Rutgers Square, Mulberry Bend: These were the places where the radicals congregated. For weeks, anarchists and Wobblies had denounced Wilson and his imperialist adventure from these very streets. Factories and shops had let their workers out to view the spectacle, and the sidewalks were filled. The Secret Service men were tense, focused.

The crowds had not expected to see the president, and it took a few moments for them to realize that he had come among them. As the fact registered, the reverent silence that had endured since the early morning finally was swept away. Cheers and huzzahs grew to such a pitch, a reporter noted, that "the demonstration took on almost the appearance of a gala day, instead of one of mourning for the nation's dead." Where Canal Street intersected with the Bowery, the youngsters of the Crippled Children's East Side Free School clapped and shouted, "Hurray for the President!" In the carriage, Wilson busied himself acknowledging the accolades and seemed to momentarily forget his reverie. Then the cortege climbed onto the Manhattan Bridge and processed again in silence.

A million New Yorkers had watched the coffins travel for two hours through downtown, and thousands more awaited them at the Brooklyn Navy Yard. The president took his place on a reviewing stand along with Mitchel and Franklin Delano Roosevelt, assistant secretary of the navy. Commissioner Woods and his team of detectives surveyed the crowds anxiously for agitators. The seventeen flag-covered caskets were laid in a row on an improvised bier in front of the dignitaries. The sun parched the hard-packed parade ground; the president removed his hat and gloves, and "with head uncovered, stood looking down upon the scene with grave face."

Woodrow Wilson had previewed this scene in his mind long before it had come to pass. He had anticipated the concern and confusion he would feel if he ever was required to serve as a wartime commander in chief. Now "his strong voice trembled, and once it nearly broke" as he shared his emotions with the audience. "For my own part," he said, "I have a singular mixture of feelings. The feeling that is uppermost is one of profound grief that these lads should have had to go to their death, and yet there is mixed with that grief a profound pride that they should have gone as they did, and if I may say it out of my heart, a touch of

FUNERAL VERA CRUZ VICTIMS - CROSSING MANHATTAN BRIDGE 3083-13

Veracruz victims crossing the Manhattan Bridge.

envy of those who were permitted so quietly, so nobly, to do their duty." The dead, at least, had been spared the trauma of being president. "I never went into battle. I never was under fire," Wilson said, "but I fancy that there are some things just as hard to do as to go under fire. I fancy that it is just as hard to do your duty when men are sneering at you as when they are shooting at you." Such had been his lot as critics had called on him to take action against the nation's southern neighbor. In the end, he had ordered these men into combat, but he had not done so until he had assured himself of the full propriety of their mission. "We have gone down to Mexico to serve mankind," he explained. "A war of aggression is not a war in which it is a proud thing to die, but a war of service is a thing in which it is a proud thing to die." The decision to expose American troops to peril had been agonizing. The consequences— these caskets before them—were appalling. But it had not been in vain.

He stepped back from the rostrum. A marine rifle squad offered volley after volley in salute, and the crowd began to disperse. From a nearby barracks, a dozen telegraph machines keyed the president's closing sentiments to the nation.

"As I stand and look at you to-day," Wilson had concluded, "I know the road is clearer for the future. These boys have shown us the way, and it is easier to walk on it because they have gone before and shown us how."

A Film with a Thrill

They filed inside the Lyric Theatre, on Forty-second Street, passing beneath the stone marquee and into the cool of the lobby. Up toward the balcony climbed the fifteen-cent-ticket holders; the rest, having paid a quarter, proceeded to the orchestra. Inside, the plastered walls and ornate ceiling were hued in rose, cream, and gold. The house lights flickered down. Murmurs from the settling crowd were replaced by the clicking of a motion-picture projector, and then General Pancho Villa and his rebel army charged into view up on the screen. Cameramen had braved "more or less constant fire for twelve days" in Mexico to bring this film, *The Battle of Torreon*, to American audiences. It was an unflinchingly "grewsome" depiction, showing falling soldiers, burning corpses, devastated villages—and all authentic. The premiere, on May 10, coincided with the memorial to the Veracruz dead. Banking on the warlike yearnings of the paying public, theater managers hoped to sell out two matinees and two evening shows a day.

New York had become a city of filmgoers. The Lyric and its competitors catered to fashionable audiences near Times Square. Jewish garment workers congregated in the airless halls on Houston Street, families from northern Italy jammed the auditoriums around Bleecker Street; down on the Bowery, "chance-met" crowds consisted of any stranger who could spare a nickel. For the millions who worked twelve-hour days and then had nothing but a tenement flat to come home to, the motion pictures were a precious refuge. "Outside, the iron city roared," a patron recalled. "Before the door of the show the push-cart venders bargained and trafficked with customers. Who in that audience remembered it?" One by one, playhouses were converted into movie theaters. "Above

The Battle of Torreon.

Fifty-ninth street there is not a legitimate theatre that survives," a columnist for the *World* discovered. "On One Hundred and Twenty-fifth street, where there were four, they have all surrendered to the movies." The process would continue until vaudeville and the melodrama had been eclipsed, and a thousand screens flickered in New York from morning till midnight.

Nearly a quarter million viewers attended screenings in the city every day, and many observers feared the moral repercussions of the "moving-picture evil." The district attorney claimed that crime was rising in proportion to the popularity of Black Hand films. "It is not a rare sight to see boys and girls engaged in mimic 'hold-ups' on the street," complained a spokesman for the Society for the Prevention of Cruelty to Children. "These shows are sinks of iniquity!" a magistrate declared. "Ninety-five per cent. of them ought to be closed."

But there were others among the respectable classes who believed that films could be just as useful in teaching virtuous habits as they had been detrimental in the spread of vice. Compared to other amusements, these activists argued, the cinema was relatively wholesome. "The moving-picture show cheers, but does not inebriate," wrote the editor of the *Fra* magazine. "It never gives you that dark-brown taste the day after, nor a headache and that tired feeling." However evil the onscreen action had become, it was hardly more vicious than the bawdy trash that graced the Broadway stage. "There is to be said in favor of the moving picture," a skeptic was forced to concede, "that as yet such rank productions as 'The Girl from Rector's' . . . have not found their way to any alarming extent into films."

Produced by private foundations and philanthropic organizations, movies urging moral and spiritual improvement became common in the city's theaters. The Edison studios released *Children Who Labor*, a dramatization of the dangers of factory work. Productions depicting the hazards of crossing busy streets were created by the Safety First Society. Religious leaders—including Reverend Parkhurst, Schmittberger's old patron and a leading campaigner against vice—commissioned cameramen to shoot biblical scenes in the Holy Land. Hope spread that the balance had turned to favor good. "Not always, when gay and frivolous youth flocks to the moving-picture show, can you say that it is going merely to pass an idle hour and watch some too-too thrilling drama of wild adventure," an advocate of uplift pictures exulted. "Sometimes the young people have their minds improved even as their pulses are stirred."

And then the White Slave films appeared.

The Inside of the White Slave Traffic premiered at the Park Theater, on Columbus Circle, in December 1913. Advertisements implied that it would be yet another of the new reform-minded movies. Endorsements from reputable civic groups were prominently displayed outside the box office. Posters proclaimed that it had been "produced from actual facts" and based on the "observations of a former US government investigator." But despite these trappings of probity, audiences were ravenous to see it. And that surely was suspicious. "Long lines of men and women and of the youth of both sexes wait, day and night, at the box offices," a reporter wrote. Even with five shows daily, and an auditorium that could seat nearly two thousand patrons, hundreds had to be turned away.

"White slavery"—the kidnapping of women into prostitution—was a titillating subject indeed for a motion picture. The issue had been a persistent fixation ever since a *McClure's* article in 1911 had identified New York as the center of an international trade in young girls. Newspapers and magazines had followed with salacious stories of abduction in which immigrant girls were surreptitiously drugged, placed in captivity, and sold into a life of sexual servitude. John D. Rockefeller, Jr., had chaired a grand jury inquiry into the subject, and when it failed to reveal any evidence of an organized conspiracy, he had founded his own research foundation, the Bureau of Social Hygiene, to continue the investigations until the truth could be discovered.

The whole thing was fatuous, radicals pointed out, founded in the inability of puritanical philanthropists to imagine that one could become a prostitute through any means other than trickery. "What is really the cause of the trade in women?" Emma Goldman asked. "Not merely white women, but yellow and black women as well. Exploitation, of course; the merciless Moloch of capitalism that fattens on underpaid labor, thus driving thousands of women and girls into prostitution." But no one listened. Politicians and religious leaders mobilized around the issue; the Presbyterian Church claimed that more than a hundred thousand girls were trapped in the nation's brothels against their will. And when the Bureau of Social Hygiene finally released its findings, it concluded—unsurprisingly, though again without proof—that the commerce in flesh was "a hideous reality."

The Inside of the White Slave Traffic claimed to be an exposé of the social evil. "A film with a moral," its backers claimed. "A film with a lesson. A film with a thrill." Skeptics were not convinced, and when a social worker attended a showing, she found her suspicions confirmed. Rather than condemning the ills of prostitution, the movie appeared to glamorize the life of a fallen woman. Three fourths of the audience was male, and the prurient crowd, far from being edified by the events on the screen, instead "seemed to gloat over the horrors portrayed." Opposition spread. The Board of Censors decried it as "an illustration of the white slave traffic, thinly veiled as an attempt to educate the public." From pulpits and editorial columns came denunciations; the film, a rabbi told his congregation, had done "nothing more than stimulate an unwholesome and morbid curiosity instead of driving home a moral lesson."

Protests against the movie climaxed just before Christmas, when a Saturday-afternoon showing was abruptly halted by the arrival of half a dozen detectives. Crashing into the auditorium, they confiscated the film reels and arrested the entire staff while the crowd shouted in protest. It was priceless publicity. "The advertising the so-called white slave films have been given through the efforts of the police to suppress them," reported the *World*, "has resulted in extraordinary attendance." The next day there were eight screenings instead of the usual five, and thousands jammed the sidewalks in front of the building, "surging in and out of the doors of the theatre in increasing volumes with each succeeding exhibition."

The controversy sparked a genre; within weeks, audiences were choosing between *Traffic in Souls*, *The Exposure of the White Slave Traffic*, *The House of Bondage*, and *Smashing the Vice Trust*, while further elaborations were "coming thick and fast." Each followed the same formula of phony reformism. *Smashing the Vice Trust* advertised a fictitious endorsement by Reverend Parkhurst. And when one of the others purported to be based on the findings of Rockefeller's Bureau of Social Hygiene, Junior issued an outraged public statement of denial.*

MONTHS LATER, in April, Rockefeller again found himself victimized on screen. At the height of the Ludlow crisis, in the week before the massacre, a family friend alerted him to a movie, *By Man's Law*, which was screening at "a horrid place" in the Bronx. "The object of the picture," the correspondent wrote,

> seems to be to make the ignorant people hate the name of Rockefeller, and it succeeds well, for the people were all hissing,—of course the name of Rockefeller is not mentioned, but it represents the "oil magnate" cold and cruel and merciless, who sends the cost of oil up higher and higher, and then smiles while the people kill each other in a labor strike. There is also a son who is interested in philanthropy and social reform, so I don't think there can be any doubt as to whom the picture means to represent.

Junior was convinced that the movie had been released in order to capitalize on the crisis in Colorado. "Would you kindly look into the matter for me," he wrote to one of the researchers for the Bureau of Social Hygiene, "and if you find the pictures as represented, see what can be done looking toward the discontinuance of the films?"

The answer was nothing. Junior had no recourse but to suffer this indignity along with all the others being tossed upon him.

The White Slave pictures, at the crescendo of the scandal, had been earning more than $5,000 apiece in weekly box-office receipts. From New York they went on a national tour, generating outrage—and

---

* In Chicago, the arrival of *The Inside of the White Slave Traffic* was not welcomed. "The New York police stopped it," opponents argued, "and our police should never let it open here." In D.C., the mayor himself declared, "If it's too bad for New York, it certainly should not be shown in Washington."

profits—nearly everywhere. By comparison, *The Battle of Torreon*, depicting the Mexican war, had fallen flat. Though the film represented something truly new—the first attempt by cameras to capture a modern conflict as it occurred—audiences were unimpressed. A two-week run at the Lyric netted little more than half of the anticipated revenue. The picture was pulled and future installments canceled. Reality was just not dramatic enough; long shots of distant maneuvers, no matter how authentic, could never compete with the studio-made war stories, where the action could be captured in close-up, down to the anguished grimace on a dying soldier's face. This was the new vérité of war.

7.

A Sleepy Little Burg

Arthur Caron rode to Tarrytown alone on Friday, May 22. Down near the railroad tracks, a few clapboard tenements housed the village workforce. Trudging up steeply rising streets, he was soon passing tidy brick storefronts and prosperous-looking commercial buildings. Then—and it didn't take long—he was on tree-lined paths flanked by the Gothic and Queen Anne homes where local professionals raised their children. After less than a mile, he was in a countryside not of farms but of estates. High walls stood on either side of the road, hiding secluded mansions belonging to some of the wealthiest families in America.

Accustomed by now to this route and no longer so awed by the scenery, Caron again approached the gates to the Pocantico Hills property. This time, he made a careful survey of the defenses, probing for entry points and vulnerabilities. With the Free Silence pickets abandoned in the city and New York authorities meting out revengeful sentences, he was scouting other means to pressure the Rockefellers. He had briefly mulled a plan to hold a mock funeral march, complete with hearse and coffin, on the road to the estate. But it had proven unfeasible. Now, after a few hours' investigation, he was convinced it would be equally impossible to trespass on the grounds. He strolled back down to the village and called on the local authorities. At each office, he requested permission to hold a meeting in the public square. These applications were denied—agitators were not welcome in Tarrytown—and Caron departed in defeat.

He promised to return, however, permit or no, to instigate in Westchester County the same sort of free-speech fight that he had led down in Union Square. Caron's imagination teemed with grand ideas, but his visions never manifested themselves quite as he had planned. In April, he had urged the unemployed to order meals in restaurants and then leave without paying. Nothing had come of it. Then there had been the mock funeral. And now this proposed mass invasion of Tarrytown. So far, few of his schemes had amounted to much of anything. Looking back at his life to date, none of his dreams, really, had come out as he had hoped.

Arthur Caron was thirty years old. Born to French-Canadian parents, he claimed to have American Indian ancestry on his mother's side. As a boy he had lived in New York State up to around the turn of the century, when the family moved to Fall River, Massachusetts. It was there he received his initial experience of industrial labor. Fifty miles south of Boston, with a population around one hundred thousand, Fall River was the "Queen City of the Cotton Industry," the "Manchester of America." The Caron home, on Thomas Street, stood near a cluster of factories where Arthur, and many of his seven siblings, soon found work. Most children in the community left the classroom following the fourth grade to take jobs as bobbin boys or sweepers. Deciding this was not the life he wanted, Arthur determined to better his condition. After his ten-hour shift at the cotton mill ended, he would drag himself to a commercial night school to study engineering, and then finally stagger home and lose himself in his books.

When he was eighteen, Caron left home for a disastrous stint in the navy. As a low-ranking landsman he had served aboard the *Constellation*, a training vessel stationed in Newport Harbor. The stern discipline had not been to his taste. He was cited repeatedly for "leaving ship without permission" or for returning late from shore leave; a third of his time in the service was spent in hospitals getting treatment for gonorrhea. After fourteen months, to everyone's relief, he was declared "unfit for service" and discharged.

A civilian once more, Caron remained in Rhode Island and found success. His studies at home qualified him for positions above the mass of laborers; he served as an inspector at the Providence Engineering Works and as an expert mechanic at the Alco automobile factory. His social life thrived as well. He made a reputation as an athlete and married a woman named Elmina Reeves. After a few years they were ready to start a family, and on December 2, 1912, their son, Reeves, was born. Arthur's fortunes crested here. The child was significantly premature, and three days after its birth, the mother died. Leaving the fragile newborn with his in-laws, Caron returned to the crowded house in Fall River and an unskilled job in a cotton mill.

Since the time he had first entered the factories as a teenager, Caron had been a believer in trade unions, but he had never been the sort to demonstrate or to rant against the owners. His hope had always been to join the managerial class. Back on the work floor again, he came to identify more strongly with his fellow laborers. And in 1913, when I.W.W. locals in Fall River campaigned for higher wages, Caron involved himself with the protests. He did not officially join the Wobblies, but he became known to the police as an agitator. At the height of the conflict, he had gone to City Hall to request a permit to speak in public—much as he would later do in Tarrytown—and when his appeal was denied, the *Boston Journal* reported, Caron had "made a veiled threat to the effect that his organization would 'get' the mayor."

As a result, he lost his job and fell out with his family. He drifted to Boston, seeking employment, and then arrived in New York City sometime during the winter. Of course, there was no work there either. Despite years of effort and tantalizing moments of promise, he had failed to escape a toiling life. As winter worsened, he sank even lower than before. It had been months since he had held a paying position. Jobless, homeless, and hungry, he stayed at the University Settlement House on the Lower East Side or slept on the street. Some nights, his friends let him use a mattress on the floor of their apartment, on the top story of a tenement on Lexington Avenue at 103rd Street.

Arthur Caron.

Dark and broadly built, he was "about six feet tall" with a well-knit sportsman's frame. High cheekbones and "a slightly dark complexion" added credence to the rumor of his Indian ancestry. He had a wide, unself-conscious smile that he showed frequently, despite the setbacks he had suffered. "Caron," a *Tarrytown Daily News* reporter observed, "appeared to be a jolly, good natured fellow and was continually cracking jokes." Upton Sinclair thought him "the most level headed and intelligent chap he had known in a long time." Those who knew him only in passing rarely noticed anything other than this cheery first impression. Trusted comrades observed the other side. To them, he confessed certain details of his past. The stories changed in the telling and retelling, but always they centered around the death of his wife, the loss of his son.

These deeper resentments revealed themselves through his actions. He courted, and even craved, danger. It was a rare protest that did not feature him among the most froward participants. When Craig Sinclair, who had taken a motherly interest in his well-being, warned him against these risks, he had replied, "I made up my mind sometime ago that they would kill me before they got through. I am prepared for whatever happens." Since March, he had been a leader of the I.W.W.'s Conference Committee of the Unemployed and a frequent orator at Anti-Militarist League meetings across the city. More recently, he had spent much of his spare time with the revolutionaries of the Ferrer Center, and even that bunch was sometimes taken aback by his militancy. "His views were far more extreme than mine," claimed Marie Ganz, the woman who had stormed into 26 Broadway threatening to murder Rockefeller Junior. "He was a pronounced anarchist who preached the most extreme views."

Certain themes came up again and again in his speeches. He despised the idea of begging for a reformer's handout. "If you wanted anything," he'd say, "the way to get it was to go and get it." For the authorities, he felt a hatred born of hard experience; nothing pleased him more than provoking an officer of the law. He would point to the men on duty at his rallies and sneer, "When St. Patrick drove the snakes out of Ireland they all came over to America, and from them the breed of policemen were derived." The cops who thrashed him at Union Square had not been acting at random. "Believe me, when they were clubbing me, they were out to get me," Caron explained. "When they caught me with Joe O'Carroll and their clubs began to come down on my head they knew what they were about."

No foe roused in him the kind of hatred that he harbored for the owners of Standard Oil. "'To hell with Rockefeller!' was the sentence on which most of his explosive spirit would spend itself," an audience member recalled. "Caron would flare up till his cheeks and forehead were flaming red upon the theme of Rockefeller." Week after week, he urged himself to escalate the demonstrations. Dissatisfied by Sinclair's pickets at 26 Broadway, he had moved the protest to West Fifty-fourth Street, and then pressed on to Tarrytown itself. "Of all the young men and women who came into public notice during the Union Square riots," a reporter for the *Times* observed, "Caron was noticed for a constantly growing aggressiveness."

But the effort came with a hard private cost. He was hungry and tense. All his emotional and physical stamina poured into his work, and the exertions left him shattered and empty; after making his speeches, he would slink down from the soapbox in exhaustion. His wounds had been poorly tended to and misdiagnosed. In between trips to Tarrytown, he checked himself into Lebanon Hospital, where doctors discovered that his nose was broken and infected from neglect. By late May, Marie Ganz was shocked to find him "wild-eyed, haggard, ragged," and looking "as if he had neither slept nor eaten for days."

CARON HAD PROMISED to return in force to Tarrytown. But days passed, then a week, and nothing came of it. Rockefeller Senior tested out a system of flashing electric lights that would warn him if any trespassers approached, but so far it had not been put to use. Downstate, where New York City was also enjoying a lull from its troubles, the respite allowed the mayor a chance to manage his critics. To hardliners who believed he had given too much leniency to dissent, he had, in advance of the Veracruz memorial, offered some arrests and a tougher stance against provocations. Confronted by those who believed "no night-stick government is needed in New York," Mitchel had hedged. He favored tolerance that stretched only so far: harshness, but only as needed. "While it is necessary sometimes for the police to use a certain amount of force in overcoming violence," he elaborated, "the Police Commissioner and I will stand unalterably against the use of any more force than is absolutely necessary to prevent crime and overcome violence."

Since February, the radical agitation in New York City had adapted and changed emphasis repeatedly. First, there had been Tannenbaum and the unemployed raids on the churches. Berkman and Edelsohn had then shifted the focus to the conflicts in Mexico and Colorado. Finally, Sinclair and Caron had directed these energies at Rockefeller Junior.

Rockefeller's mansion, Kykuit.

The Mitchel administration had responded early on with a persecution that had merely spread the troubles. Taking charge of the police in April, Arthur Woods had attempted more humane methods. But with the Ludlow Massacre occurring just weeks after his regime began, the anger of the demonstrators had not been assuaged by a few signs of tolerance. The mayor had then sought a middle course, one that would not satisfy the radicals but that largely placated his critics among the city's businessmen and newspaper editors.

The success of these maneuvers was shown during Alexander Berkman's latest "monster mass-meeting" at Union Square. When the day came, "the afternoon was balmy, and every bench in the park was occupied. Yet, with all the favorable circumstances, Berkman brought fewer than 200 sympathizers," and the assembly "was a tame affair in which most of those present soon tired of the oratory and yawned back at the speakers." Detectives Gildea and Gegan looked on lethargically, and even Becky Edelsohn made an oration that "was much less radical than on former occasions." Affairs were even more demoralized for the Industrial Workers of the World. Local 179—Tannenbaum's own chapter—had sunk back to its former languor. "About a dozen come to the weekly business meetings now," a member confided to Frank in prison. "The Sunday meetings, held indoors, were so poorly attended as the warm weather came on that we are giving them up."

The moment seemed bleak, but at least the Industrial Workers of the World had people talking. The head worker at the University Settlement, where Caron often stayed, had been impressed by the Wobblies he had seen. "Compared to the Bowery type of hopeless 'down and outs,' the leaders of the I.W.W. are intellectually keen and are even red blooded," he said, "and since their purpose was to get publicity they may be said to have been a 'howling success.'" But with the recent malaise in radical circles, this had become a minority view. "They were after publicity, and they got it," editors at the *Tribune* admitted. "If that is the measure, they were a success. They are the most ingenious self-advertisers in the world, though they have some clever imitators in Upton Sinclair and Bouck White. But aside from self-advertising what did they accomplish?" Victor Berger, the Socialist congressman from Wisconsin, passed through New York and was besieged by questions about the local agitation. "The whole affair is absolutely foolish," he replied. "It has been an instance of fanaticism run mad. There is no reason why the Rockefellers should be afraid. They are being assailed only by some crazy, overheated, excited people, who want to talk their heads off, but who have neither desire nor intention to do anything else."

Bill Haywood was the only one able to move beyond criticism to analysis. In April, Berkman's broadsides had brought thousands of demonstrators to Union Square; a month later, the anarchists were able to draw only a few hundred listless disciples, and Big Bill knew the reason why. "With the clubbing came the converts," he explained, "and after there was no more martyrdom there were no more additions to the ranks." The Jacobins, in other words, could not succeed without an obstinate ancien régime to oppose them.

BY MAY 30, Arthur Caron was through waiting for his permit. With eleven others, including Becky Edelsohn, he took the circuitous ride northward, hopping off the trolley onto Main Street, Tarrytown, around nine P.M. It was Saturday night, but the byways were quiet and mostly empty. The group walked down Orchard Street to Fountain Square, the traditional site over the years for revival meetings and Salvation Army drives, where a few residents were enjoying the warm evening. No one really paid much attention to Caron as he stalked from the sidewalk out into the middle of

Main Street, Tarrytown.

the street, deliberately set up a soapbox, and then stepped on top of it. The others clapped as he rose, to attract attention.

"Did you ever hear the wail of a dying child and the wail of a dying mother?" he cried out. "They were murdered in Colorado while the American flag flew over the tents in which they lived, and the murderer was John D. Rockefeller, Jr., who lives in this—" and, before he could finish his sentence, a police officer dragged him from his perch and into custody. "No sooner did Caron's feet touch the ground," a witness wrote, "than another member of the band stepped up on the box, only to descend even more quickly than Caron, with the assistance of another policeman." Becky was next. She managed to say, "The only thing John D. Rockefeller ever gave away was oil to burn the mothers and babes in Ludlow," and then she too was seized. One and then the next, each anarchist was detained in turn, until all twelve had been arrested. Placed together in two cells, the eleven men immediately made themselves a nuisance. "They began to sing boisterously and kept time by pounding on the iron bars with any implement they could lay their hands on." No one in the neighborhood could get to sleep for hours. "This is a stale joke," remarked Becky when she was led into the little-used women's

Berkman arriving in Tarrytown.

lockup and introduced to her cellmate: She'd be sharing her quarters with the police department chicken.*

Alexander Berkman didn't linger when he learned the fate of Caron's party. Gathering a dozen others with him, he rode north the next morning, May 31, and arrived in Tarrytown at one P.M. Having come to agitate, he had no trouble getting the locals swarming. They awaited him at the train station and chased him with jeers and threats, hustling him ahead whenever he paused. The anarchists ended up wandering for several hours in search of a place to gather. "They kept protesting all the time that they had the right of free speech and intended to exercise it." But onlookers and police had no notion of allowing this. Berkman was chased from Tarrytown to North Tarrytown and back; he and the others were shoved and antagonized. And if a radical answered back, the officers took the chance to tackle, punch, and arrest him. Over the course of

---

* The chicken belonged to one Ned O'Neill, who had recently been arrested; the bird was serving an indeterminate sentence.

Becky Edelsohn under arrest.

the day, three additional anarchists were seized. With his forces dwindling, Berkman called for aid. Twenty more men hurried up on an evening train, but by then the mob had lost patience. Unconstrained by the police, the locals attacked. "What followed," thought a reporter, "looked like a scrimmage between half a dozen football elevens. Men were swept from their feet and kicked and stepped on." It was ten P.M. before the authorities were at last able to calm their own neighbors enough to reinstate some order. Berkman and the others were paraded to the station and forcibly loaded aboard a southbound train.

The village courtroom was hushed and tense when Caron, Edelsohn, and the rest of the original twelve agitators were brought in for their arraignment that evening. Officials had been working for hours on their case; most of the men in town, and all twelve members of the police force, had been on duty for days without a break. Clerks consulted in whispers with attorneys; spectators slumped exhausted across the benches. No one spoke. "This is a solemn occasion," Becky said, breaking the silence. "I would like to borrow a handkerchief from some kind soul to weep on."

"Becky—" called a reporter, with some query.

"My name is not Becky to you," she snapped back. "It's Miss Edelsohn."

The sheriff noticed a book she was carrying—*Beyond Good and*

Evil—and asked who the author was. "It's by a well-known convict," she hissed. And after that, no one else asked her any more questions. When the town justice informed the defendants that they had been charged with "disturbing the peace, blocking traffic and endangering the public health," Miss Edelsohn leaped up in a fury.

"What do you mean charging us with blocking traffic, when you haven't got any traffic in this town to block?" she demanded. "This whole charge is fictitious and a gross lie. There ain't enough people in this town at nine o'clock to block anything. You would have to come here at two o'clock in the afternoon and then you would find half the town asleep." As for the accusation of threatening public safety, she had some choice words on that matter, too. "My God! Endangering lives!" she said, as the court officers swapped nervous looks and shrank into their seats. "You endangered lives of our men by locking six in a cell. And you placed me in a lockup which you used as a chicken coop. Why don't Tarrytown build a hencoop of its own? But we don't expect any better justice in this town, which is owned by John D. Rockefeller."

The defendants refused to have attorneys appointed, demanding to be returned to their cells; they would make the village accommodate them until the trial. The vision of eleven noisy anarchists banging on the bars night and day was not a good one for the sheriff. But the prospect of spending more time with Miss Edelsohn—the "tarter" with "an awful tongue," as a local reporter described her—went far beyond evil. Pleading inadequate accommodations, the police decided to transfer their prisoners to White Plains, the county seat. At midnight, relieved townsfolk watched as five automobiles, carrying the agitators, disappeared down the dark roads and out of sight.

CLUBS HIT HEADS WHEN I.W.W. RAIDS J.D.'S "OWN TOWN" was the big headline in the *World* on the morning of June 1. "Twelve I.W.W. agitators in jail, Alexander Berkman sent back to New York with his gang of anarchists; the whole police force of Tarrytown on continuous duty for twenty-four hours," called the *Sun*. "This, in brief, tells the story of the most riotous night and day this Sleepy Hollow country has ever known." Nearly a century had passed since Washington Irving had chosen this area as the setting for his stories. "A drowsy, dreamy influence," he had written in 1820, "seems to hang over the land, and to pervade the very atmosphere." Since then, the New York Central Railroad tracks had tied the village to the city, and some parts of the main street had been paved with brick. But otherwise, residents liked to think that little had changed. "Our people retain their old Dutch conservatism," the editor of the local newspaper proclaimed. "We are a steady people."

In fact, the countryside had been transformed by arriving "nomads of wealth"—flourishing industrialists in search of a place to homestead. They were drawn by the proximity to Grand Central Station, as well as the area's reputation as "an unwavering Republican stronghold." The Rockefellers had claimed the choicest parcels, but they were joined by Goulds and Beekmans until Tarrytown was believed to be "the home of more millionaires than any other town of its size in America." These families were perceived as generous benefactors—they had dedicated schools, churches, and roads to the community—and now that they were under threat from outsiders, most residents were inclined to repay their generosity. "Public opinion is with Mr. Rockefeller. It has little sympathy with the 'mourners,'" reported the local paper. "No Capitalist that ever lived . . . was ever more of a parasite upon society than this crew of hoodlums and blasphemers who preach a gospel of riot and murder in the name of labor."

Having read for months about the radical uprisings down in the city, the citizenry was primed for panic. "Unrest among the so called Industrial Workers of the World, anarchists, and other kindred organizations has never before been pitched to such fever heat as now," the *Tarrytown Daily News* had recently informed subscribers. "The anarchists have never had fuller sweep in their scope of murderous endeavor in any country or in any city than they are now being given in New York."

Terrified that these ordeals were soon to be visited on their own hometown, the local authorities lost all composure. The police chief swore in fifty deputies and outfitted them with clubs. The fire chief attached hoses to the hydrants, so that water could be pumped onto the protesters. The menfolk promised to tar and feather any outsiders and then dump them in the river. Volunteers watched the roads into town. Observers positioned themselves at the railroad station and the hotels, accosting every stranger who arrived. Paranoid reports of invading Wobblies came from all quarters: Twenty had been seen approaching from the south, they would mob the jails, they were sneaking in one by one. When Berkman suggested that he and his followers would come and slumber outside in Fountain Square, the town disfigured its own streets with a thick coat of asphalt. "They may sleep on that if they care to," a policeman laughed as he surveyed the mess with satisfaction, "but there's no telling when they'll get up."

The radicals responded with threats of their own. Berkman described a regiment of mad anarchists—from the northwestern timberlands, the Rocky Mountain coalfields, the city ghettos—that would march, unstoppable, on Sleepy Hollow. "Threats of bloodshed or ducking do not alarm us," he said. "We have been treated in Tarrytown worse than Russian Cossacks treated serfs. If any one made disorder there it was the police, not our people. The Constitution is greater than any village ordinance, and it guarantees to every man and woman the right of free speech. We mean to have this even if it costs blood and imprisonment and the peace of the Rockefellers." While his army coalesced, he wasted no opportunity to rile the city farmers of Westchester County. In *Mother Earth*, he wrote:

> A tiny village on the Hudson some twenty miles from New York has been placed on the map within the past two weeks and is now as well known as Trinidad, Col. This sleepy little burg is a suburb of one of John D. Rockefeller's estates and hitherto has been known only to commuters from Poughkeepsie and Ossining on their way to New York. The Anarchists and some members of the Ferrer Association have suddenly thrust fame upon this unoffending village by trying to hold meetings under the shadow of the town pump.

The marauding anarchists, and the panicky residents, had brought the village a notoriety it had not wanted. "Tarrytown is the laughing stock of the country today," a local editor complained. "Commuters who go to New York told us last night that they don't dare say they are from Tarrytown. New Yorkers who know them jeer and boo them. It is a pretty spectacle!" From afar, the city papers showed unbecoming glee in seeing another community undergo the troubles with which they had become so familiar. "It is impossible not to sympathize with the people of Tarrytown in their aversion to having their town made the rendezvous and forum of this I.W.W. riffraff," wrote an editor at the *World*. "Everybody has a right to a peaceful life, liberty from noisy mountebanks and the pursuit of sleep—if he can get away with it."

A week earlier, the Mitchel administration's policy of limited tolerance had brought the radical cause to a frustrated impasse. The press had lost interest. Attendance lagged worse and worse at every protest. All of this was now reversed. The anarchists, with the unintended assistance of the Tarrytown authorities, had discovered the perfect platform for their agitations. Only thirty miles north of Union Square—but

The Tarrytown train station.

a world away from the jurisdiction of Commissioner Woods—Arthur Caron had found his Bourbons.

* * *

WORKMEN AT POCANTICO HILLS reported glimpsing "a pale and haggard" Rockefeller on the occasions when he left his father's mansion. The chances to see him were rare; he had hardly strayed more than a few hundred feet from the house in weeks. He had spent years meticulously landscaping the grounds, choosing the fountains and statuary, making the gardens into places of comfort and introspection. With Caron and his threatened anarchist militia expected hourly, that serenity had vanished and the family estate had become a militarized encampment. Four guards, armed with automatic pistols, were stationed at every gate; rifles were stacked and ready in the guardhouse. Sixteen of Tarrytown's new special deputies were posted to Pocantico Hills on rotating twenty-four-hour shifts. Burns detectives loitered in the shadows.

Letters continued to appear, and not all of them offered solicitous encouragement:

You fooled us last Sunday + the Sunday before but you wont fool us much longer we will get you & your father yet Maybe next Sunday in Tarrytown, Yonkers, or wherever you go look out.

I.W.W.

Dear Sir,

I have fully made up my mind to assassinate you . . . As I am an expert rifle shot I guess I can pick you off regardless how many detectives or guards you have around you . . .

Yours, A Sufferer of Capital

These were filed away, or passed on to the Burns investigators. But letters from sympathetic strangers could be just as upsetting. People he had never met offered to commit violence in his cause. Several writers offered unsolicited advice, almost all of it corrupt and repellent. A businessman informed Junior that he was on the verge of purchasing *Century*—"the most influential, and in many respects the greatest, magazine in the country"—and in exchange for Rockefeller financing, he could promise sympathetic coverage of the Colorado events. "There is such tremendous pressure brought on writers just now to inflame class hatred," the author explained, "that it might be worth while to have a big sane organ voice the truth."

Another proposition came from Isaac Russell, the *New York Times* correspondent who had drawn the unwelcome assignment of insinuating himself among the protesters. "As a reporter for the Times," he clarified, apologetically, "I have had, of course, to keep in close touch with all the various groups who have created disorder hereabouts for several months." They, in turn, had come to accept him. Considering Russell a friend and "an honest man," Upton Sinclair had even entrusted him with secret correspondence divulging some of the future plans of the Free Silence League. Now the reporter forwarded this document to Rockefeller. "I have not shown the letter to anyone," Russell wrote to Junior, "and I shall never tell anyone that I have sent it on to you."

After all these months of passively accepting the facts that Bowers presented to him, Junior had finally lost faith in the Colorado executives. He began to cultivate alternate lines of intelligence, receiving telegrams from trusted sources in Denver that gave a more critical view of the operators' actions. But when he tried to go further—to take positive steps toward reform—his colleagues blocked him. They absolutely would not condone anything that could undercut the company's position while the strike persisted. Rockefeller had the idea of sending Raymond B. Fosdick, a researcher for his Bureau of Social Hygiene, to make an unbiased study of living conditions in the mining camps. "I feel quite strongly about this," he insisted, "and hope the idea may commend itself to the rest of you." His jaded subordinates tactfully killed the plan. "My first instinctive reaction was one of doubt as to the wisdom of this suggestion," replied Starr Murphy, his attorney. "I feel that the fight has got to be fought out to a finish. When it is finished, I should cordially favor an investigation and a report with a view to vindicating the Company if the facts justify it, or as furnishing a basis for reforms in future if the report shows changes to be necessary. But that will have to be deferred until the present fight is won."

Of all the unsettling communications he had received, none spoke more closely to his deepest concerns than a note from the secretary of the interior—one of the many officials who had tried, and failed, to convince Junior to step out from behind the actions of his counselors. "I am very sorry," the letter began. "I believe that I have urged you to a course that in the future your conscience and your intelligence will commend as the only wise one. I have spoken to you as your friend: There is no man who can decide for another what his personal course should be. Your ideal of yourself, not as a maker of money but as a doer of good, should determine every time your course of action without respect to what your advisers say." But while Rockefeller was unwilling to ignore the iniquities of business, he was equally unable to intercede against the executives of Colorado Fuel & Iron. He let his integrity dictate his choices, but not to the point where they could affect his father's interests. By refusing to make the hardest decision, he had sentenced himself to an existence of subterfuge and violence. For someone who honored probity and candor above other virtues, this was hardly a life at all.

Which is why it was such a relief to meet Ivy Lee. A southerner just a few years younger than Rockefeller himself, Lee had graduated from Princeton and attended Harvard Law School. He then worked as a reporter in New York before switching careers and revolutionizing the field of corporate publicity. He was currently engaged on a campaign for the Pennsylvania Railroad, but the Rockefeller account was too plummy to pass up. "I feel that my father and I are much misunderstood by the press and the people of this country," Junior said to Lee during an interview on June 4. "I should like to know what your advice would be on how to make

Ivy Lee.

our position clear." Junior had corresponded with several fast-talking public relations men in recent weeks, and he had been perturbed by their
willingness to manipulate and mislead their targeted audiences. Lee, the
drawling gentleman, deprecated the use of lies, or paid advertisements
masquerading as news stories. No publicity, he argued, was ever so effective as the truth. "This," an ecstatic Rockefeller replied, "is the first advice
I have had that does not involve deviousness of one kind or another." Lee
was immediately retained at the fee of a thousand dollars a month.

"Desiring as I do that you should understand some of the ideals by
which I work," Lee wrote to Rockefeller a week later, "I am venturing to
inclose you a manuscript copy of an address I delivered before the American Railway Guild in New York some weeks ago." Lee's speech presented
the outline of his philosophy of public relations. Crowds did not reason, he
argued, but were guided by symbols and stories. There was no point in
offering in-depth statistics, since the majority of Americans would be convinced by a few choice tidbits. Reduced to its simplest expression, he practiced "the art of getting believed in." Strongly denouncing the publication

of outright lies, he suggested a more nuanced approach: "We should see to it that the public learns the truth in all matters, but we should take special pains to see that it learns those facts which show that we are doing our job as best we can, and which will create the idea that we should be believed in. We must get so many good facts, so many illuminating facts, before the public that they will overlook the bad."

Putting these ideas into practice in the coal controversy, he submitted for approval Bulletin No. 1, in what would be a series of weekly pamphlets stating the truth—as Junior wanted it to be. "It is of the utmost importance that every American citizen should understand what has really been going on in Colorado," the publications explained. "The facts have been beclouded with unusual venom." The leaflets were to be "dignified, free from rancor, and based as far as possible upon documentary or other evidence susceptible of proof." Several key passages each week were underlined in black:

In the present issue we are not opposing or waging a war against organized labor as such.

The issue in Colorado has ceased to be, if it ever was, one between capital and labor.

Shall government prevail, or shall anarchy and lawlessness rule?

Junior quickly gave his endorsement, and Lee prepared to distribute the document to a catalogue of "thoughtful people" he had compiled. His list contained eleven thousand entries, including "about 3,500 newspapers, all members of Congress, all members of state legislatures, the mayors of all cities having a population of over 5,000, teachers of economics in colleges, and . . . every one whose name is mentioned in the latest issue of 'Who's Who in America.'" Lee's plan relied on convincing these people. "It is thought that by sending these leaflets to a large number of leaders of public opinion throughout the country," he wrote to Rockefeller, "you will be able to get certain ideas before the makers of that public opinion which will be of value."

But it was not enough to print the truth and then broadcast it widely. The bulletins needed to appear trustworthy. Recipients were not to realize that these reports had been composed by a publicist at 26 Broadway—the pamphlets had to come from somewhere else. "This publicity work on behalf of the operators," Junior wrote to an executive at Colorado Fuel & Iron, "while even more important in the East, as things now are, than in the West, must, of course . . . emanate from Denver. All of the bulletins and other matter which Mr. Lee is suggesting will be mailed from Denver."

And so Rockefeller set out to spread the truth.

*   *   *

UPTON SINCLAIR HAD gone to Denver to get a firsthand view of the strike zone. All it took was a few days in Colorado and he had already been denounced by the governor as a "prevaricator" and an "itinerant investigator." He had also managed to instigate a feud with local journalists as well as the Associated Press. "What next fool thing will Upton Sinclair do to get his name in the newspapers?" asked a reporter for the *Los Angeles Times*. "He comes perilously near being a pest."

Undaunted, he traveled to the mining districts, toured the ruined camps, and talked to anyone who would talk to him. The professionals and society folk he met described their anxieties during the previous months. "It was touch and go—like that!" a lawyer told him, snapping his fingers. "We almost had a revolution." The stories he heard from the miners and their wives kindled in him the same sort of ache he had felt, years earlier, for the workers of Packingtown, in Chicago. Once again he was determined to pressure Rockefeller into admitting his sins. "About a month ago I addressed a letter to you on the subject of the Colorado strike," Sinclair wrote to Junior in late May.

> At that time I had only hearsay evidence concerning the situation; but now I have been upon the scene, and have talked with scores of victims of the crimes that have been committed. I have met a mother who was made a target for militia bullets while she dragged her two children away from the blazing village of Ludlow; another whose three children were left behind to perish in that inferno. It seems to me as if the air I breathed were full of the smoke of powder and the scent of burning human flesh; as if my ears were deafened with the screams of women and children.

Sinclair returned to New York and replaced the defunct Free Silence League with a new organization that operated out of his apartment. Pausing momentarily in his protests, he assisted in a screen adaptation of *The Jungle*. The author was certain that his venture into the movies would be a success, especially since he would be appearing on screen, playing himself, in a sort of prologue to the feature. He was already spending, in his mind, the millions he would earn; it was left for Craig to make sure he did not do so in actuality. The film ended up being banned in Boston, and though it ran for a few weeks in New York City, the company went bankrupt and the Sinclairs never saw a penny.

Catching up on events, he found the city newspapers bursting over the latest agitation. "Edition after edition appeared, each one with new alarms upon the front page," he recalled. "The I.W.W. was marching upon Rockefeller's town from all over the United States! The anarchists were plotting bombs and assassinations! The authorities of Tarrytown had hired fifty special officers, each armed with a hickory club and two loaded revolvers!"

For once, the itinerant investigator hesitated. This frenzy was even greater than the furor over the mourning pickets, and after the scathing abuse he had received during the previous weeks, Sinclair feared to involve himself in Westchester County. "One had to be reckless as to his reputation," he reflected, "when he meddled in that story." Furthermore, he and Craig were destitute and exhausted, and his wife felt they had done their duty. "We had let the public know what was wrong," she argued, "and now surely it was up to the public to protect its own free institutions." But Sinclair could not bear to miss a chance to involve himself. He went to Tarrytown and demanded free speech. When the village authorities refused him the streets, he made them promise to find a private auditorium in which to hold his meeting. The owners of the Union Opera House and the Music Hall refused to rent to the radicals, and so Sinclair enlisted a wealthy village resident—Mrs. C. J. Gould—to let them use her lawn. The *Tarrytown Daily News* attacked him relentlessly, turning on its own local officials anytime they acceded to his requests. But he was no longer willing to play the victim. One morning, the editors of both local newspapers found themselves under arrest: Upton Sinclair had sued them for libel.

On June 6, he traveled to Tarrytown to see the trial of the twelve imprisoned anarchists as a correspondent for the *Appeal to Reason*. Caron, Edelsohn, and the others had spent the previous week in the White Plains jail. "To read the accounts of the arrested agitators, you would have thought they were maniacs or wild beasts," Sinclair wrote. "They howled and made pandemonium in their cells. They cursed and reviled God, and the Pope, and the chief of police of Tarrytown." Facing a year in prison, as well as $500 fines, the anarchists enlisted Justus Sheffield, who had represented Frank Tannenbaum, to conduct their defense. The attorney managed to gain a series of postponements that delayed the trial for a month. In the meantime, Berkman had scrambled to gather money for bail. On June 8 he handed twenty-four hundred-dollar bills to the village officers, and the twelve inmates were released.

"But you can bet we're coming back," Becky informed the spectators who tailed them from the jail to the station. "We are going to show them in Tarrytown that we can hold meetings there in spite of their old police force. We'll answer violence with violence . . . It's a matter of principle now." They rode the Harlem Line down to Morrisania station in the Bronx, where scores of anarchists were waiting to cheer their arrival. Then a rowdy impromptu parade took them to the Ferrer Center, where the freed agitators were greeted to a triumphant welcome.

Nothing so far had occasioned the sort of exposure that the anarchists were earning from their Tarrytown protests. "The most astonishing situation in the history of the United States exists in Pocantico Hills," the *Day Book* of Chicago asserted. "Thirty-six dollars and seventy-five cents have one billion two hundred million eighty-nine thousand dollars surrounded, blockaded and balked . . . John D. Rockefeller, the richest man in the world, and his son, John D., Jr., are today as close prisoners in their estate as are the convicts in Ossining penitentiary."

The standoff made headlines in the *Fort Worth Star-Telegram*, the *Olympia Daily Recorder*, and the *Aberdeen Daily News*, leading to a national debate over civil liberties. "The right of free speech is guaranteed under the constitution," an editor at the *Grand Forks Herald* conceded, before continuing on to say, "but there is another right that is inalienable, and that is the right of silence. If a man enters your house and wants to talk to you, and you do not want to hear him, you tell him so." While few went so far as to cheer the anarchists, there were observers everywhere who demanded they be given an opportunity to express themselves. "What these spouters were and what they spouted is immaterial," argued a writer for the *Memphis Commercial Appeal*. "They may be either fools or patriots; they may be forgotten tomorrow or have statues erected to their memory a hundred years hence. The important fact is that they have been denied their rights."

For Arthur Caron personally, none of the publicity was more satisfying than an article Sinclair had written for the June 20 issue of the *Appeal to Reason*. The author described a vaguely familiar person: a young man who had happened to be in Union Square in April, when he had witnessed the cops attacking some protesters. "He was a boy with no idea whatever about radical matters," Sinclair explained. "He had neither read nor thought about the class war. But he saw this outrage and from pure human sympathy rushed forward, crying out in protest. Instantly two policemen fell upon him, and began to club him. They did not stop until they had laid him out insensible. They broke his nose; and they also opened his eyes." This character, naturally, was Arthur Caron himself, or at least the version Sinclair had chosen to see. Despite all his empathy, the author was an appalling failure at judging others. But even for him, this characterization of his fellow radical as a naïve youth was absurd. "Caron told me that he did not know whether he was an anarchist or Socialist," Sinclair continued, "because he had had no time to find out what either meant." For the actual Caron, the episode was an absolute joke. He carried the article in his pocket when he attended protest meetings and showed it around to his comrades, laughing at the portrayal.

TWO WEEKS HAD passed since the prisoners had left the White Plains jail and returned as heroes to New York. Their trial had been rescheduled for early July, and the village police assumed that was when the next demonstration would occur. The new tar in Fountain Square had dried. The deputy policemen had returned to their civilian jobs. There had been so many false reports that nobody took seriously the dispatch on June 22 that the agitators were coming. But when the six P.M. local from Grand Central arrived at Tarrytown station, eighteen radicals stepped down onto the platform. At first they loitered, seemingly without a plan, but then the 8:20 train arrived and another forty or so disembarked. No more hesitation. The sixty anarchists marched with swift strides up Main Street, singing "The Marseillaise" and gathering a following of vengeful residents.

"Like the minute men of '76," a reporter wrote, "Tarrytown's harassed villagers went forth to repel the foe." A crowd of five hundred men trailed the demonstration as it turned left on Broadway, passed the village president's flower shop, and then veered again onto McKeel Avenue. There they paused in front of a narrow strip of lawn that formed the right-of-way for the old Croton Aqueduct. Technically, this was New York City property, and it was here that the anarchists intended—at last—to hold their meeting. The mob around them knotted tighter, an enraged semicircle, with a band of automobiles forming the outer ring. Berkman grabbed a soapbox and positioned it under the glow of an arc lamp. When he climbed on top of it, the chief of police shoved him down, but then another anarchist leapt up and the outnumbered officer hurried off for reinforcements.

Becky Edelsohn was the first to try and speak. She rose and held up a hand for silence, which prompted a chorus of jeers.

"You cowards!" she cried. "You curs!" A man in the front of the throng hurled sand in her face. Then a second handful hit her in the mouth, and she choked. And finally dirt was heaped on her from three sides, and Berkman had to hold his hat in front of her eyes to protect her. "She held her place for twenty minutes," a witness wrote, "and made a plucky fight against the hoots of the crowd and the charge of sand and sod thrown at her." When she stepped aside, at 9 P.M., Berkman himself took her place on the platform. The mob had reserved their best ammunition for this moment. "We demand the right of free—" was as far as he could get before a squall of rotten eggs, cabbage, and tomatoes flew toward him. Sods of dirt struck his face and yolks covered his clothing and ran down into his collar as a stone knocked him down from his perch into the arms of his comrades.

Then Arthur Caron stepped up. The halo from the street lamp marked him out against the night, while his persecutors all were masked by darkness. As he spoke, the taunts resumed in even greater torrents. "Caron has a strong voice," a reporter for the *Tarrytown Daily News* observed, "and when he began shouting the jeers of the crowd could hardly drown his voice so the owners of automobiles, which were stopped in the street, began tooting their horns and the din could be heard blocks away."

"I was born on American soil," he began.

"How do you like this soil?" came the response, as a sod clump struck his mouth. "This marked the beginning of a bombardment," a newspaperman wrote. "From every part of the crowd came missiles. There were eggs, many of them; stones, vegetables, clods of dirt, sticks, and uprooted sod." The police stood by, making no effort to intercede.

"I have Indian blood in my veins," Caron shouted in the midst of the onslaught, "and you cowards who are throwing this dirt are traitors to the flag." At that moment, a stick smacked him in the jaw, broadside on. Bleeding from his mouth, livid, he continued defying the mob until Berkman and the others dragged him—unwilling, resistant—from the box. They had accomplished their goal of bringing free speech to Tarrytown, in spite of itself, and now it was time to get out. The anarchists filed from the aqueduct property and headed for the station, while the police strained to hold off the throng. "We want Berkman!" they cried. "Let us have him!" "Lynch Berkman!" It took only a moment for the mob to loose themselves from restraint. One concerted rush bowled over both the anarchists and the police. "The Crowd swarmed around like bees." A passing trolley had its windows smashed. Berkman was separated from the rest, pinned against a wall, and beaten until the cops came to his aid. Then he and the others were all hustled down the hill to the station.

Hundreds of rioters packed the platforms and filled the nearby streets; passing trains skulked by to avoid the spectators who spilled out onto the tracks. Finally, the 10:50 southbound local crept up to the far end of the platform, and two rows of policemen, with clubs drawn, faced down the onlookers while other officers shoved the anarchists into the smoking coach.

"Go back to New York where you belong," the locals crowed.

"We'll be back again," shouted Becky, still defiant, as the locomotive jolted forward.

Then they were in the quiet of the car. Berkman's clothes were torn and ruined, his face smudged with dirt. Becky's eyes were red and swollen from the sand, her dress "a yellow Niagara" of egg drippings. "Caron was the most severely injured," a reporter wrote. "His jaw was badly cut and his lips were so swollen he could hardly talk."

THE NEXT MORNING, some were in the mood to gloat. "The anarchists who have been howling for any opportunity to air their views in Tarrytown had an educational experience when they took the police by surprise on Monday night," editorialized the *Sun*. "They succeeded in coming face to face with the plain people and they learned exactly what the plain people thought of them." But a writer for the *Times* better understood what he had witnessed. Most previous demonstrations had merely "defied John D. Rockefeller, Jr." Some had called "for a peaceful agitation for free speech, others for a radical movement, but the leaders usually were restrained from going as far as they liked." This latest escalation by the anarchists represented something new. There could be no reconciliation after such a battle.

Safe and Sane

Returning from work on the evening of June 22, inhabitants of New York's Lower East Side discovered a pamphlet with the words FOR YOU on the cover awaiting them at home. Inside, the pages were filled with practical tips for better tenement living:

Don't Throw Things Out the Windows.

The man who bathes every day works better, and can earn more money than the man who doesn't.

DON'T PUT THINGS DOWN THE TOILET. Use it only for what it is intended.

DON'T KEEP LODGERS. If you are keeping lodgers get rid of them as soon as you can.

The Police are Your Friends.

YOU CAN COMPLAIN if there are bad women in the house who entertain many men callers in their flat and who make their living in an immoral way.

Don't spit on the floors.

A back page featured a photograph of a Tenement House Commission inspector in full uniform. "The inspector is your friend," explained the accompanying text. "He is paid by the city to help you to have right conditions to live in . . . If you hinder him or do not tell him what is wrong, it is your own fault if the house is not fit to live in."

Moralizing tracts had been common for years, but unlike most previous broadsides, "For You" was printed and disbursed by a municipal agency—the Tenement House Commission—instead of by a private philanthropy. Tammany mayors had left uplift to others; Mitchel and his aides held the opposite belief, that "the greatest social worker of them all should be the government of the city." The pamphlet, which experts hoped would eventually reach every poor family in the metropolis, was a modest preliminary advance toward an essential shift in the relationship between authorities and citizens. Residents would find their elected officials taking an ever greater interest in the details of their lives. The booklets were a prelude of intrusions to come.

And this was only one of the initiatives taking tangible shape in New York. After six months in office, Mitchel and his cabinet leaders were advancing their plans in every field. Katharine B. Davis had filed a proposal to expand the city's correction facilities by constructing a "skyscraper jail" for women in Manhattan, as well as a Disciplinary Building on Riker's Island that could quarantine anarchists and other troublemakers from the common inmates. Commissioner Kingsbury's indignation had not diminished since his first days on the job. Investigating municipal clinics, he had discovered "shocking conditions of overcrowding": Sick patients were sleeping on benches and stone floors, and in one hospital he had ordered the immediate termination of the entire executive staff. Arthur Woods had reorganized the Detective Bureau, bringing back a "plain clothes patrol system" much like the one he had developed in the previous decade under Commissioner Bingham.

With these reforms in progress, Mayor Mitchel turned his attention to the looming crisis of Independence Day.

THE CARNAGE OF the holiday was proverbial. *Life* magazine's "Fourth-of-July" lexicon, published in late June, hinted at the state of affairs:

ORATION — A disclosure as to the identity of the greatest, grandest, biggest, noblest, finest country on earth.

PARADE — A line of patriots, banners, small boys and canines filling in the space between one Sousa march and another.

AMBULANCE — A vehicle for the transportation of the scraps and remnants of Master Willie and Little Harold on the Fourth of July.

FINGER — A fragment of small boy used as a projectile for a toy cannon.

Since 1903, when the *Journal of the American Medical Association* began keeping statistics, celebrations of the Glorious Fourth had claimed a calamitous toll. In that time, firecrackers, Roman candles, skyrockets, and pistols had killed nearly two thousand people and wounded another forty thousand more. Infected lacerations led to "patriotic tetanus"; stray bullets felled unlucky bystanders; little boys lost fingers, or eyes, to defective fuses; small girls were immolated when their dresses caught fire. What was supposed to be a national celebration of higher purpose had deteriorated into an "annual carnival of noise, smoke, and bloodshed."

There was once a time, respectable New Yorkers imagined, when things had been different. The "Old-Fashioned Fourth" had been a country affair, with the village green packed with heavy-laden tables, and orators who could really make the eagle scream. These simple joys had been sacrificed to the cities, where the laboring masses—foreigners, for the most part, unfamiliar with American customs—used the holiday as an excuse for lawless rioting. By the 1890s, "going away for the Fourth" had become axiomatic; wealthy families fled the crowds, and the holiday found the prosperous districts deserted. Each year it was the same. "There was more or less biff, zipp, sputter, and bang all over the city from early morning until late at night," a reporter wrote around the turn of the century. Animals panicked at the noise; humans coped by stuffing their ears with cotton. After a particularly lawless rendition, the *Times* editors complained, "A bombardment could scarcely have had a more disastrous effect in shattering the nerves of nervous people."

At last, a countrywide agitation arose to reclaim the nation's birthday. Endorsed by such luminaries as John D. Rockefeller and ex-president Taft, the Safe and Sane movement grew into a great campaign, with a national organization and steering committees in every state. To prevent injuries and restore order was only part of the point of these efforts. "Quite aside from the matter of safety," explained writers at the *American*

The Safe and Sane July 4 offered reformers yet another way to improve society.

City, "a saner method of commemorating our Independence Day has become necessary because of the coming of the nations into our life." The holiday could become an educational tool to inculcate immigrants with native traditions. Promoting a revival of the "Old-Fashioned Fourth," the reformers replaced explosions with concerts, speeches, and athletic competitions. Women's clubs and civic societies promoted the idea. A two-act play toured theaters, and *The Sane Fourth,* a film that dramatized the fireworks evil, was "doing well over the whole moving-picture circuit."

Twenty cities held Safe and Sane celebrations in 1909; two years later, the number had risen to 161. Cleveland, Saratoga, Providence, Racine, Tacoma all sponsored their own versions. The future seemed promising, but after decades of experience with similar crusades, activists tempered their optimism. "We are not sanguine of a sudden reform," one proponent cautioned. "The surreptitious revolver, cannon cracker, and dynamite torpedo will explode as of yore. But as ordered observances and spectacles come to replace the old anarchic celebrations the casualties will yearly grow less."

From 1907 to 1909, New York City suffered 1,339 injuries and deaths from fireworks on the Fourth, a higher toll, reformers liked to point out, than was taken "in the Revolutionary battles of Lexington, Bunker Hill, Fort Moultrie, White Plains, Fort Washington, Monmouth and Cowpens combined." In 1910, the butcher's bill in New York totaled five dead and ninety-seven injured. The next year, when Safe and Sane measures were finally instituted in the metropolis, the numbers began to decline—and since then, the city had passed through the holiday without a single fatality.

In early June, Mitchel named a Fourth of July citizens committee, which set to work planning the festivities. "In place of bombs, cannon crackers and skyrockets," the newspapers predicted, "the coming Independence Day celebration will be the 'safest and sanest' in the history of this city." Parks in every borough were to host baseball games and gymnastics exhibitions; musical performances were scheduled throughout the day. An airplane race would career around the circumference of Manhattan. And once the sun went down, the traditional fireworks would be replaced by a fantasia of illumination—as bright as a million candles. "The City Hall will be ablaze with electric lights," the organizers promised, "and altogether as lurid as some Arabian Night's dream."

Despite the plans for a "safe and ultra sane" holiday, the city's well-to-do residents still intended to leave town as usual. The New York Central Railroad offered discount two-dollar fares to the Adirondacks and Green Mountains. On June 24, John D. Rockefeller, Jr., and his family had fled Tarrytown for their summer home in Seal Harbor, Maine. The anarchists, too, had planned a daylong excursion to Leonard Abbott's country home in New Jersey.

As Independence Day approached, the multitudes who chose to stay in the city prepared for an uplifting celebration. "A noiseless Fourth—and for New York—tut, tut!" the chairman of the committee said. "We are only going to show them that a Fourth of July celebration can be a noisy affair without the assistance of gunpowder and squibs." By July 3, the preparations were complete. All the lights had been tested. Police detectives thwarted an eleventh-hour effort by fireworks dealers to smuggle their wares into the city. Only one thing was left. A final order issued from City Hall: "Show your flags!"

8.

His Own Medicine

The sliver of moon had set and midnight was long past when four men turned from 103rd Street onto Lexington Avenue. Treading the timber planks over an unfinished subway ditch, they entered a shabby yellow-brick tenement. Under the bare bulb in the vestibule. Up six dark flights of stairs. Careful, careful with the package. They crept inside apartment 34 and dropped into bed, two to a mattress, falling asleep without bothering to undress. It was the dark before dawn: Saturday, July 4, 1914.

A few hours later, at daybreak, cannon flashed from the battery in Lower Manhattan as the city saluted the Glorious Fourth for the 138th time. The report from the guns was the only explosion people expected to hear; the Safe and Sane holiday meant fireworks and combustibles were forbidden.

By seven A.M., many residents of 1626 Lexington Avenue—"one of the human rookeries characteristic of the Upper East Side"—were up and doing. Doors scraped. Murmured discussions drifted into the corridors. Feet pounded down the stairs and out into the street as early-rising families set off on long streetcar rides to Coney Island or Brighton Beach. Others planned picnics in Central Park, a few blocks away. In apartment 34, Louise Berger woke first and fixed breakfast. Feeing ill the previous night, she had been asleep when the men had come home. She sat alone eating at the table, careful not to make a noise while the others rested. As she finished, they began to stir. For one of them, Arthur Caron, it had been another restless night. With no home or family in the area, he stayed with comrades or at settlement houses. The White Plains jail, where he had recently spent a week, was the closest thing he had to a fixed address. To a swollen nose, he had now added a gash across his mouth—a gift from the Tarrytown mobs. Louise offered him coffee, but he refused. Needing respite above all else, he rose from his pallet on the parlor floor and lay back down in her recently vacated bed.

Eight A.M. The chilling nights of a few months earlier were a cold memory on this sunny morning, which was quickly maturing into a cool, clear day. "There was a fine tang in the air," a reporter wrote, "and the sky was as blue as the field that holds our forty-eight stars." Expecting a thousand dignitaries to hear the mayor's Independence Day oration, the staff in City Hall Park draped pennants and rowed folding chairs on a temporary grandstand. As they worked, a red auto braked to a halt; Mitchel sprang from the backseat and bounded into his office.

At nine A.M., a band struck up in Lincoln Square, on Manhattan's west side. The Safe and Sane celebration had begun. Almost every neighborhood had its own rally planned: In Harlem, Riverdale, and on the Lower East Side, recent immigrants would parade their patriotism. The Tammany Hall Wigwam, the organization's headquarters near Union Square, would be the site of denunciations of the mayor and his policies. And even the radicals had plans. Although, as an anarchist told a reporter, "we do not celebrate the Fourth the way you do," they had nevertheless scheduled a picnic for the afternoon.

Nothing, however, was scheduled for Fifth Avenue. Tradesmen and maids would keep busy there, but most of the grand homes in midtown were deserted, their masters having escaped the holiday festivities for vacations at Lake Placid or the Jersey Shore. Rockefeller Senior, four days from his seventy-fifth birthday, was in Tarrytown. Armed guards, high fences, and pretentious gates kept outsiders away. Junior was at his summer home in Maine's Seal Harbor. There had been talk that the anarchists would follow him even here, and detectives monitored all boats docking on Mount Desert Island, watching for suspicious strangers.

SINCE HIS RELEASE from jail, Caron's anger had grown ever more manifest. Formerly, he had kidded with comrades, sought good company, laughed easily. That part of his personality had retreated. He grew gaunt and solemn, his disfigurement only adding to the impression of brooding violence. "He looked half-starved," Marie Ganz recalled, "his cheeks sunken, his eyes glittering feverishly. When he spoke his voice was hoarse and rasping." A friend invited him for coffee. "No," he replied. "I'm too busy with something very important." His features were set "very tense." In just two days, on July 6, his trial in Westchester County was scheduled to begin, and he expected no clemency from the courts in Rockefeller's demesne.

On the night of July 3, he had attended a meeting at the Ferrer Center to discuss defense strategies. While the adults talked upstairs, youths watched the doors below, making sure no strangers entered the building. Around midnight, the conclave disbanded. Caron, Charles Berg, who had also been imprisoned in Tarrytown, Carl Hanson, a Latvian anarchist, and Mike Murphy, an I.W.W. member from the West who had just arrived in town, then met for a more intimate session at a nearby saloon. Berkman talked with them there for nearly an hour. Then, around one in the morning, he had retired and the others went their own way. Taking a small package, they traveled to Tarrytown one more time. Something on that journey had not gone as planned, because hours later, when they returned to the Lexington Avenue apartment, they still carried the bundle with them.

Having stayed up, they were now lying in. That afternoon, they planned to ride the trolley to Hastings and then take a train to New Jersey, where Leonard Abbott was hosting a picnic. Around nine A.M., they were all settled back into their beds and seemed to be asleep. Louise Berger stole quietly out to the hallway and descended the stairs. She stepped down onto the busy holiday avenue and turned uptown toward Berkman's house on 119th Street. Streetcars brimmed with summer families. Workaday cares had receded and the neighborhood was relaxing industriously. A cloudless sky stretched from Georgia to Maine. The morning weather "couldn't have been more satisfactory if it had been made and provided for by act of Congress or Presidential proclamation."

Twenty minutes passed.

Then, a thunderburst.

The roof of 1626 Lexington Avenue evaporated. Powdered stone, shivered joists, and collops of flesh clouded for a stroke of time and then rained down on the suddenly fleeing, screaming crowd. Sharded glass hailed into the street. The concussion busted windows for two hundred yards in all directions; in their apartments, people were blown off chairs, smashed into stoves, vaulted into bathtubs. A patrolman on the beat was knocked to the pavement; fearing the subway tunnel had exploded, he staggered to a telephone box and called for aid. The top half of the building's south side shivered, avalanched violently, and took minutes to finally settle. One person was hurled through a wall or window. He

1626 Lexington Avenue.

tumbled with the collapsing façade and then hung from the iron balusters of a fire escape. "The back of his head was badly shattered and the bones of his arms and legs were broken." The corpse remained suspended, doubled over, above the street. Another body atomized. Scraps of torso flew onto the rooftop of a neighboring church. A leg flopped between the Lexington Avenue streetcar lines.

In a stunned pause, survivors could hear the victims. "From inside the house came the screams of women and children, and scores of persons with bleeding faces came running out of the hallway and clambered over the sunken tiles of the sidewalk." One man had the mattress he was sleeping on crash down through the floor beneath him. Scratched and dazed, he found himself "looking up through a network of beams and mortar to the sky." On the street, police took him to the nearest precinct, gave him an overcoat, and moved him along. As residents poured out, rescuers ran in, shouldering up the blind stairwells. Trapped voices pleaded for attention. "Forms could be seen lying under beds, broken furniture and debris." Coroner's physicians, building inspectors, and a fleet of ambulances hurried to the site. The death toll, they feared, would be appalling. Firefighters banked ladders against the walls to scale the higher floors, while officers from six districts cordoned off a dozen blocks, holding back the terrified crowds.

Commissioner Woods arrived half an hour after the detonation. Noting how the wreckage cascaded down from the roof toward the street, he saw immediately that the blast had not come from the subway but from an upper level of the tenement. Perhaps a gas line had exploded. As Woods watched, rescuers disentangled the dangling body from the fire escape and carted it to the 104th Street precinct. The corridors of the old brick precinct house were jammed with displaced tenants. "Half the refugees were only thinly clad, and all were hysterical. Men, women and children, crying, and at times fainting, crowded the reserves' quarters of the station." Officers shoved through, carrying the corpse down to the basement cell block and stretching it long on a low cot. Newsmen watched the police rifle its clothes, searching for identification. From an inside coat pocket, they took a little morocco address book. On the flyleaf they found a name: Arthur Caron.

"Isn't that the I.W.W. fellow who has been leading the demonstrations against Mr. Rockefeller?" one of the reporters asked. "It looks like him." A deputy commissioner had just entered the room. Hearing this, he abandoned the idea of a utilities accident and dispatched detectives to gather up all known anarchists in New York City.

As police scattered across the boroughs, the department's combustibles expert arrived at Lexington Avenue. "There is no doubt in my mind," he said after a brief inspection, "that this explosion was caused by a large quantity of dynamite." Since TNT detonates downward, and the worst destruction was near the roof, he concluded that the touch point had been on the top floor. The subway tunnel had merely collapsed from the force of the raining debris. "The only possible conclusion," he declared, "is that some one was making, or was going to make, high explosive bombs."

When detectives arrived at Berkman's house, he and Louise Berger had already learned of the accident. She couldn't talk; she could barely walk. They carried her to the station. Authorities already had a firm identification, but they took their grieving suspects to the basement anyway. When an officer pulled back the blanket from Caron's head, Louise "strained forward, her mouth open and eyes glazed. She tried vainly to speak, but made only inarticulate murmurs, and then, jumping away from those who held her, she swooned." Seeing the mangled corpse, even Berkman pulled a "yellow face."

Back upstairs, facing a deputy commissioner and an assistant district attorney across an interrogator's desk, Berkman was "cool and collected" once more.

"Did you discuss the possibility of taking action of a violent sort against any one?" they asked him.

"Most assuredly not. It was simply a meeting to discuss the defense of the prisoners and those who are out on bail."

"Was there any talk of bombs?"

"No, of course not."

"Did you know there were any explosives in the apartment occupied by Caron and the others?"

"I did not, and do not know it yet."

"You are a very discreet man, Mr. Berkman," the commissioner acknowledged, and the anarchist bowed.

Reporters found Upton Sinclair in his apartment. "For God's sake!" he exclaimed when they told him. "I don't know what to think. What can I say?" He had considered Caron a disciple, and had convinced himself, despite all evidence, that the younger man had shared his commitment to pacifism. "He had been up here to see me and my wife and he assured us that he would follow the peaceful method," Sinclair said. "If I thought he was planning anything like force I would have had nothing to do with him."

Becky Edelsohn and fifty or so other friends of the Ferrer Center were relaxing at Leonard Abbott's picnic, drinking beer and eating corned beef and tongue sandwiches. A newspaperman arrived with news of the explosion. The guests "discussed the tragedy animatedly among themselves," the reporter wrote, "but when approached for an expression of opinion they became silent and declined to say a word." The moment required discretion. "Everyone was hushed," one picnicgoer recalled. "There was an undercurrent of excitement. No one knew what to say. Besides, we knew that there were spies among us."

The anarchists got a firsthand account of what had happened later that day, when Mike Murphy, bruised and in a borrowed coat, staggered out to New Jersey. He had been the person whose mattress had fallen through the floor of apartment 34. The police had let him go because at the time they had still believed the explosion had originated in the subway tunnels. Berkman had sent him to Leonard Abbott's house, and from there he disappeared.

THE TURNOUT AT City Hall had been disappointing. Most of the thousand seats reserved for dignitaries still sat empty at ten A.M., so what crowd there was had been allowed to fill them. A fife and drum corps emerged from the building, followed by four Sons of the American Revolution, dressed in the uniforms of the Continental Army. Mitchel appeared last, wearing a boutonniere of red, white, and blue posies. "We need no longer pay tribute to the democratic ideals of the founders of this country, with tongue in cheek or shame in our hearts," he said. "The city is free for the work of the city. We have lifted the grasping hands of selfish, little hearted men off the levers of our governmental machinery and have set about the business of preparing this great government for a new measure of productivity."

Mitchel then packed into his red car and dashed off to East Forty-sixth Street, where he spoke to the League of Foreign Born Citizens. Thousands of listeners, "all distinctly not of American ancestry," cheered "as American patriotism and freedom were upheld." Next, he was off to Brooklyn. By the early afternoon, athletic contests busied parks and sandlots around the city. Band concerts crowded the air with ragtime. Residents of the Colored Orphan Asylum and the Howard Industrial School listened to encouraging speeches.

At three P.M., policemen at the 104th Street station finally carried Arthur Caron's body to the morgue. On Liberty Island at the same moment, a starter's gun went off and an airplane spiraled to altitude, five hundred feet above the water. A few minutes later, a second racer climbed into the air. The contestants flew north over the Hudson. "From the Battery across Manhattan to Spuyten Duyvil gaping thousands with faces turned toward the sky lined the waterfront and cheered." The race covered a thirty-six-mile course, which the winner completed in forty-three minutes.

In Tarrytown, news of the explosion panicked an already anxious community. Two officers watched the train station for outsiders. "Pocantico Hills, always thoroughly guarded, was policed to the last inch as soon as news of the explosion reached there," wrote a reporter for the *Sun*. "A mouse would have had a hard time getting past the guards without a challenge." The Rockefellers' "small army" of detectives was supplemented by deputy sheriffs at the main gate. "They are quick to see and interpret callers. No one is admitted unless he is a friend of the family and can show credentials."

In Philadelphia's Independence Square, President Woodrow Wilson gave a history lecture. "The Declaration of Independence is not a Fourth of July oration," he informed the crowd. "The Declaration of Independence was a document preliminary to war. It involved a vital piece of business, not a piece of rhetoric." Pounding the very desk on which the document had been signed, he said, "Popularity is not always successful patriotism. The most patriotic man is sometimes the man who goes in the direction in which he thinks he is right, whether or not he thinks anybody agrees with him, because it is patriotic to sacrifice yourself if you think you are right."

While the president spoke, another sacrifice was honored. At Artstetten Castle in Austria, attendants carried an archduke and his wife, slain six days earlier in Sarajevo, between a line of soldiers and interred their coffins in the ancient vault. Franz Ferdinand's assassin had been a Slavic nationalist, not an anarchist, but his act had found admirers among the radicals in New York, who mourned not for the militarist heir to the Austro-Hungarian throne. "He would have practiced a million-fold the assassination that he suffered," Berkman wrote in *Mother Earth*. "He had to swallow his own medicine—that's all."

As night fell, New Yorkers strolled the parks, marveling at the display of electric lights. At City Hall, an illuminated baton kept time as thousands sang "Yankee Doodle" and "My Old Kentucky Home." Onlookers on Lexington Avenue pressed against the police lines at both ends of the block. During the day more than one hundred thousand spectators had visited the scene. As the last light faded, they watched inspectors emerge from the building "carrying grewsome bundles wrapped in newspapers." Detectives searching for clues inside discovered a hand press and some bulletins. "Why wait longer for these money tyrants to come to our terms?" one broadsheet proclaimed. "We must employ force. Force is our remedy." It had been the most powerful dynamite explosion in city history, yet because so many families had left their apartments early to celebrate the holiday, the casualties had been miraculously light. So far, police had found only three bodies in the apartment. A next-door neighbor, Marie Chavez, had also been killed. A fifth person was still missing.

July 5 was a new morning in New York. Early editions arrived at newsstands before dawn; in every paper, the screaming headlines announced that the bomb, which had accidentally detonated too early,

City Hall illuminated.

had been meant for the Rockefellers. The explosion was being called a "sensation such as has not been known before in many months." Ever since the beginning of the year, the city had been arguing amongst itself, debating, among many things, the ties between militant speech and actual violence. For the moment, that question appeared to be settled. Officials declared "that the city was perhaps on the eve of a reign of terror such as culminated in the Haymarket riots in Chicago in the 80's." As residents reckoned with the damage that had been done—and contemplated what could have happened if the bomb had been properly constructed—most concluded that this result had been the inevitable consequence of all the unrest that had come before.

Each faction then had to decide its own response. The anarchists remained adamant in their protests, telling reporters that "Caron's death won't end it." Berkman was considering plans for a mass funeral for his martyrs. Most others sought to distance themselves from the victims. The I.W.W. denied involvement and repudiated the claims that any of the victims had been members of the One Big Union. Mayor Mitchel ordered Woods to step up the surveillance and infiltration of radicals. Across New York, anxious minds were contemplating their futures in light of the explosion. But in the morgue at Bellevue Hospital, Arthur Caron's sleepless nights were over.

* * *

ON BLACKWELL'S ISLAND, the Fourth of July began like every other day—with the prison bell bawling before sunrise. Frank Tannenbaum stirred on the cot in his blank cell. Three months inside had hardened him to the raspy, unwashed clothes, the stench from the toilet bucket, the bed-bugs and lice. Approaching in the corridor, he heard clanking keys, and then the keeper arrived, beating the walls with his baton and calling every-body up. The doors opened and the prisoners hustled out, jostling to get toward the front of a ragged column for the washroom, and then break-fast. It was Saturday, the least pleasant period in the penitentiary. Toiling in the trade shops was tedious, routine work, but at least it passed the time. On the weekend, with no exercise or recreation, the hours spanned out interminably. The toilet pails would not be emptied till Monday, and the air would be befouled, unbearable, long before then.

At other jails, some special provisions were being made for the Fourth. Inside the Tombs, guards played a phonograph for the male inmates and even allowed the women to dance in the corridors. On Blackwell's Island, in former years, the prisoners had been allowed to celebrate the holiday with parades and parties. But Commissioner Davis had canceled that tradition. The men felt wronged. All day their frustra-tions grew; restive complaints came from all sides, scuffles erupted in the suffocating cells.

But Frank, at least, was grateful for the long, quiet hours and the chance to pursue his reading. Having begun with books strictly related to anarchism, he had since graduated to a more general course of study: literature, history, sociology, voraciously consuming everything he could. Carlyle's *French Revolution*, Gibbon's *Decline and Fall of the Roman Empire*, Herbert Spencer's *Education*, the novels of Tolstoy, whatever his support-ers could send him. He spent so many hours squinting over the pages, with only a flickering lightbulb for illumination, that his sight had begun to fail. Comrades had seen too many imprisoned Wobblies go through this same ordeal. "Giovanetti's eyes were ruined in prison," an I.W.W. leader had written him in late May, "and I do not mean the same thing to happen to you."

With the new glasses that supporters had sent him, Tannenbaum was better able to read his daily letters. Unemployment was not so bad as it had been during the winter months, but many people remained out of work, and even his most optimistic correspondents could report only that "industrial conditions are slightly improving." News of the move-ment arrived in snippets and asides; through his mail, Frank heard of the Ludlow Massacre and the protests against the Rockefellers. Since his incarceration, the Wobblies themselves had been eclipsed by the an-archists. And though the daily press was heedless of the distinction, the activists themselves were acutely alive to sectarian splits. "I hope that you will bear in mind that the I.W.W. is not an anarchist group but an organization," wrote Jane Roulston, a schoolteacher and Wobbly with pronounced doctrinaire views. "I.W.W. principles have kept us from taking part in the not very *scientific* actions which have taken place in New York City, and vicinity, since you left," Roulston continued. "But we feel much sympathy for the actors in those affairs—knowing them to be driven desperate by the horrors of the capitalist regime."

Supper passed without incident that evening, though inmates were still smarting from the injustice of missing the holiday. When the lights were put out at nine P.M., Tannenbaum and the others in his ward bedded down. But in a different wing the day's anger finally broke through. There the prisoners could hear the sounds of the Safe and Sane holiday; music and cheering drifted out across the East River, a teasing reminder of their own exile. The men responded with a concert of their own— whistling, calling out, rapping the bars—and didn't quiet down until Warden Hayes appeared. Typically, one or two ringleaders might have been given a reprimand, but this time every single person in the cell block was punished, their privileges stopped indefinitely: no mail, no visitors, no tobacco.

The next week was tense and tetchy. Attendants and prisoners eyed each other, waiting for the next confrontation. It was nearly supper time a few days later, and Tannenbaum was marching toward the mess hall, when he heard the sounds of riot. Meals were supposed to be taken in total silence: Anyone who spoke risked a thrashing from the guards who patrolled the tables. A few moments earlier, a keeper had moved to punish a whispering inmate. He had raised his baton to strike, but before he could land his blow, a metal dish flew at his head. Loosed after so much pent-up fury, dinner plates began to volley in from everywhere. By the time Tannenbaum arrived with the second supper shift, the battle was at its climax. From outside, he watched the pandemonium unfold. Hundreds of prisoners, in their gray work clothes, were standing on the tables, shouting down at their oppressors, cursing and skimming their bowls into the air. The officers were in open rout, running for the doors, shielding their faces as best they could from the flying projectiles, tripping over themselves in their rush to escape.

Panicked guards scrambled out to where Tannenbaum stood and locked the doors behind them. One aimed his gun at Frank—hand shaking wildly—threatening to level him if he moved. Others fired their revolvers in the air until the defiance wilted, and the quieted men filed out and returned to their cells. For this disturbance, the warden again retaliated with an extreme decision—putting everyone in the mess hall on lockdown. The measure was too harsh; prisoners throughout the penitentiary worried they would be the next to receive an unreasonable punishment. At breakfast the next day, a whisper passed between the men: If the others were not let out, then no one would work. "It was going to be one for all and all for one," decided Tannenbaum. The inmates at Blackwell's Island were about to go on strike.

Frank seated himself at the machine in the brush shop, where, typically, he would have spent the next eight to ten hours assembling bristle heads. But this time he just sat there. The others, who had elected him spokesman, followed his lead. Attendants rushed out to inform their superiors. The penitentiary's industrial production totaled hundreds of thousands of dollars annually. With this revenue under threat, it took just a few minutes for the warden to appear.

"Why, what's the matter with you boys?" he said. "Why don't you work? I didn't do you anything. You have no grievance."

Tannenbaum started to explain to him the meaning of solidarity, but the prison chief had no intention of arguing politics with him. He turned to a nervous youth sitting nearby, who explained that he was brother to one of the men under punishment.

"Warden," Frank interjected. "He has got one brother locked up and I have got a hundred brothers locked up. And every one of them must be given a chance to wash and something to eat before we will do a stroke of work."

With that, he stood and walked out of the shop. The others followed, and then the rest of the manufacturing gangs, who had been watching to see what Tannenbaum would do, abandoned their posts as well. But first they avenged themselves on the machines: cutting the belts, smashing the apparatuses. Fires started up in the shoe shop, the paint shop, the bed shop. "The boys," said Tannenbaum, "simply avenged themselves on the system." Seeing the striking workers marching out, the men on lockdown joined the insurrection: "They broke every window in sight. Everything they could lay their hands on was destroyed." The noise of their rioting could be heard in Manhattan.

After the keepers had finally regained some control, Frank was taken by guards down to the punishment ward, known as the cooler. While they took his coat, shoes, and tobacco, he could hear voices of those who were already there begging the keepers to let them out. The barred door locked behind him. He stood in a tiny cell without a bed or a window, equipped with only a dirty blanket and an open bucket. Nothing in his previous captivity had inured him to this degree of squalor. The toilet pail was never emptied; it took days just to stop gagging from the reek. Ten-inch rats skulked through at night. Sleeping on the stone floor was uncomfortable, but the blanket was worse. Every movement raised "a cloud of dust" so vile to Frank that he would lie as still as he could, until his whole side had gone numb, before turning over. For sustenance, he received a slice of bread and a drink of water every twenty-four hours.

On July 10, Commissioner Davis arrived on the island, trailing a gang of reporters, and determined to settle the strike. Of the fourteen hundred inmates, nearly half had been confined to their cells and put on reduced rations. The eighteen chambers of the cooler were filled with ringleaders. Touring the facility, she defended the warden and took a stern, scolding tone with the sullen men. "It's true, quite true that I am a woman," she told an audience in the mess hall. "But while I wish to be human, and even a little more than human, I am not soft

Katharine Davis on Blackwell's Island.

and don't propose to be soft. I'll have order over here if I have to call out the militia, and not one of you will get a personal hearing until the whole lot of you make up your minds to be orderly."

Passing through the punishment ward, she paused in front of Frank's cell.

"Why don't you, for once," asked the commissioner, "take the side of law and order?"

"I will," Tannenbaum snapped back, "just as soon as law and order happens to be on the side of justice."

For four days, the strike in prison halted all production. But at last hunger drove the men back to work. Davis had spoken of instituting a "kindness plan" once resistance ended, but if anyone had hoped for sweeping changes, they were disappointed. As one of her ameliorations, she ordered that the men in the cooler be served bread twice a day— instead of once—so from then on the daily allotment was sliced in half and distributed morning and night. But the portion remained the same.

After seven days in isolation, Tannenbaum had finally accustomed himself to the smell. But he could tell from the way the guards flinched when they approached him that he had become as fetid as his surroundings. When he finally returned to the general cell block, he was so starved that he could hardly stand. To the other inmates he had proven his status as a good comrade. But his correspondents on the outside, who had picked up vague, distorted accounts of his actions from the newspapers, offered only qualified support. "Remember that our *real* activity must be at the 'point of production' and not in prison," an I.W.W. colleague wrote him. "I trust you will do nothing rash."

*　　*　　*

POLICE INVESTIGATORS AND newspaper reporters had meticulously gone through the wreckage at 1626 Lexington Avenue. From the evidence collected, they believed they could piece together a reconstruction of what had happened on the morning of July 4. In their story, the men had leapt from their beds as Louise Berger had left, to continue working on their "infernal machine." Carl Hanson was probably holding the bomb, with Charles Berg nearby and Caron perhaps at a little distance. From the damage, it appeared that a huge quantity of TNT had ignited. "Half a boxful of dynamite is an amount you don't often find outside an explosive factory," judged the department combustibles expert. Placed correctly, such ammunition could have "wrecked the neighborhood." Only the holiday celebrations, which had drawn people from their apartments early on a Saturday morning, had prevented a far higher death count.

Newspapers described other finds pulled from the rubble in the "death flat": pistol cartridges, dry cell batteries, bundles of wire. "There is no doubt in my mind," said the lead inspector, "that there was not only one bomb in that apartment, but that some one was manufacturing them there." The explosion of a small device had ignited the cache, causing the unbelievable destruction. On Sunday, the deputy commissioner interrogated Louise Berger for eight hours. She confessed to the printing press, but stuck to her previous statement: There had been no dynamite, or any other explosive paraphernalia, in the apartment. She was released, no charges filed.

Alternative versions of the story were also being offered. "I should not in the least be surprised," Alexander Berkman countered, if capitalist agents had been responsible for the explosion. "The Rockefellers have committed many murders; they would not stop at anything to add a few more coldblooded crimes to the long list of which they are guilty." Upton Sinclair also voiced this idea, attempting, perhaps, to salvage his own image of Caron. "Rockefeller is a very powerful man, who is accustomed to getting what he wants in this country," he wrote in the *Appeal to Reason*. "The bomb could have been set upon the roof," he speculated, "and it would have done exactly the same work as if it had been inside the room." Not surprisingly, the police scoffed at the notion, telling reporters that "if they wanted to get rid of three anarchists they could do it without risking the lives of more than 100 innocent persons."

But the vast majority of the populace was simply ready to accept the headlines. From the first editions, the papers speculated that the bomb had been meant for Rockefeller. Everything that had been reported about the anarchists suggested the plausibility, if not the inevitability, of this outcome. Before long, almost nobody still questioned the assumption that the victims were would-be assassins. And that their deaths had prevented something far worse.

During the preceding months there had been broad approval for radical agitations. But in the aftermath of "Caron's bomb," casual supporters were shocked into a swift retreat. The atmosphere of tolerance had ended. "The whole aspect of affairs has changed in the last forty-eight hours," editors at the *New York Herald* insisted. "This city is no place for further operations of the 'I.W.W.' or the Free Speech League." The *Outlook*, too, decided its dalliance with militancy was over. "It is one thing to sympathize with the struggle for industrial freedom and against industrial oppression," its pages proclaimed, "it is another thing to commit murder."

Not for the first time that year, people turned for precedent to the 1880s. The victims, suggested the *Herald*, had been "determined to carry out their ideas of force quite as desperately as the Haymarket rioters did in Chicago. That they blew up themselves instead of the Tarrytown City Hall or the New York City Hall or the Standard Oil Building was an accident." Bill Haywood worried that the anarchists would escalate the situation into "another eleventh of November," referring to the night in 1886 when the bomb had been thrown in Chicago. And Berkman was determined to do just this. "The Haymarket Bomb was followed by a terrible wave of the mob spirit," he wrote. "No Anarchist was safe from the blind fury of the murderous law-and-order hordes, in and out of uniform." This time there would be no cringing or underground hiding. On July 5, he announced the intention to hold a fitting service in Union Square for his martyrs. "We will mass the coffins, or urns—I do not know which they will be—in the street," he said firmly. "The public funeral will be held."

Thus challenged, it was time for the authorities to react. Commissioner Woods's policies, some felt, had enabled this disaster. Under his liberal eye, editorialized the *World*, radical meetings had grown "openly threatening." Orators had promised to kill and destroy in support of what they called "free speech." And the dynamite outrage proved the seriousness of these intimations. It was quite apparent that Woods had not been prepared. "The police were stunned by all that had happened," a reporter commented. They had known Caron and the others as committed agitators, and "had seen them again and again." But they had not suspected "that this daring band of long haired youths—for youths they were—was making bombs almost within the shadow of a police station and right in the very heart of one of the most thickly populated communities in the world." If the authorities had concentrated on their responsibilities, rather than condoning, even promoting, sedition, they might have prevented an escalation that ended in dynamite. Only providence had prevented a far worse catastrophe.

A few weeks earlier, Mayor Mitchel had been forced to explain comments suggesting a place for force in police procedures. Now tough talk was popular again. "Anarchy seems to have met its deserts," he said. "It seems to me to demonstrate that the police are justified in taking precautionary measures, and we are going to continue to apply such measures. I do not know what other measures the police can take. They are watching all the time." Woods, like Sinclair, had seen free speech as a safety valve; allowing dissidents to have their say was supposed to assuage the burden of their anger. That had not happened, and so the commissioner adapted, insisting that "he would not permit any one to make martyrs of the dead men, and that no parade would be allowed unless absolute assurance was given that the law would be respected."

The funeral preparations became a showdown between Berkman and Woods. Lofty constitutional principles had dominated the free-speech battle; this round would be fought through minute legal technicalities. Authorities had no power, under existing ordinances, to "disperse a strictly orderly gathering in any park or to suppress public speech in any park unless that speech incites to riot or disorder." So they simply changed the ordinances. On Tuesday, July 7, the Board of Aldermen put a new law on the docket requiring police sanction, requested thirty-six hours in advance, for any parade in the city. The bill passed unanimously and was immediately ratified by the mayor. "Fortunately," Mitchel said with relief, "the Police Commissioner now has the unquestionable power to refuse permits for parades if, in his opinion, there is likely to be disorder. We have never permitted disorder, and we are not going to permit it."

Woods had the administrative apparatus of the city at his disposal and he used it, down to the most obscure Health Department codes. Caron's mother, learning that the Catholic priest in Fall River would not bury her son in the church grounds, had yielded his remains to the anarchists. Berkman wanted to position Caron's body as the centerpiece of his demonstration. But the corpse itself lay in the morgue, and city law required its burial or cremation within four days. Extensions were granted regularly, but in this instance none could be expected. If the anarchists did not retrieve the dead men before ten A.M. on Wednesday morning, the victims would be shipped to the potter's field. The anarchists had been organizing frantically for a huge Saturday ceremony. A midweek funeral could not hope to draw the kinds of crowds they wanted. But Woods had left them no alternative.

Berkman's party arrived at the morgue on East Twenty-sixth Street just before the deadline. Fifty policemen waited outside as he and a score or so of others, wearing red carnations and mourning armbands, filed past the unpainted coffins. The caskets were loaded onto two horse-drawn hearses, wheeled to the Thirty-fourth Street ferry landing, floated across the East River, and finally trolleyed to Middle Village, Long Island, for cremation. In the chapel, Berkman spoke briefly. "Comrades, friends

The caskets bearing Caron, Hanson, and Berg.

and sympathizers," he began, "we have with us the remains of our comrades and we consider the occasion of their death requires a service that shall have a public character. The memorial will be public because our comrades were interested in work of a public nature—that of bettering the human race." The organist played "The Marseillaise," and Caron's face was uncovered for the final time. Then the coffins slid slowly toward the incineration room. "A match was applied to the jets in the ovens and flames licked the pine boxes. The furnace doors were closed and all filed out."

A radical sculptor was commissioned to create a special urn for the ashes, but this hardly replaced the symbolic power of a coffin. And Woods knew it. Concerned with maintaining order, he was also determined to prevent a parade. Experience had shown that a gathering in Union Square could be monitored and contained, but a march through crowded streets presented innumerable opportunities for mischief. Couching their words as liberally as possible, officials stated their decision on Friday. "The free speech policy of the administration will be continued," said Mayor Mitchel, "and these or other persons desirous of holding public assemblage in a peaceable manner, under conditions laid down by the statutes, will be protected by the police." But the funeral cortege would not be tolerated. "The Police Commissioner and I agree that such a parade would lead to disorder and breach of the peace." Again, Berkman had little choice in his response. Citing "evident discrimination" over the issue of the burial and police opposition to a "dignified and impressive" parade, the anarchists announced their decision "to abandon the funeral procession because we do not want to precipitate any violence at the present time, however justified resentment on our part may be."

All efforts turned to the memorial demonstration in Union Square, where police were expecting "as large a crowd as ever packed the historic spot." Determined "to take no chances," Woods had "made it clear to all that there would be no disorder if intelligent police work can prevent it." He gave the job to the same trusted deputy, Inspector Schmittberger, who had successfully quieted the previous mass meeting, held exactly three months earlier. To avoid conflict on that day, the commissioner had intentionally minimized the police presence. This time, he did the exact opposite. Every available officer—around eight hundred in all, the largest detail assigned for such a duty in the city's history—would be stationed within a few blocks of the anarchists' rally.

The crowd began to arrive around noon, hours before the speeches were to start. "They came in twos and threes and groups of a dozen and more," wrote a *Times* reporter. "For an hour all streets, it seemed, led to Union Square." Newspapers estimated attendance at between five and six thousand; *Mother Earth* claimed four times as many. The memorial finally began at two P.M. The stage was shaded by enormous floral bouquets. "Anarchists whose names are known the country over stood on or about the little platform of dry goods boxes which was constructed just north of the pavilion in the square." The crowd pressed in, a field of straw hats protecting against the afternoon sun.

Elizabeth Gurley Flynn and Carlo Tresca, national leaders of the I.W.W., gave eulogies. Emma Goldman had been horrified by the news of the explosion and blamed Berkman for allowing things to escalate so far. "Comrades, idealists, manufacturing a bomb in a congested tenement-house!" she wrote. "I was aghast at such irresponsibility." Nevertheless, for the public occasion she sent a telegram of solidarity, which was read aloud.

"Yes, we believe in violence," Becky Edelsohn told the crowd. "We will use violence whenever it is necessary to use it. We are not afraid of what your kept press says; and when we are murdered and cannonaded, when you train your machine guns on us, we will retaliate with dynamite."

Becky Edelsohn at Caron's memorial rally.

But it was Berkman's moment to lead. "Comrades, Friends and Sympathizers," he began. "We have come here this afternoon, not to mourn any calamity, but to pay our homage to three comrades whom we consider martyrs to the cause of humanity." He speculated that the men might have fallen prey to a conspiracy. "I want to go on record here today as saying that I prefer to believe that our comrades were not victims," he insisted.

> Why do I say this? Because I believe, and firmly believe, that the oppression of labor in this country, the persecution of the radical elements especially, has reached a point where nothing but determined resistance will do any good. And I believe with all my heart in resistance to tyranny on every and all occasions . . . When workers are shot down for demanding better conditions of living, when their women and children are slaughtered and burned alive, then I say that it is time for labor to quit talking and to begin to act.

"Never in the history of the city has there been a greater play of 'free speech,'" thought the *Herald*. Orations lasted for two and a half hours. The radicals "cried out that they were being crushed under the tyranny of wealth, and that revolution and dynamite are the only agencies by which the great mass of American people can come into their own." Schmittberger acknowledged that Berkman had come close to crossing the line of

Alexander Berkman at Caron's memorial rally.

"proscribed utterances," but when the memorial was over, the masses drifted peacefully away. Woods had stressed the maintenance of order, and it had been preserved. Back at the *Mother Earth* offices, the special urn was on display until late in the night. It was a simple brass pyramid, not quite two feet high, topped with a clenched fist. Inscribed on one face were the words:

KILLED
JULY 4, 1914
CARON
HANSON
BERG

IV

In no field of human relationships is the spirit of brotherhood on which the church was founded more profoundly needed than in industrial relations.

—JOHN D. ROCKEFELLER, JR.

9.

The War Has Spoiled Everything

When John D. Rockefeller, Jr., was a boy, his father used to walk with him in the forests around their home in Cleveland. Senior knew the species names for all the trees, and he would tell them off for his son as they went. All his life, Junior had cherished these moments; seeking solace in nature became his favored means of escaping the pressures of public life. In his youth, he had developed "a kind of passion for sunsets." During his early years at 26 Broadway, he would hurry home from work, have his carriage readied, and then circle the lanes in Central Park until it was too dark to see. Even as an adult, every time he caught the scent of sap running from a freshly cut branch, his mind would be transported back to soothing childhood memories. Once he had watched reverently for half an hour as twilight turned to darkness; and when the sun finally disappeared from view, he turned to his companion and asked, "How can people say there isn't a God?"

He had chosen to summer in Seal Harbor, Maine, because of its wild beauty. On the system of gravel roads he was constructing all over his property he could drive past stands of white birch, balsam fir, and red spruce trees. In the evenings, he might watch the approach of nightfall from the veranda on his cottage, the Eyrie, a mountaintop chalet with Atlantic views that stretched to the Mount Desert Light, twenty miles out to sea. But this summer the sun passed unobserved; the trees went unidentified. Junior's time was dedicated to publicity. He spent day after day indoors, poring through newspapers and magazines, harassing his staff with suggestions, painstakingly drafting memos and rebuttals. A team of secretaries clipped articles from all over the country: two newspapers from Tarrytown, the *Longmont Ledger*, the *Pueblo Chieftain*, the *Nashville Banner*, the *Monthly Bulletin of the American Iron and Steel Institute*, the *Christian Socialist*. Junior compiled them into scrapbooks and forwarded everything to Ivy Lee, his recently hired public relations expert.

No affront was too obscure to take offense at; no praise too faint to savor. He penned a full response intended to "correct some of the glaring and false" information in an article by Upton Sinclair. He sent this memo to Lee, who quietly set it aside as too confrontational. When the *Times* offered some critique, he complained about "the vacillating of the papers." Having dealt with a number of individual publications containing "infamous statements," Rockefeller obsessed over a wholesale strategy. No criticism should be allowed to stand. "We are wondering," he wrote, "whether it might not be well to make a reply to all the papers which have printed misstatements of fact" regarding the Colorado strike. "This would be quite an arduous task," he acknowledged, "and of course a good deal of time has passed since many of the articles were written." Lee promised to consider the idea.

When Rockefeller found something he liked, on the other hand, he demanded it be broadcast as widely as possible. Reading a strongly worded critique of unionism in *Popular Science Monthly*, he requested it be sent out to "every Governor and every Mayor in the United States; to the Members of every State Legislature, to every Member of the Chamber of Commerce of the United States, to the leading officials and directors of all the great Industries of the Country, to every member of the faculty of every College and University, to every minister of prominence as well as to every newspaper editor both large and small, and all of the judges higher than magistrates in the Country."

Throughout the summer and into autumn, Ivy Lee's series of pamphlets on Colorado continued to be published at weekly intervals. Printed to look like government reports, each installment was filled with important-sounding statistics, quotations from politicians or newspaper editors, and testimony by organizations with impressive names, such as the Law and Order League—all of which were more or less beholden to the mine operators' interests. The "facts" contained within ranged from half-truths taken out of context to careless misrepresentations to willful fabrications. In the edition dedicated to correcting the false impression that a "massacre" had occurred at Ludlow, Lee asserted in bold capital letters, "BOTH SIDES AGREE THAT NO WOMAN WAS STRUCK BY A BULLET FROM EITHER SIDE." Although this was technically true, it did nothing to explain the deaths of the two mothers and six girls who suffocated beneath the burning tents. Lee's claim that "the elaborate rifle pits occupied by the strikers showed that they had made deliberate preparation for battle" glossed over the fact that both sides had been living in armed camps, and that sporadic violence had been a constant reality during the previous months of the strike. And, finally, the assertion that "no machine gun was at any time directed against the colony" was just an outright lie.

Rockefeller convinced himself that this effort represented "a broad, educative campaign of publicity"—that he and his team of publicists were performing a public service akin to his other philanthropic works. By promulgating sound ideas, he believed, modern communications techniques could conceivably eliminate the class hatreds that had led to the Colorado strike in the first place. The potential for such work was just being realized, and Lee was already considering ways to use his powers constructively. "I feel that one of the important things to do as soon as possible is to get sounder teaching in our colleges," he wrote to a Rockefeller aide, "for there is no doubt that there are a large number of young men coming out of college just now with ideas of engaging in social service work, and that these young men are usually socialistically inclined." A few pamphlets detailing the "facts" about socialism and capitalism could redirect their energies along more profitable lines.

Unlike Junior's other philanthropies, however, this one had to operate in secret. Every week the bulletins went out to thousands of opinion makers, but the recipients were not supposed to know the true source of what they were receiving. They believed they were corresponding directly with the coal companies, not with a professional publicity bureau. To ensure this, Lee sent the Colorado executives a list of names, drafted cover letters, and then issued instructions regarding the precise procedure for the mailings. "I suggest that each letter be an original," he wrote. "You can doubtless have these letters duplicated on a multigraph machine and the names and addresses inserted so that there will be every appearance of each letter being an original. I would suggest also that they be signed by you personally."

The effort to alter national opinion went to the highest levels. One plan involved drafting a note purporting to be from the governor of Colorado, and having him send it to President Wilson over his own signature. Far from protesting such tactics, Rockefeller eagerly contributed to the subterfuge. For one of the articles he wanted to distribute, he considered various means to mask its origin. "Perhaps it could go out under the auspices of some great Corporation," he speculated, "perhaps through the Merchants Association or some similar organization . . . Possibly that would be entirely safe."

As July progressed, the effectiveness of their campaign became increasingly manifest. Newspapers were using the pamphlets as the basis for sympathetic editorials, and some were just plagiarizing them entirely. "Though we did not ask nor expect that our bulletins be reprinted," Lee wrote to Junior, "you will observe from the enclosed clipping from the *Chattanooga News* that the leaven is beginning to work." Even the experts were surprised by the response to a press release concerning a gift of the Rockefeller Institute for Medical Research. "In view of the fact that this was not really news," Lee reported with delight, "and that the newspapers gave so much attention to it, it would seem that this was wholly due to the manner in which the material was 'dressed up' for newspaper consumption. It seems to suggest very considerable possibilities along this line." Having been pummeled and condemned for so long, Junior was profoundly excited to feel that the counterattack had finally begun. Responding to the latest sample of encouraging results, he wrote to Lee, "Let the good work go on."

Though his campaign to burnish the family name had cost him a sunset or two, the work gave Rockefeller an excuse to avoid the social life of Seal Harbor. He certainly had little interest in mixing with his neighbors in the summer colony—the Morgans, the Astors, and the rest. Even more than that, it allowed him to stay close to the house and keep a protective eye on his wife and children. Newspapers had reported that "not the slightest preparations had been made to guard the place against a visit from the I.W.W.'s," and that Junior himself had "no fear that his tormentors will pursue him to Maine." But this was not quite true. According to the *Herald*, Rockefeller had brought twelve "special guards" with him. In addition, "two men, believed to be detectives, have been seen daily to scan all arrivals at the steamboat landings." Additional Burns operatives, supplemented by Tarrytown deputies, had increased the security at Pocantico Hills. And Pinkertons from the New York, Denver, and San Francisco offices were being paid six dollars a day, plus expenses, to gather information "at I.W.W. places" in an attempt to preempt future conspiracies.

Junior did not talk about his anxiety, refusing to discuss the bomb plot with reporters and alluding to it only obliquely in his correspondence. In this, as in so many other aspects of his personality, he was emulating Senior's standard. "I have never known Father to show the slightest fear, physical or moral," he once recalled. A few years earlier, when the Pocantico Hills estate was being constructed, Black Hand elements had appeared among the Italian workmen. Despite the presence of William Burns and his detectives, two people were killed, several more had been threatened or robbed, and an atmosphere of terror haunted the grounds. Junior was afraid for the safety of his children. "We should hesitate to have them ride or drive in the woods and would not want them to go out of sight of the house," he confided to his father. "Until we have succeeded in getting rid of certain men among the Italians . . . I fear we shall not have a condition of perfect quiet and security on the place." Since then, the sense of danger had never entirely dissipated. "We always had to live with the fear that something would happen to the children."

Senior had humored his son's concerns, allowing him, during the Black Hand troubles, to move his family from Tarrytown to another of the Rockefeller homes in the winter resort of Lakewood, New Jersey. But in the aftermath of the Lexington Avenue explosion, it was Senior who quailed, devising a plan to surround his property with barbed wire. His son talked him out of it. "I am wondering whether so obvious an effort to make entrance to the place difficult at this time," he wrote to his father, "may not challenge attention and suggest a fear and apprehension on our part which might induce, rather than help to keep out, intruders." Letters threatening assassination continued to arrive, and Junior single-mindedly worked on. Family and friends marveled at his fortitude. Nothing could distract him from the self-appointed task of convincing the nation of his own decent sincerity. "I don't know whether it is courage or not," he reminisced later. "Often a man gets into a situation where there is just one thing to do. There is no alternative. He wants to run but there is no place to run to. So he goes ahead on the only course that's open and people call it courage."

*　*　*

ON A PERFECT summer evening, scores of New York radicals received invitations to Rebecca Edelsohn's funeral. Organizers announced the location of the service; mourners were told to congregate in Union Square. But the date was left undetermined, since Becky herself remained a "very healthy girl from all appearances."

She had been in fine bloom that morning—July 20—when she had appeared at General Sessions Court to stand trial for the time, back in April, when her speech against the Mexican war had so infuriated the audience that the police had taken her into custody in order to protect

Becky Edelsohn, at right, with Louise Berger.

her from the fury of the mob. Three months later, she was just as eager to antagonize her class enemies. Dressed in mourning, carrying an enormous corsage of American Beauty roses, she playacted as if the whole thing was a great melodrama, sighing and swooning into her comrades' arms. When the magistrate revealed her punishment—three months in the workhouse on Blackwell's Island—she recovered her poise and replied sharply, "I think the sentence pronounced on me was unjust, and I announce that I intend to start a hunger strike."

Officers led her to the Tombs prison. There she spurned a dinner of vegetable soup, boiled beef, potatoes, green peas, and bread. Supper, too—bread, tea, apple sauce—she turned away. Hunger strikes were frequent in England, where they had become a favored technique for militant suffragettes, but so far no prisoner in the United States had successfully attempted to starve themselves as a political act. Upton Sinclair had tried it for a few days, but now Becky planned to make an earnest effort to sacrifice herself for the cause. Berkman mailed the funeral invitations that evening; when she succeeded in starving to death, the memorial would then proceed. Newspapers, compelled by the novelty of the story, issued detailed descriptions of the menu at every meal.

The next morning, when Edelsohn arrived at Blackwell's Island,

Katharine Davis was waiting to receive her. In the processing room, Becky refused to be examined or to answer the medical staff's questions. "She was quite pleasant about it, but exceedingly firm," declining even to give her age and background. Instead she reiterated her determination to starve. The commissioner stood by, smiling, and then left to consult with the newspapermen who had come to watch the confrontation. "Reba is an obstinate and obdurate girl," she told them. "I'm going to find out just how obdurate and obstinate she wants to be." If the fast began to threaten her health, then doctors would tie her down and force her to eat through a tube. Until then she would get no special privileges. Davis's policy seemed sensible and practical. "She has handled hundreds of cases like Reba's," a reporter wrote, "and intends to handle this one without any fuss and feathers."

For the remainder of the day, Becky stayed in her cell. She returned breakfast, luncheon, and supper untouched, and didn't drink any water. In Manhattan, Alexander Berkman hurried to form an "anti-torture committee" and hinted at the repercussions that would follow if his comrade was harmed. "We will not appeal to the law or any higher court," he said. "We can handle the situation by our own strength." City officials hired special bodyguards, and doctors stopped visiting Blackwell's Island after a rumor circulated that anarchists planned to blow up the ferries. But Berkman's private correspondence was considerably less bellicose. To Emma Goldman, touring the West Coast, he sent a telegram pleading, YOU AND FRIENDS EVERYWHERE WIRE PROTESTS FORCIBLE FEEDING TO COMMISSIONER DAVIS . . . CASE SERIOUS.

This had never happened before—a female prisoner confronting a woman of high office—and newspapers eagerly aggravated the situation. Interest in the case inspired the *New York Call* to host a contest: Readers were asked to submit two-hundred-word essays on the subject "What Would You Do With Becky?" Across the country, editors printed articles and opinion pieces offering their own answer to the question. "Blackwell's Island reveals two striking illustrations of the woman of the past and the woman of the future," noted the *Woman Rebel*. "Katharine B. Davis is the woman of the past and Rebecca Edelsohn is the woman of the future." But it was the *Tribune* that marked the story in the boldest ink, with the headline WOMAN VS. WOMAN.

"AS A PIONEER," an acolyte wrote, Katharine Bement Davis had "blazed a trail of precedents." Born in 1860, she had been the first girl to attend the Free Academy in Rochester, New York. Then, because her family could not afford tuition, she had taught high school for a decade, saving money and pursuing her own education at night, before gaining admission to Vassar College in 1890 as a thirty-year-old freshman. She continued on to receive advanced degrees in Berlin and at the University of Chicago, under the tutelage of Thorstein Veblen. In 1901, having earned a doctorate in political economy, she became the first superintendent of the New York State Reformatory for Women at Bedford Hills, in Westchester County.

Under her direction, the prison developed into a proving ground for the newest criminological theories, and Davis herself became an acknowledged expert on crime and correction. When Mayor Mitchel announced that she would become the first woman ever to hold a cabinet post in New York, reporters had understood that history was being made. The editors at *Outlook* deemed her accession "A Revolutionary Appointment" and predicted "a new era in dealing with crime" in the metropolis. But in fact she had more than a decade of experience already and was among the most qualified candidates in the nation. "Her new position is not a woman's job, nor a man's job," an advocate reminded the doubters. "It is a job for some one who knows how. Miss Davis knows how."

Fifty-four years old in 1914, she was described by one reporter as "a modest, motherly-looking, blue-eyed woman with brown hair plentifully sprinkled with gray, whom you could pick out at a glance as a crack housekeeper, if nothing more." With rectitude and resolve, she had constructed a career. Intimates remarked on her kindness; her public statements often hinted at a wicked wit. As a professional woman she had to be both commanding and self-effacing: sufficiently masculine to put down jailhouse disturbances, but also feminine enough to set newsmen and politicians at their ease. "Her sex is always kept in the background," a journalist recorded. "One can't talk with her for five minutes without forgetting entirely that she is a woman." She had been a renowned social scientist for years, yet still, because of her sex, she would never be judged by her work alone. Praise from men always carried an element of latent mockery. "She has not gotten her ideas about criminals from reading novels and seeing plays," marveled an editor at *Current Opinion*, "nor by making an occasional visit to a jail. Not at all."

As commissioner of correction, she had taken command of the city's most retrograde department. There were five district prisons, three city prisons, and penitentiaries on Riker's Island, Hart Island, and Black-

Katharine Bement Davis.

well's Island—each in a state of decrepitude, and most about a century or so behind the times in their practices and regulations. As they stood, the jails overflowed with 4,602 prisoners, and none was worse than the women's workhouse, where as many as 730 occupants jammed a facility designed for 150. "Everybody knows New York's prison institutions to be little better than medieval," Davis had acknowledged at the start of her tenure. "I hope to bring them up to something nearer to the highest modern standard." She had already dealt with a succession of radical prisoners. The uprising on Blackwell's Island had just been quelled. And now here was Becky.

EDELSOHN HAD NOT eaten for several days. She took pleasure in taunting the keepers who watched her movements, eagerly joining the mess-hall lines and then sitting quietly at the table without taking a bite. In the hospital ward, where she had been transferred from her cell, she energetically helped out with the patients and remained infuriatingly positive. "She walks around cheerfully," an exasperated observer noted, "drinks lots of water and thoroughly enjoys the publicity her alleged 'strike' has caused." So far she had been seen ingesting the juice from one lemon, but nothing else. Authorities had no idea how long it would take for someone to weaken from a fast; they expected her to be prostrate within a week. When four days passed, Davis, without any evidence, concluded, "I am now convinced that she has been getting food ever since she went to the Island." After nine days, when Becky still appeared to be in "perfect" condition, baffled officials accused her of smuggling "milk tablets," or taking some other form of "tabloid nourishment."

Everyone was waiting for her to start suffering so that they could administer the force-feeding. Davis had mentioned the possibility of using this procedure on the very first morning of the hunger strike, and it had been discussed constantly ever since. Edelsohn's opponents took a prurient glee in the thought of having her strapped down and fattened on liquid food. The *World* typographers composed a graphic to celebrate the process:

Recipe of Dr. Katharine B. Davis, Commissioner of Correction, for treatment of a woman hunger-striker:
   Roll her tightly in blankets, with arms at sides, like Indian papoose, leaving only head protruding.
   Pin blankets fast with safety pins, so that limbs are immovable.
   Insert one-third inch rubber tube through nose. Pour through this, by means of funnel, warm soup or broth.
   Operation can be performed by two persons . . .
   Repeat as frequently as necessary.

The joking masked the fact that force-feeding an unwilling subject was an ordeal equivalent to torture. Prison authorities claimed that only two female nurses would be necessary to hold down the prisoner. "It will not hurt her," Davis insisted, "not even cause her discomfort." But if Becky resisted—and she had once fought off a group of police officers who were trying to take her into custody—far more strength would be required. So interested were readers in this procedure that a female reporter for the *World* volunteered to be force-fed in order to describe the sensations. She was tied down with tape by three men.* While she was immobile, the doctor sprayed her nostrils with cocaine and disinfectant. "As it reached my throat, it burned and burned." Then he inserted the tube into her nose. "It is utterly impossible to describe the anguish of it," she wrote. "An instant that was an hour, and the liquid had reached

---

* Not, it will be noted, the two women that Davis had claimed.

my throat. It was ice cold, and sweat as cold broke out upon my forehead." And she had volunteered to suffer this. "If I, playacting, felt my
being burning with revolt at this brutal usurpation of my own func-
tions," she wrote, "how they who actually suffered the ordeal in its acut-
est horror must have flamed at the violation of the sanctuaries of their
spirits."

To Edelsohn's supporters, the act became a metaphor for the arbitrary powers of the state. "I haven't seen in the papers anywhere that
organized or unorganized anarchy, whatever it is, has threatened to
forcibly feed 'Kitty' Davis," a socialist reader wrote to the *Call*. "Rebecca only advocated violence, while 'Kitty' says she's going to carry it
out." Speaking for his anti-torture committee, Berkman railed against
the authorities. "I believe that no humane and right-thinking person,"
he said, "can retain his self-respect if he fails to voice a vigorous protest
against such official violence and worse-than-Russian brutality practiced upon a defenseless prisoner." But no one summarized the situation
better than Becky herself. "Capitalism," she wrote in a letter smuggled

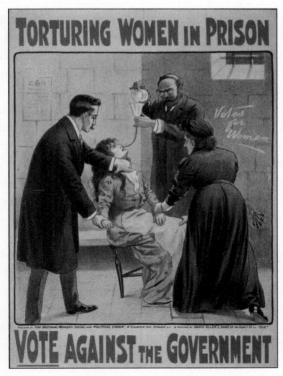

Force-feeding prisoners was considered by some to be a form of torture.

off the island, "means forcible feeding in prison and forcible starvation out of prison."

Every day, for the first week of the hunger strike, Davis had appeared to be on the verge of resorting to force-feeding. New rumors were constantly reported: The prison doctors had procured the hose; a wooden bit had been built in the penitentiary workshop; Edelsohn—though she didn't know it—was sleeping on a bed that could be equipped with straps and used for the operation. Davis had used the method many times on recalcitrant inmates at Bedford Hills. She would employ it again just as soon as Becky began to falter.

On July 31, the tenth day, Edelsohn was finally starting to flag. "Can't write much—feel very weak," she scribbled in a note that morning. That afternoon, her report was: "Very weak. Expect collapse any time." The moment was coming for Davis to fulfill her threat. "They will be forced to either forcibly feed me or let me go," Becky speculated. "They are waiting until the very last and that won't be long." Her letters to Berkman, carried off the island in secret by other prisoners, became fatalistic, morose. "Don't worry, dear," she wrote, "even if the worst comes to the worst. I can only die once. And it will make tremendous propaganda."

The time had come for Davis to make a decision. Edelsohn was weakening, and the public scrutiny was intense. For more than a week, the confrontation had received constant attention in the press. The commissioner had contributed to this by offering statements to reporters, but she had also complained of the publicity it was giving to the protest. On July 30, she made her choice, issuing a circular to the city's editors: "Hereafter I must decline to give information as to the health or conduct of Miss Edelsohn and the other members of the I.W.W., who are inmates of the institutions of the Department of Correction . . . It is not in the interest of discipline or in the interest of the democratic conduct of our institutions that these prisoners should receive consideration over that accorded to other prisoners, or be singled out for newspaper notoriety."

The anarchists were outmaneuvered. Realizing that Becky's protest relied on exposure, Davis had just ignored the controversial question of force-feeding, and had simply shut off the prisoner's access to her public. In a confidential letter to the mayor's secretary, Davis seemed as relieved at avoiding reporters as she was to have quelled the demonstration. "They have tormented the life out of me for the past two weeks for bulletins as to 'Becky's' health,' she complained. As for Edelsohn and the other inmates, "the least said about them in the papers the better. If any of them die or any other catastrophe happens I will give out information. It seems to me that the I.W.W. and their ilk simply gather strength for their cause from any material whatever expressed about them in the newspapers."

Following the commissioner's decree, the headlines ceased. The *Call* quietly canceled its contest. Reporters moved on to other sensations. And even if Davis had not sealed off access to the press, focus on the hunger strike would have diffused anyway. It was August 1, 1914, and there was news from across the Atlantic.

* * *

THE POTENTIAL FOR a European conflict had grown increasingly alarming throughout July. BRIGHT PROSPECT FOR PEACE, a headline that ran at the start of the month, had become A THREAT OF WAR a few weeks later. Then there had followed a period of anxious uncertainty: STILL IN THE BALANCE, CRITICAL DAYS. Despite the onrush of crisis, observers refused to acknowledge what they were witnessing. "A general European war is unthinkable," editors at the *Times* declared on July 28. "Europe cannot afford such a war, the world cannot afford it, and happily the conviction is growing that such an appalling conflict is altogether beyond the range of possibility." But within days, Germany and Austria, France, England, Russia, and a drove of smaller states all bound themselves for hostilities. On August 4 at six A.M., the Kaiser's field-gray infantry crossed the frontier into Belgium. At last the headlines read, THE GREATEST OF WARS.

Forthwith, the struggle spread to New York City. Two ocean liners, the *Kaiser Wilhelm II* of Germany and the British *Olympic*, both raced into the harbor at full steam, with portholes covered and deck lights extinguished, bearing stories of escaping enemy cruisers. A wireless report announced that the *Lusitania* had been sunk off the New Jersey coast. This story proved groundless, as did the repeated rumors of foreign navies operating in American waters. A village fireworks display became a burning vessel. And the residents on Riverside Drive were certain they had heard the sound of cannon. "The phantom fleet is off our coast again," the *Times* quipped. "The last time it was reported lurking near Sandy Hook it flew the Spanish flag. That was during our war with Spain. Now the fleet flag is either French, German, or British, according to the observer."

Ashore, citizens of every combatant nation intermingled with one another. Residents marched by the hundreds and thousands to their national consulates—all located on the same stretch of Lower Broadway—to volunteer for duty to their respective fatherlands. Impromptu performances of "The Marseillaise" and "Die Wacht am Rhein" arose wherever beer was poured or a street pianist played. Teutonic newsboys fought bloody combats with Slavic newsboys. Crowds massed before the bulletin boards on Park Row and in Times Square, debating each successive communiqué from Europe. "English, French, Russians, Germans, all met on common ground and argued in the language of Manhattan," a reporter wrote. "Belgian neutrality was attacked and defended. Serbs talked of what they would do when the Hapsbourgs were driven back to Budapest, Frenchmen expiated on the need for wiping out the wrong of 1870."

Occasionally bystanders erupted into arguments or minor scuffles, but if someone went too far, they were usually shouted down with the cry: "Shut up! You're in America." There had been every reason to expect worse. "Here is a general European war at white heat," newspapers marveled—yet comity prevailed. "Probably we should be amazed if we realized the seething hatreds which surrounded these new Americans at home," a *Tribune* editor observed. "But such animosities are a long way from Broadway."

As similar confrontations occurred in cities across the nation, President Wilson was determined to ensure that citizens understood their role in the growing crisis. Forcing himself to perform the duties of office—his wife had died two days after the war began—he carefully explained his vision for America's coming role. "The United States must be neutral in fact as well as in name during these days that are to try men's souls," he said in a statement to the nation. "We must be impartial in thought as well as in action."

Unsure whether such appeals would suffice for New York City, Mayor Mitchel intervened directly into residents' behavior. "The population of this city is cosmopolitan," he proclaimed two days after the invasion of Belgium. "We have people of German, of French, of English, of Italian, of Austrian, and of Russian blood. Public demonstrations of sympathy by people of a particular race, while natural from their point of view, are calculated to breed ill feeling upon the part of their fellow-citizens of other blood and sympathies, and should not take place in this cosmopolitan and entirely neutral city." By executive decree he banned all military parades and stationed police to the streets around foreign embassies. The display of any flag other than the stars and stripes was outlawed. "The wisdom and necessity of this course will, I feel sure, appeal to the natural good sense of our citizens," Mitchel con-

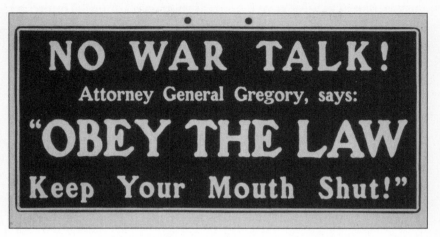

In the context of the war, free speech was severely curtailed.

cluded, "whom I ask to remember that they are after all American citizens first and sympathizers with their respective fatherlands second."

AFTER TWO WEEKS of fighting, the novelty of the Great War had diminished and New Yorkers began to recall the controversies of the previous months. "What has become of Becky?" a letter writer asked the *Times* on August 17. "Is she alive or dead? Has Commissioner Davis sent the bunch over . . . 'to fight for their country'?" Alone and ignored, Edelsohn continued to fast. While she had generated attention, the sacrifices had been justifiable. Now she was simply starving in prison, and nobody cared. "The war has spoiled everything," she wrote in a smuggled letter to Berkman. "We cannot get headlines now."

On August 20, thirty-one days into her hunger strike, a nurse handed her some street clothes and told her she was free. Her friends had paid a three-hundred-dollar bond to get her released. Preparing to depart, she thought, "I was not sorry to leave hell." Her ordeal had not seemed to affect her. "She was a little thinner in the face," a prison official reported, "but looked quite well." That afternoon she walked unsupported to the Blackwell's Island slip, was ferried to Manhattan, and then took a taxi to Berkman's apartment on West 119th Street. There, she collapsed into bed. A doctor was called for, and the few reporters who had bothered to show up were sent away.

ALEXANDER BERKMAN HAD been right about everything. "The present European catastrophe is no accident," he insisted. "It was to be foreseen as an inevitable development of existing conditions." He himself had predicted it. All the way back in January, when every other journalist in New York was certain that international peace was assured, he had written an essay about the horrid potential of the Lewis gun, which now, in the hands of British soldiers, "was giving good results at the front." For years, he had foretold that socialists, by allowing themselves to be distracted by politics—running for office, canvassing for votes—had merely been duped by their capitalist enemies. In August 1914, they proved themselves even more frail than anyone had imagined. Instead of proclaiming a general strike of workingmen in every nation, the members of the European Social Democratic parties had marched out joyously to slay one another. "You Anarchists have proved to be right in your criticism," a party leader had conceded to him recently. "The Socialist movement has broken down; there are no more Socialists; to-day we all are bourgeois." Even that old idée fixe, the *attentat*, had been vindicated. No one could now claim, as his enemies had often done, that the assassination of an individual was a futile act. Two bullets in Sarajevo—one fewer than Berkman had fired at Frick in Pittsburgh—had careened the world's empires to the brink of mutual destruction.

Gazing now—coolly, rationally—into the future, Berkman could see how all this would end. He did not embrace for a moment the soothing fiction that this was going to be the final conflict. "Vain is the hope," he wrote. "Greater wars yet will come with the newer inventions of the human mind, that will make bullets more deadly, guns more destructive, airships more perfect. War will last as long as capitalism and government last." Violence would beget violence. "Prussian militarism cannot be destroyed by the military power of other countries. Such a method must lead to national bitterness, thoughts of revenge, increased armaments and future wars."

In the meantime, the governments of the world would seize this opportunity to silence all dissenters and destroy everything that workingmen had struggled to build. Patriotism, nationalism: These were the anarchist's foremost enemies. A leading French socialist, Jean Jaurès, was murdered by a jingoist gunman on the last day of July; Berkman knew this merely to be a harbinger of the reaction to come. "The revolutionary movement of the world is now in great danger of being swept away in the general conflagration," he warned. "Let us foresee this danger. Let us combine for concerted action."

Never before had he taken so little pleasure in being correct. "Blushing in our shame we bow our heads in this hour of humiliation," he wrote. "Perturbed in our innermost feelings, distressed to our very soul." So many certainties had vanished so quickly that even he had lost his poise. "What's to be done?" he asked. The fulfillment of his predictions had shaken any faith he still possessed in society's potential to transform itself. Like so many others, he found himself in darkness. "I am sick of appeals to legality," he sighed, "sick of the hope for class justice."

10.

Who's Who Against America

By mid-August the coal war had entered its eleventh month, although it had fallen from the public view since April, when federal troops had arrived to stem the violence. Nevertheless, several thousand miners, weary and increasingly demoralized, still occupied various tent colonies in the district. But they had become little more than an inconvenience. The Colorado Fuel & Iron Company was operating its mines at three-quarters capacity, working them with replacement labor. It was apparent that the strike, though still ongoing, had failed. Surely, thought Rockefeller, the time had finally arrived to initiate reforms. He had received a settlement offer from the vice president of the United Mine Workers of America, and he inclined toward pursuing it. Bowers blocked the idea. "To move an inch from our stand at the time that defeat seems certain for the enemy would be decidedly unwise, in my opinion," he wrote to Junior. "We are encouraged to stick to the job till we win."

Through the autumn, as they had since the start, Bowers and his intransigent colleagues resisted every proposal of arbitration and reconciliation. In September, President Wilson and his secretary of labor suggested a resolution that granted every one of the coal operators' demands—it did not even require the companies to recognize their workers' rights to organize. This was the one issue that the owners had insisted upon, and now they had got their way. The union, approaching the end of its stamina, accepted the deal. Seeking only unconditional surrender, the coal operators did not.

Finally, on December 10, 1914, after fourteen months of struggle, the employees voted to end the strike. The United Mine Workers estimated it had paid out more than $3 million in benefits, while its members had sacrificed twice that amount in lost wages. At least seventy-five men, women, and children had been killed.

"The feeling of satisfaction on the part of all of us is by no means small," Bowers wrote to Rockefeller one day later. He had seen himself as waging a titanic moral struggle—opposing all attempts at interference, resisting every temptation to compromise—and now he exulted in victory. "Our rugged stand," he wrote, "has won us every foot we have gained." He had no sympathy for the families who had tried to unionize and who now faced winter in the knowledge that no company would hire them; their future, he sneered, "must be very discouraging."

Bowers did not have long to gloat. He had always said that the end of the strike would mean the time had come to examine the company's conduct. Now that this had occurred, Rockefeller made the one change he thought most pressing. On December 28, he called Bowers to his office at 26 Broadway. In a bitter and painful interview, he ordered the older man to resign his directorship, his place on the board, and every other position—official and unofficial—that he held at Colorado Fuel & Iron. Hoping to retain a scrap of his former authority, the executive suggested he might at least remain in communication with his former staff. Using the same phrase that his subordinate had so often used against him during the preceding months, Junior replied that such a decision "would be unwise." Bowers was offered a year's salary as severance, and the prospect of a nice vacation. "We want to have you take the next two or three months for unbroken rest," said Junior, soothingly. "I fancy you must feel more or less like a colt turned out to pasture."

Just as he discarded one troublesome employee, however, Rockefeller found himself accounting for the excesses of another. During government hearings in December, Colorado Fuel & Iron officials had been compelled, under oath, to reveal the true author of the series of pamphlets that had been issuing forth from their offices since June. Forty thousand had been sent, at a cost of $12,000, and the tone and scale of the effort had made scrutiny inevitable. Ivy Lee's months of work were undone in a hail of criticism. "The strike bulletins," wrote editors at the *Survey*, "were shown to be not only biased *ex parte* statements, but to contain gross misstatements of the salary and expense of the Colorado miners' leaders." A close reading revealed—among other fabrications— that Lee, attempting to discredit the opposition, had exaggerated union officials' wages by a factor of ten. IVY L. LEE—PAID LIAR, declared a story in the *Call*. Upton Sinclair dubbed him "Poison Ivy." Attempting to cover up the extent of the manipulations, the company at first denied that Rockefeller had played any part in the campaign. But internal correspondence revealed the extent of his complicity. "More systematic and perverse misrepresentations than Mr. Lee's campaign of publicity," the *Masses* proclaimed, "has rarely been spread in this country."

With anger still fresh, Rockefeller and Lee were called to testify before the Commission on Industrial Relations, the federally funded tribunal that had been traveling the country since 1912, examining the causes and consequences of labor disputes.

January 25, 1915, was a snowy, sleet-spoiled day in the midst of another hard New York City winter. Rockefeller strode through the front door of City Hall: On Ivy Lee's advice, he had abandoned the habit of sneaking in and out of back entrances. On Commissioner Woods's insistence, he was flanked by several uniformed policemen and half a dozen detectives, including the mayor's own personal bodyguard. He climbed the stairs to the Common Council chamber, where his interrogators awaited him.

Rockefeller Junior on the stand.

The audience, which the *Times* observed "was in large part frankly hostile," had come for its first glimpse of the man behind the Ludlow Massacre. During all the months of protests and persecutions, he had never allowed himself to be seen. Tense and nervous, "his platoon of shifty, active guards" kept at the ready. "Constantly they eyed every man and woman in the City Hall room where the hearing was held." The whole assembly was against him, and no one more so than the commission's chairman, Frank P. Walsh, a midwestern attorney who knew he faced one of the most important witnesses of his entire career.

The questions came quick and angry, with no purpose but to embarrass or implicate Rockefeller as a cold tyrant and a shiftless son of wealth, an autocrat and an absentee ruler. With twenty or so cameras aimed at him, Junior managed to stay poised. But his answers did not satisfy anyone. He hedged and stalled, refusing to clarify his general opinions about organized labor, trying as hard as he could to distance himself from Ivy Lee and his publicity work. "Wary and bland" was the *Times* reporter's evaluation of his performance. By the end of the first of two days of testimony, the audience had lost its savor for the spectacle; the hectoring examiners, the evasive witness—neither party could succeed in winning favor under the conditions.

No one felt the banality of the moment so acutely as Walter Lippmann, who covered the hearing as a correspondent for the *New Republic*, a magazine he had helped create a few months earlier. Here sat the inheritor of the greatest fortune in the world, a man with more responsibility over a larger part of the national economy than any other single person, a living symbol of monopoly capital and labor injustice. "Yet," to Lippmann's disgust, "he talked about himself on the commonplace moral assumptions of a small business man." No greater failure of the American system could be comprehended than that this "careful, plodding, essentially uninteresting person" should have his position—unwanted, unearned—thrust upon him. It was an absurd situation from which nobody benefited. "Those who rule and have no love of power suffer much," thought Lippmann. "John D. Rockefeller, Jr., is one of these, I think, and he is indeed a victim."

After the ordeal was over, Junior was descending the staircase when he suddenly paused. A white-haired woman in glasses stood in his path. It was Mother Jones. The guards urged him forward, but he stopped and held out his hand to her.

"We ought to be working together," he said.

"Come out to Colorado with me," she replied, "and I'll show you what we can do."

IN FACT, HE had long planned to visit the coalfields. During the strike, a trip to Colorado would have been inflammatory and detrimental to the company's position. But even as he suffered through the outbreak of criticism that accompanied the revelations of his publicity efforts, he was simultaneously working on a way to bring meaningful reforms to the mine employees.

Increasingly aware that some of Ivy Lee's "advice had been unsound on several occasions," Junior had come under the tutelage of William Lyon Mackenzie King. The former minister of labor for Canada, King had been brought in to help with the project of industrial relations—just as Lee had been hired to conduct public relations. Believing that Colorado Fuel & Iron had to offer its men more of a say in their own affairs, he suggested the creation of a grievance board where workers could seek a hearing for their complaints. While it did not go so far as to grant workers the right to unionize, it still showed a willingness to compromise that would never have been sanctioned by Bowers and the other operators. At the center of the idea was Junior's belief that personal connection between workers and bosses could overcome the perception of differences. "The hope of establishing confidence between employers and employed," he wrote to the president of Colorado Fuel & Iron, "will lie more in the known willingness on the part of each to confer frankly with the other than in anything else." Officially called "the Plan of Representation and Agreement," it would come to be known as the "Rockefeller Plan," and, in September 1915, Junior traveled to Colorado to convince both sides to ratify it.

For three weeks he toured mines, camps, and factories, speaking personally with hundreds of employees, sharing their meals, and even going so far as to don overalls and wield a pick in one of the coal shafts. "He did not dig very much," a reporter for the *Times* noted. "The miners grinned, but Mr. Rockefeller hacked away and laughed as the black lumps began to rattle down." He distributed prize money to the homes with the nicest gardens and offered to reimburse a community that wanted to construct a bandstand. At one meeting he suggested pushing the chairs to the side of the hall and then organized an impromptu dance, fox-trotting with each of the miners' wives in turn.

There had been no way to predict how the workers would receive him. Ambling through the camps and mingling with the men, Rockefeller exposed himself to reprisal. Any person in Colorado who claimed a grudge—and thousands might have done so—could have enacted a just revenge. It had been a risk to stride into the center of what had been a war zone. Senior had tried, unsuccessfully, to convince his son's secretary to carry a pistol with him for protection. But Junior encountered only warmth and generosity. The miners were in the mood to forgive, and with employment so precarious, it would have been foolhardy to make a demonstration. Few of the active strikers had been rehired, so the employees he met were almost certainly not the same people who had actually inhabited the Ludlow colony. But it was also true that Junior, with his modest and self-effacing manners, chose this occasion to show his best self. "Had Mr. Rockefeller not been the man he is," King wrote to Abby during the trip, "and had he not met his fellowmen of all classes in the manner he did . . . some situation would almost have certainly presented itself which would have made the tour of the coal fields as disastrous in its effect as, owing to his wonderful adaptability, it has been triumphant."

ROCKEFELLER WINS OVER MINERS WHO FORGET TRAGEDY AT LUDLOW, a *Denver Post* headline exulted. ROCKEFELLER TURNS HATE OF MINERS TO LOVE, reported the *Chicago Tribune*. "Enmity," wrote King, "has been changed into good-will; bitterness into trust; and resentful recollections into cherished memories." In Pueblo on October 2, Junior formally introduced his plan of management, which, according to the press, granted "practically every point which any labor union ever asked, with the one exception of recognition of the union." To illustrate his vision of the ideal corporation, Junior spilled some coins onto a small table. Each leg represented one of the four parties that made up a business: stockholders, directors, officers, workers. Because the legs were represented evenly, the tabletop was level and the money piled up. "Again," he explained, "you will notice that this table is square. And every corporation to be successful must be on the square—absolutely a square deal for every one of the four parties, and for every man in each of the four parties." When the vote was tallied, an overwhelming majority of the employees, and all the directors, had opted for the Rockefeller Plan.

"I cannot but feel," King confided to Abby at the end of the three weeks he had traveled with her husband, "that this visit is epoch-making in his own life, as it will also prove epoch-making in the industrial history of this continent."

* * *

LESS THAN ONE month after the Lexington Avenue explosion, on August 1, 1914, Commissioner Arthur Woods announced a major shake-up of the police department. Using the bomb to justify his claims that the city required a real secret service, he announced the creation of a new force: the anarchist and bomb squad. Finally, he was able to complete the task Commissioner Bingham had begun a decade earlier. Following his mentor's opinions, he explained to the city that the infiltration and surveillance of dissident organizations would be a powerful deterrent against future terror threats. The unit went to work immediately. Officers of "various nationalities" took up "residence among the various groups" of radicals and set out to "secure evidence against anarchists and followers of the I.W.W." They employed the most modern techniques, as well as elaborate disguises and subterfuges. Anything was acceptable if it allowed the secret operators to insinuate themselves among their dangerous quarry. "Detectives were carefully instructed how to act," since everyone knew that "it was the custom of the I.W.W. and anarchists to investigate carefully all new members."

Despite this specialized instruction, the new division was unsuccessful at preventing further anarchist attacks. As it happened, the most virulent bombing campaign in the city's history occurred in the squad's first years. On October 13, bombs targeted St. Patrick's Cathedral and St. Alphonsus' Church, where Tannenbaum had been arrested. On November 11, the anniversary of the Haymarket executions, unknown bombers attacked the Bronx County Courthouse. A few days later, a bomb was disabled before it exploded underneath a seat in the Tombs police court: The presiding magistrate was the same judge who had sentenced Tannenbaum to a year in prison. Despite the apparent links to radical causes and the Anarchist Squad's relentless efforts, no one was ever arrested for any of these attacks.

The secret police made their impact in other ways. New York's radicals found themselves targeted by "mosquito spies" and provocateurs. Ever since Caron's death, *Mother Earth* complained, "the Anarchist, the I.W.W. groups and the Ferrer Center have been infested by mesmerists in search of fit subjects." The school and community meeting place at the Ferrer center, plagued by informants, relocated from 107th Street to a rural farm in Stelton, New Jersey. And for those who stayed, a spreading distrust made even simple activities difficult. Undercover detectives would sidle into peaceful assemblies and declaim violent speeches advocating the use "of violence, bombs, and dynamite," trying to instigate some attack that could then be thwarted. For the most part, their presence was little more than an annoyance for the veteran agitators. "Naturally they dared not approach experienced people," Emma Goldman wrote. "But when they were told to get out, they turned to the young." One member of the bomb squad convinced two youths, Carmine Carbone and Frank Abarno, to detonate a bomb in St. Patrick's Cathedral. The provocateur planned the attack, provided the explosives, and, according to the radicals, even lit the fuse, only to have other detectives race in and "prevent" the attack. Despite the obviousness of the frame-up, a judge sentenced the two defendants to six to twelve years in Sing Sing.

Other infiltrators inadvertently revealed themselves. The anarchists discovered one when he failed to stamp a report, and his letter, addressed to the Burns Detective Agency, was returned to the Ferrer Center. Another gave himself away when his dentist noticed a revolver under his jacket. A third agent, Dave Sullivan, had served a prison sentence during the Free Silence agitation and had gone further into the radicals' confidence by becoming Becky Edelsohn's lover. He was discovered only after his outraged wife finally caught on and exposed him. Despite the clumsiness of these attempts, at least one spy did manage to inflict actual damage. Donald Vose, the son of one of Goldman's closest friends, had lived in the *Mother Earth* offices for most of 1914. Unbeknownst to the anarchists, he was a paid informant of the Burns detective agency, and information he gleaned from their conversations allowed him to lead police to arrest two suspects who were still wanted from the 1910 *Los Angeles Times* bombing case.

Even as the conflict with radicals intensified, police investigators found themselves distracted by a new and greater threat. In spite of Mayor Mitchel's pleas, it was proving impossible for New Yorkers to avoid entirely the repercussions of the Great War in Europe. By 1915, panicky reports were already warning of German saboteurs in the city. Police prepared for draft riots. "Plans have been laid by the Commissioner for almost any emergency that might arise out of alien plots or the exigencies of war," Edward Mott Woolley informed the readers of *McClure's*. "Every block in the city has at least one citizen who is a special agent of the police, and whose duty it is to communicate instantly any evidence of danger from enemies." The Anarchist Squad became the neutrality squad. Just as the old Italian detectives had tried to find links between radicals and the Black Hand, the new division came to

The breath of the Hun.

understand its various enemies as part of one single conspiracy. Inspector Thomas J. Tunney, the unit's chief, told his men to divide their attention between "the Prussian, the Bolshevik, and the Anarchist."

WHILE OVERSEEING THESE infiltrations, Commissioner Woods continued his public agitation for free speech. During 1916, when a traction strike in the city brought streetcars, elevated trains, and subways to a halt, he insisted that the police had a responsibility only to keep the peace, and that the department would not allow itself to serve as hired muscle for corporate bosses. "The question [of] who won the strike" did not interest the police, Woods wrote: "Their duty, and their sole duty, was to maintain order, to protect life and property, to ensure to all concerned—the companies, the workers, the public—the enjoyment of their full legal rights." As he had done two years earlier, and in strikingly similar language, the commissioner stressed the sanctity of free speech; "there was no law to prevent one man from talking to another on the street," he wrote. Only if strikers "became disorderly the police would take action."

As usual, however, Woods's defense of constitutional rights reflected just one aspect of his method. Two months before the transit strike, he had testified before state legislators in defense of his use of wiretaps in criminal investigations. "Eavesdropping—the most objectionable sort of thing is eavesdropping," he admitted. "We all object to it, we all revolt at the very idea of it." And yet, he argued, it was absolutely necessary in certain cases. The politicians worried that surveillance might accidentally be used against respectable citizens. But Woods said that he personally decided when the technique could be used, and, of course, he was confident in his own discretion. When it came to more abstract concerns about civil liberties, he was simply dismissive. "There is altogether too much sappy talk about the rights of the crook," he scoffed. "He is a crook. He is an outlaw. He defies what has been put down as what shall be done and what shall not be done by the great body of law-abiding citizens. Where does his right come in?"

∗　∗　∗

IN ONES AND TWOS, by elevated train and limousine, the gathering massed along the piers at Fifty-third Street along the East River on the morning of March 10, 1915. Chatting and laughing, the good-humored crowd kept its attention focused on the water. Shortly after nine A.M., their eyes were drawn to an approaching ferry; then, as the boat drew nearer, someone spotted a thin figure on the upper deck, madly waving a handkerchief. "It's Frank!" they shouted. "It's Frank!" As he stepped onshore, looking pale and, thanks to his spectacles, older than they remembered him, the welcoming committee thrust a bouquet of red carnations in his hand. After minutes of hugs and exclamations, they all departed for a celebratory breakfast; no one had noticed the member of the Anarchist Squad who had been lurking nearby the entire time.

"Tannenbaum was, I guess, a rather unruly prisoner," Lincoln Steffens reluctantly conceded. In total, he had served three stints in the cooler and had spent his final two months in solitary confinement. At a reception in the *Mother Earth* offices on his first evening of freedom, Frank described for the reporters some of the abuses he had seen. "For monumental ignorance allow me to commend Warden Hayes," he said. Not only had he overseen beatings and starvations; the tyrant of Blackwell's Island had proven to be more or less illiterate, at least in his role as censor. He had banned Goethe's *Faust*, as well as various works of bourgeois history and the *Nation* magazine, while obliviously allowing Frank to read the entire Kropotkin library in his cell. "I see no reason why any remarks of Tannenbaum should call for comment from me," Commissioner Davis had indignantly replied when reporters contacted her for a response, "and I am not going to enter into any controversy with Tannenbaum."

But she was mistaken. Frank went to work for the *Masses* magazine; in the summer of 1915 he published a series of exposés revealing the worst of what he had seen. Spurred to outrage, the state launched an investigation into conditions on the island. Warden Hayes testified to turning pressure hoses onto inmates and forcing them to sleep on the soaked floor, and he seemed surprised by the idea that healthy prisoners should be separated from those with syphilis or tuberculosis. The cooler he defended as a necessary evil. When Commissioner Davis was called in for questioning, she scolded the examiners and questioned their expertise, confronting them face-to-face, refusing to remain seated. Asked if she agreed with the warden's tactics of shattering an inmate through punishment, she replied, "Not until the prisoner's spirit is broken, but until he behaves."

Davis defended her subordinate's integrity, though she admitted his ideas of penology had not quite kept pace with the times. The damage was done, however, and a week after she testified, the Department of Correction announced that Warden Hayes was out: He had been put on leave through the end of the year, at which point he would retire. On Blackwell's Island, the prisoners gave three cheers for Tannenbaum. "The state prison commission has found Warden Hayes unfit for his position," the *Masses* cheered. "By how many months do we anticipate the findings of another commission when we say that Commissioner Davis is unfit for hers?"

TANNENBAUM'S COMRADES IN the Industrial Workers of the World, who believed that prison improvements were a distraction from the real work of factory struggle, worried that his success as a reformer might dull his agitations. "Am glad you are ready for work on 'The Masses,'" Jane Roulston wrote soon after his release, "but am sorry you have no time to affiliate with the I.W.W." Frank retained fond memories of his time with the One Big Union. "The I.W.W. that I knew I shall always look back upon with the greatest reverence," he would later write. "Nowhere have I found that idealism, that love of one's kind, that social mindedness and sincerity." In his first week of freedom he spoke to a rally in Union Square. But even though conditions in the city remained desperate—unemployment and homelessness had only increased since the previous year—the context had changed. Thanks to his agitations, there were now jobless commissions and church-organized bureaus for those who were out of work. A whole infrastructure of relief was beginning to emerge. "That may not be much to accomplish," Frank modestly conceded, "but it at least means that a little bit of conscience has been awakened."

Tannenbaum's time as a revolutionist was over; still smarting from a feeling of intellectual inadequacy, his consuming interest was to further his education. Most of his entire first day of freedom was spent on the campus of Columbia University, in Morningside Heights in northern Manhattan. With the assistance of friends he was allowed to pass the "character test," and he enrolled for classes in the summer of 1915. Not surprisingly, his former associates were aghast. "I hear you intend going to Columbia," wrote Alexander Berkman, who was in San Francisco. "Of course, advice, is never in place, but I'm sure you are going to waste several years in learning things mostly not worth knowing, partly that 'ain't so', + a small balance of which worth knowing you could acquire more thoroughly with much less expenditure of time, effort + money. In other words, it's a relic of ignorance to worship a 'college education.'"

But Frank ignored all remonstrance. Every morning he woke up at five A.M. to study. Through "work—everlasting plugging," he managed to make up for the reading he had missed out on and started to catch up with his colleagues. It was a struggle at first. In his first two semesters, he received a D in English composition, a C in German, and a B for various courses in history. The former revolutionist received his best mark—an A—in Business.

*   *   *

"I THINK YOU have the town with you," Mayor Mitchel's secretary wrote to Katharine B. Davis in early August 1914. The commissioner had just quelled the Independence Day prison riots, and she was on her way to resolving Becky Edelsohn's hunger strike. But within a year most of that support had vanished. Criticism made Davis defensive; it amplified the authoritative tendencies that had already made her despised among her prisoners. Whatever goodwill she retained was eroded by shocking revelations of maltreatment and neglect within the city's jails. Tannenbaum's investigation had exposed the worst of Blackwell's Island, the Department of Health condemned conditions in the Tombs, and the state Board of Charities did the same for Hart Island. Having begun her tenure with such headstrong ambition, Davis now spoke of the necessity of gradualism. "I am, I assert, a conservative radical," she explained. "Changes have to be made slowly. I have tried to conduct an educational campaign, and I have been reorganizing slowly . . . I have to move slowly."

Not all of these failures were hers alone. Like her colleagues in the administration, she had come to her post with advanced ideas about social science but scant experience in governing. Her main problem had nothing to do with temperament, caution, or conservatism: It was a matter of money. All the grandiose visions of the Mitchel government's earliest days had been concocted without the slightest care for appropriations and budgeting. The jails in particular needed enormous improvements, and most should have just been demolished. Davis had pleaded for increased funding. "I shouted until I was hoarse," she explained. "I know how to economize, but I can't do the impossible. It is the same proposition that Charities Commissioner Kingsbury is up against. The population we care for has increased 50 per cent. and the appropriation 4 per cent."

But public opinion, outraged by the stories of abuse, focused its anger on Davis herself. Her sex only accelerated her fall. At the time of her appointment, most people had approved of the idea of a female prison commissioner. Now the doubters appeared. "Admirable women, put in places of authority and long retained there," theorized the editors at *Life*, "are often seen to cripple the lives they dominate by excessive exercise of control. They get over-development of the will, scare off the people who ought to work with them and come lonely to saddened ends." Militant feminists were skeptical, too, but for different reasons. "Women," argued Margaret Sanger, "have been too ready to admire other women who, with inflated ideas of self-importance, are willing to degrade themselves and their sex by assuming the barbaric posts that decent men are giving up—in short by becoming detectives, policewomen and commissioners of correction. Let us proclaim such women as traitors and enemies of the working class!"

In the end, the prediction by the *Masses* about Davis's imminent removal proved accurate. In December 1915 she resigned as commissioner of correction and took a new position as the head of the newly created Board of Parole. Press releases once again lauded her as the "best-fitted person" for the job. And Mayor Mitchel supported her to the last. But the tenure of the first woman to hold a cabinet post in a New York City administration had ended in failure and controversy after only two years.

* * *

JOHN ADAMS KINGSBURY had been a perpetual headache to the mayor, his Department of Charities "the storm centre" of the administration. Sure of his ideas, the commissioner had scythed the malefactors and wastrels from his jurisdiction, cutting costs, improving care—and amassing enemies. "There was this fatal streak in him of no compromise," thought Frances Perkins. Another member of the government recalled how every one of his manic initiatives created "some new little gang of people that had their knives out for him." But no confrontation in his tenure had proven so damaging as his clash with the Sisters of Mercy.

The city spent millions each year in public subsidies for private orphanages. The Catholic Church was the largest benefactor from these payments, receiving $2.50 a week for each of the twenty-three thousand children enrolled in its parochial schools and orphanages. In former years, Tammany administrations had disbursed this largesse without much in the way of accounting and oversight. Kingsbury changed that. Scrutinizing every dormitory, bathroom, and kitchen, he discovered the inevitable disgrace: "Beds were alive with vermin," he reported to the mayor at the end of 1914; "antiquated methods of punishment prevailed . . . the children were given little else save religious instruction." In one institution, two hundred children were said to be sharing the same toothbrush and cake of soap. What they had seen, investigators concluded, was "worse than anything in *Oliver Twist*."

Although his investigations had not focused solely on Catholic facilities—more than half of the criticized schools had been run by Protestants—the diocese nevertheless detected "a nasty anti-Catholic animus" in the inquiry and responded with a campaign in self-defense. Mitchel was denounced as a betrayer of his own faith; Kingsbury and his fellow social scientists were accused of operating a "highly-organized agency of paganism." Taking a lesson from the practices of Ivy Lee, hundreds of thousands of pamphlets were printed and distributed on church steps each Sunday after mass. "The Church is from God," parishioners read. "Modern sociology is not."

Kingsbury was not patient with impediments. Finding his efforts thwarted, he immediately began to suspect a criminal conspiracy. With the assistance of Commissioner Woods and the consent of the mayor, he took the extreme step of having the police install wiretaps on the telephones of several prominent church spokesmen. When word of this measure inevitably leaked, the officials found themselves denounced everywhere. Civic and religious groups demanded Mitchel's impeachment; the governor launched an investigation. William Randolph Hearst's *New York American* was especially eager to press the assault; "in making this arbitrary and unlawful invasion and incursion upon the privacy of citizens' homes and businesses," its editors wrote, the government was "not one bit better morally than any thief who climbs in the window to steal a householder's papers or money." The administration—at first—denied any knowledge of the affair, then it clumsily attempted to destroy the evidence. But in May 1916 a Brooklyn grand jury indicted Kingsbury and considered doing the same for others. "If, as it does appear," the court declared, "Mayor Mitchel and Police Commissioner Woods approved of the conduct of those responsible for the tapping of the wires . . . they merit severe condemnation."

After more than a year of controversy, Kingsbury was acquitted. But to his—and the mayor's—list of enemies had been added many of the million Catholic voters who lived in New York City.

* * *

ALEXANDER BERKMAN WAS restless. He had hardly left New York in eight years, and with police spies everywhere, the city was less hospitable than ever before. Toward the end of 1914, he began to plan a cross-country lecture tour. As the date to leave approached, the prospect shone brighter. "Too long in one place, at the same kind of work, has a tendency to stale one," he wrote. "Again, living many years in New York one is apt to regard the Metropolis as a criterion of the whole country, in point of general conditions and revolutionary activity—which is far from correct." Then, on the night before departure, his farewell party was interrupted by the cops. Berkman was arrested and missed his train. "Man proposes, and the police impose," he wrote good-humoredly; this latest outrage delayed his start by only a single day.

His first stop, Pittsburgh, brought old recollections hurtling back. Twenty-two years had passed since his attack on Frick. A lecture in the city was well attended. But in Homestead, site of the 1892 steel strike, he was depressed to find the workers cowed and dispirited; riddled with informers, they were unwilling, he concluded, to risk their jobs to hear his speech. Elyria, Detroit, Buffalo, Denver: At every destination he faced petty injunctions. Auditorium owners reneged on their contracts; police disturbed the meetings. Even when he was allowed to talk, the results tended to be disappointing. "The poor boy seems to have absolutely no luck with lectures," Goldman wrote. "He is terribly discouraged, which I can readily understand." His gloom transmitted itself to his impressions of the country. "Kansas City is depressing: the sky is drab, the air smutty, the streets haunted by emaciated and bedraggled unemployed," he wrote. "Cleveland, Chicago, Minneapolis, St. Louis— everywhere I find the same situation." His enthusiasm for travel rapidly diminished. After two months on the road, the city he had escaped with such relief had already been transformed by wistful memory into "dear old Gotham."

The life of the itinerant missionary did not suit him; he had to be agitating. But somehow anger—the rage that had driven his politics all along—no longer felt appropriate. Sorrow was the only appropriate response to the war and its effects. Just as he had foretold, the governments of every nation had used the conflict as an excuse to persecute its dissidents; the citizenry, in its patriotic fury, had acquiesced to assist in this effort. Lifelong advocates of peace and cooperation now joined the nationalists. Even Kropotkin, the greatest anarchist teacher, had succumbed to the fallacy of ethnocentrism, writing a pamphlet declaring the need for the Slavic Russians to defeat Prussian militarism. Berkman could only take it philosophically. "Time tempers the impatience of Youth," he wrote. "Slowly, but imperatively, life forces us to learn to conceive of the Social Revolution as something less cataclysmic and mechanical, something more definite and humanly real."

He was in California during the summer of 1916, editing a magazine he had dubbed the *Blast*, when a new outrage relieved his stupor. The war was in its second year, and Americans were growing frustrated with neutrality. The *Lusitania*, which had escaped from New York Harbor in the first days of the conflict, had since been sunk by a German torpedo, costing more than a hundred American lives. A campaign for "Preparedness" found civilians marching and camping out, training themselves for the possibility of fighting. On July 22, a pro-military parade in San Francisco scattered in panic when a bomb, thrown by an unknown hand, detonated in the midst of the crowd, killing eight people and wounding dozens more.

Berkman and Goldman learned about the attack over the telephone, and their initial thought was, "I hope we anarchists will not again be held responsible." They were. Just like thirty years earlier in Chicago, the government indicted labor leaders for the crime—in this case Thomas Mooney and Warren Billings—ignoring the fact that no evidence linked them to the crime. When a hostile judge ordered Mooney to be executed, Berkman, who was himself facing imminent indictment, fomented national and international opposition. Most crucially, by using his contacts in Russia, he was able to organize street protests in Petrograd and Kronstadt. Word of the demonstrations passed from the American ambassador to Woodrow Wilson, who, mindful of the diplomatic impact on the war, personally requested that the California governor commute Mooney's sentence to life imprisonment.

That was a small but vital victory—and it was also the last.

* * *

ON APRIL 2, 1917, Washington, D.C., prepared for battle. President Wilson had called the Congress into extraordinary session, and it was widely expected that he would be asking the legislature to ratify a declaration of war. After all the years of hesitation—and a reelection campaign waged on the promise of keeping the United States out of the conflict—he was finally ready to make the dreadful decision. Antiwar groups had mobilized to show their disapproval, assaulting government offices with angry telegrams and sending thousands of delegates to the city. Outside, the Capitol was surrounded by encampments occupied by irate pacifists; inside, "the building swarmed with Secret Service men, Post Office inspectors, and policemen." Protesters rallied through the streets wearing white armbands and waving streamers that read WE WANT PEACE and KEEP OUT OF WAR. Advocates for women's suffrage, in an unrelated rally that had been ongoing since January, added their pickets to the general turmoil.

Wilson's speech was prepared; he was ready, and none could accuse him of taking this step lightly. After the disastrous occupation of Veracruz, he had kept steadfast in refusing to commit American arms to foreign soil. In 1916, he had reluctantly—and only after repeated provocations—agreed to send an expeditionary force into northern Mexico in an unsuccessful attempt to capture the renegade Pancho Villa. Since then, and despite the far greater pressures of the European war, he had dedicated himself to the moral righteousness of neutrality. "There is such a thing as a man being too proud to fight," he had said after a German torpedo sank the *Lusitania*. "There is such a thing as a nation being so right that it does not need to convince others by force that it is right." Always at the heart of his thinking was the remembrance of those coffins he had seen in New York City. "I have to sleep with my conscience in these matters," he explained, "and I shall be held responsible for every drop of blood that may be spent."

Afternoon turned to evening, but the streets remained too chaotic for the president to appear. Onlookers jeered as police and army reservists were called in to clear a thousand pacifists from the stairs on the eastern side of the Capitol building. By nightfall, peace had finally been restored. The remaining spectators applauded as two troops of cavalry, their "sabres glittering under the arc lights," cantered into the plaza. Behind them, the president's automobile stopped by the entrance. Flanked by Secret Service agents and clutching a few sheets of typewritten notes, Woodrow Wilson strode inside. The senators, Supreme Court justices, and members of the diplomatic corps had only just found their seats in the chamber of the House of Representatives when the speaker rose to announce, "The President of the United States." Everyone stood again; the congressmen "not only cheered, but yelled" an ovation unlike any he had ever before received in Washington.

Wilson held his speech in both hands, concentrating on the words and not looking up from the pages. He began with a litany of German misdeeds, starting with the invasion of Belgium and ending with the recent belligerency on the high seas. "He spoke slowly at first," a reporter observed, "then faster than usual. His voice was clear and grew stronger as he proceeded." He built his case methodically, gradually approaching the decisive point. There were no interruptions; "the close attention deepened into a breathless silence, so painfully intense that it seemed almost audible." Finally, he came to it. "With a profound sense of the solemn and even tragical character of the step I am taking," he asked Congress to "formally accept the status of belligerent which has been thrust upon it."

Further on, nearly at the end of his oration, Wilson added one last justification for the choice that he had made. "The world," he explained, "must be made safe for democracy." This remark almost passed without notice. But one senator realized it was the keynote of the entire address. Alone, he clapped his hands—"gravely, emphatically"—and then the ovation spread. "One after another," noted a *Times* reporter, others "followed his lead until the whole host broke forth in a great uproar of applause."

WORD OF THE president's decision began spreading through New York during the midst of the evening's entertainments. At the Metropolitan

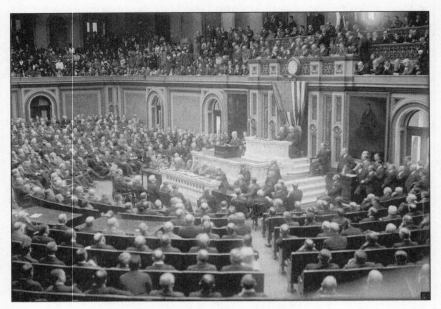

Woodrow Wilson addressing Congress.

Opera, the audience stood throughout the intermission to sing the anthem and cheer the armed forces. News of impending war flashed onto the moving-picture screen at the Rialto, on Forty-second Street, and at other cinemas throughout the city. Crowds streamed from the cabarets and theaters, crying "Hurrah for Wilson!" and "Down with the Kaiser!" In the streets, vendors did a roaring business in flags; noisy impromptu parades materialized on Fifth Avenue and Broadway.

No special announcements were made at Lüchow's or the Hofbrau Haus, two of New York's leading German restaurants. In the midst of the celebrations, socialists who spoke out against the conflict were beaten and arrested. At Rector's, the orchestra broke into "The Star-Spangled Banner" and the patrons rose to their feet. When diners at one table refused to stand, they were attacked and had to be rescued by the waiters. For these residents of the city, it was not the part of Wilson's speech about making the world safe for democracy that seemed to be the central issue, but another phrase that had gone largely unremarked upon. "If there should be disloyalty," the president had told Congress, "it will be dealt with with a firm hand of stern repression."

Having entered the war, the United States rushed to outdo its European peers in the silencing of dissent. In the months following Wilson's declaration, tyrannies of every degree and pitch undid the progress of decades of progressive agitations. Citizen vigilance committees insti-gated neighborly mob justice. Pacifists were attacked and jailed. The *New York Tribune* offered its readers a weekly column entitled "Who's Who Against America," which spotlighted William Randolph Hearst, Victor Berger, the entire state of Wisconsin, and anyone else who pub-licly doubted the virtues of the war. The Espionage and Sedition acts criminalized "disloyal, profane, scurrilous or abusive language about the form of government of the U.S. or the constitution of the U.S.," effec-tively ending free speech across the nation. Radical publications were banned from the mails, with *Mother Earth* and the *Blast* atop the list. Under the new statutes, almost every word spoken by anarchists, social-ists, or progressives during the previous thirty years—as well as most of the works of Lincoln, Thoreau, and any number of quintessentially Amer-ican thinkers—now constituted a criminal felony. "They give you ninety days for quoting the Declaration of Independence," said Max Eastman, editor of the *Masses*, "six months for quoting the Bible, and pretty soon somebody is going to get a life sentence for quoting Woodrow Wilson in the wrong connection."

Public figures of every stripe had to reexamine their beliefs.

Upton and Craig Sinclair, who had fled Manhattan soon after Caron's death, were now living in a ramshackle house in Pasadena, California. Through 1916, they had collaborated on his new novel, *King Coal*, based on the Colorado strike. The book appeared in September 1917 and proved to be another commercial failure. By then the United States had entered into war. Unlike most socialists, Sinclair enthusiastically sup-ported the president's crusade against German militarism, a position that forced him to split from the party he had championed for the previous decade. Since radical publications, including the *Call* and *Appeal to Rea-son*, had been the only dependable outlet for his writings, he was left with no way to share his thoughts with the public. This was not acceptable, so he founded a journal of his own, *Upton Sinclair's* magazine. But despite his prowar stance, his troubles continued even then. Citing his associa-tion with Caron, the post office refused to grant him a second-class mailing permit.

Walter Lippmann had demurred, back in 1914, when Sinclair had tried to recruit him for the Free Silence League. "A man has to make up his mind what his job is and stick to that," he wrote. "I know that agita-tion isn't my job." Three years later, with the country in the conflict, the twenty-seven-year-old found another role that would not suit his liking: that of soldier. "I'm convinced," he wrote to the secretary of war, "that

I can serve my bit much more effectively than as a private in the new armies." Bored with his work at the *New Republic* and eager to be nearer to the center of power, he lobbied for and received an official post at the War Department. From the heights, he then watched as repressions struck at his former associates. As usual, he viewed the matter dispassionately. "So far as I am concerned," he wrote to Colonel Edward House, adviser to the president, "I have no doctrinaire belief in free speech. In the interest of the war it is necessary to sacrifice some of it."

ON JUNE 15, 1917, New York City police arrested Berkman and Goldman in their Harlem offices. Even as repressions mounted, the two anarchists had never paused in their work, founding the No Conscription League and continually speaking publicly against the war. At their trial, they presented their own defense, turning the proceedings into an indictment of the persecutions that the war paranoia had engendered in America. Neither expected to be acquitted, and in fact they were both given long sentences in federal prison, to be followed by deportation. Their ordeal would be imposed on others again and again in the following months. Prosecutors had ceased to make any distinction between the varied gradations of protest, classifying all dissenters as "German auxiliaries in the United States." Wobblies were pilloried and attacked; the *Times* editors demanded that the Ferrer School curriculum be scrutinized. Big Bill Haywood was jailed. Eugene V. Debs, the Socialist Party's presidential candidate in 1912, was arrested for stating the obvious fact that Wall Street had benefited from the war.

Berkman spent the next two years in the Atlanta Federal Penitentiary; Goldman was held in Jefferson City, Missouri. Beyond the walls, the Russian revolution, in November 1917, offered a tantalizing hope that all their efforts had not been wasted. "The Boylsheviki alone," Berkman wrote in *Mother Earth* during the early days of the new regime, "have the faith and strength of actually putting the program of the Social Revolution into operation." At home, the armistice immediately brought the prewar antagonisms back into view. The conflict between capital and labor reemerged more dramatically than before. The tumultuous year 1919 began with a general strike in Seattle and a police strike in Boston. As May Day approached, a mail bomb exploded in a senator's house; then thirty-six identical packages, each addressed to a leading government figure, were discovered by a postal worker and defused. In June, dynamite exploded on the front porch of Attorney General A. Mitchell

Alexander Berkman in 1919.

Palmer's Washington townhouse. Gripped by a full-fledged Red Scare, the government instituted vicious retaliations. Palmer ordered a campaign of raids against any radical organization that was still standing; thousands were arrested.

On October 1, 1919, Berkman was released from prison and returned to New York City. For the next two months, he and Goldman joined together in a final agitation, but this time it was their own rights they were defending. Federal authorities demanded their deportation to Russia, and at the height of antiradical feeling, there was little they could do to fight it. "Now reaction is in full swing," wrote Berkman. "The actual reality is even darker than our worst predictions. Liberty is dead, and white terror on top dominates the country. Free speech is a thing of the past." After thirty years of living and working in the city, the anarchists could not even find a hall to rent, or a single benefactor to support them.

For most of December, Berkman was held in a cell on Ellis Island while immigration officials made their arrangements. Then, on the twenty-first, he and Goldman, as well as about 250 other undesirables, were hustled down to the *Buford*, a leaky transport ship that would carry them to Russia. The press dubbed her the "Soviet Ark." Before dawn their journey began; the vessel steamed past the Statue of Liberty and out toward the lower bay. "Slowly the big city receded, wrapped in a milky veil," wrote Berkman of his last sight of dear old Gotham. "The tall skyscrapers, their outlines dimmed, looked like fairy castles lit by winking stars and then all was swallowed in the distance."

During the final rush of events, when he had been hurried from prison to prison with little chance to gather his things or make arrangements, there had at least been one satisfying moment. In the midst of his farewell gala in Chicago, a clutch of reporters had burst in with startling news: Henry Clay Frick, the ancient nemesis, had died. Pressed for a quote, Berkman replied, "Just say he was deported by God."

* * *

TWO PAIRS OF boots, medium-weight socks, olive drab breeches and shirts, a pair of leggings and a campaign hat: Mayor Mitchel had the clerk wrap these purchases before departing for a month-long vacation in Plattsburg, in the Adirondack Mountains near the Canadian border. On August 9, 1915, he arrived and received the rest of his gear—canteen, poncho, pup tent—while the first of more than a thousand others joined him. Like the mayor, they were not quite young, of the gentry—lawyers, brokers, bankers, journalists, college men, "our kind of people"—and all toting the same unlikely equipage.

Although he had urged neutrality on the citizens of New York City, the mayor had not personally been satisfied by that policy for long. In 1914 he had been frustrated by Wilson's vacillation toward Mexico, but standing aside during the Great War was proving to be far worse. There was something dishonorable in remaining aloof in a time of crisis. With his close proximity to Wall Street, which had loaned millions to the allies, Mitchel understood that each day found American interests more tightly linked to the fortunes of England and France. He was certain that the nation would be drawn into the struggle, and yet the pretense of impartiality kept Wilson from taking the necessary measures. New York's defenses were a travesty, but the national government declined to invest in their improvement; the army was undermanned and ill equipped, but nothing was done about it—all because the president, looking ahead to his postwar role as peacemaker, feared any step that could "destroy the calm spirit necessary to the rescue of the world from a spell of madness."

So Mitchel went to Plattsburg for a month of army drills to publicize the need for universal military training, to urge preparedness on an unwilling president, and, most of all, to prove his mettle to himself. Reveille was 5:45 A.M., followed by calisthenics and maneuvers that lasted till evening. The schedule featured a nine-day hike, which the privates undertook while carrying forty-two pounds of gear on their backs. Arthur Woods was present, along with forty of his police officers, and when the mayor bested them all in a riflery competition, the whole country heard about it. Newspaper photographers captured every blister and jumping jack, publicizing the activities of the gentlemen soldiers—and annoying the president with every story. "We are having a thoroughly enjoyable and I believe a thoroughly useful time of it here," Mitchel wrote to a colleague in the city. "The spirit of the camp is fine, and all of us believe that the experiment is going to prove thoroughly worth while."

By the time New York's 1917 municipal election approached, Wilson had abandoned what the mayor had come to see as a "painful neutrality," and the nation was fully engaged in wartime exertions. Mitchel

pined to go to France with the army; he "chafed under the responsibility of his office because it prevented him from enlisting." Four years of political service had sapped his health; with a salary that hardly covered his expenses, he was in financial trouble as well, and his work had forced him to turn down several lucrative positions. No reform mayor had ever won reelection against Tammany Hall, and Mitchel's own chances were hardly certain. Only the thought of what Tammany boss Charles Murphy and his chosen candidate, John Hylan, would do to the metropolis kept him from abandoning politics altogether. Finally, picturing his office as a kind of "Western front" in the fight against corruption—and himself "as a good soldier"—he realized there was no choice but to go over the top once more.

Once again, as in 1913, all of America awaited the result. "The whole Nation has an interest in the New York City election which it feels in no other municipal contest," editors at the *World's Work* explained. "This is not only because New York is our largest city . . . but because it has for a generation symbolized all that is worst and also all that is best in American local government." The boy mayor transformed himself into the fighting mayor; campaign posters featured him in his Plattsburg khakis with the motto A VOTE FOR MAYOR MITCHEL IS A VOTE FOR THE U.S.A. He made loyalty and patriotism the center of his platform, promising to "make the fight against Hearst, Hylan, and the Hohenzollerns," as well as anyone else "who raise their heads to spit venom at those who have taken a strong, active stand with America against Germany." Trying to court an electorate that was largely of Irish and German descent, it was a disastrous strategy. President Wilson, recalling the mayor's criticism of his neutrality stance, refused to endorse him. After the uproar over the orphanages, Catholic voters were already his implacable enemies—during the campaign, opponents referred to Mitchel as the "ear-at-the-telephone candidate" in reference to the wiretapping scandal—and his association with the elite soldiery of the Plattsburg camp allowed Tammany spokesmen to accuse him of being a silk-stocking leader who had ceded "control of the city to the Rockefeller and the Morgan interests in Wall Street."

In 1913, John Purroy Mitchel had been elected mayor with the largest plurality in the history of Greater New York. Four years later, he was defeated by an even greater margin. Though it had spent more than a million dollars on the campaign—an unprecedented sum, raised mostly in large contributions from rich donors—Fusion earned less than half of the votes it had received in the previous election. John Hylan's victory was crushing. Mitchel had only avoided the ultimate ignominy of finishing behind the Socialist Party candidate by a few thousand votes. Tammany Hall, which reformers had once thought beaten, now mocked their efforts, returning to power as if nothing had changed. "We have had," the new mayor said to his constituents, "all the reform that we want in this city for some time to come."

There were several explanations for Mitchel's failure: He had barely campaigned, and had never been able to connect personally with his constituents. But the most important objection to him was his insistence on extending the administration into the private lives of the city's residents. They had never asked for the mayor's guidance. They did not want to be studied and tested at the Municipal Lodging House. They resented having their saloons shut down at one A.M. while the cabarets stayed open till dawn. They did not want to be told how to clean their homes, or worship, or raise their children. "The humbler people of New York revolted against the consequences to themselves of government by capable and disinterested experts," the *New Republic* concluded after the election. "Mr. Mitchel's downfall was greeted by a wild outburst of popular enthusiasm on the East Side. It was interpreted as the overthrow of an autocracy of experts which interfered egregiously and unnecessarily with the customs and the privacies of the common people."

Eager as the voters were to have him gone, their relief hardly matched his own impatience to depart. Mitchel had campaigned only out of a sense of duty, and now his one ambition was to get himself to the fighting lines in France. Citing his Plattsburg training as qualification, he applied for an officer's commission to every branch he could think of—infantry, artillery, cavalry. All turned him down. He even considered enrolling as a private soldier in the army. The War Department tenaciously blocked his appointment: President Wilson was taking his revenge. With all other options exhausted, Mitchel had no choice but to accept an invitation to join the air service. A thirty-eight-year-old mayor was still youthful, but a pilot trainee at that age was already past his peak. Friends worried about how the competitive enlistee would react to the sudden reversal. "Don't break your silly neck trying to be young," cautioned Frank Polk, the former corporation counsel who had been shot in April 1914. The air service lacked the cachet of the older military divisions. Worst of all, it meant months of preparation before he could go overseas. But it was the only route to combat. "Isn't it a damnable style of uniform?" Mitchel said, sighing, as he gazed in the mirror at the airman's costume he had purchased from Brooks Brothers. "Ugly and uncomfortable."

Mitchel in uniform.

In February 1918, he and Olive journeyed to an airfield near San Diego, where Mitchel had been sent for his primary flying course. He approached his first takeoff with trepidation, exuding a fatalistic sense of "resolute courage without cheering hope." His early ascents were accompanied by an instructor; then he began to solo. Occasionally he would experience bouts of nausea or a migraine in the air, but otherwise it was not so terrible. "The thing really goes much better than I had expected," he reported. "If you don't hurry, and keep your head," he wrote, reassuringly, to his mother, "there is practically no danger in this business of learning to fly as they teach it here." By April, he had graduated from basic flight to stunt work. Reporters watched in amazement as he "successfully executed the side slip, full loop, half loop, Immelmann turn, and tail spin." With increasing confidence, he looked forward to the pending opportunity to prove himself in battle. "At all events," he wrote to a friend in May, "flying is really pretty good fun and as I have more or less unexpectedly lived through the initial stages I believe I am now likely to be preserved for the Hun."

With a pilot's degree in hand, Mitchel could brook no more delays. He expected orders imminently that would send him overseas. But days, and then weeks, passed. "I thought they wanted flyers," he complained, "but apparently killing time is the prime objective. Inscrutable are the ways of military administration." In the meantime, he had the galling experience of seeing his former subordinates all engaged in useful service. Frank Polk had a position at the State Department. Katharine Davis was with the War Department, coordinating women's work. As a colonel in the air service, Arthur Woods now outranked his former chief. But these people all had office jobs. If Mitchel had wanted to remain deskbound, there would have been no difficulty; that, however, was not what he had in mind. "It is not so bad to be lost in the fighting end of the game," he wrote to his former fire commissioner, "but God protect me from being sunk in the dust of a Bureau at Washington."

Finally, in mid-June, he received his orders, but they were not the ones he had been counting on. Instead of sending him to France, they directed him to Gerstner Field in Lake Charles, Louisiana, for advanced pursuit training. He hated it from the first. The temperature reached 120 degrees at noontime, with no shade to be found. Suffocating in the heat, Mitchel was stricken by a series of migraines. He and Olive rented a bungalow near the base and he obsessed about her health. "This place is an unmitigated hell," he wrote in a letter home. "It was a crime to put a field here. It is a crime to keep men in such a climate." Hurricanes, malaria, and dysentery were a constant threat. Frequent accidents and a dissolute atmosphere had lowered morale; the officers' mess was deep in debt, and instructors verged on nervous collapse. Mitchel flew thirty-three times at the field, logging more than twenty-three hours in the air. Despite illness and a growing sense of foreboding, he tried to keep focused on his goals. "If I live through the next two weeks of acrobatic flying," he wrote on June 28, halfway through his course, "I guess I can live through most anything."

MAJOR MITCHEL REPORTED to the airfield a few minutes after seven A.M. on the morning of July 6, 1918; he had been sick the previous day and had awakened with a headache. He appeared high-strung and mentioned in the mess hall that he did not feel like flying. But when the instructor called his name, he dutifully followed him outside. All the machines had been assigned, so they walked to the center of the landing zone to wait for one to return. The Thomas Morse scouts, lithe biplanes used for advanced training, roared in circles above. As he stared upward at the others, his mood improved; he "laughed and joked when the men in the air made a false move." One of the officers, a New Yorker, apologized for having voted against him in 1917. "That's all right," Mitchel replied, "it's all over now."

The ships from the first group started coming down. Mitchel hurried to the nearest one and clambered in, but the instructor called him back: The mechanic had reported it unsuitable for flight. About a hundred yards off they found a second plane, but this one had a malfunctioning engine valve. Then another craft landed nearby; they hurried over as the pilot extricated himself from the cockpit. This one was in good order. Mitchel climbed into the seat and looked over the unfamiliar controls of the scout.

This was only his third time in this type of machine. He had taken two short flights the previous day, and they had not gone well. The first time, he had forgotten to buckle his safety harness. The experience had rattled him, and his second attempt had been nervous and indecisive. Both landings had been "exceptionally poor." After the previous day's unpromising start, the other pilots were surprised to see him back in

The Thomas Morse scout plane.

a scout plane the next morning. Actually, they thought most of his attempts were below standard. In their opinion, only his social connections had allowed him to qualify for advanced training. Alternately headstrong and overcautious, "he was not sure of himself when in the air and always seemed to be worried." Another veteran flyer agreed, saying "he was a bunch of nerves, and nerves are bad things for aviators to have." Not that Mitchel himself harbored any illusions about his own expertise. Despite investing months in training, he was still trying to find a way to transfer to the army.

While a flustered Mitchel was trying to orient himself for takeoff, the instructor was distracting him with final guidelines: Climb to six or seven thousand feet, he shouted, and then execute some glides and spirals in order to get a thorough feel for the craft. Don't try anything tricky. Mitchel throttled up the 100-horsepower engine and the plane began to skip across the grassy field. He lifted into the air and banked left, rising steeply as he circled the base. It would have taken several spirals before he could achieve the required altitude, but after one single circuit, at about a thousand feet, he turned back, shut off the engine, and attempted to glide to a landing. The unusual movement caught the attention of several mechanics and officers on the ground.

As they watched, the plane dived and then began to plummet. There was a sudden lurch—a "peculiar quick snap" that occurred when a panicking or inexperienced pilot pushed the stick forward with too much force—and a dark form catapulted from the cockpit. With horror, the onlookers realized it was the pilot. For five infinite seconds, the figure writhed uselessly, "struggling and grasping and clutching with his hands in the air." The body struck and tumbled twenty feet across the earth. John Purroy Mitchel, the former boy mayor of New York City, died on impact. For the second time in two days, he had forgotten to fasten his safety belt.

December 31, 1919

With more defiance than joy, the city confronted one last New Year's Eve. Even the preparations were businesslike. Instead of the usual kick of anticipation, the afternoon streets were filled with brisk travelers, anxiously clutching satchels and valises. "The number of suitcases and traveling bags in sight was extraordinary," noted a reporter. Men in evening dress were spotted by the *Sun* "carrying paper parcels of unmistakable shape, or handbags for which there could be no use except a certain one."

In less than a month—on January 17, 1920—the Eighteenth Amendment would become official, perpetual, law. And there were those who blessed the day. "For twenty years we Prohibitionists have labored ceaselessly and prayed God incessantly that this rum demon might be cast from our midst," a letter writer exulted in the *World*. "At last our efforts are crowned with glory; our prayer is heard." A partial ban on the sale of alcohol had already been in effect since July. But the legislation did not forbid the consumption of liquor, a loophole that made it legal for patrons to bring their own supply to a restaurant and drink it there. Hence the parcels. All those suspicious packages were filled with spirits.* At cabarets and theaters, coat-check rooms overflowed with precious bundles. "Automobiles filled with cases of wet goods rolled up to hotels," a *World* reporter observed, "and thousands of bottles of champagne and fine whiskies were carried into the supper rooms and roof

---

* The cost of alcohol had risen dramatically as Prohibition approached. Rye whiskey had gone from five dollars a quart in August to twelve dollars in September; by October, champagne was selling for fifty dollars a bottle—ten times its prewar price.

gardens." At Shanley's, near Times Square, the head waiter sprained his arm carrying suitcases. Reisenweber's nightclub, in Columbus Circle, hired private detectives to keep its customers' stock under twenty-four-hour guard.

Toward 1919, there was a collective feeling of good riddance. "The year just past," a *Times* editor ruefully declared, "to which so many of us looked forward as the portal of enduring peace, and of a prosperity more deeply grounded in righteousness, has seemed a devil's garden." Nearly eight hundred New Yorkers had been felled by automobile accidents; the city's infant-death rate remained abominably high, at eighty-four per thousand. President Wilson had suffered a stroke that left him housebound and helpless. His cherished peace treaty languished in the Senate, and hopes were fading for its eventual passage. Returning soldiers had found little work available to them, and the grinding industrial conflicts that resulted had become another source of disillusionment. "1919 will have few mourners," editors at the *World* concluded. "It has been a year of disappointed hopes and frustrated ideals, a year of the profiteer and the reactionary, a year of greed and sordidness and base partisanship."

Agents pour liquor into the sewer.

The malaise was compounded by a sense of betrayal, tinged with repentance, for the excesses of the war. Alexander Berkman and Emma Goldman, along with the hundreds of other radicals aboard the Soviet Ark, had sailed from Ellis Island during the previous week. Their departure had evoked sarcastic parting shots from the press. "Briefly summed up," a *World* reporter wrote in an unintentionally fitting tribute, "Alexander Berkman spent 33 years in this country. Eighteen and a half of them were spent in jail. He is now 49 years old, quite bald, and his eyesight is very poor. But he still believes in anarchy." But such sophomoric exultations were no longer so universal as they had recently seemed. They were countered by a growing resistance to continued governmental persecutions. The war was over, after all, and eternal warnings about national security sounded less credible each day. "We have heard a great deal of the Reds in this country," wrote editors at a midwestern labor journal. "The capitalistic press has done its best to paint for us a crimson situation. In our view, pale pink is the more suitable color." Even the *Times* tended to agree. "A few bombs, with pamphlets and speeches of the long familiar kind, have afforded material for a multitude of sensations," noted its increasingly skeptical editors. "We have never been a people inclined to anarchy and are not likely to become so."

Around seven P.M. in the subway station beneath Grand Central Terminal, an unhandy traveler dropped his parcel. With a pop of shattered glass, the amber contents of his bottle—as well as any hopes for an amusing evening—rippled out across the concrete platform. When his fellow commuters raised their eyes back to their evening newspapers, they read of that day's grand jury investigation into "Criminal Anarchism," directed at progressive schools. In upstate New York, during the afternoon, police had ransacked several Communist Party headquarters, arresting scores of "Reds." These were the last acts of paranoia to crown a year of raids and bombings.

After everything that had passed in the interim, 1914, with its sufferings and chaos, had acquired a nostalgic luster that no one who had lived through it could ever have predicted. "There were times during 1919," wrote an editor at the *Times*, "when the era leading up to the war seemed, in the casual retrospect, like some far-off Golden Age." And so, stalked by Prohibition's impending onset and dogged by regrets and fears, the city exerted itself to celebrate the holiday. For just one night, perhaps, what was lost could be recovered. A proper party was required to evoke the joyous recollections of a more innocent time, and people set out to celebrate "at least one final grand and glorious New Year's Eve, such as there used to be before the war."

* * *

ON DECEMBER 27, John D. Rockefeller, Jr., had stood in a blue suit on the south-facing porch of the Breakers, the Palm Beach hotel where he and his daughter were vacationing, to watch the day's expiry. "The setting sun was splashing its splendid colors on the sky in the west," a local reporter wrote, "the cerulean of the sky was reflected among the hues in the gently moving waters of the ocean, the temperature of the air was at just that stage where no thought is given to temperature." Asked to comment on the moment, Junior—lover of sunsets—had replied, "It is very beautiful."

For him, it had been another year of growth. His involvement with industrial relations had only deepened since Ludlow and his visit to the coalfields, so that now he was nationally known as an advocate of coopperation between bosses and employees. In October, when President Wilson had convened a national conference to bring labor, capital, and the public together to discuss possible solutions to the economic crisis, he had asked Rockefeller to attend. It was a testament to just how well Junior had distanced himself from the stigma of his fortune that he was asked to join the public delegation rather than to sit at the table alongside the other capitalists.

During the war, the labor movement had been granted an unprecedented voice in economic planning; for the peace, its leaders intended to maintain that power and expand it. "We shall never again go back to prewar conditions and concepts," insisted Samuel Gompers, president of the A.F. of L., who argued that his form of moderate trade unionism was all that stood between America and Bolshevism. The capitalist deputation, which included executives from Bethlehem Steel, General Motors, and Standard Oil, wanted to ensure the open shop and to ban union organizers from the factories and mines, hoping to go back not just to the circumstances of 1914 but to the conditions of autocratic feudalism that had reined before there even was a labor movement. After two futile weeks of rancorous accusations, the union men walked out and the conference disintegrated without having passed a single resolution.

The squabbling delegations presented an unlovely picture to a nation truly in need of solutions. In contrast, Rockefeller's dedication to reconciliation had looked especially attractive. Lillian Wald, a longtime

Rockefeller Junior in 1919.

advocate for social reform, thought he had "represented the true Christian spirit at the conference better than anybody else." It was not only his ideas but his modest and frank sincerity that had impressed onlookers and the press. "He looked as though he might have gone down to the corner grocery and discussed the price of prunes with anybody," remarked an observer. "He didn't look like a stuck-up plutocrat at all." From the wreckage of the summit, he emerged as the foremost voice for progress. "We believe that if it were left to John D. Rockefeller, Jr.," wrote editors at the *Mondavi Herald* of Wisconsin, "he could produce a solution which would be equally satisfactory to Capital and Labor."

When the conference ended he had embarked on the southern vacation that took him to Palm Beach. The "happiest days" of the trip were spent at his father's home in Ormond, Florida, two hundred miles up the coast. For Christmas they had exchanged the usual presents. Junior had given Senior two gold tiepins from Tiffany's. In exchange, he received a check for a thousand dollars. But this little ritual of presents was dwarfed by the massive transmission of wealth that was actually occurring. During the previous months, hundreds of thousands of shares of stock had been transferred to Junior's accounts, vastly increasing his personal fortune and making him, at last, the true head of the family. "As I review the year it seems as though it registered a continuous succession of wonderful gifts from you," he would write to his father. "How deeply I appreciate them all . . . is beyond the power of words to express."

This largesse marked the ultimate proof of the old man's trust. Junior had proved himself worthy of the responsibilities of his position. "There was reason," his son David would recall, "for Grandfather to feel uncertain in terms of how much Father could handle until Ludlow came along. I think it was a searing but very much a learning experience for him as well as one that toughened him." This was another sign of the distance Junior had traveled. He was the established philanthropist whose gifts, though still given in his father's name, were continually growing more generous. For Christmas, the family had disbursed $100 million, the largest charitable donation in history, and he had received most of the credit. These days, when newspapermen attended his Bible class speeches, they no longer ridiculed his sentiments. "If John D. Rockefeller, Jr., does not look out," a reporter wrote around the new year, "he is going to find himself clothed with a very attractive reputation one of these days." Forty-six years old now, he was Junior no longer. When people referred to Mr. Rockefeller, at last, this was the man of whom they spoke.

* * *

ACCORDING TO THE White House, the president planned "no special observance" for the new year; he would be asleep long before the bells pealed midnight. This was true, insofar as it went. The announcement, however, obscured the reality of the situation: that Woodrow Wilson was bedridden, incapacitated, and in no way able to perform his public duties. In early October, a calamitous stroke had left him shattered and helpless. The public knew he was ill, but only close advisers realized the actual extent of the injury. His new wife, Edith, whom he had married in 1915, had spent the previous three months serving as intermediary between the government and her husband, keeping away all distresses and intrusions, handling transactions that couldn't be postponed, and making sure the severity of his condition stayed secret.

The crisis had come in September, when he had undertaken a national tour to rally support for the Versailles peace accords. While opponents in the Senate callously distorted the issues, claiming that to join the proposed League of Nations would mean the end of American sovereignty, Wilson and Edith had boarded the special train *Mayflower* to convey his own message directly to the nation. After three weeks, he had traveled eight thousand miles and delivered thirty-two major speeches in seventeen states. Again and again he described his position in the most intimate terms. He felt personally responsible for the casualties incurred in the war; to void the treaty now would be to betray the sacred trust of the dead.

The tour reached Pueblo, Colorado, on September 25. Spectators jammed the depot long before the president arrived. Prominent among the crowd were thousands of steelworkers currently on strike against their employer—the Colorado Fuel & Iron Company. With Secret Service men on the running boards and others jogging along beside, Wilson's motorcade visited the county fairgrounds and then pushed slowly through two dense lines of cheering onlookers toward the auditorium. Already that morning, he had delivered a speech in Denver to fifteen thousand people. For nineteen days he had maintained this pace, but his strength was flagging. Words no longer came so gracefully. Bitterness at

President Wilson speaking from a train car.

his enemies threatened to overwhelm the affirmations he was hoping to convey. Yet his venture appeared to be succeeding. He was welcomed everywhere he went; increasingly, he felt confident that the people were with him. But he stumbled as he stood on the platform in downtown Pueblo. When he began, he spoke indistinctly and he paused between phrases. But he gathered strength as he continued and carried on.

Molding his message to his audience, Wilson first stressed the relevance of his fight to working people. He was championing democracy: political democracy and industrial democracy. "We had a great international charter for the rights of labor," he said to resounding cheers. "Reject this treaty and . . . there is no international tribunal which can bring the moral judgments of the world to bear upon the great labor question of the day." Shifting emphasis, he revealed the toll the war had taken on himself. There were some people, he said, who "do not know to what extent it pained me to order the armies of the United States to the fields of France." The isolationists in the Senate had not faced the anguish he had experienced during his stay in Paris when, for instance, he had visited a military cemetery. "I wish that some men in public life who are opposing the sentiment for which these men died could visit such a spot as that," he said. "I wish that that feeling which came to me could penetrate their hearts."

And then he finished with the oratorical set piece that had been drawing sobs from Columbus, Ohio, to Reno, Nevada:

> Again and again, my fellow citizens, mothers who lost their sons in France have come to me and taken hold of my hand and shed tears upon it. Not only that, but they have added "God bless you Mr. President." Now, why should they, my fellow citizens, pray God to bless me? I advised the Congress of the United States to create the situation that led to the death of their sons. I ordered their sons overseas . . . Why should they then, take my hand, and pray God to bless me? Because they believe their boys died for more than the ending of the war. They believe that their sons saved the freedom of the world, and they believe that this sacrifice was made in order that other sons should not be called upon for the same work.

When he had finished, even his wife was crying. "Loud uproarious cheering" followed him from the stage to his automobile, where hundreds of people who had been unable to find seats inside the auditorium were awaiting his departure. His head was throbbing. His hands felt numb. Secret Servicemen had to fight back the crowds as the procession made its way back toward the depot. That night, in his train car, Wilson suffered "a severe nervous attack" and did not sleep until after four A.M. He rallied slightly in the morning but then collapsed again while trying to dress. By then they had arrived in Wichita, Kansas, and fifty thousand people were already gathering to hear him speak. The waiting crowds quieted when the physician appeared. "The tour's off," he said.

All remaining appearances were canceled; the *Mayflower* sped directly back to Washington, D.C., and Wilson was driven to the White House through empty streets. A week later, he suffered his devastating stroke. Edith found him collapsed on the bathroom floor, with cuts on his face from where he had hit the fixtures. "My God," exclaimed the doctor, after a brief examination, "the President is paralyzed!" For the next three weeks, the patient lay silently in bed, unable to rise or talk. The treaty fight in the Senate, which he had seemed to be winning, slipped further from his hands. By November he had made small gains, and a few highly choreographed visits were allowed. At Christmas, he took his first halting, cane-aided steps. On New Year's Eve, he was able to spend more than an hour sitting in a chair out of doors. He had lost the use of his left arm; he could no longer speak clearly or follow complex arguments. Woodrow Wilson would never wholly be well again.

* * *

PAST SUNDOWN IN New York City that night, the religious-minded and sober at heart began to congregate at the churches. St. Patrick's Cathedral and St. Marks-in-the-Bouwerie were holding late-night services. At Calvary Baptist, an evangelical preacher would highlight a full program of events. Thousands packed Madison Square Garden to hear a choir of three thousand voices perform the Hallelujah Chorus. Messages of somber humility came from the pulpits. "With unlimited money to squander and the will to spend it, New Yorkers refuse to be downcast," ran one such homily. "Yet the passing thought may come to some few that in other countries misery and hunger reign among countless millions. It would be well if many to whom New Year's Eve is a time for unrestrained merriment and excess paused to ponder the lesson."

A troupe of carolers from the military recruiting center paraded with a sign that read, THE ARMY WISHES A HAPPY NEW YEAR TO EVERY AMERICAN CITIZEN. Athletic events in Brooklyn and Staten Island entertained servicemen who had nowhere else to be. "For wounded soldiers (there still are lots of them, you know)," the *Evening Post* announced, "there is to be a special party at the Cheer Canteen given by the National League for Woman's Service." Carry-On Dances, held all week in the hotels, paired injured veterans with fashionable partners, including Olive Mitchel, who, since her husband's death, had redirected her grief to volunteering with crippled survivors of the war.

In the streets outside, two thousand uniformed police reserves idled on sidewalks from Madison Square to Columbus Circle. Hawkers found few customers for their rattles, ticklers, tin horns, or cowbells. The night was mild, and yet midtown was as quiet—or quieter, even—than it would have been on a typical Saturday evening. "Any one traversing the length of Broadway," marveled a reporter for the *Sun*, "must have been struck by the entire lack of the New Year's spirit of our predecessors in that same thoroughfare on New Year's Eves of the past. Never was a crowd so decorous, so mirthless, so without noise." More people attended special midnight moving-picture shows than caroused in the streets. Shortly after twelve o'clock, the souvenir vendors folded their tables and stomped off in disgust. The police, who in former days would have been on duty till dawn, were sent home at one A.M. "New Year's Eve as an institution," concluded the *Times*, "that caused thousands in other years to gather into a great Broadway maelstrom, has passed into the city's history."

The cabarets, charging entrance fees ranging from seven to fifteen dollars, presented a different spectacle. "Only in the hotels and the restaurants," a reporter observed, "was there any hint last night of the old prewar New Year's Eve, with its ear-rending, noise-making machines, its feather ticklers, its confetti, its trumpets, its immovable crowds, and its good cheer." Rector's had closed its doors a year earlier, but the lid was off in the Café de Paris, which had opened at the same location on Forty-eighth Street. Maxim's, Murray's, and the Palais Royal quaked with music and fun; inside the Waldorf-Astoria there was not "space for another chair or another table."

But this was only a gilding of excitement; even these celebrations fell short of the deep insouciance of former nights. Everything was more expensive than it had ever been before. Rumors that deadly grain alcohol was being passed off as whiskey had tipplers nervous. Diners at adjacent tables scrutinized one another closely; it was said that revenue officers, and members of the Anti-Saloon League, had decided to dress in dinner clothes and infiltrate the hotels, taking note of anyone who violated the dry laws.

The traditional acknowledgments of midnight passed, and a pall descended along with memories of auld lang syne. Bottles emptied; anxious eyes watched each draft pour out, all too aware that the morrow's replenishment was not assured. Supplies diminished; parties begged cups of kindness from their neighbors, swearing to return the favor once Prohibition was repealed. A new decade had begun, and rarely had a change of years seemed so ominous. For those whose minds retained any clarity at that late hour, the thought of the moment went something like the *Tribune*'s verdict on the era: "Bohemia is passing, whether for good or ill."

* * *

WHILE OLD NEW York sought its youth in the dregs of a cup, Alexander Berkman stood at the rail of the *Buford*, squinting toward the horizon. "It is hard to be torn out of the soil one has rooted in for over thirty years," he wrote, "and to leave the labors of a lifetime behind. Yet I am glad: I face the future, not the past." New Year's Day found the Soviet Ark tracking a ragged course through the North Atlantic. The horizon bobbed and tumbled, and somewhere beyond the swell lay his homeland. More than three decades had passed since Berkman had fled the most repressive empire of Europe; now he was returning to a nation in the thrall of revolution. "To think that it was given to Russia, enslaved and tyrannized over for centuries, to usher in the New Day!" he wrote ecstatically in his diary. "It is almost beyond belief, past comprehension. Yesterday the most backward country; today in the vanguard. Nothing short of a miracle."

He was one of the few passengers who had not succumbed to seasickness. The *Buford*, a thirty-year-old transport that had seen service in the Spanish-American War, shipped water with every wave. It poured through the hatches and sloshed the floors in steerage, where the 246 male deportees bunked in three overcrowded compartments. Emma Goldman and her two female companions were isolated in a separate cabin above. Hostile sentries, their minds filled with dreadful stories about the prisoners, guarded the doors and patrolled the decks.

By January 1, eleven days out from New York Harbor, enough comrades had recovered for Berkman to call a meeting. His fellow passengers were mainly Russian and Ukrainian immigrants who had been gathered by Attorney General Palmer from across the United States: miners, bakers, factory workers, anarchists, socialists. They represented a variety of trades and creeds, but all had been forcibly detained by

The *Buford*.

government agents, held incommunicado, and then deported without forewarning. Some had been completely surprised by these dislocations— shipped to Ellis Island with just the suits they were wearing—while others had been given enough time to gather a trunk filled with clothes. Such inequality could not stand. A committee was named to assess everyone's belongings. The "possessing" members donated their excess clothing to the general supply; "suits, hats, shoes, winter underwear, hosiery, etc.," piled up in the center of the cabin for redistribution. "There is much shouting, laughing, and joking," Berkman wrote. "It's our first attempt at practical communism. The crowd surrounding the committee passes upon the claims of each applicant and immediately acts upon its verdict. A vital sense of social justice is manifested."

After another stormy week, the *Buford* lurched from the Bay of Biscay to the Kiel Canal. By the time the vessel entered the North Sea, Berkman had converted most of the soldiers to anarchism, and the worried officers requested a British destroyer to escort them for the rest of the journey through the North Sea. Afterward, the radicals alighted in Finland for another harrowing trip, this time locked inside unheated train cars, across the frozen wastes of Scandinavia. Finally, on January 19, the deportees stepped out into the frigid air and found themselves separated from the Soviet frontier by an icy stream and a few hundred meters of hard-packed snow. No one was exactly sure how they would be received, but the Finns wanted them gone, and the anarchists were desperately eager to see the revolution for themselves.

Alexander Berkman was chosen to serve as delegate for the party. Shouting "Comrades!" he crossed over into revolutionary Russia.

Afterword

John Purroy Mitchel's body arrived in New York by train a few days after his death. For one night, he lay in state within the City Hall rotunda. The coffin had to be closed, thanks to a botched autopsy at the airfield, but nevertheless fifty thousand people had filed silently past by morning, when it was loaded onto a flag-draped caisson and led through the streets. His former commissioners marched together as a group in the procession. Residents who had impatiently rejected the mayor's leadership less than a year earlier now filled the sidewalks to proffer their respects. Airplanes dropped flowers from above, so that the parade followed a path of roses to Woodlawn Cemetery in the Bronx. Riflemen clipped three volleys toward the gray sky, a bugler sounded taps, and the casket lowered into the grave.

A "brilliant and valiant knight of civic virtue," said eulogists of Mitchel, and so he had been. But the qualities of a knight-errant are not often those best suited to a mayor. The personae had been in conflict within him from the start: the diligent bookkeeper who was also a daring sportsman, the politician who abhorred the public, the long-suffering victim of physical pain who had no patience for contradiction or debate. Four years of coping with the frustrations of the mayoralty had accentuated his volatile side. The Great War offered him a tantalizing escape. To fight became his fixed idea; he craved the totalizing experience of action. And then, when that opportunity was blocked, he lost what remained of his self-possession. The man who forgot to buckle his safety belt twice in a row while piloting a skittish, unfamiliar scout plane was not the poised and steady Mitchel of 1914.

Dedicated to economy, he had died a profligate death, the victim of a

Soldiers load Mitchel's coffin onto a carriage.

careless accident incurred on behalf of an unworthy cause. To achieve such prominence so young only to be cheated of his future meant that Mitchel was denied the privilege of regretting his own mistakes. Unlike those who had survived the Great War, he would never realize the folly of the crusade that had cost his life. Nor could he redeem himself for his other failures—acquiescence in the repressive measures of wartime, defeat in a humiliating election. His record would have to stand incomplete. When people mourned, therefore, they were grieving for his lost chance to mature and improve. "A brilliant career was finished off before it was over," Frances Perkins would later recall. "He would have ripened with life. He should have been Governor of New York. He should have been a Senator. He should have been various things. He had a very great future and he would have been a tower of strength."

Mitchel had helped pioneer a modern form of governance that would eventually become the ideal for striving cities across the nation. Many of the young officeholders who got their start in his service would go on to prominent careers, furthering the good work that he had begun. But in the short term, his hard-won gains were easily effaced by a Tammany machine devoted to old ways of business. The new mayor, John Hylan, had assured the voters he would not put experts into positions of power, and this was one campaign promise he kept. "Cigar-Smoking,

Top-Hatted, Frock-Coated" loyalists returned to their jobs. Investigations lapsed; regulations went unenforced. In the first twelve months of the new administration, the city's budget rose by $100 million, or one third of the total. Three years later, the voters gleefully reelected Hylan by a margin of nearly two to one.

Efficiency in and of itself—the motto emblazoned on Mitchel's banner—had proven to be of dubious value politically. Even a friendly observer acknowledged that the mayor and his commissioners were "scientific highbrows" who "got up early in the morning and counted one-hundred and sixty-six superfluous jobs in the Department of Bridges, and abolished them and made one-hundred and sixty-six enemies, and put it into a report quite unintelligible to nine out of ten citizens, and went home and called it a grand day's political work."

Robert Moses, the future parks commissioner who had worked on civil-service reform for the Fusion administration, had little but scorn for his former boss. "Almost all the . . . Mitchel proposals were pipe dreams," he wrote. "It was an honest outfit committed to saving rubber

Mitchel and Moses at Lake Placid.

bands, using both ends of the pencil and similar efficiency devices, and to the impossible promise of making vast physical improvements without spending more money."

Working families knew all about efficiency. Their lives depended, to a degree that affluent reformers could never know, on constant calculations of income and expenditure. It was not frugalness they objected to, therefore, but the biased forms it took under Mitchel's control. Streamlining was unfairly applied. Again and again excesses of the working masses were targeted while the extravagance of the wealthy was preserved. Police inspectors enforcing the Lid begrudged the poor their saloons, but condoned the glittering all-night cabarets of the Tenderloin. Moving-picture houses were subjected to perpetual scrutiny, while the Broadway stage, though far more lascivious, escaped notice. Fireworks were banned on Independence Day, while Mitchel and his peers escaped the city to blast away in the Catskills or Adirondacks. The administration had tried to uplift New York from the top down. Few of its policies had ever considered the perspective of the people toward whom they were directed. Perhaps the reformers themselves acted without quite realizing the partiality inherent in their works, but the people knew. Spied upon by Woods's men, prodded and questioned by Kingsbury's experts, brutalized by the prison officers under Davis's direction: Really, there could be little doubt.

The Fusion leaders had attempted to separate governance from politics, but that does not work in a democracy. Mitchel's cabinet had been something like Walter Lippmann's dream of administration by experts—by the trained few whose greater knowledge entitled them to guide the masses toward the light. There was no talk of reallocating society's wealth, nor of guaranteeing the dignity of work or the security of health and well-being. It was a parsimonious philanthropy, offering moral injunctions but little else.

IT TOOK A full decade after Mitchel's death for supporters to overcome Tammany obstructionism and complete a civic monument to his memory: a gilded bust of the mayor, affixed to the reservoir embankment near Central Park's East Ninetieth Street entrance. Among the most faithful visitors to the memorial was a man whose career simultaneously honored and repudiated Mitchel's legacy. Fiorello La Guardia won the mayoralty in 1933 as a Fusion candidate, ending sixteen uninterrupted years of Democratic control in City Hall. He had also joined the air service during the Great War, and every Memorial Day he led the commemorations held before the Mitchel monument in Central Park. Though a Republican, he considered his predecessor an inspiration and was conscious that his tenure was continuing the work that the earlier reformers had begun. "The La Guardia administration," his secretary believed, "would have been impossible if it had not been for 'the trail Mayor Mitchel blazed.'"

But La Guardia was superb at the sort of politics that Mitchel had scorned. He cultivated a persona as the people's champion. Even though his own upbringing had been cosmopolitan and solidly middle-class, his background—Italian and Jewish—helped make him a friend to the city's immigrant population. But the main difference between the two administrations was La Guardia's willingness to spend. Freed from the dictates of economy, he took advantage of New Deal disbursements to make sure that the city received more than its share of the federal largesse. Parks, playgrounds, schools, hospitals, housing developments: Pipe dreams for Mitchel became reality under La Guardia.

The role of benefactor, which had once been filled by Tammany's informal networks, was assumed by the government in the 1930s as well. People who were homeless or out of a job no longer asked a favor from the local ward heeler, they went to the Housing Authority or the Works Progress Administration. Mitchel's work had suggested an important element that would lead to success, but it was left for La Guardia to discover the working formula for governing a twentieth-century metropolis. Roughly speaking, it was a combination of the two previous models, incorporating the professionalism and management of experts with the political savvy and welfare services of Tammany Hall. With this arrangement in place, La Guardia was able to accomplish something that no reform mayor in New York City had ever done before. He was reelected— twice.

* * *

ARTHUR WOODS NEVER stopped telling his two favorite stories—the one about his successful handling of the Union Square demonstration, the other concerning the time when his patrolmen had defended a female radical's right to speak against a hostile audience. But by the end of the war, these homilies were sounding increasingly implausible.

During the conflict, New York's bomb squad had utilized every manner of subterfuge and coercion in its campaign to rid the city of anarchist, Prussian, and then Bolshevik influence. As commissioner, Arthur

Woods had overseen these investigations. And when his subordinate, Thomas J. Tunney, published *Throttled!*, a melodramatic account of the unit's activities, Woods contributed the introduction. "I believe the police methods in these times were wholesome and effective," he wrote. The agents "proved themselves to be Americans all the way through, aggressive, loyal, bound to put the job through, no matter what the difficulties might be." He then proceeded to elaborate his mature views on the subject of national security. "The lessons to America are clear as day," he wrote: "We must not again be caught napping with no adequate national Intelligence organization. The several Federal bureaus should be welded into one, and that one should be eternally and comprehensively vigilant. We must be wary of strange doctrine, steady in judgment, instinctively repelling those who seek to poison public opinion."

For all Woods's success in quashing revolutionary saboteurs, he knew he could not take on Tammany Hall. He had already seen a secret police force undone by a machine administration—in 1909, Bingham's Italian squad had been disbanded soon after the commissioner's termination—and he was not planning to let it happen again. Therefore in December 1917, just a few weeks before Mitchel's tenure ended, Woods engineered the transfer of the municipal bomb squad to the control of the federal government: Twenty-four out of the thirty-four officers, including Tunney, enlisted in the army together. The move, explained the *Tribune*, was made out of "the fear that when the Tammany regime takes over the affairs of the city Tammany's favorites would be placed in charge of the bomb squad."

Forming the core of military intelligence in New York, which was considered the center of radicalism nationwide, Woods's former disciples were strategically placed to affect postwar policy. With memories of the 1914 anarchist street demonstrations formative in their experience, they intended to prepare the federal government against future subversive threats. The army amassed information about the nation's dissidents, overstating the strength and influence of leftist organizations and seeing threats everywhere. A catalog of "Red and Pink" publications for censorship included the *New Republic*, the NAACP's *Crisis*, the *Survey*, and *Upton Sinclair's*. Convinced that an insurrection was imminent and assuming they were "in no way restrained by any statute," the general staff compiled War Plan White, an armed response to domestic protests that called for the requisition of transportation networks, the declaration of martial law, and the mass arrest of dissident leaders.

While his protégés busied themselves applying his methods in ever-widening fields, Woods himself emerged from the Great War with a colonel's rank and national renown for his successful tenure as police commissioner. "The best New York ever had," declared Theodore Roosevelt, who had personal experience with the position. "I used to think that honor belonged to me, but it no longer does—Woods has been a better man than I was." What he did not have was a job. He moved between temporary positions with the American Legion and the Automobile Club of America, never finding a perfect match for his skills. He came close to being appointed Prohibition commissioner, and then during the first years of the Depression, his unemployment expertise was called into service by President Hoover, who named him to lead an Emergency Committee for Employment. But nothing permanent emerged.

It was not until Arthur Woods began to work for John D. Rockefeller, Jr., that he finally found a career. They had known each other since the Free Silence agitations, when Woods was attempting to placate the city's businessmen while still allowing the radicals to vent their anger. At their very first meeting Rockefeller had been so impressed with him that he had promised to hire Woods if he ever returned to private life. In the late 1920s, Woods accepted the offer, serving as trustee and director for several Rockefeller philanthropies. In 1934, he became chairman of the board of Rockefeller Center.

But these official posts were secondary to the personal connection that developed between the two. Over time, Woods became Rockefeller's trusted private adviser and confidant, serving his new boss in much the same capacity as he had once done for Mayor Mitchel. "The association," Junior recalled, "was one of the happiest of my life and one of the most productive." Both men had been born on January 29, though Woods was almost half a decade older, and each year they playfully wished one another "many a happy return of our birthday." There was a serious side, too. Whenever Rockefeller had a problem requiring a discreet response, he turned to the former police commissioner. Over the years, a steady succession of con men and blackmailers tried to bully or threaten Junior and his family, and Woods handled these affairs, hiring several of his former associates from the force—including Thomas Tunney, the former head of the bomb squad—to track down potential dangers and silence them.

Arthur Woods was in his early seventies when he died in 1942. Known for his early commitment to civil liberties, he was rarely credited with the other innovations of his policing career: surveillance of citizens, infiltration of dissident organizations. His commitment to tolerating free speech had been a tactic rather than an ideal. He believed that allowing agitators to discuss their grievances was the most effective way to ensure that their protests would not escalate into violence. He also realized that the overt police repression favored by his predecessors was the surest means of attracting sympathy of such independent types as Mabel Dodge and Walter Lippmann to the radicals' causes. By espousing freedom of expression in public while silently working to undermine threatening movements, Arthur Woods had devised a blueprint that would be put into practice again and again in American politics for decades to come.

WOODS AND HIS police associates were by no means alone in finding Junior a worthy successor to Mitchel. Katharine Davis, who had collaborated with Rockefeller in the years before her appointment with the city, returned to his employment afterward, pursuing a groundbreaking study of female social behavior. The resulting monograph, *Factors in the Sex Life of Twenty-Two Hundred Women*, was published in 1929 and was shocking enough that the Bureau of Social Hygiene immediately distanced itself from its findings and its author. Although Kingsbury did not find a place among the Rockefeller philanthropies, in 1921 he became director of the Milbank Fund, a foundation focused on the implementation of socialized medicine in the United States. The same "stormy petrel" he had been as a commissioner in New York City, Kingsbury parted ways with his employers in the 1930s.

Kingsbury and Davis were among the first generation of specially trained social scientists, and though their research methods and results fell far short of later standards, they nevertheless had a crucial task to perform, one that was illustrated by developments in New York City.

Advanced university degrees, prestigious governmental positions, and the praise of journalists such as Edward Mott Woolley all combined to imbue these professional reformers with enormous moral authority. Between radicals on the one hand and plutocrats on the other, it was the reformers in the middle whose support would decide the questions of the hour. In 1914, no one had been sure how this powerful force would be deployed. Progressives formed their own distinct bloc. Many among them—Davis, for instance—had loyalties to the Rockefellers or other affluent families. But there were others—Kingsbury was one, Ida Tarbell and Lincoln Steffens were others—who were deeply suspicious of plutocratic influence. Thus in April 1914 the *Globe* could write of the

Mitchel administration standing as a bulwark between two equally malignant forces, "the anarchistic rich as well as the anarchistic poor."

Into this fragile equilibrium had stormed Berkman and his followers. They represented a threat that was frightening enough to drive the other two groups together. Facing widespread enmity, the Rockefellers and their peers were forced to humanize their fortunes, diverting large amounts of wealth into foundations, universities, and other institutions of social benefit. To impart credibility to these organizations, they turned to their erstwhile critics, the reformers. Arthur Woods, Katharine Davis, John Adams Kingsbury, and their counterparts in cities across the nation lent their professional standing to these endeavors. Henceforth, the social equation would no longer consist of three independent factors. Once formed, this alliance joining the expertise and authority of professional Progressives with the limitless affluence of the plutocrats would present a nearly insuperable obstacle against the demands of radical activism.

* * *

DURING HIS FIRST trip to Colorado, in 1915, Junior had promoted the Rockefeller Plan as a vision for industrial harmony. The scheme, which he optimistically believed would render future strikes "unnecessary and impossible," had offered employees an opportunity to voice complaints but did not include the right to unionize. With its paternalistic tenor and limited concessions, it had not proven to be the economic milestone Junior had initially hoped for. Workers only bothered to vote on it under duress, complaining that taking a grievance to the owners was "like bringing suit against the devil and holding the court in hell." Management was downright recalcitrant in its implementation. Labor leaders denounced it. "Imagine," said Samuel Gompers, head of the A.F. of L., "an organization of miners formed by the richest man in the world, who employs its members!"

But the Rockefeller Plan had merely been Junior's first foray into labor politics. In the following years, he expanded his vision of workers' rights to accommodate the need for independent unions as well as collective bargaining—although he never quite conceded the necessity of the closed shop. And even Gompers had to acknowledge that Rockefeller had "grown both in comprehension of fundamental problems and particularly in the esteem of the people." By involving himself in the public debate over industry, he acquired an international reputation as an enlightened plutocrat. "Mr. Rockefeller, more so, perhaps, than any other man of immense wealth in America, is conscious of the principle of 'richness oblige,'" the *San Jose News* declared. "He is a good type of the new money king," asserted the *London Sunday Pictorial*, "the man who controls incredible wealth and seeks to use it as a public trust for the public good."

In the years after 1915, Rockefeller spent a quarter of a million dollars to improve the conditions in the mining camps, funding the construction of bathhouses, bandstands, community centers, gardens, and schools. In exchange, he earned the right to consider himself the miners' patron and to use their story as he saw fit. He elided the violence, as well as the continued suffering, to create a parable of the Golden Rule. "In no field of human relationships," he observed, "is the spirit of brotherhood on which the church was founded more profoundly needed than in industrial relations." He crafted for himself a parable out of his experiences with the Ludlow crisis. "The men in the Colorado coal fields," he liked to believe, "who some years ago had been on strike for many months and in whose minds the most intense bitterness had grown up, responded to the genuine spirit of brotherhood when it was made manifest among them, while personal contact and the rubbing of elbows soon dispelled hatred and bitterness and established mutual confidence and good will."

In effect, Junior succumbed to the efforts of Ivy Lee and Mackenzie King: He had come to believe his own publicity.

The reality was different. In 1918, he and his wife returned to Colorado to attend the opening of his latest bequest, a new YMCA clubhouse. During their visit they learned that the United Mine Workers of America was about to unveil a monument to the victims of the Ludlow Massacre. Confident that he was as well liked as the newspapers said he was, Junior wanted to be present—and even to speak—at the ceremony. A chauffeur drove his party to the place where the tent encampment had once stood. Three thousand people had already arrived to bear witness to the memory of those who had died on this bare stretch of prairie. Rockefeller had a messenger convey his card to the organizers. He was sure that the crowd here would welcome him. The union leaders were just as certain that if he tried to address them, the audience would react with hostility or violence. They told him as much, and the Rockefeller automobile disappeared from the scene; few there ever realized that he had been present.

Junior did not allow this incident to affect his belief that he had made himself a friend to the workingman. The Rockefeller Plan became a model of welfare capitalism; other companies followed suit, offering their employees pensions, stock-sharing opportunities, and other benefits without actually binding themselves to any commitments or sacrificing authority to organized labor. The system worked, more or less, as long as the economy was thriving; the Great Depression bankrupted the pensions and decimated the stocks. Without independent unions, the workers had no means to protect the privileges they had been promised. At Colorado Fuel & Iron, the 1930s brought mass layoffs, the shuttering of the YMCA, and eventually the bankruptcy of the company.

By then Junior had lost interest in the industrial question. His focus flitted between a series of passing enthusiasms. In the 1920s, he became a spokesman for the Interchurch World Movement, an attempt to unite various Protestant sects into one unified body. Then there was the refurbishment of Colonial Williamsburg, the construction of Riverside Church, and the development of Rockefeller Center—each couched with millennial purpose. Senior, who was determined to live to one hundred, came remarkably close to his goal, dying in 1937 at the age of ninety-seven. Junior lived on for more than twenty years. He died on May 11, 1960, while wintering in Tucson, Arizona. Newspapers described his "serious and studious" character, recalled his Bible class lessons and religious work, and tallied the staggering generosity of his philanthropic donations. In Tarrytown, the flags lowered in mourning. John D. Rockefeller, Jr., was eighty-six years old.

In the spate of praiseful obituaries that followed on his death, no major newspaper made anything but oblique references to the Ludlow Massacre. And yet if it had not been for the experiences of 1914, none of the rest could have taken place. At the beginning of that year, Rockefeller had known only the cloistered privilege of his position. He was not qualified to intervene meaningfully in a labor dispute, and was utterly unprepared to be the target of national criticism. The anarchist threats and the Free Silence pickets, the crushing betrayal of colleagues and friends, the abuse from newspapers and magazines had been the greatest trauma of his life. Blocked by his advisers from intervening, he had relied on publicity to restore his good name. When the disingenuousness of his efforts was revealed, he finally attempted to ameliorate the circumstances of the Colorado miners. Though the actual reforms themselves were not enough to compensate for the conditions in the coalfields, the narrative as a whole, with its dramatic arc of hubris, scorn, and redemption, had transformed the Rockefeller name forever.

Junior understood the importance of his trial. In the course of it he had grown into himself and had learned how to manage his role in life. He had taken a variety of lessons from the experience about the power

Rockefeller Junior.

and malleability of public opinion, as well as the opportunities and hindrances that his fortune provided him. And there were other morals as well. "I never read the papers when there's apt to be any trouble," he would later recall. "I learned that in the old days during the strike out west." All in all, he believed that the whole journey, culminating in his visit to Colorado, had been "one of the best things that ever happened to the family."

As time passed, the coalfield strike and the Free Silence movement that attended it joined the growing catalog of industrial troubles. For those who had participated, however, they represented a never-to-be-forgotten epoch in American life. "Forty-eight years have passed since you and I had a brief encounter," Upton Sinclair wrote to Rockefeller during the 1950s. "Many times I have wondered what it meant to you . . . I will merely say—which I think is a Christian action—that your public career since that . . . episode has earned our sincere regards." Sinclair had pondered the question before. "I have often thought what must have been the effect of that event upon the Rockefeller family," he wrote of the Lexington Avenue explosion in his autobiography. "There has been an enormous change in their attitude to the public since that time." Even as he approached his ninetieth birthday, and despite a prosperous literary career that had recovered remarkably from the disappointments of the 1910s, Sinclair continued to weigh the propriety of the actions he had taken half a century earlier. In 1966, he wrote the last in a long series of letters to a member of the Rockefeller family, this time to Nelson, Junior's son, who was serving as governor of New York State:

Dear Mr. Rockefeller:

I am 89+ and my memory is no more. This is to tell you I am flying to NY tomorrow . . . to address a dinner of writers who have received the Pulitzer Prize.

Look forward to meeting you + making amends for what I did to your grandfather!

Sincerely,
Upton Sinclair

* * *

THOUGH CRITICALLY DIMINISHED, in 1920 Woodrow Wilson had been eager to seek his party's presidential nomination for the third time. Carefully staged photographs and disingenuous newspaper stories attempted to assuage concerns about his physical well-being. But in the end, the problem was not his health: It was him. After nearly a decade of his lectures and scolding, his never-ending concern for the state of his own conscience had grown tiresome. The Senate had refused to ratify the Versailles treaty, and the patriot fervor of the war years had subsided into disillusionment and repentance. Fellow Democrats did not intend to follow him further, and the selection went to James M. Cox, governor of Ohio, and, as vice president, Franklin D. Roosevelt. In November, voters repudiated his party—and the politics of morality for which he had stood—by electing Republican Warren G. Harding, who had campaigned on the promise of returning to normalcy and represented nothing but the chamber of commerce and an end to millennial movements and causes.

Wilson spent the last years of his life in private retirement. He died in 1924. Looking back on the former president's legacy, Walter Lippmann wrote:

Woodrow Wilson in 1923.

Woodrow Wilson left behind him a country which was divided
between those who swore by him as a prophet and those who
firmly believed that his ideals were a threat to the integrity and independence of the country. Was this controversy which wracked
us and paralyzed us for a generation a real and irreconcilable issue;
I venture to think it was not, and that it arose originally from the
fact that Wilson chose mistakenly to state his war aims in the language of a philanthropic crusade. He told the people what they
ought to fight for, but he shrank from telling them prosaically why
in fact they were compelled to fight.

But Wilson could fight for only one thing: unequivocal moral righteousness. And during the Progressive years, the country could be convinced to engage in a foreign conflict only on those terms. The nation as
a whole had taken on the president's personal self-conception as the conscience of the world.

*

WHILE AMERICANS HASHED out their daily differences—soldiering through the war, coming to grips with the conflicts of labor, adjusting to Prohibition—a fundamental shake-up had occurred without anyone particularly noticing. The fighting spirit of the era had been sparked by a sense of the inhumane scale of twentieth-century life: Monopoly corporations left no space for independent entrepreneurs, colossal cities degraded the families who lived among the jumbled tenements, sprawling factories reduced labor to anonymous routine. To protest against these conditions had been the central motive behind both Progressivism and anarchism; both movements, though they used different strategies and cherished divergent goals, had been based on a shared sympathy for the individual's plight in a mass society.

In 1914, anything suggestive of large-scale agglomeration had immediately been suspect. "Everything askew—all the frictions of life are readily ascribed to a deliberate evil intelligence," Walter Lippmann wrote that year in *Drift and Mastery*, "and men like Morgan and Rockefeller take on attributes of omnipotence, that ten minutes of cold sanity would reduce to a barbarous myth." This skepticism had been eroded by familiarity and frustration. Progressives gradually applied the methods of monopoly and centralization in their own attempts at reform, until their solutions were hardly distinguishable from the problems they had initially been trying to resolve. These experiments had reached their height during the war, when President Wilson and his advisers had instituted national control over food, fuel, and transportation. After the armistice, business leaders had reasserted themselves to ensure that economic conditions returned to their previous hectic state. Widespread suspicion of corporate influence was written off as a naïve and somewhat ridiculous habit of the past. "The allegations that 'the Rockefeller interests' are stealthily scheming to 'put over' this, that and the next nefarious plot to shackle or enslave the people," scoffed a writer for *Forbes* in 1920, "are so ludicrous that even the wildest-eyed revolutionaries are beginning to doubt not only their truth but their power to poison the minds of the masses."

To speak out for the essential dignity of the individual had been the anarchists' greatest contribution to American society. For decades, Emma Goldman and Alexander Berkman had performed this task with principled conviction. But they were gone now, their movement scattered and destroyed, and no comparable voices remained to protest the increasing interference of state and corporate power into private lives. Their successors on the left certainly had no interest in the role. Communists had replaced anarchists as the new Red Menace, but their party was much more concerned with realizing the dream of Soviet-style central planning than it was with defending individual freedoms. Despite their inherent differences, communists and leading capitalist businessmen—as well as the Rockefellers and, eventually, the New Dealers—all tended to believe that the good of society took priority over personal liberation. Individual expression was subsumed into a discipline that was deemed to be good for the whole community. Without the anarchists to remind them of what they were sacrificing, Americans by the 1920s had learned to accept the unacceptable. The previous decade's fears of powerlessness in the face of centralized control had come to seem as outmoded as its silent films and tango parties.

BY THE TIME the new decade was half over, it seemed incredible that a radical movement had ever thrived in the United States. The bygone anarchists and socialists became an object of curiosity and nostalgia, and magazines across the nation bestirred themselves to inquire into the lives of the men and women whose protests had dominated the headlines in 1914. "That was a time when a tidal wave of unrest swept the world," the *Literary Digest* reminded its readers. "Soap boxes were to be seen in almost every public square . . . Strikes flourished. Bombs were manufactured and set off. The army of rebels, under Emma Goldman and Alexander Berkman, the arch-anarchists, grew and grew. Wild pop-eyed radicals they were—most of them fiercely sincere in their beliefs. And wild and insane were the things they did or tried to do for the thing they called their 'cause.'"

"What has become of this movement that promised so much twenty years ago?" asked the *Survey* in 1925. "What has become of the pre-war radicals?" Perhaps because their protests no longer posed an apparent threat, it was suddenly safe to wonder about them. "What changes . . . have come over these rabid Reds, and their various and sundry philosophies?" editors everywhere wondered. "What are they doing now, as compared with that day of rampant Socialism, Radicalism, Communism, Anarchism—a period which knows no parallel in our history?"

A correspondent from *Collier's* magazine was duly assigned the task of seeking out the agitators and reporting back on their circumstances. First he journeyed to Brooklyn, where he discovered Marie Ganz "wheeling a baby carriage, a little stouter than she was in her stormiest days—a picture of complete domestication." She had long since parted with the anarchists, joining the patriotic rush to war and afterward writing a breathless memoir entitled *Rebels: Into Anarchy—And Out Again*. At the height of the Ludlow protests, she had stormed the inner offices of Standard Oil brandishing a handgun and threatening to assassinate John D. Rockefeller, Jr. For her, those days were over. "'Sweet Marie' dabbles not with pistols and violence, but with such absolutely necessary things as rompers," the reporter continued. "The volcanic little firebrand of 1914 is now a rebel in retirement—one of the millions of plump mothers whose sole absorbing occupation is motherhood."

Next came Rebecca Edelsohn. "She, too, was young and spectacular," the *Collier's* man wrote. "Becky spoke through a black scowl of indignation. She was vituperative, direct, defiant." And she also was "a rebel in retirement." Whereas Marie had regaled the reporter with tales of her redemption, Becky refused to be interviewed. Since her release from Blackwell's Island, she had married and divorced Charles Plunkett, one of the anarchists who had been arrested in Tarrytown with her and Caron. In 1919 they had a son, Robert. It was the height of the Red Scare, and Becky worried about her security. As a notorious radical who had never bothered to apply for citizenship, she was excruciatingly vulnerable to the whims of Attorney General Palmer and his associates. Deportation loomed as a distinct threat, and she was determined to escape her fame. On her son's birth certificate she had given her name as "Rebecca Edwards."

In 1961, Becky Edelsohn Crawford was living with her second husband in Winston-Salem, North Carolina.

Whether she feared exposure or her ideas had changed, the woman whom the press had formerly called "one of the nicest girls that ever rode in a patrol wagon" was finished with agitation. She was attracted to artistic circles, serving in the 1920s as business manager for the Provincetown Players and having a brief affair with the playwright Eugene O'Neill. After marrying her second husband, John Crawford, a copy editor for the *New York Times*, she made a living selling stocks over the telephone. Believing her own pitch, she became an investor herself and lost everything in the 1929 crash. When her husband was fired they moved around, eventually ending up in California. For them it was hard to get money. She sold lightbulbs, stockings—anything—over the phones, smoking heavily while she made her calls. She was warm and generous, usually surrounded by friends. And everyone always referred to her as Becky. But she rarely talked politics, nor did she tell her son about her youthful exploits. The image of her on a soapbox in Union Square, urging on twenty thousand ragged anarchists to acts of revolutionary violence, was a picture out of another lifetime.

Professor Frank Tannenbaum.

Her smoking led to emphysema. Rebecca Edelsohn Plunkett Crawford died in Los Angeles in August 1971.

None of the former rebels had transformed themselves so dramatically as Frank Tannenbaum. "I have broadened considerably since then," he reported. "I have added many things to my intellectual make-up. In 1914 I was convinced I had the key to heaven and that no one else's key would fit the lock. Now I know that others will." After his first difficult semesters at Columbia, he had learned to master academic life. At graduation, he was elected to Phi Beta Kappa with honors in history and economics. His first book, *The Labor Movement*, had appeared in 1921, and he was in the midst of researching a dissertation on the economic structures of Mexico. Over the next four decades he would establish himself as a prominent historian, writing important studies on Latin America, labor politics, and slavery. When he died in 1969 at the age of seventy-six, his obituary in the *New York Times* devoted two full columns to his scholarly work while making only one general reference to his involvement with "the Industrial Workers of the World movement."

ALEXANDER BERKMAN'S EUPHORIA upon arriving in Russia lasted about as long as any of his other fleeting spells of optimism. At first he had suspended judgment of the Bolsheviki's methods, seeing the harsh strictures of proletarian dictatorship as the necessary consequences of civil strife and foreign aggression. But gratuitous injustices soon became apparent. He and Goldman met with Lenin and were treated as dignitaries, while most of the people they saw were starving. Everywhere, they came upon the same disparity of conditions between party favorites and common workers. As anarchists, they were quicker than most foreign guests to recognize the Soviet regime for what it was—and Goldman proved more adroit in this than Berkman. Lincoln Steffens had visited in 1919, returning home famously to pronounce, "I have seen the future, and it works." John Reed and Big Bill Haywood both died while serving the Soviet Union, and their remains were given honorary interment within the Kremlin walls.

It took only a few months for Berkman to see his fondest hopes for Russia disappointed. But it was the crushing of the Kronstadt rebellion that broke his heart. In the winter of 1921, sailors and workers in the port near Petrograd, including many anarchists, demanded that the Bolsheviks honor their promises to create a people's democracy. Instead Red Army soldiers, led by Leon Trotsky, besieged the town and pitilessly crushed the uprising. The reprisals crested on March 18, 1921, the fiftieth anniversary of the creation of the Paris Commune. For Berkman, it was another doleful prediction confirmed. He had spent a lifetime denouncing the inherent brutality of state power, and here it was again, unmistakable, despite its revolutionary trappings.

After two years in Russia, Berkman and Goldman escaped to the West in January 1922. A permanent exile now, living without papers and under scrutiny—first in Sweden, then in Germany, and finally in France—he publicized his critique of the Soviet Union and found a new cause to fight for in the murder trial of Nicola Sacco and Bartolomeo Vanzetti, anarchists facing execution by the state of Massachusetts. When global appeals failed to save the two men, it was another dismaying loss. Nevertheless he worked on, publishing his last book, *What Is Communist Anarchism?*, in 1928. Intended to speak to uneducated readers, the treatise was clear and direct in its answer. "It is not bombs, disorder or chaos," Berkman wrote. "It is not robbery and murder. It is not a war of each against all. It is not a return to barbarism or to the wild state of man." Anarchism, he asserted after a lifetime lived by its tenets, was "the finest and biggest thing man has ever thought of."

With no citizenship, his final decade was plagued by bureaucratic annoyances. Long years in prison had ruined his health; he suffered from stomach ulcers and kidney disease. After two failed prostate operations had left him in unceasing pain, Alexander Berkman decided to commit suicide. On the morning of June 28, 1936, he fired a pistol at his heart. For the second crucial time in his life, he missed his aim. The bullet shredded his lung and lodged in his stomach. It took several excruciating hours before he died. He was sixty-five years old.

* * *

ARTHUR CARON HAD emerged from obscurity in March 1914; for a few short months he had become a figure of notoriety and speculation, an icon of rebelliousness and anger, and then, in July, he was gone. As far as those who knew him were concerned, he was best forgotten. Twice a failure, he had conceived of a grievous deed and had then botched its execution. Upton Sinclair and his wife distanced themselves from any association with him. The Industrial Workers of the World repudiated his actions. Emma Goldman thought he was little better than a criminal. And Berkman, too, had soon moved on to other causes, discovering new martyrs.

The tenement at 1626 Lexington Avenue was hastily repaired. Today few residents know the story of the most shocking day in the building's history, but they all realize that something is not quite right there. Floors are buckled and creaky; windows and doors don't close properly. Otherwise, things are much as they were. Families still overcrowd the small apartments, throwing mattresses on the floor when there is not enough space in the bedrooms. And early in the morning each Fourth of July, they come down to the street toting loaded picnics to celebrate the holiday.

Arthur Caron's son, Reeves—the boy who had been born in 1912 and whose mother had died shortly after childbirth—also seems to have never known the truth about his father. He had been sent to live with his in-laws as a newborn, and when the notorious Arthur had died two years later, his keepers had presumably seen no reason to tell him the truth about his parentage. Reeves moved to San Francisco and worked for the post office. He died in 1978. If he had ever learned that there were anarchists in the family, it was a story he did not share with his daughter, Nancy, who knew only that her ancestry was clouded in silence and mystery.

The urn holding Caron's remains, shaped like a pyramid and topped with a clenched fist, resided briefly in the offices of *Mother Earth*. When police raids and arrests rendered the city uninhabitable, comrades held a short ceremony and scattered the ashes in an open field. The emptied vessel made the trip from Harlem to New Jersey when the Ferrer Center was forced to relocate. There, for years, it served "the peaceful function of a bell to call children to school and adults to meetings."

ACKNOWLEDGMENTS

I presented Anna Ghosh, my agent, with a proposal about an intimate history involving marginal politics and populated by obscure characters; she took a deep breath, helped me broaden its scope, and then worked untiringly to connect the project to the right people. At Walker & Co., Margaret Maloney was a diligent and enthusiastic editor; she adopted this book as her own and consistently pushed to make it better and more ambitious. Lea Beresford, Michelle Blankenship, and Mike O'Connor always made me feel that my work was their top professional priority, offering a commitment to this project that went far beyond my expectations. The latter stages of my research would have been impossible but for a generous grant from the National Institute of Social Sciences.

Committed archivists are essential to any work of nonfiction, and I was fortunate to benefit from the assistance of great researchers at numerous libraries. I would like to thank Eric Wakin and Susan Hamson at Columbia University's Rare Book and Manuscript Library, Lea Osborne at the New York Public Library, Candace Falk at the Emma Goldman Papers Project, James Folts at the New York State Archives, Fernanda Perrone at Rutgers University Special Collections, Kathryn Kulpa at the Fall River Public Library, Bonnie Coles at the Library of Congress, Sara Mascia at the Sleepy Hollow Historical Society, and Patti Fink at the National Personnel Records Center. I was also aided by librarians at the UCLA Special Collections library, the Western Reserve Historical Society Library, and the International Institute of Social History, in Amsterdam. I thank Robert Plunkett and Thomas Krieg for their willingness to confide their family histories to me. In particular, I wish to acknowledge the generous assistance given to my research by the late Kenneth Rose at the Rockefeller Archive Center.

Important sections of this book were developed in Columbia University seminars conducted by Professors Elizabeth Blackmar, Kenneth T. Jackson, Alice Kessler-Harris, Sarah Phillips, and Simon Schama. Chelsea Szendi Schieder read the manuscript as it was being written, and then reread the whole after its completion. Her perspective was always sharp and inspiring, and she made the work seem fun. My fellow doctoral candidates in Columbia's Department of History have provided guidance and solicitude in equal measure. Jessica Adler, Melissa Borja, Victoria Geduld, Elizabeth Hinton, Sarah Kirshen, Justin Jackson, Ben Lyons, Tamara Mann, Yuki Oda, Nick Osborne, Matt Spooner, Mason Williams, Mike Woodsworth—thank you all—and now get back to work!

A book on anarchism would be mere chaos without constructive feedback from critical readers. Zayd Dohrn, Rachel DeWoskin, Chesa Boudin, Jonah Hoyle, and Nick Miroff read parts of the manuscript and offered useful suggestions. Samuel G. Freedman, mentor and role model, read and edited the entire proposal—seemingly overnight—and his notes were keen and learned, as always. Billy Herbert and the profoundly missed Margaret Black Mirabelli were insightful and enthusiastic supporters. Bernardine Dohrn, Bill Ayers, Kathy Boudin, and David Gilbert provided their political acumen and experience in ways that fundamentally shaped my understanding of the street demonstrations and prison conditions of the past. Sean and Hudson Jacke provided expert technological assistance. Harry Kellerman, Tom Meredith, Aisha Ayers, Camila Piñeiro Harnecker, Carole Armel, Jane Hirschmann, Richard Levy, Michael Ratner, and Karen Ranucci all graciously offered their homes as places for me to write, research, and revise.

Finally, the people who have contributed the most to this effort: Eleanor Stein, my mother, whose erudition continually amazes me, and Jeff Jones, my father, a political thinker without peer, offered loving support and priceless encouragement at all times. My brother, Arthur Bluejay, not only had to read each and every word, but was often forced to read them out loud. *More Powerful Than Dynamite* never could have been written without him.

SOURCES AND NOTES

Abbreviations

LOC: Library of Congress
OMR: Office of Messrs. Rockefeller
RAC: Rockefeller Archives Center
RBML: Columbia Rare Book & Manuscript Library

December 31, 1913

1 **"wildest"**: "Multitude Dins Welcome to 1914," *New York Tribune* (Jan. 1, 1914); "'Happy New Year!' Shouts Broadway," *New York Tribune* (Jan. 1, 1914); "Quieter Throngs See 1914 Come In," *New York Times* (Jan. 1, 1914). The *Times*'s assessment that this was a quiet New Year's Eve is contradicted everywhere else.

1 **the city air popped**: "Multitude Dins Welcome to 1914"; **Singer Tower**: O.F. Semsch, *The History of the Singer Building: Its Progress from Foundation to Flag Pole* (New York: Shumway & Beattie, 1908); **clothing**: "The Well Dressed Man," *Vanity Fair* (Dec. 1913); **cherub**: "Cigar Clad Man a New Year Emblem," *New York Tribune* (Jan. 1, 1914).

1 **"Safe and Sane"**: "Horns and Hymns, Texts and Trots, Are 1914's Ushers," the *World* (Jan. 1, 1914); "1914 Dances Into Favor as Chimes Tinkle 12 and Populace Shouts Welcome," *New York Herald* (Jan. 1, 1914); "Carnival as City Greets New Year," the *Sun* (Jan. 1, 1914).

2 **"raspy throated tin horns"**: "Multitude Dins Welcome to 1914."

2–3 **Rector's**: George Rector, *The Girl from Rector's* (Garden City, NY: Doubleday, Page & Company, 1927), 114; **"It was dance-dance-dance"**: "Horns and Hymns"; **waltz craze**: Mark Knowles, *The Wicked Waltz and Other Scandalous Dances: Outrage at Couple Dancing in the 19th and Early 20th Centuries* (Jefferson, NC: McFarland, 2009); **Couples spun**: "'Happy New Year!' Shouts Broadway"; "Champagne Yields to Dance in New Year's Eve Festivities," *New York Herald* (Jan. 1, 1914); "Broadway's Automatic Merrymaking," *Evening Post* (Dec. 31, 1913); "New Year Trots In as Old Tangoes Out," the *Sun* (Jan. 1, 1914).

3 **The toughest reservation in town**: "Champagne Yields"; "Quieter Throngs."

3–4 **a man of authority**: William B. Ellison, "A Young Man of New York," *Hearst's Magazine* (April 1913); **"infectious kind"**: Raymond B. Fosdick, *Chronicle of a Generation: An Autobiography* (New York: Harper, 1958), 82; **"a young knight"**: Reminiscences of Robert Binkerd (1949), Columbia University Oral History Collection, 43.

4   **pocket watch:** Henry N. Hall, "The Young Mayor of the Greatest American City; What He Thinks of the Office and Its Opportunities; Responsibility and Danger; Still Favors Free Speech," the *World* (April 26, 1914).

4–5   **"probably near the north pole":** "Carnival as City Greets New Year"; **"blaze of glory":** "Multitude Dins Welcome to 1914."

5   **"kick out the old":** Emma Goldman to Theodore Dreiser, Dec. 27, 1913, The Emma Goldman Papers Project Web site.

5–6   **procession of friends:** Emma Goldman, *Living My Life, Volume II* (New York: Dover Publications, 1970), 521; **scores of women:** Bob Brown, "Greenwich Village Gallops," *American Mercury* (Jan. 1934); **"Tin cans":** Alexander Berkman, *Prison Memoirs of an Anarchist* (New York: Mother Earth Publishing Association, 1912), 309.

6   **"a rubber of whist":** "Cities of Westchester and Her County Seat," *New York Times* (May 3, 1903).

6–7   **"a noisy, happy time":** John D. Rockefeller, Jr., to Laura Spellman Rockefeller, Dec. 26, 1913, box 4, folder 43, John D. Rockefeller, Jr., Personal series, Record Group 2, Office of the Messrs. Rockefeller (OMR), Rockefeller Family Archives, Rockefeller Archives Center (RAC); **"as happy as their parents":** John D. Rockefeller, Jr., to Laura Spellman Rockefeller, Jan. 7, 1914, box 4, folder 44, John D. Rockefeller, Jr., Personal series, Record Group 2, OMR, Rockefeller Family Archives, RAC.

7   **"I am so glad":** Quoted in Ron Chernow, *Titan: The Life of John D. Rockefeller, Sr.* (New York: Random House, 1998), 188; **handkerchiefs . . . queer I am about presents":** John D. Rockefeller, Jr., to Laura Spellman Rockefeller, Dec. 23, 1913, box 4, folder 43, John D. Rockefeller, Jr., Personal series, Record Group 2, OMR, Rockefeller Family Archives, RAC.

7–8   **"You can never forget":** Quoted in Chernow, *Titan*, 357; **"a very poor opinion":** Quoted in Raymond B. Fosdick, *John D. Rockefeller, Jr., A Portrait* (New York; Harper, 1956), 191; **"They can prove":** Fosdick, *John D. Rockefeller, Jr.*, 87.

8–9   **"a busy life":** John D. Rockefeller, Jr., to W.H.P. Faunce, Dec. 26, 1913, box 60, folder 448, John D. Rockefeller, Jr., Friends and Services series, Record Group 2, OMR, Rockefeller Family Archives, RAC; **"cares should sit lightly":** W.H.P. Faunce to John D. Rockefeller, Jr., Dec. 24, 1913, box 60, folder 448, John D. Rockefeller, Jr., Friends and Services series, Record Group 2, OMR, Rockefeller Family Archives, RAC. **Safe and Sane:** Jacob A. Riis to John D. Rockefeller, Jr., Dec. 11, 1912, box 4, folder 41, Cultural Interests series, Record Group 2, OMR, Rockefeller Family Archives, RAC; **"rowdyism":** "Sane New Year's Eve Plans," *New York Times* (Dec. 24. 1912).

9   **"no social diversions":** "President Wilson Spends Happy Day," *New York Times* (Dec. 26, 1913); **"life just as easy":** "President 57 Today," *Washington Post* (Dec. 28, 1913); **Wilson's journey:** "President Off for a Rest," *New York Times* (Dec. 24, 1913); "Flock to See Wilson," *Washington Post* (Dec. 25, 1913).

9   **"ruddy glow":** "President 57 Today"; "Life in Pass Christian," *Washington Post* (Dec. 22, 1913); **life in Mississippi:** "Extra Guards for President Wilson," *New York Tribune* (Dec. 30, 1913).

10   **Kaiser Wilhelm:** "Mystery in Lind's Visit," *New York Times* (Jan. 1, 1914).

10 **snowdrifts stood shoulder-high:** "Snow Piled Four Feet on Streets of Denver," *Los Angeles Times* (Dec. 6, 1913); "Slip! Slip! Everybody's Slipping on Sidewalks," *Denver Post* (Dec. 30, 1913); "The Weather," *Colorado Springs Gazette* (Jan. 1, 1914); "Coal Production in U.S. for 1913 Record Breaker," *Denver Post* (Dec. 29, 1913); "Important Coal Notice!" *Denver Post* (Dec. 30, 1913).

10–11 **Two hundred miles south:** Scott Martelle, *Blood Passion: The Ludlow Massacre and Class War in the American West* (New Brunswick, NJ: Rutgers University Press, 2007), 144–145; **"candies":** "Striking Miners Not Forgotten," *El Paso Herald* (Dec. 25, 1913).

11 **"Lavish" decorations:** "Striking Miners Not Forgotten"; "Saloons in Coal Strike Zone are Ordered Closed," *El Paso Herald* (Dec. 26, 1913); **"If John D. lives":** "'Cigarettes Out,' John D.'s Order to C.F. & I. Men," *Denver Post* (Dec. 30, 1913).

12 **this gruff and vicious atmosphere:** "Troops Take Arms from Strikers," *El Paso Herald* (Dec. 31, 1913).

12 **"census takers":** "Multitude Dins Welcome to 1914"; **"stellar observation":** "1914 Flashed by Wireless," *New York Times* (Jan. 1, 1914).

12 **"half delirious":** Gerald Mygatt, "Celebrating Nothing on New Year's Eve," *Evening Post Saturday Magazine* (Dec. 27, 1913).

13 **"devotee of the dance":** "Dance the 'Twinkle Step' with Mayor Mitchel," the *World Magazine* (July 5, 1914); **"ear to the ground":** "Greenwich Village Gallops."

13 **the accounting began:** "One Big City Yawn Amid $250,000 in 'Dead Soldiers'," the *World* (Jan. 2, 1914); Rector, *The Girl from Rector's*, 119.

1. So the New Year Opens in Hope

17 **"cold and blustery":** "Cold Bothers Rockefeller," *Los Angeles Times* (Jan. 2, 1914); **Cleveland winter:** "The Weather," *Cleveland Plain Dealer* (Jan. 2, 1914).

17 **"slowest back-swing":** Ron Chernow, *Titan: The Life of John D. Rockefeller, Sr.* (New York: Random House, 1998), 400; **"clear gray blue eyes":** "John D. Rockefeller Discusses Big Questions," *New York Sun* (Jan. 11, 1914); **"finally he arrives":** "The Two John D. Rockefellers," *Current Literature* (Nov. 1908).

17 **"about the ninth hole":** Chernow, *Titan*, 365; **"constantly hunted":** Frederick T. Gates, quoted in Raymond B. Fosdick, *John D. Rockefeller, Jr., A Portrait* (New York: Harper, 1956), 94.

18 **"drizzly Winter day":** Elbert Hubbard, "A Week Off," the *Fra* (Feb. 1914).

18 **"as good as eggs":** "John D.'s Wit Well Oiled," *New York Tribune* (Jan. 5, 1914); **"mad wag":** Franklin Pierce Adams, "The Conning Tower," *New York Tribune* (Jan. 5, 1914).

19 **"Glorious old John D.":** Chernow, *Titan*, 412; "A Week Off"; **"moneymaniac":** Ida Tarbell, "John D. Rockefeller, A Character Study: Part Two," *McClure's Magazine* (Aug. 1905); **A CLAM:** Chernow, *Titan*, 426, 450.

20 **"socialists and anarchists":** "John D. Rockefeller Discusses Big Questions," *New York Sun* (Jan. 11, 1914); **"let the world wag":** Chernow, *Titan*, 434; John Ensor Harr and Peter J. Johnson, *The Rockefeller Century* (New York: Scribner, 1988), 60.

20 **"Mr. Hyde"**: "Persons in the Foreground: The Two John Rockefellers," *Current Literature* (Nov. 1908); Chernow, *Titan*, 412–413; **"diabolical"**: "Persons in the Foreground: The Two John Rockefellers"; Chernow, *Titan*, 412–413.

20 **"We are all socialists"**: "John D. Rockefeller Discusses Big Questions."

21 **"So the new year"**: "The New Year's Greatest Happiness," *New York Times* (Jan. 1, 1914).

21 **"On the contrary"**: "Life's Little Optimisms," *Life* (Jan. 1, 1914); **"What 1914 may disclose"**: "Hopes of Peace," *New York Post* (Dec. 31, 1913).

21 **"good hopes of peace"**: Ibid.

21 **lynched**: Booker T. Washington, "A Decrease in Lynchings," *New York Times* (Jan. 14, 1914).

22 **live poultry**: "New York Is Greatest Live Poultry Market," *New York Sun* (Jan. 1, 1914); "City's 1913 Butter Bill Is $64,700,000," *New York Sun* (Jan. 1, 1914); Frederick L. Hoffmann, "Pauper Burials and the Interment of the Dead in Large Cities," *An Address Read at the National Conference of Social Work, Atlantic City, N.J., June 4, 1919*, 107; "To Be Babies' Paradise," *New York Tribune* (Oct. 27, 1913); "Lower Death Rate in City for 1913," *New York Herald* (Jan. 4, 1914); **auto deaths**: "Motors Kill 302 in City," *Evening Post* (Jan. 2, 1914).

22 **statistical wonder**: "The Foreign Carrying Trade of the Port of New York for the Fiscal Year Ending June 30, 1913," *Chamber of Commerce of New York, Fifty-Sixth Annual Report, Part II*, 126; *Statistical Abstract of the United States, 1912*; "New York and Other Cities," *New York Times* (Oct. 8, 1907); "$164,000,000 Earned by the Pennsylvania," *New York Times* (March 3, 1908); "Gov. Hughes Cuts Budget $4,488,886," *New York Times* (May 24, 1909); "How New York City Spends Its Money Every Year," *New York Times* (Oct. 2, 1911); "The Increasing Burden of Taxes," *New York Times* (Nov. 19, 1911).

22–23 **Municipal government**: Henry Bruère, *New York City's Administrative Progress, 1914–1916: A Survey of Various Departments Under the Jurisdiction of the Mayor* (New York: M.B. Brown Printing Co., 1916); **public workers**: Bureau of Municipal Research, *Municipal Year Book of the City of New York* (New York: Municipal Reference Library, 1917), 35; **jails**: "Foreign Criminals Crowd Our Prisons," *New York Times* (Jan. 24, 1910); "Prison Population Grows," *New York Times* (Aug. 27, 1915); **police**: Foster Ware, "Fusion's Finest Makes Good: The Regeneration of the New York Police," the *Independent* (Aug. 18, 1917).

23 **New York has had a history**: Sydney Brooks, "New York: A Triumphant Essay on Art of Saving Time and Space," *New York Times* (Jan. 25, 1914).

24 **long felt inferior**: See James Bryce's influential study of nineteenth-century American institutions, quoted widely, and particularly employed by Richard Hofstadter. James Bryce, *The American Commonwealth* (New York: The Macmillan Company, 1902), 422; **"representative government"**: "The Wilson Administration Closes Its First Year," *Current Opinion* (April 1914).

24 **"Politics today"**: "Election Results Send Cheer to the Occupant of the White House," *Current Opinion* (Dec. 1913).

24 **"American political lexicon"**: "The Defeat of Tammany—A National Service," the *Independent* (Aug. 7, 1913).

24–25 **"terrible ogre"**: "Murphy—The Terrible Ogre of American Politics," *Current Opinion* (Dec. 1913); **"days of Tweed"**: "What Are You Going to Do About It?" *Outlook* (Oct. 25, 1913).

25 **"Graft, graft, graft"**: "Sulzer Gives Graft Clues," *New York Times* (Jan. 22, 1914).

26 **"without regard"**: "Tammany Versus the People," *Outlook* (Oct. 4, 1913).

26 **"Spectacularly"**: "Mitchel: A Young Man with a Chip on His Shoulder," *New York Times* (Aug. 3, 1913); **fads and nostrums**: "Fusion and Folly," *New York Times* (July 31, 1913); **"make things easier"**: "Republicans Mark Time on Mitchel," *New York Tribune* (Aug. 2, 1913); "The Great Duty of Defeating Tammany," *New York Tribune* (Aug. 5, 1913).

26 **"a smashing statement"**: "Mitchel to Stick to 'Bitter End,'" *New York Times* (Aug. 31, 1913); **strong hands**: Henry N. Hall, "The Young Mayor of the Greatest American City," the *World* (April 26, 1914). **"to hit the ceiling"**: Reminiscences of Frances Perkins (1955), Columbia University Oral History Research Collection, 287; **"analytical mind"**: William B. Ellison, "A Young Man of New York," *Hearst's Magazine* (April 1913).

26–27 **"When he sits"**: William Hard, "John Mitchel," *Everybody's* (June 1917); **"greatest thing"**: Hall, "The Young Mayor of the Greatest American City"; **"straight stretch"**: Statement of Mrs. W.B. Meloney, made to Capt. P.H.B. Frelinghuysen on Sept. 14, 1918. John Purroy Mitchel Papers, box 24, Library of Congress (LOC); **"Yes, I dance"**: Quoted in Edwin R. Lewinson, *John Purroy Mitchel, Symbol of Reform* (doctoral thesis, Columbia University, 1961), 147.

27 **Gaelic hands**: Lewinson, *Symbol of Reform*, 5; **"great capacity"**: "Death of H.D. Purroy," *New York Times* (Aug. 23, 1903).

27 **"hatred of expediency"**: "John Purroy Mitchel," *National Municipal Review* (Sept. 1918); **"growing interest"**: Lewinson, *Symbol of Reform*, 93; **"probably no man"**: "John Purroy Mitchel," A Man Who Eats Up Figures," *Current Opinion* (Sept. 1913).

27–28 **"Whirlwind"**: "Mitchel Makes First 'Whirlwind' Tour," *New York Tribune* (Oct. 9, 1913); **"better-than-thou"**: "Fitzgerald Makes New Attack Upon Mitchel," *New York Tribune* (Oct. 15, 1913); **simple words**: Memorandum, no date. William B. Meloney Papers, box 4. folder "Miscellaneous mss. About Mitchel, including material on the charities controversy," Columbia University Rare Book & Manuscript Library (RBML); **"The issue is Murphy"**: "No Secret Pledge, Declares Mitchel," *New York Tribune* (Sept. 30, 1913).

28 **"flashing eyes"**: "No Secret Pledge, Declares Mitchel"; **"evidently suffering"**: "Mitchel Has Proxy Read His Speech," *New York Tribune* (Oct. 15, 1913); **"the electorate"**: Francis Hackett, "The Sacred Cow," *New Republic* (June 3, 1916); **"be a 'fan'"**: Theodore A. Bingham to John Purroy Mitchel, Oct. 3, 1913, box 5, folder 3, John Purroy Mitchel Papers, LOC; **"that he should 'Look pleasant'"**: "My Dear S.V.," Memo, Sept. 16, 1913, box 5, folder 3, John Purroy Mitchel Papers, LOC.

28 **Fusion's accounts**: Lewinson, *Symbol of Reform*, 127; "Spent $129,519 to Whip Tammany," *New York Tribune* (Nov. 24, 1913).

28–29 **Half a million:** "Election Throngs in Times Square," *New York Times* (Nov. 5, 1913); **"one ambition":** Lewinson, *Symbol of Reform*, 123; "Mitchel and M'Call Vote Early, Then Rest," *New York Tribune* (Nov. 5, 1913); "Almost Mob Mitchel to Shake His Hand," *New York Tribune* (Nov. 5, 1913).

29 **the most overwhelming victory:** "Tammany," *Morning Olympian* (Nov. 6, 1913); quoted in "The Elections: A Poll of the Press," *Outlook* (Nov. 15, 1913); "Mr. Mitchel," *Anaconda Standard* (Nov. 5, 1913); **"with all my heart":** Woodrow Wilson to John Purroy Mitchel, Nov. 6, 1913, Memorandum, Meloney Papers, box 4, folder "Biographical Notes" (RBML).

30 **staggering survivors of the previous night:** "Horns and Hymns, Texts and Trots, Are 1914's Ushers," the *World* (Jan. 1, 1914); "Mitchel Takes Office, Advises Silent Policy," *New York Tribune* (Jan. 2, 1914).

30–31 **he turned to the commissioners:** John Purroy Mitchel to Mr. Mullins, Jan. 6, 1914, box 6, folder "January 1914," John Purroy Mitchel Papers, LOC; **the experts:** "Mitchel Names 18 and Tells of Efficiency Plan," the *World* (Jan. 1, 1914); **"Run up and down":** "Mayor Mitchel's Appointments," *Evening Post* (Jan. 2, 1914).

31 **importance of teamwork:** "Mitchel Slogan Work, Not Talk," *Evening Sun* (Jan. 2, 1914).

32 **"It's been hell":** George S. Hellman, *Lanes of Memory* (New York: Knopf, 1927), 175.

32 **Faugh! Stupidity:** Alexander Berkman, "Observations and Comments," *Mother Earth* (July 1913, Oct. 1913, March 1913, Aug. 1913); "A Message of Optimism," the *World* (Jan. 1, 1914).

33 **"Wonderful human achievement":** Alexander Berkman, "Observations and Comments," *Mother Earth* (Jan. 1914).

33 **The holiday season:** Alexander Berkman, "Observations and Comments," *Mother Earth* (Oct. 1913); "Black Haired Dance," *New York Tribune* (Dec. 25, 1909).

33 **especially aggravating:** Alexander Berkman, "Observations and Comments," *Mother Earth* (Oct. 1912, Nov. 1913).

34 **bald, bespectacled, and short:** Maurice Hollod interview, in Paul Avrich, *Anarchist Voices: An Oral History of Anarchism in America* (Princeton: Princeton University Press, 1995), 206; **creating an elaborate taxonomy:** Alexander Berkman, "Observations and Comments," *Mother Earth* (Sept. 1912, March 1913, April 1913, May 1913, July 1913, Nov. 1913, Dec. 1913, June 1914).

34–35 **"friends with somewhat similar aims":** Alexander Berkman, "Reflections," the *Blast* (Dec. 15, 1916); **"be patient . . . present 'victory'":** Alexander Berkman, "Observations and Comments," *Mother Earth* (April 1910).

35 **"at heart had no faith in himself":** Gabriel Javsicas interview in Avrich, *Anarchist Voices*, 67; Roger Baldwin interview, *Anarchist Voices*, 62–63; Alexander Berkman, *Prison Memoirs of an Anarchist* (New York: Mother Earth Publishing Association, 1912), 7–8.

36 **Yet human, too:** Candace Falk, *Love, Anarchy, and Emma Goldman* (New Brunswick: Rutgers University Press, 2000), 20–21; Berkman, *Prison Memoirs*, 201.

36 **"There can be no peace":** Berkman, *Prison Memoirs*, 32.

37 **"One such act":** "The Spirit of Revolt," in Peter Kropotkin, *Kropotkin's Revolutionary Pamphlets* (New York: Dover Publications, 1970), 40.

37 **The halfway anarchists:** Berkman, *Prison Memoirs*, 7, 32.

37–38 **He saw his enemy seated:** No two renditions of this scene are identical. Berkman, *Prison Memoirs*, 33–35; Falk, *Love, Anarchy*, 24–25; "Shot in His Office," *Washington Post* (July 24, 1892); "Henry C. Frick Shot," *New York Tribune* (July 24, 1892); "Frick Shot Down by an Anarchist," *Philadelphia Inquirer* (July 24, 1892); "Chairman Frick Shot," *New York Times* (July 24, 1892).

39 **Berkman was sentenced:** Alexander Berkman to Emma Goldman, Oct. 1892, reprinted in Candace Falk, ed., *Emma Goldman: A Documentary History of the American Years, Vol. I* (Berkeley: University of California Press, 2003), 129; Berkman, *Prison Memoirs*, 263.

39 **"I found the world changed":** Alexander Berkman, "A Greeting," *Mother Earth* (June 1906); **cold deliberation":** Berkman, *Prison Memoirs*, 492–493.

39 **could still inspire love:** Marie Ganz, *Rebels: Into Anarchy—and Out Again* (New York: Dodd, Mead and Company, 1920), 231; John J. Most, Jr., in Avrich, *Anarchist Voices*, 19; "Exploded in Apartment Occupied by Tarrytown Disturbers," *New York Times* (July 5, 1914); "Tarrytown Police Rout I.W.W. Forces," *New York Times* (June 1, 1914); Hutchins Hapgood, *A Victorian in the Modern World* (New York: Harcourt, Brace and Company, 1939), 204–205.

41 **the applied details of utopia:** Berkman to Havelock Ellis, 1925, quoted in Linnea Goodwin Burwood, *Alexander Berkman: Russian-American Anarchist* (doctoral thesis, SUNY Binghamton, 2000), 20–21; **radical the treatment":** Berkman, *Prison Memoirs*, 7; **Berkman's uncle was Max Nathanson:** Paul Avrich, "Berkman's Uncle," *Freedom* (Jan. 17, 1973).

41 **"Bombs and anarchists are inseparable":** Guido Bruno, "Anarchists at Close Range," *Current Opinion* (Sept. 1916); **"When compared":** "For Legislation Against Anarchists," the *Independent* (April 16, 1908).

41 **"Do we build warships":** Alexander Berkman, "Violence and Anarchism," *Mother Earth* (April 1908); **"Our whole social life":** Alexander Berkman, "Observations and Comments," *Mother Earth* (Aug. 1914); **"Of all paradoxes":** Earle Labor and Robert C. Leitz III, "Jack London on Alexander Berkman: An Unpublished Introduction," *American Literature* (Oct. 1989).

42 **"a *man*, a complete man":** Berkman, *Prison Memoirs*, 7–8.

Statistical Abstract

44 **Edward Mott Woolley was typical:** Edward Mott Woolley, *Free-Lancing for Forty Magazines* (Cambridge, MA: The Writer Publishing Company, 1927), 241–242.

44–46 **Of all the magazines in the United States:** Ibid., 166, 243; **"existence and supremacy":** Ibid., 166, 147; **"money sticking out":** Edward Mott Woolley, "Money Sticking Out: The Story of a Man Who Sold Groceries," *McClure's Magazine* (Jan. 1914); **"Every industry":** Edward Mott Woolley, "Buttons: A Romance of American Industry," *McClure's Magazine* (Feb. 1914).

46 **believed that his own rise:** Gary Scharnhorst with Jack Bales, *The Lost Life of Horatio Alger, Jr.* (Bloomington: Indiana University Press, 1985), 149; "Topics of the Week: Perpetual Best-Sellers," *New York Times* (May 28, 1910); Woolley, *Free-Lancing*, 79; "Runaways Find City Isn't Like Books Say," *New York Tribune* (Jan. 23, 1915).

46–47 **Frank Wiegel:** Frank Wiegel was photographed by Lewis Hine for the National Child Labor Committee records. Photographs from the records of the National Child Labor Committee (U.S.), Library of Congress Prints and Photographs Division.

2. The Jobless Man and the Manless Job

48 **"i wisht they'd hurry up":** Theodore Dreiser, *The Color of a Great City* (New York: Howard Fertig, 1987), 228–230. In his sketch "The Men in the Storm," written around 1910, Dreiser describes the men waiting outside a Lower East Side hotel. There were between sixty and one hundred thousand homeless in the city, according to a State Excise Department investigation. **Toward the front:** "Rehabilitation of the Homeless Man," John Adams Kingsbury Papers, box 1:34, folder 8, LOC; "Big Crowd of Applicants Gets Work Through New City Bureau," the *World* (Feb. 15, 1914); "Yale Slummers Seeing the Town," *New York Times* (May 13, 1910); "Summary of the Report of William Alberti Whiting on the Investigation of the Homeless Unemployed Which Was Held at the Municipal Lodging House in March, 1914," Kingsbury Papers, box 1:10, folder 3; "Vagrancy" paper read at the National Conference of Charities and Corrections, May 15, 1914, by Stuart Rice, Confidential Inspector, Department of Public Charities, New York City: Kingsbury Papers, box 1:34, folder 8.

49 **Those who made it inside:** Dreiser, "The Men in the Snow"; "Isaac Russell to John A. Kingsbury," Nov. 24, 1917, Kingsbury Papers, box 1:10, folder 2; "New Municipal Lodging House," *New York Tribune* (Feb. 28, 1909); "In the matter of a 'John Doe' investigation of the Municipal Lodging House," Kingsbury Papers, box 1:10, folder 3; Memorandum from Miss Mason to Mr. Folks, Dec. 27, 1914, Kingsbury Papers, box 1:10, folder 3; Chief City Magistrate's Court, First Division, City of New York, The People of the State of New York, Complainant, Against William C. Yorke and Others, April 11, 1914, Kingsbury Papers, box 1:10, folder 3; W. Frank Persons to Kingsbury, April 2, 1914, Kingsbury Papers, box 1:10, folder 2.

50 **too many to ignore:** "Zero Weather Kills Six Here," *New York Times* (Jan. 14, 1914); "The Church and the Unemployed," the *Masses* (April 1914); John Purroy Mitchel, "Introductory Address," *American Labor Legislation Review* (May 1914); Alexander Berkman, "Observations and Comments," *Mother Earth* (Feb. 1914).

50–51 **feeling rather homeless himself:** John D. Rockefeller, Jr., to Laura Spellman Rockefeller, Oct. 16, 1913, box 4, folder 43, John D. Rockefeller, Jr., Personal series, Record Group 2, OMR, Rockefeller Family Archives, RAC; **"We slept":** John D. Rockefeller, Jr., to Laura Spellman Rockefeller, Jan. 7, 1914, box 4, folder 44, John D. Rockefeller, Jr., Personal series, Record Group 2, OMR, Rockefeller Family Archives, RAC.

51 **He had hated working here:** Fosdick Research Notebooks, vol. 26, box 57, folder 503, John D. Rockefeller, Jr., Personal series, Record Group 2, OMR, Rockefeller Family Archives, RAC; Raymond B. Fosdick, *John D. Rockefeller, Jr., A Portrait* (New York: Harper, 1956), 84.

51 **his focus had shifted to philanthropy:** William H. Allen to Frederick T. Gates, April 1, 1912, box 2, folder 6, Civic Interests series, Record Group 2, OMR, Rockefeller Family Archives, RAC.

52 **"a much more important man":** *Current Literature*, quoted in Fosdick, *John D. Rockefeller, Jr.*, 142; **"you poor dear":** Abby Aldrich Rockefeller to John D. Rockefeller, Jr., probably Oct. 4, 1914, box 1, folder 7, John D. Rockefeller, Jr., Personal series, Record Group 2, OMR, Rockefeller Family Archives, RAC; Chase, Mary Ellen, *Abby Aldrich Rockefeller* (New York: Macmillan, 1950), 32.

52–53 **the incoming administration:** John D. Rockefeller, Jr., to John Purroy Mitchel, Dec. 15, 1913, box 92, folder 694, Friends and Services series, Record Group 2, OMR, Rockefeller Family Archives, RAC; **too many of his own:** "May Retain Waldo; Few Want His Place," *New York Times* (Dec. 24, 1913); "Mitchel Faces Row Over Spoils," *New York Tribune* (Dec. 24, 1913); **"a known large fund":** R. Fulton Cutting to Starr J. Murphy, Jan 12, 1914, box 2, folder 6, Civic Interests series, Record Group 2, OMR, Rockefeller Family Archives, RAC.

53 **the Colorado Fuel & Iron Company:** Research Notebooks, vol. 26, box 57, folder 503, John D. Rockefeller, Jr., Personal series, Record Group 2, OMR, Rockefeller Family Archives, RAC; Charles O. Heydt to John E. Sykes, May 30, 1914, box 20, folder 173, Business Interests series, Record Group 2, OMR, Rockefeller Family Archives, RAC.

53–54 **Lamont Montgomery Bowers:** Raymond B. Fosdick conversation with John D. Rockefeller, Jr., Oct. 28, 1953, vol. "Biographical Works," box 57, folder 503, Record Group 2, OMR, Rockefeller Family Archives, RAC; *Final Report and Testimony Submitted to Congress by the Commission on Industrial Relations, Vol. 9* (Washington: Government Printing Office, 1916), 8428.

54 **"Mother" Jones was back:** Scott Martelle, *Blood Passion: The Ludlow Massacre and Class War in the American West* (New Brunswick, NJ: Rutgers University Press, 2007), 152; "Colorado Troops Oust Mother Jones," *New York Times* (Jan. 5, 1914).

54–56 **the business of the antiques:** John D. Rockefeller, Jr., to Thomas B. Clarke, Jan. 12, 1914, box 132, folder 1309, Homes series, Record Group 2, OMR, Rockefeller Family Archives, RAC; **surely he was justified:** Fosdick Research Notebooks, vol. 26, box 57, folder 503, John D. Rockefeller, Jr., Personal series, Record Group 2, OMR, Rockefeller Family Archives, RAC.

56 **An infinitesimal movement:** William Morris Davis, *Elementary Meteorology* (New York: Ginn and Company, 1894), 58–59; Willis Isbister Milham, *Meteorology: A Text-Book on the Weather, the Causes of Its Changes, and Weather Forecasting for the Student and General Reader* (New York: The Macmillan Company, 1918), 359; "Keeping Tabs on Gales That Buffet New Yorkers," *New York Tribune* (March 7, 1915); "Bitter Cold Here on Wings of Gale," *New York Times* (Jan. 13, 1914); Ernest Harvier, "What Daybreak Means in the City," *New York Times* (Nov. 11, 1923); "Shipping and Mails," *New York Times* (Jan. 12, 1914); Horatio

Alvah Foster, *Electrical Engineer's Pocket-Book: A Hand-Book of Useful Data for Electricians and Electrical Engineers* (New York: D. Van Nostrand Company, 1903), 415. Foster lists New York City's streetlight illumination and extinguishment schedule. In January, as of 1903, the lights would have been switched off approximately half an hour before sunrise; on Jan. 12, that would have corresponded to 6:52 A.M. "Dark City Streets Make Crime Easy," *New York Times* (July 25, 1915); "375,037 Buildings in Greater City," *New York Tribune* (Nov. 29, 1914). This article reports that the greater city's 102,400 houses contained 919,000 individual apartments. Vance Thompson, "Women of New York's Smart Set Live in Limelight of Publicity, Says Vance Thompson," *Evening Sun* (Feb. 1, 1914).

56–57 **Above their heads:** "Bitter Cold Here"; "Bear Panic Hits Weather Market," *New York Tribune* (Jan. 13, 1914); Milham, *Meteorology*, 155; **By sundown:** "The Bowery Cleared of Idle Hosts," *New York Call* (Feb. 12, 1914).

57–58 **after everyone else was settled:** "Zero Weather Kills Six Here," *New York Times* (Jan. 14, 1914); **"His good faith":** Reminiscences of Robert Binkerd, Columbia University Oral History Collection, 51–52; "One Time 'Hobo' Plans Big Reforms to Help City's Needy," *New York Times* (Feb. 1, 1914).

58–59 **Abuses tainted every division:** "Children Infected in City Hospitals," *Evening Sun* (Jan. 17, 1914); Letter from Kingsbury to Dr. Ray Nelson, May 9, 1914, Kingsbury Papers, box 1:9, folder 1, LOC; Letter from Mr. Percy R. Pine to Kingsbury, Jan. 24, 1917, Kingsbury Papers, box 1:9, folder 8; "Memorandum of Visit to City Home," Dec. 14, 1914, Kingsbury Papers, box 1:9, folder 8. These particular thefts were committed during the month of Sept. 1914. "Conditions Reported on Blackwell's Island by Joseph H. Stoltzenburg, Steward, City Home," Nov. 6, 1914, Kingsbury Papers, box 1:9, folder 8; **In the morgue:** Letter from John W. Armstrong to Kingsbury, Oct. 15, 1915. The note reads: "I hereby recommend the dismissal of Frank Idane+? Kelly helpers at Mortuary caught with a woman in exposed state 1:30 am. Idane brings woman in I caught Kelly on top of woman." Kingsbury Papers, box 1:9, folder 2.

59 **the largest social welfare system:** Dorothy Marie Brown, *The Poor Belong to Us: Catholic Charities and American Welfare* (Cambridge: Harvard University Press, 1997), 49; Winthrop D. Lane, "Children and the City's Purse-Strings," the *Survey* (Jan. 1, 1915); **"in the dead of night":** "The Care of the City's Poor," speech by Kingsbury, Kingsbury Papers, box 1:34, folder 8, LOC; Frances Perkins, Columbia University Oral History Collection, interview 1, session 1, 260.

59 **falling toward zero:** "Six Perish in Intense Cold," *Evening Sun* (Jan. 14, 1914); **"prostrate forms":** "The Care of the City's Poor."

60–61 **a tour of the Municipal Lodging House:** "Mayor Visits City Shelters to Aid in Care of Homeless," the *World* (Jan. 17, 1914); **"become panicky":** "Mayor Appeals for Work for the Idle," *Evening Sun* (Feb. 11, 1914).

61 **A condition of "industrial leanness":** H.N. Gardner, "Democratic Prosperity," *Outlook* (Oct. 18, 1916); Roger W. Babson, "The Ups and Downs of Wall Street," *New York Times* (Dec. 31, 1916); Henry Litchfield West, "American Politics: Business Depression and the Popular Mind," *Forum* (Oct. 1908); John B.

Andrews, "Introductory Note: Organization to Combat Unemployment," *American Labor Legislation Review*, vol. IV, no. 2 (May 1914): 209–220; "Nation Faces Panic," *Appeal to Reason* (Dec. 27, 1913).

61–62 **made for a charming diversion:** John D. Rockefeller, Jr., to Laura Spellman Rockefeller, Jan. 19, 1914, box 4, folder 44, "Personal Correspondence, Rockefeller, Laura Spellman, 1914–1915. Rockefeller Family JDR, Jr. Personal," Record Group III2Z, RAC.

62 **an opportune crisis:** Marie Ganz, *Rebels: Into Anarchy—and Out Again* (New York: Dodd, Mead and Company, 1920), 154; "Six Perish in Intense Cold"; "Two Ice Maidens Dance with Gale," *New York Tribune* (Jan. 13, 1914); "Frozen Bodies Are Found in Streets—Mercury Falls to Four Below," *New York Times* (Jan. 14, 1914); "The Cry Has Meaning," *Appeal to Reason* (Jan. 17, 1914); Fred D. Warren, "Things as I See Them," *Appeal to Reason* (Jan. 17, 1914); Alexander Berkman, "Observations and Comments," *Mother Earth* (Feb. 1914).

63 **Mitchel appealed to the public:** Mayor John Purroy Mitchel Records, box 49, folder 439, "Subject Files—Unemployment," New York City Municipal Archives.

63 **everyone was dictating to the unemployed:** Helen Marot, *American Labor Unions* (New York: Henry Holt and Company, 1914), 255–260; Melvyn Dubofsky, *We Shall Be All: A History of the Industrial Workers of the World* (Chicago: Quadrangle Books, 1969), 64, 115, 155, 164.

64 **the Industrial Workers of the World:** Marot, *Labor Unions*, 263; Henri Handwirth, "What IS to Be Done for the I.W.W. in New York City?" *Solidarity* (March 21, 1914). The I.W.W. meeting halls are described in a letter from Estelle to Frank Tannenbaum, April 12, 1914. Of Grand Street, she wrote, "Gee what a place, but the place in West St. has that beat." Frank Tannenbaum Papers, box 5, RBML; Thomas Flynn and John Sandgren, "New York City and the I.W.W.," *Solidarity* (Feb. 7, 1914); Joe Ettor, "New York City and the I.W.W.," *Solidarity* (Jan. 24, 1914); New Yorker, "Big Meeting in New York City," *Solidarity* (Nov. 22, 1913); "191 I.W.W. Raiders Arrested in Church; Court Holds Tannenbaum in $5,000 Bail," the *World* (March 5, 1914).

65 **many chose to be optimistic:** "I.W.W. War on Waiters," *New York Tribune* (Nov. 9, 1913); "The New Year," *Solidarity* (Jan. 10, 1914); **Frank Tannenbaum's faith:** "Unemployed 'Army' of 100 Decline Places at $3 a Day; Demand Turkey and Wine," *New York Herald* (March 4, 1914); Estelle to Frank Tannenbaum, April 11, 1915, Tannenbaum Papers, box 5, RBML; Frank Tannenbaum, *The Labor Movement: Its Conservative Functions and Social Consequences* (New York: Putnam, 1921), 21, 50–51; "The $1,000 Fund," *Solidarity* (Feb. 7, 1914); Frank Tannenbaum to Dr. Grant, April 21, 1914, Tannenbaum Papers, box 3, RBML; Mary Heaton Vorse, "The Case of Adolf," *Outlook* (May 2, 1914), 30.

65–67 **He had been born in Austrian Galicia:** There is a unanimous uncertainty concerning the early years of Frank Tannenbaum's life. Every source offers a different version of events. These dates are based on census and military records. The newspapers reported that he was twenty-one in the spring of 1914, but his birthday was Nov. 23, 1894. Tannenbaum, *The Labor Movement*, 50; Estelle to Frank Tannenbaum, Sept. 25, 1914, Nov. 1, 1914, Oct. 17, 1914, Tannenbaum Papers, box 5, RBML; Joseph Maier and Richard W. Weatherhead, *Frank Tannenbaum: A Biographical Essay* (New York: Columbia University, 1974); **"restless, dissatisfied"**: Tannenbaum, *The Labor Movement*, 51–52, 96–97; "Tannenbaum's Speech," the *Masses* (April 1914); Emma Goldman, *Living My Life, Volume II* (New York: Dover Publications, 1970), 523; Harry (?) to Tannenbaum, July 9, 1914, Tannenbaum Papers, box 4, RBML; **"inarticulate hunger"**: George Palmer Putnam, "The New Tannenbaum," *New York Times* (June 26, 1921); **his ordinariness was agony**: "Tannenbaum's Speech"; Tannenbaum, *The Labor Movement*, 4; Estelle to Frank Tannenbaum, April 11, 1915, Tannenbaum Papers, box 5, RBML; "The $1,000 Fund," *Solidarity* (Feb. 7, 1914); Violet Maxwell to Frank Tannenbaum, March 29, 1914, Tannenbaum Papers, box 3, RBML; Charles Willis Thompson, "So Called I.W.W. Raids Really Hatched by Schoolboys," *New York Times* (March 29, 1914).

67–68   **The next storm rolled up along the tracks:** "8 Die in Icy Blast with Storm Near," *New York Tribune* (Feb. 13, 1914); "Snow Falls Thick as Cold Departs Heavy Storm Spreads Over Country and Gas Pressure Grows," *Cleveland Plain Dealer* (Feb. 14, 1914); "Snow 20 Inches Deep in Scranton," *Philadelphia Inquirer* (Feb. 15, 1914); "Cincinnati Recovers from Storm," *Philadelphia Inquirer* (Feb. 15, 1914); "Worst Since Blizzard of 1888," *Philadelphia Inquirer* (Feb. 15, 1914); "City in Snow Storm Grip Traffic Held Up While Business Is Paralyzed," *Wilkes-Barre Times Leader* (Feb. 14, 1914); "East Snow-Swept; Two Ships Ashore," *New York Times* (Feb. 14, 1914); "City Snow-Bound and Eight Perish in 75-Mile Gale," *New York Times* (Feb. 15, 1914); "Below-Zero Cold Kills Four in City; Thousands Suffer," the *World* (Feb. 13, 1914); "Much Suffering, Tho' Snow Comes After Zero Spell," the *World* (Feb. 14, 1914); "Ten Inches of 'Dry Sleet' Cover City; 6 Deaths in Storm," the *World* (Feb. 15, 1914); "Trains Snowed Up; Many Commuters Fail to Reach City," the *World* (Feb. 15, 1914).

68   **the city's first municipal employment bureau:** 320 of the city's private job agencies reported 27,062 jobs available, but only 11,268 filled. The *Evening Sun* says the bureau opened from seven A.M. to seven P.M. "Mayor Hunts Jobs for Unemployed," *New York Tribune* (Feb. 11, 1914); "Big Crowd of Applicants Gets Work Through New City Bureau," the *World* (Feb. 15, 1914); "16,000 Only Lift Corner of City's Mantle of Snow," the *World* (Feb. 16, 1914); "City Finds Jobs for 570 on First Day," *Evening Sun* (Feb. 15, 1914).

68–69   **Ten inches of snow:** The full-time sanitation employees were the "white wings," named after the snowy uniforms that cost each man a dollar a week to keep clean. "Mayor Hunts Jobs for Unemployed"; "Big Crowd of Applicants Gets Work Through New City Bureau"; "16,000 Only Lift Corner of City's Mantle of Snow"; **Up in Tarrytown:** "Rockefeller Plies Shovel," *New York Times* (Feb. 18, 1914).

70   **"a comedy of inefficiency":** "New Snowstorm Clogs City; 4 Die, 5 Hurt, As Result," the *World* (Feb. 17, 1914); "Snow-Bound New York," the *World* (Feb. 17, 1914); "Mitchel Himself Takes a Hand in Heavy Snow Job," the *World* (Feb. 18, 1914); "The Snow-Removal Problem," the *World* (Feb. 18, 1914); Roy L. M'Cardell, "Snow Shoveling as Homeless 'Chowder' O'Brien Sees It," the *World* (March 8, 1914).

70–71 **"The Jobless Man and the Manless Job":** "1,000 Jobless Seek Shelter in Church," *New York Times* (Feb. 28, 1914); "To Bring the Jobless Man to the Manless Job," *New York Times* (Feb. 22, 1914).

The Social Evil

72 **Wickedness had specialized:** Rev. Edwin Whittier Caswell, "The Right Use of Wealth," *New York Observer and Chronicle* (Jan. 27, 1910).

72 **"a wave of moral house cleaning":** "Progress," *New York Tribune* (March 1, 1913); **"Everything is":** "Reforming the Republican Party," *Palladium* (Nov. 21, 1913); **catalogue the eighty-seven:** "Introducing 'The Society for Improving the Condition of the Rich,'" the *World* (Feb. 22, 1914).

73 **the catchword . . . "social hygiene":** Havelock Ellis, *The Task of Social Hygiene* (Boston and New York: Houghton Mifflin, 1912), 2; "Books and Authors," *Living Age* (Nov. 2, 1912).

73 **A geography of uplift:** Harry P. Kraus, *The Settlement House Movement in New York City, 1886–1914* (New York: Arno Press, 1980); 34; Theodore Dreiser, *The Color of a Great City* (New York: Howard Fertig, 1987), 129; Karl K. Kitchen, "Why Not Join the Uplift Movement," the *World* (May 3, 1914).

74 **it was necessary to advertise:** "The Spectator," *Outlook* (Feb. 26, 1910); **charities trust:** "The Spectator," *Outlook* (Feb. 26, 1910). The couplet is from the 1886 poem "In Bohemia," by John Boyle O'Reilly; it was quoted by Walter Lippmann. Lippmann, *Drift and Mastery* (New York: Mitchell Kennerley, 1914), 290.

74–75 **The proliferation . . . was baffling:** "Union of Reform Societies Needed," *New York Tribune* (Jan. 4, 1912).

75 **Down that road lay madness:** "Is 'Reform' Sensationalism Responsible for the Apparent Increase of Insanity?" *New York Times* (May 13, 1906); Tom P. Morgan, "The After Effects," *Puck* (Feb. 9, 1910); "Cult of the Half-baked," *New York Tribune* (Feb. 11, 1913); Lippmann, *Drift and Mastery*, 184–185.

75–76 **when *The Charity Girl* premiered:** "'The Charity Girl' Is Disappointing," *New York Times* (Oct. 3, 1912); "'The Charity Girl' Sung," *New York Tribune* (Oct. 3, 1912).

3. A New Gospel

77 **"If the ladies will form in line":** Lew Quinn, "Teaching the Tango to John D. Rockefeller, Jr.," the *World Magazine* (Feb. 22, 1914); **became merely details:** Fosdick Research Notebooks, vol. 26, box 57, folder 503, John D. Rockefeller, Jr., Personal series, Record Group 2, OMR, Rockefeller Family Archives, RAC.

78–79 **The latest revelations:** John D. Rockefeller, Jr., to Laura Spellman Rockefeller, Jan. 24, 1914, box 4, folder 44, John D. Rockefeller, Jr., Personal series, Record Group 2, OMR, Rockefeller Family Archives, RAC; John D. Rockefeller, Jr., to James Bronson Reynolds, Dec. 24, 1913, box 6, folder 30, Rockefeller Boards series, Record Group 2, OMR, Rockefeller Family Archives, RAC; John D. Rockefeller, Jr., to George J. Kneeland, Feb. 13, 1914, box 6, folder 30, Rockefeller Boards series, Record Group 2, OMR, Rockefeller Family Archives, RAC;

John D. Rockefeller, Jr., to John Purroy Mitchel, Jan. 16, 1914, John Purroy Mitchel Papers, box 6, folder 1, LOC.

79 **the Young Men's Bible Class:** "Bible Class Prays for Rockefeller, Jr.," *New York Times* (May 22, 1905); **pass along his insights:** Albert F. Schenkel, *The Rich Man and the Kingdom: John D. Rockefeller, Jr., and the Protestant Establishment* (Minneapolis: Fortress Press, 1995), 22–29; "Fixing Life's Standards," box 1, folder 38, Speeches series, Record Group 2, OMR, Rockefeller Family Archives, RAC; "'Young Men Who Try to Win Don't Drink,'" the *Sun* (Jan. 19, 1914); **Under his leadership:** Ron Chernow, *Titan: The Life of John D. Rockefeller, Sr.* (New York: Random House, 1998), 509, 510; Raymond B. Fosdick, *John D. Rockefeller, Jr., A Portrait* (New York: Harper, 1956), 126.

80 **yet another . . . blizzard:** Robert S. MacArthur, *History of Calvary Baptist Church, New York* (New York: E. Scott, 1890); "Rockefellers Face Storm," *New York Tribune* (March 2, 1914); "Mob Threat for Calvary Church Brings Out Police," *New York Herald* (March 2, 1914); "The Calvary Baptist Church," *New York Times* (Dec. 24, 1883); "Snow Can't Keep John D. from Church," the *World* (March 2, 1914).

80–81 **the old First Presbyterian Church:** "Unemployed Invade Fifth Av. Church," *New York Times* (March 2, 1914); **they had chosen his church:** The newspaper accounts of the interaction between Tannenbaum and the Rev. Duffield vary, but this version, from the *World*, is most in keeping with the tendencies of the participants. Other papers, particularly the *Times* and the *Herald*, depict a more hostile conversation. "Invading Church, I.W.W. Mob Gets Money by Threat," the *World* (March 2, 1914); "Mob in Church in Fifth Avenue Assails Pastor," *New York Herald* (March 2, 1914). This was the third straight evening that Tannenbaum had descended on a place of worship, demanding food and rest. First, he and a few score of others had attempted to storm the Old Baptist Tabernacle on the East Side, but a beat cop had happened by and moved them along. Then, on Saturday, February 28, he had brought hundreds of unemployed men to the Labor Temple, a mission church on Fourteenth Street, where they had crept in during a movie screening. When the lights came up and the rector ordered them out, Frank had declared, "We are honest men. We have come here to sleep and eat. If you attempt to force us from this hall, the floor of the Labor Temple will be covered with blood." Scuffles sparked up between some of the men and the church workers. The police had come, and it looked like trouble. As a last resort, the pastor asked all those who truly had no place to stay to make themselves known. Sixty or so hands went up, and he agreed to let them sleep in the basement. The cops shooed the rest back into the streets.

81–83 **This was the third straight night:** "Homeless Army Lodged and Fed in Old St. Mark's," the *World* (March 3, 1914); "Urges Workless on to Anarchy," *New York Times* (March 3, 1914); "Unemployed Mob of 200 March to St. Mark's Church," *New York Herald* (March 3, 1914); "'We Will Work if You Wake Us at 9,'" *New York Tribune* (March 3, 1914); **in the headlines every morning:** Tannenbaum and his friends provided the inspiration and leadership for the tactic of church invasions. Although more prominent I.W.W. leaders, including Bill Haywood, Carlo Tresca, and Elizabeth Gurley Flynn, were in New York and offered their support, Frank angrily denied receiving any funds or direct instruction from the national office. In *Footnote to Folly*, her memoir of New York City life, Mary Heaton Vorse wrote, "The shifting mass of unemployed workers was run by a Committee of Ten, the ablest of the group. This committee consulted daily with Haywood and Elizabeth Gurley Flynn." This was not the case. Tannenbaum himself identified the leaders as Henry Landwirth, Frank Strawn Hamilton, Sam Hartman, Moses Bell, Sam Wallace, Frank Shafer, Joseph Secunda. "Shall It Be Capitalist Bread Line or Socialist Voting Line?" *Appeal to Reason* (March 14, 1914); "500 Jobless Spend Night in St. Paul's," the *Call* (March 4, 1914); "Unemployed 'Army' of 100 Decline Places at $3 a Day; Demand Turkey and Wine," *New York Herald* (March 4, 1914); **Wilson's cabinet:** "Tells Unemployed to Adopt Force," *New York Times* (March 4, 1914); "Mutiny in Ranks of I.W.W. Army at Old St. Paul's," the *World* (March 4, 1914).

83 **inside the Willard Hotel:** "President Wilson Guest of His Cabinet Officers," *Washington Post* (March 7, 1914).

84 **end-of-year retrospectives:** "The Administration's First Year," *New York Tribune* (March 3, 1914); "The First Year of the Wilson Administration: A Review," *Outlook* (March 7, 1914); **heightened the conviviality:** "President Wilson Guest of His Cabinet Officers"; Edwin A. Weinstein, *Woodrow Wilson: A Medical and Psychological Biography* (Princeton: Princeton University Press, 1981), 255; Arthur S. Link, *Wilson: The New Freedom* (Princeton: Princeton University Press, 1956), 460; Arthur S. Link, ed., *The Papers of Woodrow Wilson: Volume 29* (Princeton: Princeton University Press, 1979), 347.

85 **a diplomatic quandary:** James Creelman, "Armed Intervention in Riven Mexico by United States Alone Can Stop Savage Battle for Power and Plunder, Says James Creelman in Message from Huerta's Capital," *Washington Post* (March 1, 1914); **Wilson chose to remain aloof:** "Says Wilson Policy is 'Deadly Drifting,'" *New York Times* (Feb. 26, 1914); **the president relaxed his position:** "Carranza Plays for Recognition," *New York Times* (March 3, 1914); "United States May Abandon Benton Inquiry," *New York Tribune* (March 3, 1914).

86 **the longed-for thaw:** "With Old Sol Chief Aid, 20,687 Do Big Day's Work," the *World* (March 4, 1914); "City Freed by Thaw from Snow Fetters," *New York Tribune* (March 4, 1914).

86–87 **"Get in the real breadline":** The newspapers were oddly contradictory about the number of men who left the breadline to join the march. Some said none at all left the queue, but the *Tribune*, normally the most hostile to Tannenbaum's movement, reported a mass exodus. "500 Jobless Spend Night in St. Paul's"; **arrived at the parish house:** It is not clear whether Frank made this speech in the parish house at St. Paul's, or earlier in the evening. "Unemployed 'Army' of 100 Decline Places at $3 a Day"; "I.W.W. Mob Splits on Leaders; Ranks Dwindle," *New York Herald* (March 4, 1914); "Tells Unemployed to Adopt Force"; "The Unemployed Raid St. Paul's"; "Mutiny in Ranks of I.W.W. Army at Old St. Paul's."

87 **Vacationing in the Adirondacks:** "Governor and Mayor Snowbound," *New York Herald* (March 3, 1914); "Mayor Among Snowbound," *New York Tribune* (March 3, 1914).

87–89 **the administration's voice on unemployment:** "Lest We Forget," *New York Times* (Dec. 22, 1913); John A. Kingsbury, "Our Army of the Unemployed," reprinted in Julia E. Johnson, ed., *Selected Articles on Unemployment* (New York: H.W. Wilson Company, 1921), 8; **"the basement of any church":** "Unemployed Invade the Labor Temple," *New York Times* (March 1, 1914); "Mitchel Will Deal with Work Problem," the *World* (March 1, 1914); **"The great man":** "Jail Them All, Mayor Mitchel," the *Call* (March 6, 1914); "Homeless Army Lodged and Fed in Old St. Mark's"; "Help to Salvation Army," *Evening Post* (March 5, 1914); "Tells Unemployed to Adopt Force."

89 **In public he downplayed the Tannenbaum issue:** "What the Authorities Should Do," the *Sun* (March 3, 1914); "A Criminal Menace," the *World* (March 3, 1914); "Women Scout for I.W.W.," *Evening Post* (March 4, 1914); "Tannenbaum's Idle 'Army' Trapped in a Church Raid; 190 Men, 1 Woman, Seized," *New York Herald* (March 5, 1914); "Tells Unemployed to Adopt Force."

90–93 **St. Alphonsus' Catholic Church:** There were several detectives assigned to keep watch on the unemployed activists. But the two most prominent were Detective Sergeant Gegan (sometimes spelled Geoghegan) and Detective Lieutenant Gildea. At the time, Tannenbaum claimed that he had chosen St. Alphonsus' on a whim, but during his trial Charles Plunkett, anarchist and future husband to Becky Edelsohn, testified that he had suggested the church for the night's destination, having heard—incorrectly, as the events showed—that the unemployed had been offered sanctuary there. **"the best meeting I've had yet":** For a description of the Night Court, see "A Taste of Justice," in John Reed. *John Reed: Adventures of a Young Man: Short Stories from Life* (San Francisco: City Lights, 1975), 32; "Tannenbaum's Speech," the *Masses* (May 1914); "I.W.W. Invaders Seized in Church," *New York Times* (March 5, 1914); "Unemployed Storm Church; 190 Arrested," *New York Tribune* (March 5, 1914); "Tannenbaum's Idle 'Army' Trapped in a Church Raid"; "191 I.W.W. Raiders Arrested in Church; Court Holds Tannenbaum in $5,000 Bail," the *World* (March 5, 1914); "Army of Jobless Arrested After It Is Denied Shelter at St. Alphonsus Church," the *Call* (March 5, 1914); "Big Bail for Unemployed," *Evening Post* (March 5, 1914).

93 **a late evening for . . . McKay:** "191 I.W.W. Raiders Arrested in Church."

94 **in no mood for anniversaries:** "Observations and Comments," *Mother Earth* (March 1914); **"severest struggle":** Mabel Dodge Luhan, *Intimate Memories, Vol. 3: Movers and Shakers* (New York: Harcourt, Brace, 1936), 61. For Berkman's vision of the ideal revolutionist, see Alexander Berkman *Prison Memoirs of an Anarchist* (New York: Mother Earth Publishing Association, 1912), 73.

96 **had witnessed this all unfold before:** "I.W.W. Slurs Mayor; Calls Him 'Bell Hop,'" *New York Times* (March 7, 1914); "Shocking Abuse by Police, He Says," the *World* (March 16, 1914); Alexander Berkman, "The Movement of the Unemployed," *Mother Earth* (April 1914).

96 **a rally at Union Square:** Berkman "The Movement of the Unemployed"; "Anarchists Spread Alarm in 5th Ave.," *New York Times* (March 22, 1914); "Anarchists Rout Fifth Ave. Throng," *New York Tribune* (March 22, 1914); "Bearing Black Flag, Mob Raids Fifth Ave.," the *World* (March 22, 1914); "Those Signs of Spring," *New York Times* (March 18, 1914); "The Weather," *New York Times* (March 23, 1914).

96 **the slightest indication of unrest:** "Police Awe Orators at I.W.W. Meeting," *New York Times* (March 24, 1914); "Mitchel Warns the I.W.W.," *New York Times* (March 25, 1914); "Mayor Doesn't Fear I.W.W. Outbreak," the *World* (March 25, 1914); **"damned nonsense":** "Anarchists Spread Alarm in 5th Ave."

99–100 **cell number 813 of the Tombs:** For details about the prison in the 1910s, see Carlos Furnaro, *A Modern Purgatory* (New York: Mitchell Kennerley, 1917), 5–28. Officials had refused to allow known sympathizers into the courtroom. **never wanted to submit:** "Tannenbaum's Speech," "Lawyers' Wrangles Mark Opening of Tannenbaum Trial," the *Call* (March 25, 1914); "Tannenbaum Fails to Draw a Crowd as Trial Begins," the *World* (March 25, 1914); "Says I.W.W. Leader Expected Violence," *New York Times* (March 25, 1914); "Tannenbaum Trial for Church Attack," *New York Tribune* (March 25, 1914); "Women Flock to Trial of Tannenbaum, Curious to See Leader of Church Raid," *New York Herald* (March 25, 1914); **justice would prevail:** Max Eastman, "The Tannenbaum Crime," the *Masses* (May 1914); "Priests Accuse Young Leader of I.W.W. at Trial," the *World* (March 26, 1914); "Priests Testify to Idle Mob Raid at St. Alphonsus'," *New York Herald* (March 26, 1914); "Tannenbaum's Side to Be Heard To-day," *New York Tribune* (March 26, 1914); "I.W.W. Mob Forced Church Door Lock," *New York Times* (March 26, 1914); "Reporters Spring Sensations at the Tannenbaum Trial," the *Call* (March 27, 1914); "Tannenbaum Was Lured into Church, His Witnesses Say," the *World* (March 27, 1914); "Church Riot Laid to Police, Not I.W.W. Men," *New York Sun* (March 27, 1914); "German Reporter Aids Tannenbaum," *New York Herald* (March 27, 1914); "Tannenbaum's Men Testify for Him," *New York Times* (March 27, 1914); "Tannenbaum Is Guilty; Gets Year and Fine of $500," the *World* (March 28, 1914); "Tannenbaum Guilty: Gets a Year in Jail," *New York Times* (March 28, 1914); "Tannenbaum Guilty; Year in Prison and $500 Fine," *New York Herald* (March 28, 1914); "Tannenbaum Guilty Is Jury's Verdict," the *Call* (March 28, 1914).

The Possibility of a Revolution

103 **mussed white linens:** Mabel Dodge Luhan, *Intimate Memories, Vol. 3: Movers and Shakers* (New York: Harcourt Brace, 1936), 4, 44, 80–81, 83; **"their passions":** Ronald Steel, *Walter Lippmann and the American Century* (Boston: Little, Brown, 1980), 50.

103–4 **Insurrections were everywhere:** Luhan, *Movers and Shakers*, 55–75; John Reed, *Adventures of a Young Man: Short Stories from Life* (San Francisco: City Lights, 1975), 139; **"bourgeois pigs":** The cook was Hippolyte Havel. Gerald W. McFarland, *Inside Greenwich Village: A New York City Neighborhood, 1898–1918* (Amherst: University of Massachusetts Press, 2005), 197.

104–5 **The Francisco Ferrer Center:** Leonard Abbott, quoted in Avrich, *Modern School*, 70, 114; **portraits and speakers:** Florence Tager, "Politics and Culture in Anarchist Education: The Modern School of New York and Stelton, 1911–1915," *Curriculum Inquiry* (Winter 1986); **the Modern School:** Paul Avrich, *The Modern School Movement: Anarchism and Education in America* (Oakland, CA: AK Press, 2006).

105–6 **the devilish Walter Lippmann:** Luhan, *Movers and Shakers*, 103; **"expects to be president":** Letter from Mabel Dodge to Gertrude Stein, May 18, 1914, Patricia R. Everett, ed., *A History of Having a Great Many Times not Continued to be Friends: The Correspondence Between Mabel Dodge and Gertrude Stein, 1911–1934* (Albuquerque: University of New Mexico Press, 1996); **"cleanest strokes":** "Confidential Book Guide," *Life* (Sept. 25, 1913); **Tenderloin:** Walter Lippmann, "The Taboo in Politics," *Forum* (Feb. 1913); Lincoln Steffens, *The Autobiography of Lincoln Steffens* (Berkeley, CA: Heyday Books; Santa Clara: Santa Clara University, 2005), 655; **"categories," "a fine poise":** Quoted in Steel, *Walter Lippmann*, 50, 51, 53.

106 **devoting herself to political pursuits:** Luhan, *Movers and Shakers*, 57–58, 110.

108 **inviting them to her apartment:** Steel, *Walter Lippmann*, 51, 53.

108–9 **"As rulers of American industry":** Walter Lippmann, "Dynamite Versus Revolution," the *International* (January 1912); **"Wilson doesn't really fight":** Lippmann, *Drift and Mastery*, 137–138; **"wild in . . . deeds":** Ibid., 180; **"weak unions . . . weakness":** Ibid., 89; **"heated powder mine":** "Dynamite Versus Revolution"; **"his second book":** Letter from Mabel Dodge to Gertrude Stein, May 18, 1914, Patricia R. Everett, ed., *A History of Having a Great Many Times*.

109–10 **Dodge and Berkman just could not communicate:** Luhan, *Movers and Shakers*, 40, 58–61.

4. "Three Cheers for the Cops!"

111–15 **Saturday . . . in Union Square:** Details of Caron's beating come from his testimony in Magistrates Court, which is reprinted in Mary Heaton Vorse, *A Footnote to Folly* (New York: Farrar & Rinehart Inc., 1935), 71; "Police Battle with I.W.W. in Union Sq. Riots," *New York Tribune* (April 5, 1914); "Police Use Clubs on I.W.W. Rioters," *New York Times* (April 5, 1914); "Police Clubs, Fists and Horses Rout I.W.W. Rioters in Fierce Battle at Union Square," the *World* (April 5, 1914); "Mounted Policemen Ride Down I.W.W. Rioters in Union Square, Club Leaders, Arrest O'Carroll and Eight Others," *New York Herald* (April 5, 1914); "Police Club Big Anarchist Mob," the *Sun* (April 5, 1914); Alexander Berkman, "The Movement of the Unemployed," *Mother Earth* (April 1914); "Police Called Off I.W.W. by Mayor," *New York Herald* (April 8, 1914); "Writer Once Jailed with I.W.W. Describes Meeting," the *World* (April 12, 1914).

115–18 **the telegram from Washington:** Telegram from M.D. Foster to John D. Rockefeller, Jr., March 31, 1914, and the reply, April 2, in Rockefeller Family, OMR, Business Interests, Record Group III2C, box 21, folder 196, RAC; John D. Rockefeller, Jr., to John D. Rockefeller, April 3, 1914, quoted in Joseph W. Ernst, ed.,*"Dear Father"/"Dear Son"* (New York: Fordham University Press, 1994), 51; **"the word 'satisfaction' ":** *Industrial Relations Committee, Vol. 9*, 8441; **"happy day for the business man":** Bowers to Charles M. Cabot, April 8, 1912, quoted in Scott Martelle, *Blood Passion: The Ludlow Massacre and Class War in the American West* (New Brunswick, NJ: Rutgers University Press, 2007), 41; **"society in general":** Casualty figures and quotations are from ibid., 156–157, Appendix B; **"You may give your name and residence"**: *Conditions in the Coal Mines of Colorado: Hearings Before a Subcommittee of the Committee on Mines and Mining, House of Representatives, Sixty-Third Congress, Second Session, Pursuant to H. res. 387, A Resolution Authorizing and Directing the Committee on Mines and Mining to Make an Investigation of Conditions in the Coal Mines of Colorado* (Washington: Government Printing Office, 1914); **how all the family operations worked:** Welborn to John D. Rockefeller, Jr., Aug. 20, 1914, "Colorado Memorandum," 18, Rockefeller Family, OMR, Business Interests, Record Group III2Z, Series V, Biographical Works, box 54, folder 484, RAC.

120 **If Junior was concerned:** Charles M. Schwab to John D. Rockefeller, Jr., April 9, 1914; **"exceedingly amusing":** J. P. Morgan, Jr., to John D. Rockefeller, Jr., April 7, 1914. Rockefeller Family, OMR, Business Interests, Record Group III2C, box 21, folder 196, RAC; **"a bugle note":** Laura Spellman Rockefeller to John D. Rockefeller, Jr., April 7, 1914; John D. Rockefeller, Jr., to Laura Spellman Rockefeller, April 7, 1914, Rockefeller Family, JDR, Jr. Personal—Record Group III2Z, box 4, folder 44, RAC; John D. Rockefeller to E. B. Thomas, April 11, 1914, Rockefeller Family, OMR, Business Interests, Record Group III2C, box 10, folder 103, RAC.

121 **Perhaps he had delegated too much:** L. M. Bowers to John D. Rockefeller, Jr., April 7, 1914: "You have rendered a service for the entire country in your testimony before the Congressional Committee, that cannot be over estimated for its value just at this period in our industrial history: As the writer anticipated, these biased political wire pullers utterly failed in their attempt to trip you and every word you said simply brought out clearer and clearer your genuine American loyalty to stand against all comers, to protect every man who seeks employment in the enterprises in which you have a commanding interest in the enjoyment under the stars and stripes, of life, liberty and the pursuit of happiness. I believe that the hours you gave to the committee and the position you so ruggedly maintained . . . will do more for the cause of the millions of laboring men, than all the efforts of social reformers in as many years . . . I cannot put into words my satisfaction, I will say boundless delight with your magnificent and unshaken stand for principle, whatever the cost may be. Now for an aggressive warfare to 1916 and beyond for the open shop." Rockefeller Family, OMR, Business Interests, Record Group III2C, box 21, folder 190, RAC; THINK IT IMPORTANT: John D. Rockefeller, Jr. (telegram) to L.M.. Bowers, April 11, 1914, Rockefeller Family, OMR, Business Interests, Record Group III2C, box 20, folder 182, RAC.

122 **And then Arthur Caron took the stand:** "Caron on Trial in I.W.W. Case," *Globe and Commercial Advertiser* (April 7, 1914); "Mitchel Watching the Rioters' Trials," *New York Times* (April 8, 1914); "I.W.W. Rebellion Drives Out Chiefs," *New York Times* (April 10, 1914).

122 **McKay had . . . watched the burnish fade:** "Arthur Woods Police Commissioner," *Outlook* (April 18, 1914); "Investigate the I.W.W. Clubbing," *New York Tribune* (April 8, 1914); "Magistrates and the Police," *New York Times* (April 8, 1914); **"no unnecessary clubbing":** "Police Called Off I.W.W. by Mayor," *New York Herald* (April 8, 1914).

123–24 **"the hardest job in the entire city"**: Mayor John Purroy Mitchel to Douglas McKay, April 1, 1914, John Purroy Mitchel Papers, "Police Department Received," box 69, folder 723, Municipal Archives; **"The surest way"**: "Police," in Kenneth T. Jackson, ed., *The Encyclopedia of New York City,* 2nd edition (New Haven: Yale University Press, 2010), 1008. Mitchel also approached two of John D. Rockefeller, Jr.'s close associates, Raymond B. Fosdick, a criminologist for Rockefeller's Bureau of Social Hygiene, and Henry Bruère, director of the Bureau of Municipal Research. London's Scotland Yard, by contrast, had replaced its commissioner five times in the previous eighty-five years. Reminiscences of Henry Bruère, Columbia University Oral History Collection, 88; Foster Ware, "Fusion's Finest Make Good," the *Independent* (Aug. 18, 1917); "The New Police Commissioner," the *World* (April 8, 1914); **Police (noun)**: Campbell MacCulloch, "Commissioner Woods and the New Police Power," *Outlook* (Feb. 10, 1915); "The Cleanest Big City in the World," *Outlook* (Jan. 26, 1916); Gregory Mason, "The City or the System?" *Outlook* (March 7, 1914); "The New Police Commissioner," *New York Tribune* (April 8, 1914); **"Once more"**: William Brown Meloney, "Our Police Disease," *Outlook* (Oct. 5, 1912).

124 **six times as many murders**: Raymond B. Fosdick, *American Police Systems* (New York: The Century Co., 1921), 11, 20; **"collusion between exploiters of vice"**: "The Cleanest Big City in the World"; **"clean streets"**: Clinton Rogers Woodruff, ed. *Proceedings of the Chicago Conference for Good City Government and the Tenth Annual Meeting of the National Municipal League* (Philadelphia: National Municipal League, 1904), 385; **"The police 'system' in New York"**: "The City or the System?"

125–26 **The speaker's name was Arthur Woods**: Arthur Woods, "The Control of Crime," *Journal of the American Institute of Criminal Law and Criminology* (Jan. 1914); **"as if the occasion were a picnic"**: "Woods Sworn In; Plans No Shake-Up," *New York Tribune* (April 9, 1914); **"pray for me"**: "Say a short prayer for me, will you?" is how the *World* reporter noted this line. "Police 'System' Hit at in Order by Commissioner," the *World* (April 9, 1914); "No Shake Up in the Police Department," *New York Herald* (April 9, 1914); Arthur Woods, "Police Administration," *Proceedings of the Academy of Political Science in the City of New York* (April 1915), 54–61.

126–28 **"I have done a good many things"**: *Industrial Relations Final Report*, 10550; **After graduating Harvard**: "Heads Police of New York," *Boston Daily Globe* (April 12, 1914); **As a police reporter**: Charles Willis Thompson, "Woods to Bring Police Department into the Uplift," *New York Times* (April 12, 1914); **agitated for municipal reform**: Michael Pearlman, *To Make Democracy Safe for America: Patricians and Preparedness in the Progressive Era* (Urbana: University of Illinois Press, 1984), 106; Arthur W. Page, ed., *The World's Work: A History of Our Time, May to October, 1914* (Garden City: Doubleday, Page & Company, 1914), 150; "Needs More Police to Check Crime," *New York Times* (July 25, 1907); "Bingham's New Deputy," *New York Times* (July 25, 1907); **very much the gentleman**: Alfred Henry Lewis, "Sherlock Holmes in Mulberry Street," *New Broadway Magazine* (May 1908); "Woods to Bring Police Department into the Uplift"; **"Woods had ideas of his own"**: Edward Mott Woolley, "The Inner

Story of New York," *McClure's Magazine* (Nov. 1917); **"more fitly trained"**: "The Police," *Outlook* (April 25, 1914).

128 **his first day in command**: "Police 'System' Hit at in Order by Commissioner"; **five hundred angry, excited radicals**: "I.W.W. 'Martyrs' Cheered by 500, Revile Police," the *World* (April 9, 1914).

128–30 **the potential gravity of Berkman's threat**: Thomas J. Tunney and Paul Merrick Hollister, *Throttled! The Detection of the German and Anarchist Bomb Plotters in the United States* (Boston: Small, Maynard, 1919), 41; **a "splutter of sparks"**: Jim Rasenberger, *America 1908: The Dawn of Flight, the Race to the Pole, the Invention of the Model T, and the Making of the Modern Nation* (New York: Simon and Schuster, 2007), 91–94; "Bomb in Union Square," *New York Tribune* (March 29, 1908); "To Get Secret Service," *New York Tribune* (April 2, 1908); "Bomb Thrower Talks," *New York Tribune* (April 7, 1908); **released with a warning**: Berkman relates the judge's sermon slightly differently: "As long as you persist in calling yourself an Anarchist, and evidently take pride in it, it is the duty of the police to keep you under surveillance." Quoted in "A. Berkman Arrested," *New York Tribune* (March 31, 1908); Alexander Berkman, "Violence and Anarchism," *Mother Earth* (April 1908); "Berkman on Anarchy," *New York Times* (March 31, 1908); "Alexander Berkman Freed," *New York Times* (April 4, 1908); **"mightier than the Constitution"**: Or, as it was alternately rendered, "This, at times, is over the Constitution." "Over Constitution," *New York Tribune* (March 29, 1908); "Complain of Schmittberger," *New York Times* (April 12, 1908).

130 **Woods recalled the lessons he had learned**: "Lincoln Steffens and Woods Make an I.W.W. Truce," the *World* (April 10, 1914); Lincoln Steffens, *The Autobiography of Lincoln Steffens* (New York: The Literary Guild, 1931), 636–640; **"the crowd would undoubtedly be most provocative"**: Arthur Woods, *Policeman and Public* (New Haven: Yale University Press, 1919), 74–75.

131–32 **"Free speech was beginning"**: John Reed, "Writer Once Jailed with I.W.W. Describes Meeting," the *World* (April 12, 1914); "Bait the Police Now the Order to the I.W.W.," *Globe and Commercial Advertiser* (April 9, 1914); **"the whacks of the police clubs"**: "Lets I.W.W. Talk in Union Square," *New York Times* (April 12, 1914); **"Three cheers for the cops"**: *Industrial Relations Final Report*, 10551.

132 **"With such a man as police commissioner"**: *The Story of John Purroy Mitchel*, unpublished typescript, 2, William B. Meloney Papers. RBML; Reminiscences of Robert Binkerd, Columbia University Oral History Collection; **black hair . . . turning gray**: "The Young Mayor of the Greatest American City, Henry W. Hall," the *World* (April 26, 1914).

133–34 **workdays usually began at breakfast**: Reminiscences of Robert Binkerd, 53; **Peter Stuyvesant**: "A $500,000 Project," *New York Tribune* (April 30, 1908); "Newest Riverside Structure," *New York Times* (Jan. 3, 1909); **"Mayor Mitchel's friends"**: Edwin R. Lewinson, *John Purroy Mitchel, Symbol of Reform* (doctoral thesis, Columbia University, 1961), 137, 143–144; **"Quite a lot of time of this office"**: Reminiscences of Robert Binkerd, 54; Reminiscences of William H. Allen, Columbia University Oral History Collection, 233; Hall "The Young Mayor of the Greatest American City"; **mayor warned reporters**: "Mayor's Headache Gone," *New York Tribune* (March 15, 1914); "Mitchel Was Subject to

Intense Headaches," *New York Times* (July 7, 1918); **"mental incompetents"**: "Half of New York's Insanity Cases Could Be Prevented," *New York Times* (Sept. 18, 1910); "Mayor's Own Story of Escape From Death: 'I Had a Pistol; I Wish I Had Used It,'" the *Sun* (April 18, 1914).

135–36 **descending . . . onto City Hall Plaza:** Moses King, *King's How to See New York* (New York: Moses King, Inc., 1914), 71; "Spring in City Hall Park," *New York Times* (April 4, 1907); "The Weather," *New York Times* (April 17, 1914); "The Weather," *New York Times* (April 18, 1914); **the experience of this afternoon":** "Madman Shoots at Mayor Mitchel," *Globe and Commercial Advertiser* (April 17, 1914); "Woods Sought to Prevent Shooting," *New York Tribune* (April 18, 1914); "Almost Expected Attack, Mayor Tells Press Club," *New York Tribune* (April 18, 1914); "Second Crank for Mayor," *Evening Post* (April 18, 1914); "Attempt to Kill Mitchel; Frank Polk Is Wounded," *Evening Post* (April 17, 1914); "Bullet Sent to Assassinate Mayor Misses Him and Wounds Corporation Counsel Polk," the *Sun* (April 18, 1914); "Mayor's Own Story of Escape from Death"; "Prepared for Attacks, Mayor Tells Press Club," the *Sun* (April 18, 1914); "Mahoney, Locked in with Capt. Tunney, Breaks Down and Tells His Life Story," the *Sun* (April 18, 1914).

Chief-Inspector Judas

137–38 **he parades through a perpetual ovation:** The parade route traveled from the Battery north on Broadway to Twenty-third Street, where it jagged east to Madison Avenue and then proceeded to Fortieth Street, where it turned west for a block, then back south on Fifth Avenue to the reviewing stand in Madison Square. As for the cheers, the *Tribune* reported, "Inspector Schmittberger received the most generous applause." In the *Sun* a similar view appears. "Inspector Schmittberger . . . although he made no effort to show himself . . . was picked out and cheered by the crowds at several points. At the corner of Broadway and Houston street the applause for Schmittberger was so persistent that he had to stop and raise his hat several times." The *New York Herald* writer offers a commensurate description: "The plaudits fell upon Schmittberger from sidewalk, office windows and tops of office buildings. He was the principal feature of the parade." The *Times* alone is contradictory, saying at one point that Schmittberger "did not receive as noisy or as enthusiastic a greeting" as some others earlier in the parade, but granting him "the lion's share" at the reviewing stand. "Populace Cheers Police on Parade," *New York Herald* (May 3, 1903); "Crowd Cheers the Police," the *Sun* (May 3, 1903); "Called Record Parade," *New York Tribune* (May 3, 1903); "5,000 Police in Long Line," the *World* (May 2, 1903); "Police Parade Past Cheering Thousands," *New York Times* (May 3, 1903); **"Max! Schmitzy!":** Lincoln Steffens, *The Autobiography of Lincoln Steffens* (New York: The Literary Guild, 1931), 269; "Schmittberger Best Shot," *New York Tribune* (Dec. 27, 1915); **"Police Samson":** Steffens, *Autobiography*, 266; **"big, burly six-footer":** "Lifting the Lid," the *Outlook* (Nov. 14, 1917); **brass buttons:** From photographs and the early Edison Company actuality "New York Police Parade, June 1, 1899." Also, see the chapter on uniforms in *Rules and Regulations of the*

Police Department, City of New York (New York: J. W. Pratt Co., 1908), 203–210.
Prussian Order . . . von Moltke: When Schmittberger finally visited Berlin in 1902, he found the policemen there sleepy and lackadaisical, despite their pointed helmets. "Schmittberger Chief," *New York Tribune* (Feb. 19, 1909); Bertram Reinitz, "The Evolution of the Police Inspector," *New York Times* (Aug. 25, 1929); **a crisp salute:** "M.F. Schmittberger Police Chief, Dead," *New York Times* (Nov. 1, 1917); **handiest horseman:** Lincoln Steffens describes his horsemanship; as chief of the traffic squad, he transformed the mounted branch into what one military man referred to as "the finest cavalry in the world." "Schmittberger Now Chief Inspector," *New York Times* (Feb. 19, 1909); **truest sharpshooter:** "Schmittberger Best Shot"; **"artist" with a baton:** Steffens, *Autobiography*, 278; **small mouth, blue-gray eyes:** From photos and Schmittberger's April 1902 passport application: Ancestry.com, U.S. Passport Applications, 1795–1925 (online database); **"cuffed and cursed":** "Dr. Parkhurst Defends Capt. Schmittberger," *New York Tribune* (Feb. 9, 1909); **nasty and vindictive:** "Pleads Repentance," *New York Tribune* (Feb. 8, 1903). **forbidden . . . from marching:** "Ready for the Police Parade," *New York Tribune* (May 31, 1901).

138–39 **Such curses had covered him:** "Schmittberger, Chief Inspector, Is Dead at 66," *New York Tribune* (Nov. 1, 1917); "Says Schmittberger Had to 'Squeal,'" *New York Times* (Feb. 8, 1903); **"thief and a crook":** "Philbin Backs Jerome," *New York Tribune* (Feb. 10, 1903); "Raps Schmittberger," *New York Tribune* (Feb. 7, 1903); **"marked man":** "Socialists Meet; Police in Charge," *New York Times* (April 5, 1908); "Marked for Bomb," *New York Herald* (May 13, 1908); **loathed:** "Mr. Jerome Denounces Capt. Schmittberger," *New York Times* (Feb. 7, 1903); "Schmittberger, Chief Inspector, Is Dead at 66"; Frank Marshall White, "The Chief Inspector of New York's Police," *New York Times* (March 14, 1909); **"police work of any kind":** "The Captain to Retire," *New York Tribune* (Feb. 11, 1903); **a "hard drubbing":** "Dark for Schmittberger," *New York Tribune* (Oct. 3, 1905); **"has got to go!":** "Schmittberger Attacked," *New York Tribune* (July 30, 1902).

139 **"unmarred by a single complaint":** Schmittberger was born in Bavaria in 1851; he emigrated to the United States with his family as a child. As a Bavarian, his penchant for Prussianism might seem to require explanation. But once in New York City, all Saxons were as one. Schmittberger himself was often referred to as the "Big Dutchman." "Has Served Twenty Years," *New York Herald* (Jan. 29, 1894). **shrewd and patient:** "Lifting the Lid"; "Has Served Twenty Years"; **funny things:** "Schmittberger Caught," *New York Tribune* (Oct. 12, 1894).

139 **"loud buzzing":** "The Crowning Exposures," *New York Tribune* (Dec. 22, 1894); "A Field Day Indeed," *New York Tribune* (Dec. 22, 1894); "All the City Excited," *New York Tribune* (Dec. 22, 1894); "Gloom in Mulberry St.," *New York Tribune* (Dec. 24, 1894); "The Week," the *Nation* (Dec. 27, 1894); "The Results of the Investigation," the *Independent* (Dec. 27, 1894); New York State Senate, Committee on Police Dept. of the City of New York, Report and Proceedings (Albany, 1895), 5311.

140 **"a villain . . . in two worlds":** Steffens, *Autobiography*, 274.

141–42 **he was promoted to chief inspector:** "Schmittberger Now Chief Inspector," *New York Times* (Feb. 19, 1909); **in his apartment:** "Mr. Jerome Denounces Capt. Schmittberger."

5. Somebody Blundered

143 **the magistrate had disclosed his sentence:** Frank Tannenbaum to his parents, undated, c. March 1914, box 5, Frank Tannenbaum Papers, RBML; **Department ferry:** Bouck White, *Letters from Prison: Socialism a Spiritual Sunrise* (Boston: Richard G. Badger, 1915), 115; "Gotham's Fleets," *New York Tribune* (Nov. 24, 1907).

144 **"had ceased to be a human being":** Frank Tannenbaum, "What I Saw in Prison," the *Masses* (May 1915).

144–46 **Blackwell's Island . . . A narrow two-mile-long shard:** "Blackwell's Island Uses," *New York Times* (March 16, 1902); "Blackwell's Island for Playground," the *Survey* (May 18, 1912); **"pathetic beauty":** Mary Grace Worthington, *Fifty Benevolent and Social Institutions in and Near New York* (New York: Douglas C. McMurtrie, 1915), 56; Dr. William G. Le Boutillier, "Blackwell's Island Abuses," *New York Times* (Feb. 11, 1894); **rechristen the island:** Rev. Louis Albert Banks, ed., *T. DeWitt Talmage: His Life and Work* (London: O.W. Binkerd, 1902), 91; **a report on the penitentiary:** "Blackwell's Island," *New Bedford Mercury* (Jan. 2, 1829); "Department of Correction," in Henry Bruère, ed., *New York City's Administrative Progress, 1914–1916* (New York: M.B. Brown Printing and Sending Co., 1916), 151; "Blackwell's Island a Prison Terrible," *New York Times* (March 27, 1914); Memorandum from Burdette G. Lewis, deputy commissioner of the Department of Corrections, to William A. Prendergast, city comptroller, undated, 1914, box 17, folder 172, Department of Corrections Correspondence Received, John Purroy Mitchel Papers, Municipal Archives; **"doesn't like your face":** Frank Tannenbaum, "What I Saw in Prison."

146–47 **Tannenbaum's initial discouragement:** In the original note, Berkman signed this letter "Alex B." For the sake of clarity, I have used his full name. Alexander Berkman to Frank Tannenbaum, April 1, 1914, box 2, Frank Tannenbaum Papers, RBML; **"only an ignorant boy":** George Palmer Putnam, "The New Tannenbaum," *New York Times* (June 26, 1921).

147 **his correspondents kept him informed:** Maurice Woolman to Frank Tannenbaum, April 2, 1914, box 2, Tannenbaum Papers, RBML; **The police bore down:** Helen Hill to Frank Tannenbaum, April 5, 1914, box 3, Tannenbaum Papers, RBML; **"a giant protest meeting":** Charles Plunkett to Frank Tannenbaum, April 3, 1914, box 4, Tannenbaum Papers, RBML.

147–48 **I.W.W. DEFIES POLICE:** Charles Plunkett to Frank Tannenbaum, April 3, 1914, box 4, Tannenbaum Papers, RBML; **"And this is an attack":** Charles Willis Thompson, "So-Called I.W.W. Raids Really Hatched by Schoolboys," *New York Times* (March 29, 1914).

148–49 **to rectify these misperceptions:** Mary Heaton Vorse, *A Footnote to Folly* (New York: Farrar & Rinehart Inc., 1935), 73; "Want Tannenbaum at Carnegie Hall," *New York Times* (April 19, 1914); **an authentic I.W.W. meeting:** "Haywood

Openly Stirs Sedition," *New York Times* (April 20, 1914); "Ignore Call to War Says Haywood," the *Sun* (April 20, 1914); "Strike Threat if War Is Declared," *New York Tribune* (April 20, 1914).

149–51 **Haywood . . . "leader of all poor devils":** Carl Hovey, "Haywood and Haywoodism," *Metropolitan Magazine* (June 1912); **"strength of an ox":** Quoted in Beverly Gage, *The Day Wall Street Exploded: A Story of America in Its First Age of Terror* (New York: Oxford University Press, 2009), 69; **"a scarred mountain":** John Reed, *Adventures of a Young Man: Short Stories from Life* (San Francisco: City Lights, 1975), 123; **38 Colt . . . two-gun man":** J. Anthony Lukas, *Big Trouble: A Murder in a Small Midwestern Town Sets Off a Struggle for the Soul of America* (New York: Simon & Schuster, 1997), 204, 235; **"long on talk":** "How They Love 'Big Bill,'" *Common Cause* (Dec. 1912); **preferred discussing poetry:** Hutchins Hapgood, *A Victorian in the Modern World* (New York: Harcourt, Brace and Company, 1939), 293; **an indictment against "Big Bill":** "Sedition, Says Washington," *New York Times* (April 20, 1914).

151 **in Mayor Mitchel's office:** "No Plot Involved, the Mayor Asserts," *New York Times* (April 18, 1914); **"nuts":** Woods put Sergeant Gegan on this assignment. Arthur Woods to Theodore Rousseau, secretary to the mayor, April 28, 1914, Records of the John Purroy Mitchel Administration, Police Received, box 69, folder 725, NYC Municipal Archives; Rousseau to Woods, April 27, 1914, Records of the John Purroy Mitchel Administration, Police Sent, box 19, folder 384, NYC Municipal Archives; Rousseau to Woods, May 1, 1914, Records of the John Purroy Mitchel Administration, Police Sent, box 19, folder 385, NYC Municipal Archives.

151 **a looming war with MEXICO:** Arthur S. Link, *Wilson: The New Freedom* (Princeton: Princeton University Press, 1956), 394; **"watchful waiting":** Edgar Eugene Robinson, *Foreign Policy of Woodrow Wilson, 1913–1917* (New York: The Macmillan Company, 1917), 203; Robert D. Schulzinger, *U.S. Diplomacy Since 1900* (New York: Oxford University Press, 2008), 51–59; "Tammany Prepares to Recruit Troops," *New York Times* (April 24, 1914); "Bulletins Keep Washington Posted," *New York Tribune* (April 23, 1914); "Support of Wilson Pledged by Press," *New York Times* (April 22, 1914); "Navy Yard Astir to Get Ships Off," *New York Tribune* (April 15, 1914).

152 **officials heard some . . . commotion:** "Mob Attacks I.W.W. Anti-War Agitators," the *Sun* (April 23, 1914); "Mob Woman Talker Who Decries War," *New York Times* (April 24, 1914).

152–54 **"exploits of one Becky Edelsohn":** "In a Revolt Against Established Authority Young Women of the Fiery Becky Edelson Type Take Their Share of the Labor Agitation," *New York Tribune* (May 10, 1914); **"a tremendously fiery person":** Paul Avrich, *Anarchist Voices: An Oral History of Anarchism in America* (Princeton: Princeton University Press, 1995), 206, 218; **"Becky's eyes":** "In a Revolt Against Established Authority"; **"a girl with power":** Robert E. Platt, "Becky and the Respectables," *Woman Rebel* (Aug. 1914); **Born in Ukrainian Odessa:** Telephone interview with Robert Plunkett, Becky's son, July 15, 2011. The 1910 census taker recorded her year of birth as "abt 1889." **they had become lovers:** Candace Falk, *Love, Anarchy, and Emma Goldman* (Now Brunswick: Rutgers University

Press, 2000), 38–41, 97; **"more men in a day"**: Charles H. McCormick, *Hopeless Cases: The Hunt for the Red Scare Terrorist Bombers* (Lanham: University Press of America, 2005), 52; **"a source of irritation"**: Emma Goldman, *Living My Life: Volume 2* (London: Pluto Press, 1988), 535.

155–56 **"we not merely permit free speech"**: Testimony of Arthur Woods, *Industrial Relations: Final Report and Testimony, Volume 11* (Washington, D.C.: Government Printing Office, 1916), 10550; Arthur Woods, "American Citizenship on Trial," *Harvard Alumni Bulletin* (March 18, 1920); **"Woods has nerve"**: Lincoln Steffens, *The Autobiography of Lincoln Steffens* (New York: The Literary Guild, 1931), 636–640; Walter Lippmann, *Drift and Mastery*, vx–vxi; **"graveyard work"**: State of New York, *Minutes and Testimony of the Joint Legislative Committee Appointed to Investigate the Public Service Commissions* (Albany: J.B. Lyon Company, 1916), 117.

156 **an effective plainclothes branch**: "Chief Devery's View," *New York Times* (July 31, 1900); **Hebrew colony of the great East Side**: William Howe Tolman and Charles Hemstreet, *The Better New York* (New York: The Baker and Taylor Company, 1904), 31; Raymond B. Fosdick, *American Police Systems* (New York: The Century Co., 1921), 199; **"like a child regarding a strange bug"**: George Kibbe Turner, "The Man-Hunters," *McClure's Magazine* (June 1913).

156–57 **a million and a half Italians**: Kimberly Joyce Sims, *Blacks, Italians, and the Progressive Interest in New York City Crime, 1900–1930* (doctorial thesis, Harvard University, 2006); John Foster Carr, "The Coming of the Italian," *Outlook* (Feb. 24, 1906); **"gentle drudges"**: Herbert N. Casson, "The Italian in America," *Munsey's Magazine* (Oct. 1906); "Trend of Foreigners Is from New York," *New York Times* (May 19, 1912); Mike Dash, *The First Family: Terror, Extortion, Revenge, Murder, and the Birth of the American Mafia* (New York: Ballantine Books, 2010), 104; "Desperate Gang Held in Murder Mystery," *New York Times* (April 17, 1903); **"an Italian problem"**: "Italian Crime and Police Incompetence," *New York Tribune* (Aug. 21, 1904).

158–59 **Petrosino . . . avoided headquarters**: "The Farce of 'Plain Clothes,'" *New York Tribune* (July 15, 1908); Arthur Woods, "The Problem of the Black Hand," *McClure's Magazine* (May 1909); **"bring about the end of the Black Hand"**: Gino C. Speranza, "Petrosino and the Black Hand," the *Survey* (April 3, 1909); "Petrosini, Detective and Sociologist," *New York Times* (Dec. 30, 1906); **"a dejected pretense of an Italian squad"**: Turner, "The Man-Hunters"; "Black Hand Record," *New York Tribune* (Feb. 25, 1907).

159–60 **a new police commissioner arrived**: Norris Galpin Osborn, ed., *Men of Mark in Connecticut: Ideals of American Life Told in Autobiographies of Eminent Living Americans, Volume 2* (Hartford: William R. Goodspeed, 1906), 75; "The Fateful Photograph of Duffy," *Current Literature* (Aug. 1909); "General Bingham Again," *Outlook* (May 6, 1911); "Bingham a Diplomat and Soldier as Well," *New York Times* (Dec. 30, 1905); Theodore A. Bingham, "Foreign Criminals in New York," *North American Review* (Sept. 1908); **"crowning absurdity"**: Theodore A. Bingham to Mayor McClellan, Jan. 5, 1907, Mayor McClellan Papers, Departmental Correspondence Received, Police Department, box 55, folder 542, New York City Municipal Archives; Bingham, "Foreign Criminals in New York"; **not**

just another underling: "Police Department, New York City," *The Brooklyn Daily Eagle Almanac* (Brooklyn: Daily Eagle Publication, 1909), 385; **"our own stupid laws":** Arrigo Petacco, *Joe Petrosino* (New York: Macmillan Publishing Co., Inc., 1974), 57, 67–69; **eighty men:** "Must Stop Outrages by the Black Hand," *New York Times* (Jan. 26, 1908); "A Secret Service Squad to Hunt the Black Hand," *New York Times* (Dec. 20, 1906).

160–61 **yet another justification:** David Graham Phillips, "Secret Police and Anarchy," *New York Times* (April 2, 1908); Petacco, *Petrosino*, 69; **"I have money and plenty of it":** "New Secret Service to Fight Black Hand," *New York Times* (Feb. 20, 1909); "Secret Police Fund," *New York Tribune* (Feb. 20, 1909); **"Here the police are local":** Woods, "The Problem of the Black Hand."

162 **their commitment to surveillance:** "The Fateful Photograph of Duffy," *Current Literature* (Aug. 1909); "Rogues' Gallery Is Systematized," *Philadelphia Inquirer* (Oct. 27, 1907); Raymond B. Fosdick, *Chronicle of a Generation: An Autobiography* (New York: Harper, 1958), 92; **believed that they were being followed:** In a secret hearing before Mayor McClellan, Woods denied the charge that police detectives had been assigned to follow city officials. **Bingham was dismissed:** "Mayor Removes Police Heads," *New York Times* (July 1, 1909); "Secret Service Men Must Patrol Again," *New York Times* (July 13, 1909).

163 **Pocantico Hills Lyceum:** Tom Pyle, *Pocantico: Fifty Years on the Rockefeller Domain* (New York: Duell, Sloan, and Pearce, 1964), 12; **"Workaday Religion":** "Work-A-Day-Religion," April 19, 1914, Rockefeller Family, JDR, Jr., Personal, Record Group III2Z, box 1, folder 38, RAC.

163–65 **cold and blustery in the Colorado:** Howard M. Gitelman, *Legacy of the Ludlow Massacre: A Chapter in American Industrial Relations* (Philadelphia: University of Philadelphia Press, 1988), 12; Scott Martelle, *Blood Passion: The Ludlow Massacre and Class War in the American West* (New Brunswick, NJ: Rutgers University Press, 2007), 89, 160; **"On the whole":** L.M. Bowers to John D. Rockefeller, Jr., April 18, 1914, *Industrial Relations Final Report, Vol. 9*, 8429; **the miners as "the enemy":** Martelle, *Blood Passion*, 150, 162; **"stab-stab-stab":** John Reed, "The Colorado War," *Metropolitan Magazine* (July 1914); **"ceased to be an army":** This is from a subsequent military investigation conducted by the state of Colorado, quoted in Martelle, *Blood Passion*, 173; **the maternity bunker:** One woman, Mary Petrucci, survived to tell the story of the plight suffered by those in the maternity pit.

166–68 **his summary of the battle:** *Industrial Relations Final Report, Vol. 9*, 8430–8431; **"the best answer is—*dynamite*":** "Observations and Comments," *Mother Earth* (May 1914); **"the anarchy that ensues":** "The Ludlow Camp Horror," *New York Times* (April 23, 1914).

The Lid

171–72 **illuminated sign for Rector's:** "Rector's Restaurant" entry in Ken Bloom, ed., *Broadway: An Encyclopedia* (New York: Routledge, 2004), 427–28; "The Hotel Rector, New York," *American Architect* (Jan. 18, 1911); **more infamous than Jack's:** "'The Girl from Rector's,'" *New York Times* (Feb. 2, 1909); "'The

Girl from Rector's'; Amusing Comedy Returns Again to Boston and Is Warmly Applauded at the Globe Theatre," *Boston Globe* (March 28, 1911); **It was . . . "the spot":** Geroge Rector, *The Girl from Rector's* (Garden City, NJ: Doubleday, Page & Company, 1927), 59–60.

172–73 **brazenly flouted the curfew law:** Karl K. Kitchen, "When MUST Broadway Go to Bed? That's What New York Wants to Know," the *World* (March 15, 1914); "Restaurants Split on Closing Time," *New York Times* (March 12, 1914); Rector, *Girl from Rector's*, 122; **"stringent measures":** "Committee to Plan New Closing Policy," *New York Times* (March 9, 1914); Memorandum for the Mayor by Arthur Woods, Jan. 30, 1914, John Purroy Mitchel Papers, subject file "All-Night Licenses," box 22, folder, 198, New York Municipal Archives; **"everything that they asked for":** "Favor Mitchel Closing Plan," *New York Times* (March 19, 1914).

173–74 **"investigated in two separate ways":** Arthur Woods to Mayor Mitchel, May 13, 1914, John Purroy Mitchel Papers, subject file "All-Night Licenses," box 23, folder 204, New York Municipal Archives; "Mitchel Names 7 to Uplift 'Lid,'" *New York Times* (March 9, 1914); **"no drunkenness or disorder":** The police were less convinced than the liquor-law inspector of the Marlborough's good character, since it was the site of frequent neighborhood complaints and known to "cater to the gambling fraternity." Its request for an all-night license was rejected. G.G. Freer, Marlborough-Blenheim Hotel Inspection Report, April 7, 1914, John Purroy Mitchel Papers, subject file "All-Night Licenses," box 22, folder 201, New York Municipal Archives; Investigation in the Matter of an All-Night Liquor License, the Marlborough-Blenheim Corp., no date, John Purroy Mitchel Papers, subject file "All-Night Licenses," box 22, folder 201, New York Municipal Archives; **"A female with transparent drapings":** G.G. Freer, Germania Catering Company, Inspection Report, April 1914, John Purroy Mitchel Papers, subject file "All-Night Licenses," box 22, folder 201, New York Municipal Archives; **"tiresome ballad":** G.G. Freer, Café Regent, Inspection Report, April 3, 1914, John Purroy Mitchel Papers, subject file "All-Night Licenses," box 22, folder 201, New York Municipal Archives; **"showgirls and prostitutes":** Inspector's Report Upon Periodical Inspection of Premises Occupied as a Public Dance Hall, Bustanoby's, John Purroy Mitchel Papers, subject file "All-Night Licenses," box 22, folder 201, New York Municipal Archives; **"flirts with patrons":** G.G. Freer, Circle Hotel Inspection Report, April 10, 1914, John Purroy Mitchel Papers, subject file "All-Night Licenses," box 22, folder 201, New York Municipal Archives; G.G. Freer, the Princess Restaurant, Inspection Report, date illegible, c. April 1914, John Purroy Mitchel Papers, subject file "All-Night Licenses," box 22, folder 202, New York Municipal Archives.

174 **eateries that catered to working people:** G.G. Freer, the Whip, Inspection Report, date illegible, c. April 1914, John Purroy Mitchel Papers, subject file "All-Night Licenses," box 22, folder 203, New York Municipal Archives.

174–75 **quiet entrance into Rector's:** G.G. Freer, Rector's 48th Street, Inspection Report, April 3, 1914, John Purroy Mitchel Papers, subject file "All-Night Licenses," box 23, folder 204, New York Municipal Archives; **"the most flagrant** violator": John Dwyer, inspector, 4th District, to Woods, April 17, 1914, John Purroy Mitchel Papers, Departmental Correspondence, Police Department Received, box 69, folder 725, New York Municipal Archives; Dwyer to Woods, May 4, 1914, John Purroy Mitchel Papers, Departmental Correspondence, Police Department Received, box 69, folder 726, New York Municipal Archives; John F. Dwyer to Arthur Woods, Sept. 4, 1914, John Purroy Mitchel Papers, subject file "All-Night Licenses," box 23, folder 204, New York Municipal Archives; **"Ballroom de Luxe":** "Gala Night at Rector's," *New York Tribune* (Sept. 29, 1914).

6. Free Silence

176–77 **Spring had not arrived:** "A Bad April," the *World* (May 1, 1914); **Easter:** "The Weather," *New York Times* (April 13, 1914); **"red" . . . "fur coats":** "When Spring Comes to the Middle of Manhattan," the *Sun* (April 26, 1914); **"slanting sunlight":** "Someone's First Spring Day," *Evening Post* (March 21, 1914); **"little by little":** Upton Sinclair, *Love's Pilgrimage* (New York: Mitchel Kennerley, 1911), 522; **hand-organs:** Marie Ganz, *Rebels: Into Anarchy—and Out Again* (New York: Dodd, Mead and Company, 1920), 200; **"two weeks":** Upton Sinclair, *Springtime and Harvest* (New York: The Sinclair Press, 1901), 11; **extortionate rate of ten dollars:** Upton Sinclair, *The Autobiography of Upton Sinclair* (New York: Harcourt, Brace & World, Inc., 1962), 198; **"search your soul":** "Sylvia," *McClure's Magazine* (Oct. 1913).

177–78 **He was thirty-five years old:** Will Durant, quoted in Anthony Arthur, *Radical Innocent: Upton Sinclair* (New York: Random House, 2006), 99, 132; **"eyes":** Edie Summers, quoted in Arthur, *Radical Innocent*, 88; **"by instinct shy":** Upton Sinclair, *The Brass Check: A Study of American Journalism* (Long Beach, CA: self-published, 1928), 88; **"turmoil":** "Sinclair Organizes 'Free Silence' Band," *New York Tribune* (April 30, 1914); **"haughty and powerful men":** Sinclair, *The Brass Check*, 267; **"Sinclair's intentions are so good":** Walter Lippmann, *Public Persons* (Piscataway: First Transaction Printing, 2010), 31, 33; **"Sinclair is simply an ass":** "Sinclair 'An Ass;' John D. Just 'Goat,'" the *World* (June 11, 1914); **"countless jokes":** Sinclair, quoted in Arthur, *Radical Innocent*, 105; **prolonged fasting:** Upton Sinclair, *The Fasting Cure* (New York: Mitchell Kennerley, 1911); **"monkey and squirrel diet":** Upton Sinclair, *The Book of Life* (Chicago: The Economy Book Company, 1921), 119.

178–79 **hissed at every mention of "Rockefeller":** Sinclair, *Autobiography*, 198; Arthur, *Radical Innocent*, 150; **"horsewhip him":** "Pickets to Haunt J.D. Rockefeller, Jr.," *New York Times* (April 29, 1914); **picturesque protesters:** Sinclair, *Brass Check*, 144; **"'social chill'":** "Sinclair Mourners Split by Discord," *New York Times* (May 3, 1914); **"They will surely arrest you":** Mary Craig Sinclair, *Southern Belle* (Jackson: University Press of Mississippi, 1999), 153; **"Someone will put up the money":** Sinclair, *Autobiography*, 198.

179–80 **the entrance to 26 Broadway:** "To Enlarge Its Building," *New York Tribune* (July 14, 1895); **"known in every part":** "'26 Broadway,' Standard Oil's

Headquarters, Is to Be the World's Largest Business Office," *New York Tribune* (March 6, 1921); **second note:** "Pickets to Haunt J.D. Rockefeller, Jr.," *New York Times* (April 29, 1914); **"no answer":** Sinclair, *The Brass Check*, 144; **thirty feet of sidewalk:** "To Enlarge Its Building"; **"behave like a gentleman":** Sinclair, *Autobiography*, 199; FREE SILENCE LEAGUE: "Fighting Continues Between Miners and State Troops," *New York Herald* (April 30, 1914); "Sinclair Organizes 'Free Silence' Band"; "Rockefeller Balks Sinclair Mourners," *New York Times* (April 30, 1914).

180–81 **slaughter climaxed in the coalfields:** John D. Rockefeller, Jr., to Woodrow Wilson, April 27, 1914, Rockefeller Family, OMR, Business Interests, box 23, folder 210, RAC; **"defiance":** "Rockefeller, Jr. Rejects Peace; Mine War Grows," *New York Times* (April 28, 1914).

181–85 **soppy and bleak in New York:** "Sinclair Organizes 'Free Silence' Band"; **ice cream:** "Mrs. J.D. Rockefeller, Jr., Causes 'Mourners' Arrest; Home Is Heavily Guarded," *New York Herald* (May 1, 1914); **court:** "'Mourners' Mob Begins Torment of Rockefeller," *New York Tribune* (May 1, 1914); **"shoot him down like a dog":** "Night Picketing at Rockefeller's," *New York Times* (May 1, 1914); **supper . . . "I took one look":** "This Tombs Feast Not Kind to Tempt Sinclair," the *World* (May 1, 1914); **"languisihing in jail":** "Death Like Dog's, Girl's Threat for Rockefeller, Jr.," the *World* (May 1, 1914).

185 **Night was falling in midtown:** "Mrs. J.D. Rockefeller, Jr., Causes 'Mourners' Arrest"; "'Mourners' Mob Begins Torment of Rockefeller"; "Night Picketing at Rockefeller's"; "Two Agitators at Rockefeller Home Arrested," *Evening Sun* (May 1, 1914); "Death Like Dog's, Girl's Threat for Rockefeller, Jr."

186 **"the busiest day he has experienced":** "'Mourners' Mob Begins Torment of Rockefeller"; **Calvary Church:** "Attack in Church on Rockefeller," *New York Times* (May 2, 1914); "Socialists Make Church Attack on Mr. Rockefeller," *New York Herald* (May 2, 1914); "Socialists Invade Church," *Evening Sun* (May 1, 1914); **"multi-murderer":** "May Day's Riot of Talk," *Evening Post* (May 1, 1914); **"guilty conscience":** Ibid.; "May Day Parade for Socialists," *New York Tribune* (May 1, 1914); "Anarchists Menace May Day Paraders," *New York Times* (May 1, 1914); "5,000 Stampeded by Police Clubs," *New York Times* (May 2, 1914); **"Rockefeller's War":** "The Rebellion in Colorado," *New York Times* (April 28, 1914); **"The suspicion":** "The Bloodshed in Colorado," *New York Herald* (April 30, 1914); **back door:** Sinclair, *Autobiography*, 199; **bronchitis:** John D. Rockefeller, Jr., to Richard S. Aldrich, May 7, 1914, Rockefeller Family, OMR, Business Interests, Record Group III2C, box 19, folder 170, RAC; **"seriously troubled":** "Rockefeller, Jr., Weary, Seeks a Rest from Mob," *New York Tribune* (May 2, 1914).

186–87 **Junior had avoided the office all week:** "Rockefeller, Jr., Weary, Seeks a Rest from Mob"; **"sharp outlook":** "Rockefeller Workmen Promise Protection," *New York Herald* (May 3, 1914); **"much affected":** Carl Heydt, in "Rockefeller Back; I.W.W. Siege Raised," *New York Tribune* (May 20, 1914); **"last two weeks":** John D. Rockefeller, Jr., to Charles M. Thoms, May 14, 1914, Rockefeller Family, OMR, Business Interests, Record Group III2C, box 20, folder 173,

RAC; **Calvary Baptist:** John D. Rockefeller, Jr., to A. LeRoy Chapman, May 1914, Rockefeller Family, OMR, Business Interests, Record Group III2C, box 19, folder 171, RAC; **"Those who are":** John D. Rockefeller, Jr., to Dr. Cornelius Woelfkin, May 5, 1914, Rockefeller Family, OMR, Business Interests, Record Group III2C, box 20, folder 173, RAC.

187–88 **the same official position:** "Colorado," *New York Times* (April 29, 1914); **"disinterested men . . . such a scheme":** "Colorado Memorandum," Rockefeller Family, OMR, Business Interests, Record Group III2Z, series V, Biographical Works, box 54, folder 484, RAC; **"IF IT IS TRUE":** John D. Rockefeller, Jr., to L.M. Bowers, April 29, 1914, *Industrial Relations, Vol. 9*, 8434; **"conservative":** L.M. Bowers to John D. Rockefeller, Jr., Jan. 15, 1913; **"labor union agitators":** L.M. Bowers to John D. Rockefeller, Jr., Feb. 23, 1912, Rockefeller Family, OMR, Business Interests, Record Group III2C, box 21, folder 190, RAC.

188–90 **Junior might have acted:** "To Call It 'Rockefeller's War' Is Infamous, John D. Jr. Protests," the *World* (May 1, 1914); **"fair and broad-minded":** John D. Rockefeller, Jr., to Oswald Garrison Villard, May 7, 1914, Rockefeller Family, OMR, Business Interests, Record Group III2C, box 20, folder 173, RAC; **labor unions:** John D. Rockefeller, Jr., to Adolph S. Ochs, June 5, 1914, Rockefeller Family, OMR, Business Interests, Record Group III2C, box 20, folder 175, RAC; **Ralph Pulitzer:** John D. Rockefeller, Jr., to Ralph Pulitzer, April 29, 1914; Ralph Pulitzer to John D. Rockefeller, Jr., April 30, 1914, Rockefeller Family, OMR, Business Interests, Record Group III2C, box 20, folder 173, RAC; **Andrew Carnegie:** Andrew Carnegie to John D. Rockefeller, Jr., May 7, 1914, Rockefeller Family, JDR, Jr. Personal - Record Group III2Z, box 8, folder 78, RAC; **every man:** John S. Montgomery to John D. Rockefeller, Jr., April 30, 1914; **"crazy anarchists":** John W. Woodward to John D. Rockefeller, Jr., May 2, 1914; Rockefeller Family, OMR, Business Interests, Record Group III2C, box 20, folder 173, RAC; **"no more 'Americans' ":** Frank A. Egan to John D. Rockefeller, Jr., May 1, 1914; **"God vs. Anti-God":** Andrew O. Nash to C.O. Heydt, April 28, 1914, Rockefeller Family, OMR, Business Interests, Record Group III2C, box 20, folder 174, RAC; **"Jesuits":** J.S. Hurst to John D. Rockefeller, Jr., May 4, 1914, Rockefeller Family, OMR, Business Interests, Record Group III2C, box 19, folder 170, RAC.

190–91 **they disembarked in Tarrytown:** "Trolley Trips in the Vicinity of New York," *New York Times* (July 7, 1912); **"have him worried":** " 'Mourners' Go to Rockefeller Estate at Tarrytown; Invade Church in City," *New York Herald* (May 4, 1914); "Mourners March on Rockefeller Homes," *Evening Sun* (May 4, 1914); " 'Mourn' at Gates of Country Home of Rockefeller," the *World* (May 4, 1914); "Spies Hound Rockefeller at Pocantico Hills," *New York Tribune* (May 4, 1914); "I.W.W. Pickets Pen Rockefellers," *New York Times* (May 4, 1914); **"most pretentious in the country":** "John D's Estate Is Still Under Guard," *Tarrytown Daily News* (May 5, 1914); "Rockefellers Are Guarded," *New York Times* (May 7, 1914); "Costly Rockefeller Entrance," *New York Times* (May 16, 1914).

191–92 **Sinclair was crafting plans:** "That Pedal War on Young John D. Is Getting Slow," the *World* (May 5, 1914); "Leaders Abandon Silence Mourning," *New York Times* (May 10, 1914); "Rockefellers Fear to Attend Church," *New York Tribune* (May 10, 1914): **"Why should":** "New York from the Suburbs," *New York Tribune* (May 17, 1914); **"job of violence":** "Silence League Disbands," *New York Times* (May 11, 1914).

192–93 **Rockefellers . . . abstain from Sunday services:** "What the Great Metropolitan Churches Are in Business," *New York Times* (Jan. 10, 1909); "Bouck White Fights in Oil King's Church," *New York Tribune* (May 11, 1914); "Rockefeller's Foes Invade His Church," *New York Times* (May 11, 1914); "Church Battle of Social Revolution a Police Victory," the *World* (May 11, 1914); **"real God":** "Taking the Bible as the Text-Book of the Social Revolution," *Current Opinion* (June 1914).

193–94 **"Almost enough of the I.W.W.":** "The I.W.W. in Union Square," the *Sun* (May 3, 1914); **"nightsticks . . . mouse":** "Is Mr. Mitchel a Mayor or a Mouse?" *New York Herald* (May 2, 1914); **"extremely liberal":** "Rockefeller, Jr., Weary, Seeks a Rest from Mob," *New York Tribune* (May 2, 1914); Ganz, *Rebels*, 200; "Jail for 'Silence' Picket in a Shroud," *New York Times* (May 8, 1914); **"kid gloves":** "'Vigorous'—But Lawful," the *World* (May 13, 1914).

194–96 **marines placed the first coffin:** Robert E. Quirk, *An Affair of Honor: Woodrow Wilson and the Occupation of Veracruz* (Lexington: University of Kentucky Press, 1962), 103; Mark Benbow, *Leading Them to the Promised Land: Woodrow Wilson, Covenant Theology, and the Mexican Revolution, 1913–1915* (Kent, Ohio: Kent State University Press, 2010), 68; **The military spectacle:** "Vera Cruz Dead Here on Warship," *New York Times* (May 11, 1914); "President Voices Nation's Tribute," the *World* (May 12, 1914); "Throng Hears Wilson's Eulogy," *New York Tribune* (May 12, 1914); "Nation, State and City Honor Vera Cruz Dead," the *Sun* (May 12, 1914); "Nation Honors Vera Cruz Dead in Grieving City," *New York Times* (May 12, 1914); "War Is a Symbol of Duty, Says President; 'Hard to Do Duty When Men Are Sneering,'" *New York Tribune* (May 12, 1914); "Wilson in Parade, Despite Warning," *New York Tribune* (May 12, 1914); "Thousands Silent in City Hall Park," *New York Tribune* (May 12, 1914); **The greatest shock for Wilson:** Cary Travers Grayson, *Woodrow Wilson: An Intimate Memoir* (Washington: Potomac Books, 1977), 30; Arthur S. Link, ed., *Wilson: The New Freedom* (Princeton: Princeton University Press, 1956), 402.

A Film with a Thrill

199 **They filed inside the Lyric Theatre:** *The Battle of Torreon* was screened as part of a double feature, along with *The Life of General Villa*; **twelve days:** "Parlous Times," *New York Tribune* (May 10, 1914); **"grewsome":** "The Broadway Pictures," *New York Tribune* (May 17, 1914); "New York's New Theaters," *Carpentry and Building* (Feb. 1903); Joseph E.J. Clark, "'Real War and No Make-Believe': The Spectacle of the Mexican Revolution on Screen" (master's thesis, the University of British Columbia, 2001).

199–200 **a city of filmgoers:** Mary Heaton Vorse, "Some Picture Show Audiences," *Outlook* (June 24, 1911); **"Fifty-ninth":** Roy L. McCardell, "There Are Some Rare and Wondrous Goings On in the Famous Theatres of the 'Good Old Days' Since New York Became a 'Movie Town,'" the *World* (March 15, 1914).

200 **"moving-picture evil . . . 'hold-ups'":** "Picture Shows Menace," *New York Tribune* (Nov. 16, 1911); **sinks of iniquity:** Alphonsus P. Haire, "Motion Pictures as Educators," *New York Tribune* (Nov. 6, 1910).

200 **"cheers, but does not inebriate":** "The Moving Pictures," the *Fra* (Jan. 1914); **Rector's:** Haire, "Motion Pictures as Educators"; **moral and spiritual improvement:** "Children Who Labor," the *Edison Kinetogram* (Feb. 15, 1912), in National Child Labor Committee Records, box 3, RBML; "Films to Flash Clean-up Warning!" *New York Tribune* (May 11, 1914); "Films to Teach Caution," *New York Tribune* (May 15, 1914); "Churches Plan Moral 'Movie' Propaganda," *New York Tribune* (June 13, 1914).

201–2 **the White Slave films appeared:** Shelley Stamp Lindsey, "'Oil Upon the Flames of Vice': The Battle Over White Slave Films in New York City," *Film History*, vol. 9, no. 4 (1997); **"Long lines":** "The Inside of the White Slave Traffic," *New York Times* (Dec. 26, 1913); **"What is really the cause":** Emma Goldman, *The Traffic in Women, and Other Essays on Feminism* (Ojai, CA: Times Change Press, 1971), 20; **"hideous reality":** George J. Kneeland, *Commercialized Prostitution in New York City* (New York: The Century Co., 1913), 99.

202 **Skeptics were not convinced:** "'Oil Upon the Flames of Vice'"; **"through the efforts of the police":** "Enjoin Police in 'Slave' Film War," *New York Tribune* (Dec. 21, 1913); "John D. Rockefeller, Jr., Repudiates Vice Films," *Duluth News-Tribune* (Dec. 28, 1913).

203 **again found himself victimized:** John D. Rockefeller, Jr., to Raymond B. Fosdick, April 18, 1914, Rockefeller Family Rockefeller Family, OMR, Rockefeller Boards, Bureau of Social Hygiene, box 7, folder 53, RAC.

203 **at the crescendo of the scandal:** "Parlous Times"; "The War Pictures," *New York Tribune* (May 24, 1914); "Real War and No Make-Believe," 35.

7. A Sleepy Little Burg

205 **Caron rode to Tarrytown:** "Fake Hungry Boy Can't Start Riot at I.W.W. Bidding," the *World* (March 24, 1914).

206 **Caron was thirty years old:** John T. Cumbler, *Working-Class Community in Industrial America: Work, Leisure, and Struggle in Two Industrial Cities, 1880–1930* (Westport: Greenwood Press, 1979), 99; **Indian ancestry:** "Caron's Career in Anarchy," *New York Times* (July 5, 1914); **disastrous stint in the navy:** Arthur Caron, personnel files, National Personnel Records Center; **A civilian once more:** I have pieced together Arthur Caron's life story, fragmentary as it is, through a variety of sources. And there is no detail that is not disputed. Even Caron's family and closest friends give widely divergent accounts: "He was a Canadian Irishman"; "born of French parents in Connecticut"; "it was said that his grandfather on his mother's side had been an Indian chief." **lived in New York:** Arthur Caron's sister told a reporter

for the *World* that he, and she herself, had been born in New York. His naval records list Quebec as his birthplace. There is no extant record of his birth, nor does he figure in the family's 1910 census entry—presumably because he was living with his wife or serving in the navy. However, the census does register that the Caron children were all born in New York until the year 1901, when the youngest, Blanche, was born in Massachusetts. **married a woman:** Several accounts agree that Caron married Elmina Reeves in Providence, but the 1910 census lists her as living (under her married name) with her family in Fall River. So they might have been moving around. **their son, Reeves:** Reeves Caron's death certificate lists his date of birth. **the mother died:** "Deaths," *Pawtucket Times* (Dec. 6, 1912).

207 **I.W.W. locals in Fall River:** Cumbler, *Working-Class Community*, 99–164; Henry M. Fenner, ed., *History of Fall River: Compiled for the Cotton Centennial* (Fall River: Fall River Merchants Association, 1911); "Accidents in Mills," *Wade's Fibre and Fabric* (Oct. 30, 1886); "Relief Work in the Fall River Strike," *Charities: A Review of Local and General Philanthropy* (Jan. 21, 1905); **the protests:** "I.W.W. Enter Strike," *New York Times* (Nov. 21, 1913); **as an agitator:** "Arthur Caron Killed by Anarchist's Bomb," *Fall River Evening News* (July 6, 1914); **" 'get' the mayor":** "Suffrage Rider Meets Repulse in Fall River," *Boston Journal* (July 9, 1914).

207–9 **failed to escape a toiling life:** "Goes for Caron's Body," *Boston Daily Globe* (July 6, 1914); Marie Ganz, *Rebels: Into Anarchy—and Out Again* (New York: Dodd, Mead and Company, 1920), 136, 198; **Jobless, homeless:** "Women Flock to Trial of Tannenbaum, Curious to See Leader of Church Raid," *New York Herald* (March 25, 1914); **"six feet tall":** Rose Goldblatt, in Paul Avrich, *Anarchist Voices: An Oral History of Anarchism in America* (Princeton: Princeton University Press, 1995), 210; **"slightly dark":** Charles Plunkett, in Avrich, *Anarchist Voices*, 216; **jolly . . . fellow:** "7 'Mourners' Appear at Rockefeller Estate and March in Silent Protest," *Tarrytown Daily News* (May 4, 1914); **"level headed":** "Anarchists Prepare for Public Funeral," *New York Herald* (July 6, 1914); **"they would kill me":** Upton Sinclair, "Free Speech Fight in John D.'s. Town," *Appeal to Reason* (June 20, 1914); **"they knew what they were about":** "Caron's Career in Anarchy," *New York Times* (July 5, 1914); **nose was broken:** "Mayor on Police Clubs," *New York Times* (May 17, 1914).

209 **electric lights:** "John D. Doubles Guard About His House," the *World* (May 19, 1914); **"no night-stick government":** " 'Vigorous'—But Lawful," the *World* (May 13, 1914); **"necessary sometimes":** "Mayor on Police Clubs."

209–11 **radical agitation . . . had adapted:** "Jane Est Rebels Against Threat in Union Square Talk," the *World* (May 17, 1914); "Raid Taft Meeting, Jane Est's Threat," *New York Times* (May 17, 1914); Helen Hill to Frank Tannenbaum, May 24, 1914, Frank Tannenbaum Papers, box 3, RBML; **head worker at the University Settlement:** About a month after he publicly praised the mettle of the I.W.W. activists, the head of the University Settlement was forced to resign his position. **"intellectually keen":** "Gilman Praises the I.W.W.," *New York Times* (June 2, 1914); **"after publicity":** "The Publicity Graf," *New York Tribune* (June 2, 1914); **Victor Berger:** "Sinclair 'An Ass;' John D. Just 'Goat,'" the *World* (June 11, 1914).

212–13 **"Did you ever hear the wail":** "Mayor on Police Clubs"; "Riotous Scenes as I.W.W. Agitators and Anarchists Fight on Streets for Free Speech in Tarrytown," *Tarrytown Daily News* (June 1, 1914); "I.W.W.'s in Tarrytown Jail," *New York Tribune* (May 31, 1914); **Having come to agitate:** "12 Agitators Put in Cells," the *Sun* (June 1, 1914); "Tarrytown Police Rout I.W.W. Forces," *New York Times* (June 1, 1914); "Clubs Hit Heads When I.W.W. Raids J.D.'s 'Own Town,'" the *World* (June 1, 1914); Leonard D. Abbott, "The Fight for Free Speech in Tarrytown," *Mother Earth* (June 1914).

215–16 WHEN I.W.W. RAIDS J.D.'S "OWN TOWN": "12 Agitators Put in Cells"; **drowsy:** This is from "The Legend of Sleepy Hollow." **paved with brick:** "Bricking Broadway," *Tarrytown Daily News* (May 24, 1914); **"Dutch conservatism":** "Cities of Westchester and Her County Seat," *New York Times* (May 3, 1903).

216 **the countryside had been transformed:** Frederic Shonnard, quoted in Marcus D. Raymond, ed., *Souvenir of the Revolutionary Soldiers' Monument Dedication at Tarrytown, N.Y.* (Tarrytown, 1894), 34; **"Public opinion":** "Imprudent Language," *Tarrytown Daily News* (May 11, 1914); **"No Capitalist":** "I.W.W. 'I Won't Work,'" *Tarrytown Daily News* (May 5, 1914).

216–17 **authorities lost all composure:** "Anarchy Causes Great Unrest," *Tarrytown Daily News* (May 22, 1914); **"sleep on that":** "Hose and Tar Await Agitators at Tarrytown," *New York Herald* (June 4, 1914); **"Threats of bloodshed":** "Will Fool Reds at Tarrytown by a Secret Trial," the *World* (June 6, 1914); **"tiny village":** Alexander Berkman, "Observations and Comments," *Mother Earth* (June 1914); **"Commuters who go to":** "Home Rule Isn't for Tarrytown People," *Tarrytown Daily News* (June 12, 1914); **"sympathize":** "Free Speech in Tarrytown," the *World* (June 9, 1914); **"if he can get away with it":** "Tarrytown and the I.W.W.," the *World* (June 4, 1914).

218–20 **"a pale and haggard" Rockefeller:** "Is Judge Lindsey with Rockefeller?" *New York Times* (May 23, 1914); **Four guards:** "Tarrytown Sleeps Now on Its Arms," *New York Herald* (June 7, 1914); "Armed Squad Joins Rockefeller Guard," *New York Times* (June 8, 1914); **"you fooled us":** "I.W.W." to John D. Rockefeller, Jr., June 10, 1914; **"to assassinate you":** "A Sufferer of Capital" to John D. Rockefeller, Jr., no date, Rockefeller Family, OMR, Business Interests, Record Group III2C, box 21, folder 191, RAC; **alternate lines:** Jerome D. Greene to John D. Rockefeller, Jr., May 6, 1914, May 7, 1914; Rockefeller Family Papers, Record Group 2, OMR, Business Interests Series, box 20, folder 176, RAC; **"I feel quite strongly":** John D. Rockefeller, Jr., to Starr J. Murphy, June 29, 1914; **"My first instinctive reaction":** Starr J. Murphy to John D. Rockefeller, Jr., July 10, 1914, both letters in Rockefeller Family, OMR, Business Interests, Record Group III2C, box 20, folder 178, RAC; **"I am very sorry":** Franklin K. Lane, secretary of the interior to John D. Rockefeller, Jr., June 6, 1914, Rockefeller Family, OMR, Business Interests, Record Group III2C, Box 20, folder 179, RAC.

220–22 **such a relief to meet Ivy Lee:** Lee had worked for the *Times*, the *Journal*, and the *World*. **"misunderstood":** Ron Chernow, *Titan: The Life of John D. Rockefeller, Sr.* (New York: Random House, 1998), 584; **"Desiring as I do":** Ivy Lee to John D. Rockefeller, Jr., June 14, 1914, *Industrial Relations Committee, Vol. 9,* 8871; **"We

should see to it": Ivy L. Lee, "The Relation of the Railroad to Human Nature," *Railway Age Gazette* (June 5, 1914); **stating the truth:** "Bulletin No. 1," *Facts Concerning the Struggle in Colorado for Industrial Freedom: Series I* (Issued by the Coal Mine Managers, 1914); **"dignified . . . It is thought"**: Ivy Lee to John D. Rockefeller, Jr., June 5, 1914, *Industrial Relations Committee, Vol. 9,* 8867; **"thoughtful people"**: Jerome D. Greene to John D. Rockefeller, Jr., July 6, 1914, Rockefeller Family, OMR, Business Interests, Record Group III2C, box 20, folder 176, RAC; **"This publicity work"**: "Colorado Memorandum," Rockefeller Family, OMR, Business Interests, Record Group III2Z, series V, Biographical Works, box 54, folder 484, RAC.

223–24 **Upton Sinclair had gone to Denver:** Upton Sinclair, *Brass Check: A Study of American Journalism* (Long Beach, CA: self-published, 1928), 162; **feud:** Upton Sinclair, "The A.P. Must Answer," *Appeal to Reason* (June 20, 1914); **A "pest":** "Pen Points: by the Staff," *Los Angeles Times* (May 19, 1914); **"touch and go":** Upton Sinclair, "Was There Civil War in Colorado?—What Upton Sinclair Saw," the *Day Book* (June 3, 1914); **"About a month ago":** William A. Bloodworth, Jr., *Upton Sinclair* (Boston: Twayne Publishers, 1977), 82–83; **a screen adaptation of *The Jungle*:** "Filming the 'Jungle'," *New York Tribune* (May 17, 1914); Mary Craig Sinclair, *Southern Belle* (Jackson: University Press of Mississippi, 1999), 171; "Tarrytown Armed to Thwart I.W.W.," *New York Tribune* (June 6, 1914); **"Edition after edition . . . reputation":** Upton Sinclair, "Free Speech Fight in John D.'s Town," *Appeal to Reason* (June 20, 1914); **"let the public":** Sinclair, *Southern Belle,* 163–164; **libel:** "Sinclair to Start Criminal Actions," *Tarrytown Daily News* (June 15, 1914); "Arraign Three Editors This Morning to Answer Criminal Libel Charges," *Tarrytown Daily News* (June 17, 1914).

225 **"you can bet we're coming back":** "Tarrytown Loses I.W.W. Martyrs," *New York Tribune* (June 9, 1914); **"most astonishing":** Hugh Fullerton, "Siege of Tarrytown! John D. and Son Prisoners on Big Estate," the *Day Book* (June 1, 1914); **"right of silence":** reprinted from the *Commercial Appeal,* "The Right of Silence," *Grand Forks Herald* (July 3, 1914); **"spouters":** "Denying Free Speech," *Grand Rapids Press* (June 8, 1914).

225–26 **For Arthur Caron, personally:** Upton Sinclair, "Free Speech Fight in John D.'s Town"; "Caron's Career in Anarchy," *New York Times* (July 5, 1914).

226–28 **Two weeks had passed:** "I.W.W. Agitators Pelted with Rotten Eggs, Stones and Dirt, as They Hold Free Speech Meeting on Aqueduct," *Tarrytown Daily News* (June 23, 1914); "Anarchists Egged in Tarrytown Riot," *New York Times* (June 23, 1914); "60 Agitators Storm Tarrytown to Speak," the *Sun* (June 23, 1914); "Bad Egg Volleys and Sand in Eyes Rout the I.W.W.," the *World* (June 23, 1914); "Tarrytown Mob in 3-Hour Riot Routs the I.W.W.," *New York Tribune* (June 23, 1914); "I.W.W. Stoned by Tarrytown Force After Egg Shower," *New York Herald* (June 23, 1914).

228 **some were in the mood to gloat:** "Anarchy and Law at Tarrytown," the *Sun* (June 24, 1914); **a writer for the *Times*:** "Anarchists Egged in Tarrytown Riot."

Safe and Sane

229–30 **"Don't Throw Things Out the Windows":** *For You. It Is Hard to Get Money. It Is Harder to Spend It Right. Health Is Wealth* (New York: Issued by the Tenement House Department of the City of New York and the Tenement House Committee of the Charity Organization Society, 1917); **"greatest social worker":** This was said by George McAneny, president of the Board of Aldermen. "City Plans to Uplift Tenement Livers," *New York Times* (June 22, 1914); **a prelude of intrusions to come:** "A Primer for Tenement Dwellers," *New York Tribune* (June 22, 1914).

230 **only one of the initiatives:** "'Skyscraper Jail' for Women Is Soon to Be Begun," *New York Times* (March 22, 1914); "Anarchist Prison on Riker's Island," *New York Times* (Nov. 29, 1914); "Kingsbury Hopes to Save $666,000," *New York Times* (June 4, 1914); "Detective Force Reorganized," the *World* (June 16, 1914).

230–31 **The carnage of the holiday:** "A Fourth-of-July Lexicon," *Life* (July 2, 1914); "Fourth of July Tetanus," the *Medical Standard* (July 1901); William B. Bailey, "The Glorious Fourth," the *Independent* (June 29, 1914); **"annual carnival":** Raymond W. Smilor, "Creating a National Festival: The Campaign for a Safe and Sane Fourth, 1903–1916," *Journal of American Culture* (Winter 1980); **"more or less biff":** "The Glorious Fourth Comparatively Quiet," *New York Times* (July 5, 1901); **"A bombardment":** "The Fourth in the City," *New York Times* (July 5, 1896).

231–33 **a countrywide agitation:** "Taft for a Sane Fourth," *New York Times* (July 6, 1909); **John D. Rockefeller:** "Sane Fourth Idea Pleases John D.," *Chicago Daily Tribune* (July 5, 1909); **"Quite aside":** "The New Fourth," *American City* (June 1912); **"doing well":** "How to Celebrate 'A Safe and Sane Fourth'—A Series of Contrasts," *New York Times* (June 25, 1911); **Twenty cities held Safe and Sane celebrations:** Roy Rozenzweig, *Eight Hours for What We Will: Workers and Leisure in an Industrial City* (New York: Cambridge University Press, 1983), 153; **Revolutionary battles:** "A Revolution in Celebrations," *Boston Medical and Surgical Journal* (June 27, 1912); "Fewer Injuries Mark Sane Fourth," *Chicago Tribune* (July 6, 1910); "No Lives Lost in 4th Celebration," *New York Tribune* (July 5, 1914).

233 **"In place of bombs":** "New York's 'Safety First' Celebration of the Fourth," the *World* (July 4, 1914); "Safe and Sane Fourth," *New York Times* (June 7, 1914); "Safe, Sane Fourth Without Fireworks," *New York Times* (June 28, 1914); **"City Hall will be ablaze":** "Fourth Committee Takes in Lighting Rehearsal," the *World* (July 4, 1914); **"safe and ultra sane":** "'Show Your Flags!' Is Final 4th Order," *New York Times* (July 3, 1914); "More Rockefeller Guards," *New York Times* (June 25, 1914); Display ad, "Fourth of July Excursions," the *World* (June 24, 1914); **"TUT, TUT!":** "Noisy Fourth Sure, but Minus Powder," *New York Tribune* (June 29, 1914); "Ship Fireworks by Mail," *New York Times* (July 4, 1914).

8. His Own Medicine

234–35 **"one of the human rookeries":** "'Reds' Slain by Bomb They Were Making; Woman Also Killed," *New York Tribune* (July 5, 1914); **"we do not celebrate the Fourth":** "Caron's Death Won't End It," *New York Times* (July 5, 1914).

235 **Nothing . . . scheduled for Fifth Avenue:** "Rockefellers Go Away," *New York Herald* (June 25, 1914).

235 **Caron's anger had grown:** Marie Ganz, *Rebels: Into Anarchy—and Out Again* (New York: Dodd, Mead and Company, 1920), 174. **very tense:** Paul Avrich, *Anarchist Voices: An Oral History of Anarchism in America* (Princeton: Princeton University Press, 1995), 222–223.

236 **still carried the bundle with them:** "Anarchists Are Questioned Closely at Police Station," *New York Herald* (July 5, 1914).

236–37 **Then, a thunderburst:** "I.W.W. Bomb Kills Three Foes of John D. Rockefeller and Wrecks Big Apartment House in Harlem," *New York Herald* (July 5, 1914); "Explosion Hurls Debris Through Church Windows," *New York Herald* (July 5, 1914); "I.W.W. Leader and 2 Others Killed in Bomb Explosion," the *World* (July 5, 1914); "'Reds' Slain by Bomb They Were Making; Woman Also Killed"; "Anarchist Bomb Believed for Rockefeller, Kills Three I.W.W. Makers and Woman—Injures Many—Wrecks Tenement House," the *Sun* (July 5, 1914); "Police Find Body of Berg in Ruins," *New York Tribune* (July 6, 1914); "Fourth Body in Debris of Bomb Shop," *New York Herald* (July 6, 1914); **gave him an overcoat:** Avrich, *Modern School*, 221.

238–39 **Commissioner Woods arrived:** "Anarchist Bomb, Believed for Rockefeller"; **grieving suspects:** "Anarchists Are Questioned Closely at Police Station"; "I.W.W. Leader and 2 Others Killed in Bomb Explosion." Most papers concurred that Berkman retained his famous insouciance at this moment. However, the *Herald*, one of the most hostile papers in the city, disagreed: "Berkman was plainly distressed. His naturally sallow face was pasty in color and he wet his lips continually as he spoke. His remarks were delivered slowly and with an effort and he paused several times in the middle of a sentence as if to formulate his remarks."

239 **found Upton Sinclair in his apartment:** "Anarchist Bomb Believed for Rockefeller."

239 **Becky Edelsohn and fifty or so others:** "Caron's Death Won't End It"; Moritz Jagendorf in Avrich, *Anarchist Voices*, 221.

240–41 **In Tarrytown, news of the explosion:** "Survivor of Bomb Explosion Eludes Police," the *Sun* (July 6, 1914); "J.D. Rockefeller's Tarrytown Estate Surrounded by a Cordon of Guards," *New York Herald* (July 5, 1914).

241 **In Philadelphia's Independence Square:** "Wilson Demands High Patriotism," *New York Times* (July 5, 1914).

241 **"He would have practiced a million-fold":** Alexander Berkman, "Observations and Comments," *Mother Earth* (Aug. 1914).

241 **New Yorkers strolled the parks:** "All Sang 'Yankee Doodle,'" *New York Times* (July 5, 1914).

242–44 **On Blackwell's Island:** "Chapter Six: Vacations in the Workhouse," in Isidore Wisotsky, *Such a Life,* unpublished typescript, Tamiment Library, New York University; Frank Tannenbaum, "What I Saw in Prison," the *Masses* (May 1915); **squinting over the pages:** "Books I Read in Jail," Frank Tannenbaum Papers, box 3, RBML; Jane Roulston to Frank Tannenbaum, May 28, 1914, Frank Tannenbaum Papers, box 4, RBML; **"industrial conditions":** Harry Rappaport to Frank Tannenbaum, July 9, 1914, Frank Tannenbaum Papers, box 4, RBML; **"I.W.W. principles":** Jane Roulston to Frank Tannenbaum, July 30, 1914, Frank Tannenbaum Papers, box 4, RBML.

244–47 **The next week was tense:** "New York Penitentiary, Blackwell's Island," *Twentieth Annual Report of the State Commission of Prisons for the Year 1914* (Ossining, NY: Sing Sing Prison, 1915), 137–138; **could be heard in Manhattan:** Frank Tannenbaum, "A Strike in Prison," the *Masses* (July 1915); **"700 Join Mutiny; Island Shop Fired,"** *New York Times* (July 10, 1914); **the cooler:** Frank Tannenbaum, "The Blackwell's Island Hell," the *Masses* (June 1915); Tannenbaum, "A Strike in Prison"; **Commissioner Davis arrived:** "Woman Calms Blackwell's Mutiny Gang," *New York Tribune* (July 11, 1914); "Quiet on Island; Miss Davis Here," *New York Times* (July 11, 1914); Tannenbaum, "A Strike in Prison"; "How a Woman Commissioner Deals with Prison Problems," *Outlook* (July 25, 1914); "Correction Dep't After 6 Months Under Miss Davis," the *World* (Aug. 2, 1914); **After seven days in isolation:** George Palmer Putnam, "The New Tannenbaum," *New York Times* (June 26, 1921); "Jail Ban on Goethe Enrages Tannenbaum," *New York Tribune* (March 10, 1915); **"do nothing rash":** Jane Roulston to Frank Tannenbaum, July 14, 1914, Frank Tannenbaum Papers, box 4, RBML.

247 **the wreckage at 1626 Lexington Avenue:** "Anarchistic Printings, a Press and Cartridges Found in Flat," the *World* (July 6, 1914).

248 **Alternative versions of the story:** "Alexander Berkman's Opening Address," *Mother Earth* (July 1914); Upton Sinclair, "Bomb Tragedy a Mystery," *Appeal to Reason* (July 18, 1914); "Survivor of Bomb Explosion Eludes Police."

248–49 **"The whole aspect of affairs":** "Need of Another Sort of 'Clean Up Week,'" *New York Herald* (July 6, 1914); "Anarchy and Dynamite," *Outlook* (July 18, 1914); Avrich, *Modern School,* 223; Alexander Berkman, "A Gauge of Change," *Mother Earth* (July 1914); "Anarchists Prepare for Public Funeral," *New York Herald* (July 6, 1914); **it was time for the authorities to react:** "Dying by Their Own Dynamite," the *World* (July 6, 1914); "Fourth Body in Debris of Bomb Shop," *New York Herald* (July 6, 1914); **"Anarchy seems to have met its deserts":** "I.W.W. Jeered by Tarrytown Throng," *New York Herald* (July 7, 1914). The *World* had the mayor's statement slightly differently: "Anarchy seems to have got its just deserts. It was a lamentable accident, of course, but it seems to have justified fully the action of the police in taking precautionary measures. The police will continue to take such measures." From "Mayor and Woods to Enforce Order at Reds' Funeral," the *World* (July 7, 1914).

250 **a showdown between Berkman and Woods:** "Anarchists at Cremation of Three Bomb Victims," *New York Herald* (July 9, 1914); "Will Seize Bodies of

Bombmakers if Unburied To-Day," the *World* (July 8, 1914); "Mayor Signs New Law for Parades," the *World* (July 9, 1914); "Bodies of the Dead Anarchists Burned," *New York Times* (July 9, 1914).

250–51 **"Comrades, friends, and sympathizers":** "The Lexington Explosion," *Mother Earth* (July 1914); "Anarchists at Cremation of Three Bomb Victims," *New York Herald* (July 9, 1914); "'Reds' Cremated; Leader Announces Funeral Saturday," the *World* (July 9, 1914); "Bodies of the Dead Anarchists Burned," *New York Times* (July 9, 1914); **A radical sculptor:** "800 Police Ready to Quell Anarchy in Union Square," *New York Herald* (July 11, 1914); "The Lexington Explosion."

252–54 **All efforts turned to the memorial:** "Anarchists Insist on Marching for Bomb Makers," *New York Herald* (July 10, 1914); "5,000 at Memorial to Anarchist Dead," *New York Times* (July 12, 1914); "Anarchists Hold Memorial Meeting for Bomb Makers in Union Square; Violent Speeches May Cause Arrests," *New York Herald* (July 12, 1914); **"Comrades, idealists":** Quoted in Beverly Gage, *The Day Wall Street Exploded: A Story of America in Its First Age of Terror* (New York: Oxford University Press, 2009), 103; **"we believe in violence":** "Rebecca Edelsohn's Speech," *Mother Earth* (Aug. 1914); **"proscribed utterances":** "Anarchists Hold Memorial Meeting for Bomb Makers in Union Square."

9. The War Has Spoiled Everything

257 **his father used to walk with him:** "Research Notebooks," 60–61, 124, Rockefeller Family Papers. John D. Rockefeller, Jr., Personal Files, Record Group III2z, series V, Biographical Works, box 57, folder 503, RAC; **isn't a God:** Raymond B. Fosdick Interview with Rev. Charles Schweikert; Rockefeller Family Papers, Record Group II, OMR, series V, Biographical Works, box 57, folder 502, RAC; Lydia Bodman Vandenbergh and Earle G. Shettleworth, Jr., *Revisiting Seal Harbor and Acadia National Park* (Charleston: Arcadia Publishing, 1997), 66–69.

258 **No affront was too obscure:** John D. Rockefeller, Jr., to Ivy Lee, June 10, 1914, quoted in *Industrial Relations Committee, Vol. 9*, 8869; **"vacillating":** John D. Rockefeller, Jr., to Ivy Lee, June 5, 1914, *Industrial Relations Committee, Vol. 9*, 8868; **"infamous statements":** Refers to a story in *Everybody's* written by George Creel; John D. Rockefeller, Jr., to Ivy Lee, June 11, 1914, *Industrial Relations Committee, Vol. 9*, 8871; **"every Governor":** The article he liked was John J. Stevenson, "Labor and Capital," *Popular Science Monthly* (May 1914), quoted in John D. Rockefeller, Jr., to Starr J. Murphy, June 29, 1914, Rockefeller Family, OMR, Business Interests, Record Group III2C, box 20, folder 178, RAC.

258–59 **Ivy Lee's series of pamphlets:** "No 'Massacre' of Women and Children in Colorado Strike," *Struggle in Colorado for Industrial Freedom* (July 26, 1914); **"educative campaign":** "Letter to Wilson Rockefeller's Idea," *New York Times* (May 17, 1915); **"teaching in our colleges":** Ivy Lee to Starr J. Murphy, July 3, 1914.

259 **Unlike Junior's other philanthropies:** Ivy Lee to J.F. Welborn, July 17, 1914, Rockefeller Family, Record Group 2, OMR, Business Interests, Record Group III2C, box 22, folder 200, RAC; **"under the auspices":** John D. Rockefeller, Jr., to Starr J. Murphy, June 29, 1914, Rockefeller Family, OMR, Business Interests, Record Group III2C, box 20, folder 178, RAC; **to President Wilson:** John D. Rockefeller, Jr., to Ivy Lee, June 10, 1914, *Industrial Relations Committee, Vol. 9*, 8869, 8875, 8876.

260 **his campaign . . . had cost him a sunset:** "Bar Harbor: Mr. and Mrs. John D. Rockefeller, Jr., Among Arrivals," *New York Tribune* (July 5, 1914); **"not the slightest":** "At Bar Harbor," *New York Tribune* (July 1, 1914); "Guarding John D. Rockefeller, Jr., from I.W.W. Invaders at Seal Harbor," *New York Herald* (July 6, 1914); "Police Find Body of Berg in Ruins," *New York Tribune* (July 6, 1914); Pinkerton's National Detective Agency invoice, July 31, 1914, Rockefeller Family Papers, Record Group I, John D. Rockefeller, series A, box 267, folder 1784, RAC.

260–61 **did not talk about his anxiety:** "Recollections of My Father," Rockefeller Family Papers, Record Group 2, OMR, series I: "Correspondence," box 7, folder 72, RAC; Robert F. Dalzell, Jr., and Lee Baldwin Dalzell, *The House the Rockefellers Built: A Tale of Money, Taste, and Power in Twentieth-Century America* (New York: Henry Holt and Co., 2007), 111–116; **"We should hesitate":** John D. Rockefeller, Jr., to John D. Rockefeller, Aug. 31, 1912, Rockefeller Family Papers, Record Group 2, OMR, Series I: "Correspondence," box 2, folder 15, RAC; **"live with the fear":** Rockefeller Family JDR, Jr., Personal: Speeches, Record Group III2Z, series V, box 57, folder 503, Research Notebooks, vol. 26, RAC; **"I am wondering":** John D. Rockefeller, Jr., to John D. Rockefeller, Aug. 7, 1914, Rockefeller Family Papers, John D. Rockefeller, Jr., Personal: Record Group III2Z, box 2, folder 15, RAC; **"people call it courage":** "Research Notebooks," 30, Rockefeller Family Papers, John D. Rockefeller, Jr., Personal Files, Record Group III2Z, series V, Biographical Works, box 57, folder 503, RAC.

261–63 **On a perfect summer evening:** The temperature that day ranged from 73 to 79 degrees; **to the Tombs:** "To Break 'Starving' of Becky Edelson," *New York Times* (July 21, 1914); "Reba's Bill of Fare to Contain Force," the *Sun* (July 22, 1914); "Reba Edelson, in Jail, Begins Hunger Strike," the *World* (July 21, 1914); **The next morning:** "Forcible Feeding Awaits Edelson Girl's Need of It," the *World* (July 23, 1914). The *Times* version of this encounter implies less reserve on Becky's behalf, saying she "objected in noisy tones" to her examination. "Becky Edelson Begins Her Strike," *New York Times* (July 22, 1914); "Reba Edelson May Be Fed in Prison by Force," the *World* (July 22, 1914); "Becky Edelson Begins Her Strike," *New York Times* (July 22, 1914); "Hunger Strike Means Matteawan," *New York Tribune* (July 22, 1914); **For the remainder of the day:** "Reds May Use Force for Hunger Striker," the *Sun* (July 23, 1914); Mary Harris, *I Knew Them in Prison* (New York: Viking Press, 1936), 12; telegram, July 24, 1914, Alexander Berkman to Emma Goldman, the Emma Goldman Papers.

263 **newspapers eagerly aggravated the situation:** "What Would You Do with Becky?" *New York Call* (July 23, 1914); "The Old and the New," *Woman Rebel* (Aug. 1914).

263–64 **"blazed a trail of precedents"**: Mabel Jacques Eichel, "Katharine Bement Davis," *Woman's Journal* (April 13, 1928). Katharine Davis has been discussed as one of several characters in two important group biographies. Ellen F. Fitzpatrick, *Endless Crusade: Women Social Scientists and Progressive Reform* (New York: Oxford University Press, 1990), and Estelle B. Freedman, *Their Sisters' Keepers: Women's Prison Reform in America, 1830–1930* (Ann Arbor: The University of Michigan Press, 1981). She was also featured in Antonia Petrash, *More Than Petticoats: Remarkable New York Women* (Guilford, CT: TwoDot, 2002). Thomas C. McCarthy, historian for the New York City Department of Correction, wrote a mini-history of her life. See McCarthy, *New York City's Suffragist Commissioner: Correction's Katharine Bement Davis* (Department of Correction, 1997). Important studies of women's penal history include Estelle B. Freedman, *Their Sisters' Keepers*; Nicole Hahn Rafter, *Partial Justice: Women in State Prisons 1800–1935* (Boston: Northeastern University Press, 1985); Eugenia C. Lekkerkerker, *Reformatories for Women in the United States* (The Hague: J.B. Walters, 1931).

264 **the prison developed into a proving ground**: "A Revolutionary Appointment," *Outlook* (Jan. 17, 1914); quoted in Edward Marshall, "New York's First Woman Commissioner of Correction," *New York Times* (Jan. 11, 1914).

264 **Fifty-four years old**: "Katherine B. Davis, the Tamer of Rebel Souls," *Current Opinion* (Nov. 1914); Fitzpatrick, *Endless Crusade*, 101; "A Revolutionary Appointment"; "Miss Davis Takes Hold of Her Work," *New York Times* (Jan. 3, 1914); Jean Henry Large, "A Man's Job," in Fitzpatrick, *Katharine Bement Davis*.

265 **"little better than medieval"**: Katharine Bement Davis, "Charities and Correction," in *The Government of the City of New York* (The New York State Constitutional Convention Commission, 1915), 86–97; Edward Marshall, "New York's First Woman Commissioner of Correction," *New York Times* (Jan. 11, 1914); Harris, *I Knew Them*, 6.

265–66 **Edelsohn had not eaten for several days**: "Rebecca Doesn't Let Up on Her Hunger Strike," the *Call* (July 25, 1914); "It's Hunger Strike of Doubt in Reba's Case," the *World* (July 25, 1914); "Lemon Fattens Becky Edelson," *New York Herald* (July 25, 1914); "Says Reba Fakes Food Strike," the *Sun* (July 25, 1914); "Becky Edelson 'Fasts' Well on Tabloid Food," the *World* (July 30, 1914); **recipe**: "Forcible Feeding Awaits Edelson Girl's Need of It," the *World* (July 23, 1914); **"It will not hurt her"**: "Hunger Strike Means Matteawan"; **a female reporter**: Djuna Barnes, "How It Feels to Be Forcibly Fed," the *World Magazine* (Sept. 6, 1914). This essay's sensational tone requires a careful interpretation. For such an exegesis, see Barbara Green, "Spectacular Confessions: 'How It Feels to Be Forcibly Fed,'" *Review of Contemporary Fiction* (Sept. 1993).

267 **metaphor for the . . . powers of the state**: Robert Carlton Brown, "What Call Readers Think: Forcible Feeding," *New York Call* (July 24, 1914); "Rebecca Doesn't Let Up on Her Hunger Strike"; "On Hospital Cot, Becky Shuns Food," *New York Call* (July 24, 1914).

268 **finally starting to flag**: Rebecca Edelsohn, "One Woman's Fight," *Woman Rebel* (Aug. 1914).

268–69 **"Hereafter I must decline"**: Katharine Bement Davis, "To the Press of New York City," John Purroy Mitchel Papers, box 17, folder 174, New York Municipal Archives; **confidential letter to the mayor's secretary**: Katharine Bement Davis to Theodore Rousseau, July 30, 1914, John Purroy, Mitchel Papers, box 17, folder 174.

269 **The potential for a European conflict**: "Bright Prospect for Peace," *New York Times* (July 10, 1914); "A Threat of War," *New York Times* (July 24, 1914); "A General European War Still in the Balance," *New York Tribune* (July 28, 1914); "Critical Days," *New York Times* (July 31, 1914); **"unthinkable"**: "The Man of the Hour," *New York Times* (July 28, 1914).

269–70 **the struggle spread to New York City**: "Spook Fleet Off the Hook," *New York Times* (Aug. 7, 1914); **"all met on common ground and argued"**: "Reserves Throng to Answer Calls," *New York Times* (Aug. 4, 1914); "Mayor Bars All but Stars and Stripes," *New York Times* (Aug. 7, 1914); "Women to March in Funereal Black," *New York Tribune* (Aug. 7, 1914); **"Belgian neutrality"**: "Wait in Times Sq. for News of War," *New York Times* (Aug. 17, 1914); **"Shut up"**: Mary Chamberlain, "The Clutch of Militarism," the *Survey* (Oct. 3, 1914); **"white heat"**: "Our Peaceful Land of Many Tongues," *New York Tribune* (Aug. 7, 1914).

270–71 **"impartial in thought"**: "The American People and the Great War: Address of President Wilson to the People of the United States, Aug. 18, 1914," the *Independent* (Aug. 31, 1914); Edwin A. Weinstein, *Woodrow Wilson: A Medical and Psychological Biography* (Princeton: Princeton University Press, 1981), 256; **"American citizens first"**: "Mayor Bars All but Stars and Stripes."

271 **"Is she alive or dead"**: John Jones, "Becky Edelson Submerged," *New York Times* (Aug. 17, 1914); Harris, *I Knew Them*, 13; **thirty-one days**: Rebecca Edelsohn, "Hunger Striking in America," *Mother Earth* (Sept. 1914); "Becky Edelson Out; Says She Fasted Whole Month," the *World* (Aug. 21, 1914); "Free Becky Edelson; Funeral Plans Off," *New York Times* (Aug. 21, 1914).

272–73 **Berkman had been right**: Alexander Berkman, "Observations and Comments," *Mother Earth* (Aug. 1914); "The War in Photographs: Indian Troops Encamped in France," *Manchester Guardian* (Oct. 8, 1914); **"You Anarchists"**: "The Reckoning," *Mother Earth* (Sept. 1914); **Two bullets**: "Heir to Austria's Throne Is Slain with His Wife by a Bosnian Youth to Avenge Seizure of His Country," *New York Times* (June 29, 1914); **"Vain is the hope"**: Alexander Berkman, "Observations and Comments," *Mother Earth* (Aug. 1914); **"Prussian militarism"**: Alexander Berkman, "Observations and Comments," *Mother Earth* (Oct. 1914); **"great danger"**: Alexander Berkman, "War on War," *Mother Earth* (Aug. 1914); **"Blushing in our shame"**: "The Reckoning," *Mother Earth* (Sept. 1914); **"I am sick of appeals"**: Alexander Berkman, "Observations and Comments," *Mother Earth* (Aug. 1914).

10. Who's Who Against America

274–75 **the coal war had entered its eleventh month**: L.M. Bowers to John D. Rockefeller, Jr., Aug. 16, 1914, *Industrial Relations Committee, Vol. 9*, 8441;

Bowers and his intransigent colleagues: John A. Fitch, "Law and Order the Issue in Colorado," the *Survey* (Dec. 5, 1914); **employees voted to end the strike:** Scott Martelle, *Blood Passion: The Ludlow Massacre and Class War in the American West* (New Brunswick, NJ: Rutgers University Press, 2007), Appendix B; "Miners' Board Ends Colorado Strike," *New York Times* (Dec. 9, 1914); **"satisfaction . . . discouraging":** L.M. Bowers to John D. Rockefeller, Jr., Dec. 11, 1914, *Industrial Relations Committee, Vol. 9,* 8444; **"rugged stand":** L.M. Bowers to John D. Rockefeller, Jr., Dec. 11, 1914, *Industrial Relations Committee, Vol. 9,* 8442.

275 **Bowers did not have long to gloat:** "Memorandum of talk with Mr. Bowers in my office, Dec. 28, 1914," Rockefeller Family Papers, Record Group 2, OMR, Friends and Services, box 49, folder 359; **"turned out to pasture":** John D. Rockefeller, Jr., to Bowers, Jan. 20, 1915, Rockefeller Family Papers, Record Group 2, OMR, Friends and Services, box 49, folder 359.

275–76 **discarded one troubled employee:** "Lee Wrote 'Colorado Facts,'" *New York Times* (Dec. 9, 1914); **"The strike bulletins":** "The End of the Colorado Coal Strike," the *Survey* (Dec. 19, 1914); *Industrial Relations Committee, Vol. 8,* 7903; Jonathan Rees, *Representation and Rebellion: The Rockefeller Plan at the Colorado Fuel and Iron Company, 1914–1942* (Boulder: University Press of Colorado, 2010), 23; "Letter to Wilson Rockefeller's Idea," *New York Times* (May 17, 1915); **"systematic and perverse":** Herbert J. Seligmann, "A Skilled Publicity Man," the *Masses* (Aug. 1915).

276–77 **Rockefeller and Lee were called:** Kirk Hallahan, "Ivy Lee and the Rockefellers' Response to the 1913–1914 Colorado Coal Strike," *Journal of Public Relations Research*, vol. 14, issue 4 (2002); "Rockefeller, Jr., Wary and Bland," *New York Times* (Jan. 26, 1915); **"he is indeed a victim":** Walter Lippmann, "Mr. Rockefeller on the Stand," *New Republic* (Jan. 30, 1915).

278 **he had long planned to visit:** "Conference at Mr. Rockefeller's Apartment January 7, 1953," Rockefeller Family Papers, Record Group II, OMR, series V, Biographical Works, box 57, folder 502, RAC; **"He did not dig very much":** "Rockefeller Plies Pick in Coal Mine," *New York Times* (Sept. 22, 1915); Rees, *Representation and Rebellion*, 28–36; Raymond B. Fosdick, *John D. Rockefeller, Jr., A Portrait* (New York: Harper, 1956), 160–165; **There had been no way to predict:** Fosdick, *John D. Rockefeller, Jr.*, 160; **"Had Mr. Rockefeller":** William Lyon Mackenzie King to Abby Rockefeller, Oct. 6, 1915, Rockefeller Family Papers, Record Group 2, OMR, Abby Aldrich Rockefeller, box 3, folder 38, RAC; ROCKEFELLER WINS OVER MINERS: Headlines quoted in Rees, *Representation and Rebellion*, 32; **"good-will":** William Lyon Mackenzie King to Abby Rockefeller, Oct. 6, 1915; **"practically every point":** Rees, *Representation and Rebellion*, 33; **"this table is square":** Rees, *Representation and Rebellion*, 37; **"I cannot but feel":** William Lyon Mackenzie King to Abby Rockefeller, Oct. 6, 1915.

280 **after the Lexington Avenue explosion:** Jennifer Fronc, *"I Led Him On": Undercover Investigation and the Politics of Social Reform in New York City, 1900–1919* (doctrial thesis, Columbia University, 2005), 230, 231; "Quick Results Follow Detective Squad Change," *New York Herald* (Aug. 2, 1914); "New Detective Branches," *New York Times* (July 30, 1914); **"Detectives were carefully**

instructed": From an untitled report in the National Civic Federation records, Manuscripts and Archives Division at the New York Public Library, series X, "Subversive Activities Files, c. 1907–1942," reel 405: 1; **Despite this specialized instruction**: Paul Avrich, *Sacco and Vanzetti: The Anarchist Background* (Princeton: Princeton University Press, 1991), 100–101; Fronc, *"I Led Him On,"* 223–224; "Lighted Bomb Put in Tombs Court," *New York Times* (Nov. 15, 1914).

280–81 **made their impact in other ways**: Thomas J, Tunney and Paul Merrick Hollister, *Throttled! The Detection of the German and Anarchist Bomb Plotters in the United States* (Boston: Small, Maynard, 1919), 39–69; "Many Explosions Since War Began," *New York Times* (July 31, 1916); "Detective Lit Bomb, Abarno Tells Court," *New York Times* (April 3, 1915); "Bomb Plotters Get 6 to 12 Years," *New York Times* (April 20, 1915); **revealed themselves**: Emma Goldman, "The Barnum and Bailey Staging of the 'Anarchist Plot,'" *Mother Earth* (April 1915); Avrich, *The Modern School*, 231–232; Emma Goldman, *Living My Life, Volume II* (New York: Dover Publications, 1970), 550–551.

281–82 **draft riots**: "Arthur Woods Urges Man-to-Man Contact," *New York Times* (June 21, 1920); **"The Prussian, the Bolshevik, and the Anarchist:"** Edward Mott Wooley, "The Inner Story of New York," *McClure's Magazine* (Nov. 1917); James Lardner and Thomas Reppetto, *NYPD: A City and Its Police* (New York: Henry Holt and Co., 2000), 177.

282–83 **While overseeing these infiltrations**: Melvyn Dubofsky, *When Workers Organize: New York City in the Progressive Era* (Amherst: The University of Massachusetts Press, 1968), 130–147; Arthur Woods, *Policeman and Public* (New Haven: Yale University Press, 1919), 71–72; **"too much sappy talk"**: State of New York, *Minutes and Testimony*, 109–110.

283 **"It's Frank!"**: "Jail Ban on Goethe Enrages Tannenbaum," *New York Tribune* (March 10, 1915); "Tannenbaum, Church Raider, Fine Remitted, Is Free Today," *New York Tribune* (March 9, 1915).

284–85 **Frank went to work for the *Masses***: "State Investigates Blackwell's Prison," *New York Times* (July 15, 1915); **"until he behaves"**: "Warden Hayes Quits Blackwell's Island," *New York Times* (July 23, 1915); **three cheers for Tannenbaum**: "Katharine B. Davis' Little Hell," the *Masses* (Sept. 1915); **"Am glad you are ready"**: Jane Roulston to Frank Tannenbaum, March 12, 1915, Frank Tannenbaum Papers, box 4, RBML; **"I.W.W. that I knew"**: Frank Tannenbaum to Dr. Grant, April 21, 1917, Frank Tannenbaum Papers, box 3, RBML; **"much to accomplish"**: "Jail Ban on Goethe Enrages Tannenbaum," *New York Tribune* (March 10, 1915).

285 **time as a revolutionist was over**: Frank Tannenbaum's Columbia University Transcript, 1915–1916, Frank Tannenbaum Papers, box 5, RBML; *Columbia University in the City of New York Catalogue, 1915–1916* (New York: Columbia University, 1916).

285–87 **"I think you have the town with you"**: Theodore Rousseau to Katharine B. Davis, Aug. 6, 1914, John Purroy Mitchel Papers, box 6, folder 10, New York Municipal Archives; "Penitentiary Cells Called Dangerous," *New York Times* (April 26, 1915); "Warden Hayes Quits Blackwell's Island"; **"I shouted until I** was hoarse": "Warden Hayes Quits Blackwell's Island"; **"Admirable women, put in places of authority"**: E.S.M., "Are Women Despots?" *Life* (July 29, 1915); "One Woman's Fight," *Woman Rebel* (Aug. 1914); **ended in failure:** "Miss Davis Heads New Parole Board," *New York Times* (Dec. 29, 1915).

287–88 **a perpetual headache to the mayor:** Lyman Beecher Stowe, "Waifs Now Well Treated in City's Institutions," *New York Tribune* (Nov. 4, 1917); Reminiscences of Frances Perkins; Reminiscences of Robert Binkerd, 51; **"Beds were alive with vermin":** Quoted in Francis Hackett, "The Sacred Cow," *New Republic* (June 3, 1916); Winthrop D. Lane, "Children and the City's Purse-Strings," the *Survey* (Jan. 1, 1915); Edwin R. Lewinson, *John Purroy Mitchel, Symbol of Reform* (doctoral thesis, Columbia University, 1961), 247; **"Oliver Twist":** "A Campaign of Calumny: The New York Charities Investigation" (New York: The America Press, 1916), 29; **"agency of paganism":** Ibid., 6; Lewinson, *Symbol of Reform*, Chapter X; "Father Blakely States the Issue," *New Republic* (July 29, 1916); **"arbitrary and unlawful":** Quoted in Lewinson, *Symbol of Reform*, 262; "A Campaign of Calumny," 56; **role in wiretaps:** "Appendix," 14, box 4, Meloney Papers, RBML.

288–89 **Alexander Berkman was restless:** Alexander Berkman, "An Innocent Abroad," *Mother Earth* (Jan. 1915); **"The poor boy":** Quoted in Beverly Gage, *The Day Wall Street Exploded: A Story of America in Its First Age of Terror* (New York: Oxford University Press, 2009), 107; **"Kansas City is depressing":** Alexander Berkman, "An Innocent Abroad II," *Mother Earth* (Feb. 1915); **"dear old Gotham":** Alexander Berkman, "Anniversary Musings," *Mother Earth* (March 1915); **"Time tempers":** Alexander Berkman, "Anniversary Musings," *Mother Earth* (March 1915); **"something more definite":** Alexander Berkman, "In Reply to Kropotkin," *Mother Earth* (Nov. 1914).

289 **He was in California:** Richard Drinnon, ed., *The Blast: Volumes 1–2* (New York: Greenwood Reprint Corporation, 1968).

290–92 **Washington, D.C., prepared for battle:** Inez Haynes Irwin, *The Story of the Woman's Party* (New York: Harcourt, Brace and Co. 1921), 205; "Pacifists in Riots; Lodge Is Assaulted," *Washington Post* (April 3, 1917); "Must Exert All Our Power," *New York Times* (April 3, 1917); **Wilson's speech was prepared:** Arthur S. Link, *Wilson: Confusions and Crises: 1915–1916* (Princeton: Princeton University Press, 1964), 233; John Milton Cooper, *Woodrow Wilson: A Biography* (New York: Alfred A. Knopf, 2009), 287; **Afternoon turned to evening:** "Pacifists in Riots; Lodge Is Assaulted"; "Wilson's Plea Provides for Full Warfare," *New York Tribune* (April 3, 1917); **Wilson held his speech:** "Wilson's Plea Provides for Full Warfare"; "Must Exert All Our Power"; "The President Calls for War Without Hate," *New York Tribune* (April 3, 1917); **Word of the president's decision:** "Call for War Stirs All City," *New York Times* (April 3, 1917); "Fight in Rectors; Diner Refuses to Sing U. S. Anthem," *New York Tribune* (April 7, 1917).

292 **rushed to outdo its European peers:** "Who's Who Against America: News Garbler Hearst," *New York Tribune* (Oct. 21, 1917); "Who's Who Against America: Victor L. Berger, of Milwaukee," *New York Tribune* (Nov. 4, 1917); Quoted in Ronald Steel, *Walter Lippmann in the American Century* (Boston: Little, Brown, 1980), 124.

293 **Upton and Craig Sinclair:** Anthony Arthur, *Radical Innocent: Upton Sinclair* (New York: Random House, 2006), 163–171; **"agitation isn't my job":** Steel, *Walter Lippmann*, 74, 116, 125–126.

294–96 **police arrested Berkman:** "Anarchists and Socialists," *New York Times* (July 11, 1917); **Berkman spent the next two years:** Charles H. McCormick, *Hopeless Cases: The Hunt for the Red Scare Terrorist Bombers* (Lanham: University Press of America, 2005), 36, 41; Alexander Berkman, "The Boylsheviki Spirit and History," *Mother Earth* (Nov. 1917); **"Now reaction is in full swing":** Alexander Berkman and Emma Goldman, "Deportation, Its Meaning and Menace: Last Message to the People of America by Alexander Berkman and Emma Goldman"; **"Slowly the big city receded":** Alexander Berkman, *The Bolshevik Myth* (New York: Boni and Liveright, 1925); **"deported by God":** Goldman, *Living My Life*, 709.

296 **Two pairs of boots:** John Garry Clifford, *The Citizen Soldiers: The Plattsburg Training Camp Movement, 1913–1920* (Lexington: The University Press of Kentucky, 1972), 63, 45; "Mayor Joins Camp for Military Drill," *New York Times* (Aug. 9, 1915).

297 **So Mitchel went to Plattsburg:** Lewinson, *Symbol of Reform*, 271; "City Rookies Make Good Rifle Score," *New York Times* (Aug. 17, 1915); Michael Pearlman, *To Make Democracy Safe for America: Patricians and Preparedness in the Progressive Era* (Urbana: University of Illinois Press, 1984), 58.

297–99 **1917 municipal election:** Pearlman, *To Make Democracy Safe*, 125; **"chafed":** Lewinson, *Symbol of Reform*, 354; **"The whole Nation":** "A Final Blow at Tammany Hall," *World's Work* (Feb. 1917); A VOTE FOR MAYOR MITCHEL . . . **Hearst:** Lewinson, *Symbol of Reform*, 329; **"ear-at-the-telephone":** Lewinson, *Symbol of Reform*, 341; **"control of the city":** " 'Billionaire Band' in Fusion Ranks Assailed by Hylan," *New York Tribune* (Oct. 10, 1917); **"all the reform":** Robert A. Caro, *The Power Broker: Robert Moses and the Fall of New York* (New York: Alfred A. Knopf, Inc., 1974), 84; **"an autocracy of experts":** "The Obstacle to Fusion Success," *New Republic* (Aug. 17, 1921).

299–301 **private soldier:** "Gen. Wood Reveals Mitchel Wanted to Enlist as a Private," *New York Tribune* (July 12, 1918); **"Don't break your silly neck":** Frank Polk to John Purroy Mitchel, Meloney Papers, box 4, folder "Biographical Notes," RBML; **"a damnable style of uniform":** Memorandum on Mayor Mitchel, April 18, 1922, Meloney Papers, box 4, folder "Biographical Notes," RBML; **"resolute courage . . . better than I had expected":** Lewinson, *Symbol of Reform*, 358–359; **"keep your head":** John Purroy Mitchel to Mrs. Mitchel (mother), no date, c. May or June 1918, John Purroy Mitchel Papers, box 24, LOC; **"succesfully executed":** "Ex-Mayor Mitchel in Air Stunts," *New York Times* (April 19, 1918); **"flying is really pretty good fun":** John Purroy Mitchel to Mr. Hedge, May 20, 1918, Meloney Papers, box 4, folder "Biographical Notes"; **"I thought they wanted flyers":** John Purroy Mitchel to Mr. Hedge, May 20, 1918, Meloney Papers, box 4, folder "Biographical Notes"; "Girls Can Help Soldiers," *New York Times* (May 29, 1918); "Arthur Woods Flies Higher Than Mitchel," *New York Tribune* (March 3, 1918); **"God**

protect me": John Purroy Mitchel to Robert Adamson, June 3, 1918, John Purroy Mitchel Papers, box 22, folder "June 1918."

301 **directed him to Gerstner Field:** *Aircraft Production: Hearings, Sixty-fifth Congress, Second Session, Parts 1–2. By United States. Congress. Senate. Committee on Military Affairs* (Washington: Government Printing Office, 1918), 560; **"unmitigated hell":** John Purroy Mitchel to Samuel L. Martin, no date, received June 26, 1918, John Purroy Mitchel Papers, box 22, folder "June 1918"; **deep in debt:** Memorandum for Colonel Arthur Woods, Dec. 13, 1918, John Purroy Mitchel Papers, box 24; **"If I live through":** Mitchel to Samuel L. Martin, June 28, 1918, John Purroy Mitchel Papers, box 22, folder "June 1918."

301–3 **a few minutes after seven** A.M.: Lewinson, *Symbol of Reform*, 362; **all over now:** "Mitchel Killed by Fall from Aero; Safety Belt Loose," *New York Tribune* (July 7, 1918); Testimony of Lt. Myers, Gerstner Field, Lake Charles, LA, Feb. 3, 1919, John Purroy Mitchel Papers, box 24, folder "General Correspondence Relating to the Death of JPM and Memorials to Mitchel"; **"exceptionally poor . . . not sure of himself":** Memorandum for Colonel Arthur Woods, Dec. 13, 1918, John Purroy Mitchel Papers, box 24, LOC; **"he was a bunch of nerves":** Untitled note, possibly from a biography that William Brown Meloney wrote of Mitchel but never published, no date, Meloney Papers, box 4, RBML; **transfer to the army:** John Purroy Mitchel to General Leonard Wood, June 13, 1918, John Purroy Mitchel Papers, box 22, folder "June 1918," LOC.

303 **he had forgotten to fasten his safety belt:** For obvious reasons, this explanation of Mitchel's death did not satisfy his family and friends. At the urging of his wife and mother, successive investigations into the accident lasted for well over a year. The first one, conducted by Captain P.H.B. Frelinghuysen, interviewed Mitchel's close associates but was stymied by the fact that Gerstner Field had suffered first a dysentery outbreak and quarantine and then a hurricane in the months since the crash. Everyone who had actually known Mitchel there—or had witnessed his death—had been reassigned. The second inquiry, coordinated by Arthur Woods, had more success. Its agents were able to interview several witnesses, including the flight instructor who had given Mitchel his final commands.

The main question being disputed concerned the explanation for why Mitchel's safety harness was unfastened. His wife believed that German saboteurs were to blame. One suggestion argued that the plane had caught fire shortly after takeoff and that Mitchel had unfastened his belt in order to fight the flames. This theory was supported by the fact that the fire extinguisher was not with the plane where it crashed, but landed at a distance from the wreckage. Furthermore, Mitchel's mother had heard that there were burn marks on her son's body. However, other reports denied this fact. And there were no signs of fire found on the airplane. Fire extinguishers were intentionally fastened loosely—so as to be easily accessible in an emergency—and it was not unusual for them to come free during a reverse tailspin. Others suggested that Mitchel had experienced a headache inflight and had unhooked his safety harness for relief—something he is said to have done on previous occasions—but since the entire flight lasted less than five minutes it seems unlikely that he was suddenly struck with a migraine in that time. The most likely explanation, and the one that multiple investigations finally, and reluctantly, accepted, is that Mitchel merely forgot to attach his harness. Then, noticing this, he had turned to land. But because he was in an unfamiliar plane, and panicking about the safety belt, he worked the controls too rapidly and was thrown clear by a sudden jolt.

The conductors of the inquiry were sympathetic with the family's desires. But nevertheless they came finally to accept that it was Mitchel's carelessness that cost his life. "On concluding my investigation," the army's agent wrote, "it is my personal opinion that Major Mitchel came to his death by falling out of his plane, on account of having failed to fasten his safety belt, and I made every effort in conducting this investigation in the hopes of finding that his death was caused by some other reason." (Lewinson, *Symbol of Reform*, 363–364.) In February 1919, having reviewed the findings of a second inquiry, Arthur Woods came to the same conclusion. "This is the last report on Major Mitchel's death," he wrote. "I know of nothing further to be done."

December 31, 1919

304 **With more defiance than joy:** "'Dry' Eve of 1920 Is Wet and Merry; Wine Given Away," the *World* (Jan. 1, 1920); **"except a certain one":** "1920 Welcomed in Wine Oceans by Joyous Folk," the *Sun* (Jan. 1, 1920); **"For twenty years":** "Outlaw Citizens," the *World* (Dec. 31, 1919).

305 **feeling of good riddance:** "The Old and the New," *New York Times* (Jan. 1, 1920); "Automobiles in City Kill 1,270," *Evening Post* (Jan. 2, 1920); Ernst Christopher Meyer, *Infant Mortality in New York City* (New York: The Rockefeller Foundation, 1921), 130; **"few mourners":** "The Task for 1920," the *World* (Jan. 1, 1920).

306 **a sense of betrayal:** No Title, *Mondavi (Wis.) Herald* (Jan. 2, 1920), John D. Rockefeller, Jr. Personal Papers, series IX, Scrapbooks, volume 9, RAC; **a few bombs:** "The Old and the New"; **"Briefly summed up":** The reporter mistook Berkman's age, asserting that he was fifty-one years old. It has been changed in the text for clarity. "The Kind of Man Alex. Berkman Is," the *World* (Dec. 28, 1919); **dropped his parcel:** "1920 Welcomed in Wine Oceans by Joyous Folk," the *Sun* (Jan. 1, 1920); "Scores of 'Reds' Arrested Up-State," *Evening Post* (Dec. 31, 1919); "Jury to Resume Anarchy Inquiry," *Evening Post* (Dec. 31, 1919).

306–7 **After everything that had passed:** "The Old and the New"; **"at least one final":** "Last Hopes of the Beaten 'Wets,'" *New York Tribune* (Dec. 28, 1919).

307–9 **John D. Rockefeller, Jr.:** "John D. Rockefeller, Jr. Visiting Palm Beach," *Palm Beach Post* (Dec. 28, 1919), John D. Rockefeller, Jr., Personal Papers, series IX, Scrapbooks, volume 9, RAC; **After two futile weeks:** Haggai Hurvitz, "Ideology and Industrial Conflict: President Wilson's First Industrial Conference of October 1919," *Labor History* (Fall 1977); **"corner grocery":** "What Rockefeller's Like," *San Jose News* (Dec. 26, 1919), John D. Rockefeller, Jr., Personal Papers, series IX, Scrapbooks, Volume 9, RAC; **"We believe":** No Title, *Mondavi (Wis.)*

Herald (Jan. 2, 1920), John D. Rockefeller, Jr., Personal Papers, series IX, Scrapbooks, Volume 9, RAC; **"happiest days":** John D. Rockefeller, Jr., to John D. Rockefeller, Jan. 5, 1920, John D. Rockefeller, Jr., Papers, Record Group III.2.Z, Correspondence, box 2, folder 19, RAC; **gold tiepins:** John D. Rockefeller, Jr., to John D. Rockefeller, Feb. 16, 1920, John D. Rockefeller, Jr., Papers, Record Group III.2.Z, Correspondence, box 2, folder 19, RAC; **"wonderful gifts":** John D. Rockefeller, Jr., to John D. Rockefeller, Jan. 12, 1920, John D. Rockefeller, Jr., Papers, Record Group III.2.Z, Correspondence, box 2, folder 19, RAC; Ron Chernow, *Titan: The Life of John D. Rockefeller, Sr.* (New York: Random House, 1998), 623–624.

309 **"no special observance" for the new year:** "Big New Year Feast Decreed for Wilson," *New York Tribune* (Jan. 1, 1920); Edwin A. Weinstein, *Woodrow Wilson: A Medical and Psychological Biography* (Princeton: Princeton University Press, 1981), 357.

309 **The crisis had come in September:** J. Michael Hogan, *Woodrow Wilson's Western Tour: Rhetoric, Public Opinion, and the League of Nations* (College Station: Texas A&M University Press, c. 2006); Weinstein, *A Medical and Psychological Biography*, 353; "Keep Faith with the World, Wilson's Appeal to America," *Boston Globe* (Sept. 5, 1919).

310–12 **The tour reached Pueblo:** Philip Kinsley, "'Act, Then I'll Decide,' Wilson Word to Senate," *Chicago Tribune* (Sept. 26, 1919); "Huge Crowd Sees Wilson Arrive at Depot in Pueblo," *Pueblo Chieftain* (Sept. 26, 1919); "Pres. Wilson Attracted Big Crowd to Fair," *Pueblo Chieftain* (Sept. 26, 1919); "Wilson Closely Guarded by the Federal Detectives," *Pueblo Chieftain* (Sept. 26, 1919); "Steel Committee and Welborn Hold a Secret Conference," *Pueblo Chieftain* (Sept. 26, 1919); **Molding his message:** "President Wilson's Address on League as Delivered in the City of Pueblo," *Pueblo Chieftain* (Sept. 26, 1919). This transcript of the speech is as it was transcribed by a team of stenographers, working in relays, at the auditorium in Pueblo. It is slightly truncated compared with the version that is usually published in collections of the president's speeches. "Extra Work Getting News of Wilson's Visit Here to World," *Pueblo Chieftain* (Sept. 26, 1919); **wife was crying:** "'Act, Then I'll Decide,' Wilson Word to Senate"; "Huge Crowd Cheers Wilson Leaving Hall," *Pueblo Chieftain* (Sept. 26, 1919); "Grayson's Order Ends Tour," *New York Times* (Sept. 27, 1919); **appearances were canceled:** Hogan, *Woodrow Wilson's Western Tour*, 162; Weinstein, *A Medical and Psychological Biography*, 356.

312–13 **in New York City that night:** "New Year Services in Churches Here," the *World* (Dec. 31, 1919); **"With unlimited money":** "New Year's Here and There," the *World* (Dec. 31, 1919); THE ARMY WISHES . . . **"For wounded soldiers":** "Wine Can't Be Sold So Hotels Say They Will Give It Away," *Evening Post* (Dec. 31, 1919); "'Carry On' Dances to Be Given at Hotels," *New York Tribune* (Jan. 11, 1920); "New Year's Eve Gay in Hotels, Quiet on Streets," *New York Times* (Jan. 1, 1920); **"so without noise":** "Crowds in Streets Strangely Silent," the *Sun* (Jan. 1, 1920); **"New Year's Eve as an institution":** "New Year's Eve Gay in Hotels, Quiet on Streets"; **"Only in the hotels":** "New Year's Eve Gay in Hotels, Quiet on Streets"; **"another chair":** "Hotel Throngs to Greet New

Year in Usual Fashion," *New York Herald* (Dec. 31, 1919); **"Bohemia":** "Last Hopes of the Beaten 'Wets'" *New York Tribune* (Dec. 28, 1919).

314 **Berkman stood at the rail of the** *Buford:* Alexander Berkman, *The Bolshevik Myth* (New York: Bone and Liveright, 1925), 16–27.

Afterword

317–18 **John Purroy Mitchel's body:** "Nation and City Unite in Honors to Honor Mitchel," *New York Times* (July 12, 1918); "Mitchel Laid to Rest as All in City Mourn," *New York Tribune* (July 12, 1918); **"valiant knight":** Quoted in "Honoring a Mayor," *New York Times* (Nov. 16, 1928); **"A brilliant career":** Quoted in Reminiscences of Frances Perkins (1955), Columbia University Oral History Collection, 264.

318–19 **hard-won gains were easily effaced:** Charles T White, "Hylan Appointees Typical of Old Tammany Day," *New York Tribune* (Jan. 2, 1918); **budget rose:** "A $316,000,000 City Budget," *New York Tribune* (Oct. 16, 1919); **reelected Hylan:** Kenneth T. Jackson, ed., *Encyclopedia of New York City,* 2nd edition (New Haven: Yale University Press, 2010), "Mayoralty."

319 **Efficiency in and of itself:** William Hard, "John Mitchel," *Everybody's* (June 1917); **"saving rubber bands":** Robert Moses, *Working for the People: Promise and Performance in Public Service* (New York: Harper, 1956), 29–30.

320–21 **a full decade after Mitchel's death:** "Memorial Tributes Paid to J.P. Mitchel," *New York Times* (July 20, 1937); **visitors to the memorial:** "La Guardia Honors Mitchel at Shrine," *New York Times* (May 31, 1934); **it was left for La Guardia:** Mason Williams, *City of Ambitions: Franklin Roosevelt, Fiorello La Guardia, and the Rise of Liberal New York* (New York: W.W. Norton, 2012).

321–22 **New York's bomb squad:** Thomas J. Tunney and Paul Merrick Hollister, *Throttled! The Detection of the German and Anarchist Bomb Plotters in the United States* (Boston: Small, Maynard, 1919), vii, xi; **"eternally and comprehensively vigilant":** Ibid., ix–x. The new mayor replaced Tunney with a Tammany man, James Gegan, the detective who had arrested Frank Tannenbaum at St. Alphonsus' Church. Gegan then justified Woods's fears by discharging all the officers assigned to the squad by the reformers. **Tammany reorganizes police:** Richard Polenberg, *Fighting Faiths: The Abrams Case, the Supreme Court, and Free Speech* (New York: Viking, 1987), 60; **Twenty-four out of thirty-four:** Tunney, *Throttled!,* 3–5; **"Tammany's favorites":** Quoted in "N.Y. Bomb Squad Drafted by U. S. for Army Service," *New York Tribune* (Dec. 13, 1917).

322 **the core of military intelligence:** Roy Talbert, *Negative Intelligence: The Army and the American Left, 1917–1941* (Jackson: University Press of Mississippi, 1991), 212; **"in no way restrained":** Quoted in Clayton D. Laurie and Ronald H. Cole, *The Role of Federal Military Forces in Domestic Disorders, 1877–1945* (Washington, D.C.: Center of Military History, 1997), 337; **amassed information:** Bruce W. Bidwell, *History of the Military Intelligence Division, Department of the Army General Staff: 1775–1941* (Maryland: University Publications of America, 1986).

323 **"The best New York ever had":** Quoted in John J. Leary, Jr., *Talks with T.R.* (New York: Houghton Mifflin Co., 1920), 226; **Arthur Woods's career:** "Arthur Woods, 72, Is Dead in Capital," *New York Times* (May 13, 1942); **"The association":** John D. Rockefeller, Jr., to Mrs. Woods, June 8, 1942, Rockefeller Family, OMR, Friends and Services, Record Group III2H, box 122, folder 909, RAC; **"our birthday":** Arthur Woods to John D. Rockefeller, Jr., telegram, Jan. 29, 1939, Rockefeller Family, OMR, Friends and Services, Record Group III2H, box 122, folder 909, RAC; **Tunney and the former police:** Raymond B. Fosdick to John D. Rockefeller, Jr., Jan. 15, 1923, Rockefeller Family, OMR, Friends and Services, Record Group III2H, box 24, folder 178, RAC.

324–25 **Junior a worthy successor to Mitchel:** Judith Sealander, *Private Wealth & Public Life: Foundation Philanthropy and the Reshaping of American Social Policy from the Progressive Era to the New Deal* (Baltimore: Johns Hopkins University Press, 1997), 185; **Milbank Fund:** J. A. Kingsbury Quits the Milbank Fund," *New York Times* (April 20, 1935); Reminiscences of Frances Perkins (1955), Columbia University Oral History Collection, 259; **"stormy petrel":** "John Kingsbury, Lecturer, Dead," *New York Times* (Aug. 4, 1956); **"anarchistic rich":** "Saturday's Disturbance," *Globe and Commercial Advertiser* (April 6, 1914).

325–26 **During his first trip to Colorado:** Jonathan Rees, *Representation and Rebellion: The Rockefeller Plan at the Colorado Fuel and Iron Company, 1914–42* (Boulder: University Press of Colorado, 2010), 3; **imagine:** Quoted in Raymond B. Fosdick, *John D. Rockefeller, Jr., A Portrait* (New York: Harper, 1956), 166; **"bringing suit against the devil":** Quoted in Rees, *Representation and Rebellion*, 5; **"grown both in comprehension":** Quoted in Fosdick, *John D. Rockefeller, Jr.*, 168; **" 'richness oblige' ":** "Mr. Rockefeller's Letter," *San Jose News* (Dec. 30, 1919), John D. Rockefeller, Jr., Personal Papers, series IX, Scrapbooks, volume 9, RAC, **"new money king":** F. A. McKenzie, No Title, *London Sunday Pictorial* (Jan. 18, 1920), John D. Rockefeller, Jr., Personal Papers, series IX, Scrapbooks, volume 9, RAC; **quarter of a million dollars:** "Rockefeller Says Good Will Reigns in Ludlow Fields," *New York Tribune* (Aug. 12, 1918); **"genuine spirit of brotherhood":** Quoted in Charles E. Harvey, "John D. Rockefeller, Jr., and the Interchurch World Movement of 1919–1920: A Different Angle on the Ecumenical Movement," *Church History* (June 1982); **Ludlow monument:** Scott Martelle, *Blood Passion: The Ludlow Massacre and Class War in the American West* (New Brunswick, NJ: Rutgers University Press, 2007), 211–212.

327–28 **He died on May 11, 1960:** "Sleepy Hollow Folk Mourn Man They Knew as 'Neighbor John,'" *New York Times* (May 12, 1960); **Newspapers described:** "John D. Jr., 86, Dies in Tucson, Nelson at Side," *Chicago Daily Tribune* (May 12, 1960); **"I never read the papers":** Ron Chernow, *Titan: The Life of John D. Rockefeller, Sr.* (New York: Random House, 1998), 584; **"one of the best things":** Rockefeller Family JDR, Jr., Personal Record Group III2Z, series V, Biographical Works, box 57, folder 503, 44b, RAC.

328–29 **Upton Sinclair wrote to Rockefeller:** Sinclair misremembered the date of the Ludlow crisis, referring to forty-eight years (it had actually been forty-five) and mentioning the year 1911. Upton Sinclair to John D. Rockefeller, Jr., Aug. 22, 1959, Rockefeller Family, OMR, Business Interests, Record Group III2C, box 20, folder 183, RAC; **"making amends"**: Upton Sinclair to Mr. Rockefeller, May 5, 1966, Rockefeller Family, OMR, Business Interests, Record Group III2C, box 20, folder 183, RAC.

329 **Though critically diminished:** Edwin P. Weinstein, *Woodrow Wilson: A Medical and Psychological Biography* (Princeton: Princeton University Press, 1981), 371–378; Walter Lippmann, *Public Persons* (Piscataway: First Transaction Printing, 2010), 139.

331 **large-scale agglomeration:** Lippmann, *Drift and Mastery*, 2–3; **"stealthily scheming"**: "Gives $100,000,000; Furnishings $20,000," *Forbes* (Jan. 10, 1920), John D. Rockefeller, Jr., Personal Papers, series IX, Scrapbooks, volume 9, RAC.

332 **that a radical movement had ever thrived:** "Sweetened 'Reds' and Rebels of Yesteryear," *Literary Digest* (Jan. 31, 1925); **What has become of the pre-war radicals?"**: Leon Whipple, "A Pilgrim's Progress in Politics," the *Survey* (Dec. 1, 1925); "Where Are the Pre-War Radicals?" the *Survey* (Feb. 1, 1926).

333–34 **Next came Rebecca Edelsohn:** "Sweetened 'Reds' and Rebels of Yesteryear"; Robert Plunkett Interview; **Whether she feared exposure:** "Death Like Dog's, Girl's Threat for Rockefeller, Jr.," the *World* (May 1, 1914); Stephen A. Black, *Eugene O'Neill: Beyond Mourning and Tragedy* (New Haven: Yale University Press, 1999), 201; Plunkett Interview; "Helen R. Crawford" Death Certificate, Ancestry .com.

335 **dramatically as Frank Tannenbaum:** "Sweetened 'Reds' and Rebels of Yesteryear"; **academic life:** Helen Delpar, "Frank Tannenbaum: The Making of a Mexicanist, 1914–1933," the *Americas* (Oct. 1988); Peter Winn, "Frank Tannenbaum Reconsidered: Introduction," *International Labor and Working-Class History* (Spring 2010); **When he died:** Carter B. Horsley, "Dr. Frank Tannenbaum, 76, Dies; Organized Columbia Seminars," *New York Times* (June 2, 1969).

335–36 **Berkman's euphoria . . . in Russia:** "I have seen the future" became Steffens's most famous refrain, and he repeated it often. Quoted in Dimitri S. von Mohrenschildt, "Lincoln Steffens and the Russian Bolshevik Revolution," *Russian Review* (Autumn 1945); **Russian sojourn:** Linnea Goodwin Burwood, *Alexander Berkman: Russian-American Anarchist* (doctoral thesis, SUNY Binghamton, 2000), chapter seven; **After two years in Russia:** Ibid., chapter eight; **"It is not bombs"**: Quoted in ibid., 332; **suicide:** "Exiled Berkman Commits Suicide," *New York Times* (July 2, 1936).

336–37 **Arthur Caron had emerged:** "Reeves J. Caron," *San Jose Mercury* (June 13, 1978); Correspondence with Thomas Krieg, Reeves Caron's son-in-law; **"the peaceful function"**: Harry Kelly, quoted in Paul Avrich, *The Modern School Movement: Anarchism and Education in the United States* (Oakland: AK Press, 2006), 208.

INDEX

Page numbers in *italics* refer to illustrations or captions. Page numbers with an "n" refer to notes.

A NOTE ON THE AUTHOR

Thai Jones is familiar with protest and its consequences. Born while his parents were fugitives from justice, he went by a series of aliases until the age of four. His first book, *A Radical Line: From the Labor Movement to the Weather Underground, One Family's Century of Conscience*, was a personal exploration of the history behind that experience. *More Powerful Than Dynamite* stems from Jones's PhD work at Columbia University. Formerly a reporter for *Newsday*, he has written for a variety of national publications, ranging from the *New York Times* to *Monthly Review*. A graduate of Vassar College and the Columbia School of Journalism, he lives in New York City.